The Creation of Deviance

Interpersonal and Organizational Determinants

Richard Hawkins
Southern Methodist University

Gary Tiedeman
Oregon State University

Charles E. Merrill Publishing Company
A Bell & Howell Company
Columbus, Ohio

Published by
Charles E. Merrill Publishing Company
A Bell & Howell Company
Columbus, Ohio 43216

This book was set in *Caledonia*.
The Production Editor was Susan Sylvester-Glick.

Library of Congress Cat. Card No.: 74–33924
International Standard Book No.: 0–675–08693–0

Printed in the United States of America
5 6 7 8 9 10 — 79 78

Contents

PREFACE

There is growing unrest in sociology today concerning theoretical traditions, methodological approaches, and implications for policy or action. This is evidenced in the discontent of undergraduate students, the radicalization of many graduate students, and a consequent re-examination of the field by its practicing members (Gouldner, 1970). Responses to this discontent take various forms: proliferation of "hip" textbooks, an increasing politicalization of professional sociological meetings, a closer scrutiny of research plans—as to topics studied, uses of knowledge, and the implications of research for exploitation, counter-insurgency (e.g. Project Camelot)—and a re-examination of value-free sociology (Gouldner, 1970). There has been a redirection by some in the field toward action sociology or the "new sociology"—e.g. organization of welfare recipients, ghetto cooperatives, rent strikes, etc. The outcome has been a bifurcation of the field into the "establishment" and the "new order" with various subgroupings in each camp.

While debates over theoretical and methodological directions have been part of the subterranean tradition of sociology for decades, recent developments have placed the division in bold relief. The "challengers" take on various titles: a sociology of the absurd, phenomenological sociology, neo-symbolic interactionism, ethnomethodology, naturalism (in the sense of David Matza's definition), the neo-Chicagoan view, and various forms of humanistic sociology. The work of such men as Garfinkel, Cicourel, Goffman, Matza, Scott, Lyman, McHugh, Lofland, Becker, Douglas, Scheff, and others have provided a many-faceted attack on establishment sociology. If one indication of norm violation is the reaction which ensues, then ethnomethodology is probably the most "deviant" group involved in the challenge. The East Coast Establishment has called this group a "sociology of marihuana smokers"—apparently intending a derogatory meaning—an evaluation of drug use which is consistent with the establishment (Dreitzel, 1970). Their work has been subject to scathing book reviews by those in power,* and their work is seen as heretical nonsense by many traditional sociologists. These examples are not invoked to point to the deviants in our midst, but rather to introduce and place in perspective these subterranean traditions. Through an examination of the work of these "deviants," we hope to demonstrate the utility of applying their ideas to the study of deviant behavior. Specifically, we will try to show how ethnomethodology can add to our theoretical understanding of deviance and reactions to it.

Plan of the Book

The first chapter will present the traditional sociologist's approach to the analysis of behavior (normative paradigm) and contrast it with the approach implied by "challengers," such as ethnomethodology (interpretive paradigm). We suggest how these two seemingly contradictory frameworks converge in some areas. The second chapter delineates the implications of the modified interpretive approach for the definition and study of norms and norm violations. Chapter III outlines extant societal reactions and labeling theory formulations, provides an analysis of the criticism which has been directed at this framework, and examines the types of questions which labeling theory either glosses or does not pose. The theory is then reconstituted in terms of the interpretive paradigm. Chapter IV examines the labeling process at the informal reactions level—i.e., how friends and relatives react to rule violations through unofficial means: by ignor-

---

* See the review symposium on Harold Garfinkel's book, *Studies in Ethnomethodology,* in the *American Sociological Review* 33 (February, 1968):122–30, especially James S. Coleman's misguided critique, pages 126–30. Full citations for the other authors cited in the Preface are found in later chapters.

ing or denying the violation, by normalizing its occurrence, or by other more punitive responses.

The next few chapters will deal with the question of formal reactions to deviance by large social-control agencies. How do large social-control bureaucracies make decisions about people passing through these processing organizations? How do agencies create and expand their definitions and jurisdiction for deviance? How are category systems developed and maintained for the handling of large numbers of cases? We will be concerned with questions of what is involved in decisions to bring rule violations to the attention of formal social-control procedures and what the role of the organization is in this process. We will examine the types of processing stereotypes which evolve for both actor and act in these large bureaucracies, and the extent to which inter-agency cooperation influences these stereotypes. Next, our analysis focuses on the deviant's reaction to the formal processing procedures and examines his role in the acceptance of the label offered by the agency. We will also investigate the influence of his experiences within the agency on his future behavior. Also, the impact of processing on the deviant's sense of injustice is described and suggested as an important factor in the reform process. The impact of the total institution is examined in Chapter X with special reference to effect on personal identity and perceptions of justice. The possibility of adaptation to the totality of the institution both during and after incarceration are explored in the remaining chapters. The final chapter summarizes the diverse ways in which societal intervention and treatment contribute to the creation of deviance. Readers desiring a preview of the themes in the book might begin by reading the first section of Chapter XII.

In writing this book, we hope to achieve the following goals:

1. To treat deviance and its subsequent reaction at a very general and broad level—i.e., to include traditional criminal behavior, mental illness, and certain types of physical illness, as well as more mundane rules of everyday interaction (e.g., deference and demeanor).

2. To develop and synthesize the labeling framework from the scattered writings of many sociologists and to assess its ability to account for patterns of deviance in the broad areas mentioned above.

3. To gather from the literature the empirical evidence bearing on the major hypotheses of labeling theory and revise the theory in light of the evidence from criminal, mental illness, and physical illness research.

4. To delineate the factors involved in the labeling or categorization process at both the informal and formal reactions level and to show how the processes are quite similar at both levels.
5. To show how the accused deviant may take an active role in the labeling process, either through various forms of self-labeling and self-referral to control agencies or through organized resistance (politicalization of deviance) to the labeling effects.

Two personal observations must be entered at this point. First, we owe a debt to Thomas Szasz, whose excellent book *Manufacture of Madness* gave us the idea for the theme developed in the following pages. We will try to show that society through its response to deviance in its midst may indeed create deviance. The term "manufacture" implies a formal assembly process which applies to the situation within control agencies; we use the term "creation" in part to stress the importance of noninstitutional settings for the production of deviance, and to emphasize the dynamic, interactional, and interpretive aspects—at times yielding ambiguity and unpredictability—which is not reflected in the more determinate term "manufacture." Second, we have been influenced in our approach and our writing by ethnomethodological works, yet perhaps due to our graduate training (at the universities of Washington and North Carolina, respectively), we find our "positivistic tendencies" surfacing throughout the book. While we do not consider ourselves ethnomethodological "turnouts," neither are we the opposite (which is much worse), ethnomethodological "turnoffs." We mention this because we do not wish to scare away those who have prejudged ethnomethodology, and also because we believe a synthesis can emerge from the dialetic which will further our theoretical understanding and generate new empirical questions in the study of deviant behavior.

ACKNOWLEDGEMENTS

Both authors wish to acknowledge the support of those sociologists who reviewed this project in its early stages for Charles E. Merrill. Their supportive comments provided significant incentive during the early going. Also, the detailed critiques by two anonymous reviewers to the entire manuscript were also helpful in producing the final form of this book. We also wish to thank the following authors and publishers for granting permission to reprint short excerpts from the following works:

Howard S. Becker, *Outsiders: Studies in the Sociology of Deviance*, copyright 1963. By permission of The Free Press of Glencoe, a division of Macmillan Publishing.

Truman Capote, *In Cold Blood*, copyright 1966. By permission of Random House, Inc.

Erving Goffman, *Asylums*, copyright 1961. By permission of Doubleday and Company, Inc.

Martin Hoffman, *The Gay World*, copyright 1968. By permission of Basic Books, Inc.

Xaviera Hollander, *The Happy Hooker*, copyright 1972. By permission of Delacorte Press.

Nicholas N. Kittrie, *The Right to be Different: Deviance and Enforced Therapy*, copyright 1971. By permission of The Johns Hopkins University Press.

John Lofland, *Deviance and Identity*, copyright 1969. By permission of Prentice-Hall, Inc., Englewood Cliffs, N.J.

David Matza, *Becoming Deviant*, copyright 1969. By permission of Prentice-Hall, Inc., Englewood Cliffs, N.J.

Karl Menninger, *The Crime of Punishment*, copyright 1966 by Jeanetta Lyle Menninger. By permission of The Viking Press, Inc.

Karl Menninger, *The Vital Balance*, copyright 1963. By permission of The Viking Press, Inc.

Thomas S. Szasz, *The Manufacture of Madness*, copyright 1970. By permission of Harper and Row Publishers, Inc.

Thomas P. Wilson, "Conceptions of interaction and forms of sociological explanation," *American Sociological Review* 35 (August 1970):697–710. Copyright 1970 by the American Sociological Association. By permission of the Association and the author.

Don H. Zimmerman, and D. Lawrence Wieder, "Ethnomethodology and the problem of order: a reply to Denzin." in Jack D. Douglas (ed.), *Understanding Everyday Life*, copyright 1970. By permission of Aldine Publishing Company and the authors.

On a more personal level, Gary Tiedeman wishes to thank his medical sociology and social psychology classes at Oregon State University for enduring "trial runs" and providing valuable feedback. Great thanks also to his wife, Libby, for assistance in manuscript typing and for tolerating the late dinners, shortened vacations, and general frustration that were all part of bringing this work to its completion. Both authors wish to thank David Hardesty of Corvallis, Oregon, for work on cover designs.

Dick Hawkins would like to thank those students at the University of Arizona and at Southern Methodist who were exposed to some parts of this material for their helpful criticisms and comments. The care and concern of Ms. Kathy Brooks, who typed most of the manuscript, is gratefully acknowledged. Finally, to Fran, for her support —though not always tenderly administered—throughout this project.

Richard Hawkins
Dallas, Texas

Gary Tiedeman
Corvallis, Oregon

T<small>O</small> F<small>RAN</small> & L<small>IBBY</small>

Two Sociological Approaches to Rules, Roles and Deviance

The very nature of this conversation of gestures requires that the attitude of the other is changed through the attitude of the individual to the other's stimulus. In the conversation of gestures of the lower forms the play back and forth is noticeable, since the individual not only adjusts himself to the attitude of others, but also changes the attitudes of the others. The reaction of the individual in this conversation of gestures is one that in some degree is continually modifying the social process itself. It is this modification of the process which is of greatest interest. . . .

George Herbert Mead

Sociology can be viewed as an attempt to answer the Hobbesian question: Why is there order in society? Why is there not a war of all against all? Chapter I begins with a brief review of the various attempts by sociologists to answer this central question. The question is often glossed or completely ignored in treatments of deviance and conformity; however, the implicit answer which is accepted by various writers radically affects their approach to the study of the phenomena which society classifies as deviant.

In a recent essay, Thomas Wilson (1970) suggests two divergent approaches to the question of social order which have evolved: the normative paradigm and the interpretive paradigm. The former is most consistent with the dominant thrust in sociology—mainly structural functionalism—while the latter is more consonant with ethnomethodology and symbolic interactionism.[1] We commence then with a detailed discussion of Wilson's paper in order to suggest the implications of each paradigm for the study of deviance.

The Normative Paradigm

The normative paradigm is a model which assumes behavior is largely a product of adherence to normative standards or institution-

Source: George Herbert Mead, *Mind, Self and Society.* Chicago: University of Chicago Press, 1934, p. 179.

3

alized expectations of behavior in various situations. In this model, social order is a given and is imposed from *outside* the interaction through socialization into a common culture. Socialization produces an internalization of rules and consensus on expected behaviors. Because social order is assumed due to socialization, interest is usually focused on the occasional violations of norms or role expectations —i.e., reasons for disorder. The interpretive paradigm, on the other hand, assumes that this order is problematic in social interaction: the interaction involves a negotiation of social order. Uniformity in interaction then is the result of each actor's work in interpreting and negotiating a basis for consensus by deciding through inference and actions the purposes and sentiments of others' behavior. Social order emerges from *within* the interaction; it is not imposed from without. Thus, the normative view suggests a rather static, structural image of behavioral expectations and resultant activities, while the interpretive view suggests a dynamic, relatively unstable process where definitions are formed, revised, or abandoned and new definitions created. Since this distinction is very critical for gaining an understanding of the confusion and conflict on the order question in the field of sociology as well as for providing a basis for our theoretical approach to deviance, let us outline more extensively the major points of each orientation, beginning with the Normative Paradigm.

The view of interaction produced by normative definition of role taking is based on the concept of role expectations. Drawing mainly on Parsons, Wilson summarizes the origins of role expectations:

> In the major current theoretical approaches in sociology, the actor is viewed on the one hand as having certain acquired *dispositions*, such as attitudes, sentiments, conditioned responses, need-dispositions and the like, and, on the other, as being subject to particular *expectations* supported by sanctions. (Wilson 1970:698. Emphasis added.)

The role expectations of each status in society are determined by (1) internalization of norms "so that to act in conformity with this internalization becomes a need-disposition in the actor's own personality structure" (Parsons, 1951:37); and (2) "conformity with a shared system of value-orientation standards" based on a concern with maximizing the favorable responses of others and avoiding sanctions of others (Parsons, 1951:38). Conformity to role expectations is assured via the "binding in" produced by internalization and socialization into a common value system. In this way the role expectations become institutionalized. This suggests the first assumption of the normative paradigm about human behavior: "interaction between actors is governed by the role-expectations of their respective statuses" (Wilson, 1970:698). Definitions, expectations, etc., are brought to the interaction and are seldom altered during the interaction sequence.

A second assumption of the normative paradigm is that one's status or position determines the form which the interaction will take (as opposed to a negotiation of form and direction):

> A person therefore enters a social situation with an identity already established. His identity refers to his *position*, or *status*, within the social structure applicable to the given situation, and establishes his rights and obligations with reference to others holding positions within the same structure. His position and consequently his identity in the particular situation result from all the other positions he holds in other major social structures, especially in the other structures most closely related to the one he is acting in at the moment. (Davis, quoted by Cicourel, 1970:14)

The idea that an actor's identity at any given time and place is the result of "all the other positions he holds in other major social structures" can be identified in the work on status inconsistency, status crystallization, distributive justice—indeed, in many areas of sociology. However, this knowledge is often assumed rather than made an empirical question.[2] This position expressed by Davis (1949) means that often the unit of study is the status, or the role set within the social structure, without regard to the behavior of individuals in these roles—e.g., studies have focused on the rights and duties of a status, or role strain induced by overlapping role sets or incompatible expectations by the simultaneous "membership" in many role sets, etc. Indeed, these role conflicts may produce structural strain which is one potential determinant of deviant behavior in the normative framework (see Parsons, 1951: ch. 7).

A third assumption of the normative paradigm is that actors share "a system of symbols and their meanings, including language and gestures, that serves as a commonly understood medium of communications" and as a basis for their interaction (Wilson, 1970:698). Socialization of members of society into commonly held value orientations is an intergal part of Parson's work: the normative paradigm assumes a consensus model of society. The recurring debate over conflict and consensus models of society will not be reviewed here (see Horton, 1966). Rather, this assumption is made explicit to suggest that the order within the interaction sequence is not seen as problematic. Actors are socialized into common expectational systems and so failure in interaction (or violations of role expectations) suggests a failure in the socialization-internalization process which produces conformity. Thus, deviance may result from structural strain (e.g., role strain) or inadequate socialization or presumably both (Parsons, 1951).

A fourth assumption of the normative paradigm involves the theorist's model of the actor. Man is seen by Parsons (1951) as motivated by a concern for optimizing gratification and avoiding negative reactions from others (see Wrong, 1961 for a critical discussion of these assumptions). There are, of course, assumptions about the nature of man in any framework; the model of actor is introduced by Wilson to show that this paradigm and its view of social interaction is consistent with previous assumptions. Through these four assumptions, the orderliness of the interaction sequence is accounted for:

> Interaction in a given situation, then, is explained by first identifying structures of role-expectations and complexes of dispositions, and then showing that the relevant features of the observed interaction can be deduced from these expectations and dispositions along with the assumptions embodied in the model of the actor. (Wilson, 1970:699)

Wilson suggests that *if* this view is an accurate characterization of interaction, then we can produce literal descriptions—statements independent of context and intersubjectively verifiable—of the interaction; we can generalize about the phenomenon and treat these descriptions in logical, deductive, theoretical frameworks which may provide abstract explanations of the behavior within the interaction sequence. Indeed this may be one reason why the Normative Paradigm has been the favored approach of sociology: its assumptions fit the deterministic, natural science model which most social sciences try to emulate (cf. Catton, 1966).

The Interpretive
Paradigm

The interpretive paradigm takes the following view of social interaction. Based mainly on the work of Symbolic Interactionists such as Ralph Turner (1962), Wilson suggests interaction involves *role mak-*

ing and remaking from within the interaction sequence. Turner highlights the difference:

> The idea of role-taking shifts emphasis away from the simple process of enacting a prescribed role to devising a performance on the basis of an imputed other role. The actor is not the occupant of a status for which there is a neat set of rules—a culture or set of norms—but a person who must act in the perspective supplied in part by his relationship to others whose actions reflect roles he must identify. (Turner, 1962:23)

Thus, the interpretive view makes the following assertions about the nature of social interaction phenomena:

First, the actor is assumed to place the behavior of others into patterns (roles) and "it is this tendency to shape the phenomenal world into roles which is the key to role-taking as a core process in interaction" (Turner, in Wilson, 1970:700). The expectations are not given from outside, but must be achieved from within the interaction by alter and actor. What takes place during the encounter—the specific behaviors, attitudes, voice intonations, and setting—signals some type of role imputation and placement. This recognition in turn triggers some type of response. Role boundaries are not clear-cut and performances are determined more by situational contingencies— the events of the moment—than strict role expectations imported to the scene. Consequently, roles and norms are important only in that they provide outer bounds which may limit some of the action. In this sense, they do not strictly determine behaviors, as implied by the normative paradigm.

Second, the assignment of a pattern to behavior is based on some imputation of "purpose or sentiment to the actor." This imputation of motives for behavior facilitates categorization of the actor into a tentative role. In the interpretive view, role is conceptualized as some coherent pattern of behavior organized via the imputation of motives to the actor by others (Zimmerman, 1969:12). The ascription of motives is a very social phenomenon; motives are of interest not as internal states which supposedly cause behavior, but as social attributions of these internal states, drives, or needs as imputed by observers of an action (Blum and McHugh, 1971).

Third, the interaction sequence is characterized by a certain level of uncertainty, of assigning and reassigning roles to alter with corresponding changes in the actor's role. Turner notes that "since the role of alter can only be inferred rather than directly known by ego, testing inferences about the role of alter is a continuing element in interaction. Hence the tentative character of the individual's own role definition is never wholly suspended" (Wilson, 1970:700). Because of the dynamic and emergent quality of the interaction sequence, actor is never quite sure of what his role vis-a-vis alter will be at various points in the course of the encounter.

Interaction provides a means whereby roles are constantly being defined, reinterpreted, etc.—in short, a process of negotiation occurs which involves accommodation, redefinition, and compromise in response to the context or setting of the interaction as well as the past and present behavior of the interactants. We would expect the negotiations to be a foremost concern where strangers and acquaintances meet (where there is no past to guide placement). At some point, the focus of interaction will shift from negotiation of identities to other topics (cf. Turner, 1970). In relational pairs (e.g., husband-wife) there may be no negotiation at all, although periodically a renegotiation may have to take place to shore up identities taken for granted (cf. Berger and Kellner, 1970; and Denzin, 1970).

At any time the role placement may be problematic for either presenter or audience (Ball, 1970). For example, police in uniform may be thought to be free of role-placement and negotiation problems. However, police may encounter individuals who are not willing to recognize and produce appropriate deference and demeanor toward the uniform. When dealing with delinquents and minority groups, police may be forced to act in an authoritarian manner in order to assure respect and legitimacy for the position. Consequently, police often justify roughing up suspects as necessary to achieve role recognition (Westley, 1953). Female physicians may have similar presentation problems, since they are often taken for nurses by hospital patients. They must present various behavioral displays to compensate for the failure of the white smock and name tag to achieve correct placement.

Failure to treat roles as broad, negotiable entities often leads to conflict. In the police example, individuals who hold stereotyped views of what the policeman's role is (e.g., bigot, oppressor, pig) will probably approach the interactional encounter with an attitudinal and behavioral set which produces the very traits complained of— in other words, the cop will be defensive, authoritarian, and dogmatic in his attempt to assert his role of law enforcer. To the extent a society fosters the view of hard and fast roles, thereby reducing negotiation possibilities, it may be planting the seeds of conflict. Indeed, the goal of some police community relations programs is to get the officer out of the stereotyped role of enforcer. Policemen are encouraged to give talks to school children, often out of uniform, or to initiate informal meetings with ghetto residents. At these meetings role playing may be utilized as a form of therapy where role reversal is staged and each individual literally takes the role of the other. Role playing can provide an insight into role-presentation problems and also teaches negotiation skills. Through such programs, ghetto residents and police may come to realize that they face similar problems—survival in a hostile environment, the problems of establishing trust, and others.

Fourth, role taking and role imputation are *accomplished* through the documentary method of interpretation:

> Documentary interpretation consists of identifying an underlying pattern behind a series of appearances such that each appearance is seen as referring to, an expression of, or a 'document of', the underlying pattern. However, the underlying pattern itself is identified through its individual concrete appearances, so that the appearances reflecting the pattern and the pattern itself mutually determine one another in the same way that the 'part' and 'whole' mutually determine each other in gestalt phenomena. (Wilson, 1970:700–701)

This mutual determination of pattern and event is a fundamental process in making sense of anything (Garfinkel, 1967). Since documentary interpretation is an ongoing process, role definitions are constantly open to change. "Later appearances may force a revision in the perceived underlying pattern that in turn compels a reinterpretation of what previous appearances 'really were.' Moreover, on any given occasion, present appearances are interpreted partially on the basis of what underlying pattern projects as the future course of events, and one may have to await further developments to understand the meaning of present appearances" (Wilson, 1970:701).

Prior to a continuation of this rather abstract discussion, let us present an example illustrating some of the points in the interpretive framework. Consider the following interaction sequence. A twenty-year-old woman (W) is waiting alone at a bus stop. A man (M) approaches and initiates a conversation. Take the role of the woman and notice how she changes her role imputation to M and also, simultaneously, her own role taking.

M approaches W and says "Say, don't I know you from some-place?" W's immediate reaction is that this is a sexual pass, that M is "on the make," so she temporarily categorizes him as a "hustler" or a "dirty old man" (depending on M's age and appearance). Simultaneously she takes the role of "threatened woman" (she resents being treated as a sex object) and sarcastically replies, "That's the oldest line around, can't you do better than that?" M protests, furnishing "evidence" that W does indeed resemble a girl he had gone to school with, describing friends they had in common, etc., to W's satisfaction that some girl does exist who looks much like herself. Finally, W is convinced and redefines M's motive (sexual advance) to a more legitimate one (honest mistake of identity) and consequently the action (initiating conversation) is less threatening. W changes her role and subsequent reactions to M: she softens and remarks that she has done the same thing on occasion—that is, made a mistake in identity. The discussion then turns to rather innocuous topics (the weather, current news stories, etc.). After five minutes of idle conversation, M asks W where she lives (picking up on W's remark that the bus was getting later everyday). W replies to the query giving the general location. She instinctively does not give her actual address and now starts vacillating between her original role placement of M and the current one. M suggests that he is on the way to his car and W lives "right on the way home." Again W starts to redefine M's intentions (and hence his role) but reviewing the previous conversation in her mind, she decides her original placement was erroneous. Also, by this time she begins to feel she might have missed the bus, so she consents to a ride home.

Halfway home, M slows down for an intersection, grabs W's purse while pushing her out the door and speeds away from the scene. W calls the police and describes M as a professional thief who took advantage of her. In describing the incident to the officer, she redefines and reinterprets all that happened in the interaction sequence, revising words and actions given knowledge of the true motives (to steal her money); she also "discovers" some new facts in light of the third role imputed to M. For example, it was the last day of the month, she had just come out of the bank across the street where she had cashed her paycheck, etc. Through reinterpretation of past events, a new imputation of motives for M's initiation of conversation at the bus stop emerges: W defines M as a professional thief and herself as an unsuspecting victim.

The police recognize M from her description and from the *modus operandi* as the one who has pulled ten similar purse snatchings in the last six months. Based on his record, the police hypothesize that

M has a sexual fetish for black purses and that his motive was not monetary gain. He usually sent back money and credit cards, but kept the purse. When W learns of this, she once again reviews and reinterprets the encounter, searching now for documentation for the sexual hangup motive. (W has problems here because the role of fetishist is relatively unknown and ambiguous—shading into the larger, catch-all categories of "pervert" or "weirdo"). Role negotiation does not end here, of course; if M is caught, then the interpretive process continues between the social-control agents and the accused.

In summary, the major difference between the normative and interpretive paradigms, as outlined by Wilson (1970:701), is that for the latter, "definitions of situations and actions are not explicitly or implicitly assumed to be settled once and for all by literal application of a preexisting culturally established system of symbols." Rather, interactants are seen as actively engaged in a social construction of reality through documentary interpretation and negotiation (cf. Berger and Luckmann, 1966). Hence "the meaning of a particular role or role-expectation is not a matter of fact, but is taken as problematic for the *actor* as well as the *observer*" (Dreitzel, 1970:xi. Emphasis added).

The study of human behavior thus involves reality construction at two levels: for the actors within the interaction sequence and for the observer (e.g., sociologist) who must decide what is going on and what it means. Thus sociologists using observational techniques are involved in an interpretive process. For example, someone using Bales' fixed observational categories to code actions within a group "must impute motives or sentiments to the actor and identify the other actors to whom the act was directed. That is, the observer must decide the meaning of the behavior in its context" (Wilson, 1970:701). For these reasons, Wilson challenges traditional sociological practices of treating interactional data as literal descriptions:

> ... descriptions of interaction are not intersubjectively verifiable in any strong sense—since the interpretations of different individuals will necessarily agree only when they are able to negotiate a common social reality ... nor are such descriptions independent of context [which determines meaning]. (Wilson, 1970:704)

Wilson says it follows from this that sociological explanations cannot be treated as deductive in any strict sense: "This conclusion does not deny the possibility of sociological investigation, but it does compel a reexamination of the nature of sociological explanation" (1970:705).

A Convergence of the Normative
and Interpretive Paradigms

Before searching for another form of explanation to replace the deductive form which Wilson has discarded, let us examine the possible grounds for a convergence between the normative and the interpretive frameworks. Wilson, in constructing his polemical argument, seems to neglect the potential similarities of these two approaches. His argument, when pushed to the extreme, suggests that the nature of social phenomena denies context-free generalizations and prohibits intersubjective verification because of variations inherent in a documentary interpretation of nature; in short, a scientific (positivistic) approach to the study of social action is untenable (cf. Douglas, 1970: Chapter 1, for a similar argument). At this point in the discourse, we will not choose sides on the controversy, but simply note the increasing dissension in the ranks.[3]

While sympathetic to Wilson's description of interaction phenomena, we suggest that the interpretive aspects of interaction over time will move toward the normative. The interpretive process contains elements of the normative in the sense that participants do not start from scratch; role making and role recognition are based on typified images of what various roles contain,—i.e., commonly held ideas and expectations of how a "hustler" or "dirty old man" looks, acts, thinks, operates and the like. These commonly held images of roles inform the construction of reality which takes place within the interaction sequence. The image of a given role may be highly accurate or it may be ambiguous or stereotyped. Stated differently, role imputation may be correct or misdirected. The role images will be "normative" (normative in the sense of average or typical) in that they will contain commonly held correlations between patterns of events and typical motives, sentiments, or moral character associated with these events —e.g., the unwed mother is seen in that stereotyped role as morally loose, sexually promiscuous, and probably ignorant or careless (of birth-control procedures). Ex-mental patients are seen as untrustworthy, potentially dangerous, and "just plain different"; ulcer patients may be viewed as anxiety-prone, tense, introspective, overworked, successful, etc. Some of these imputations may be accurate, others untrue. The point is that most people hold relatively similar views of a role and, consequently, responses *may be similar* across situations.

Convergence may be seen in another area: the interpretive process itself—the negotiations, the documentary interpretations, the role placements—may be subject to normative influences. For example, there are probably common expectations as to how long the negotiations take place, how much questioning is permitted before the interaction breaks down through violations of trust (Garfinkel, 1963). What are the conditions under which the probability of changing role imputations assigned will decrease? It could, for example, depend on the type of role assignment (deviant or conforming role), one's investment or stake in the original "diagnosis," the setting and context of the interaction, the extent to which the interactants are acquainted, etc. Thus, we might find universal patterns in the interpretive process. Indeed one of the key questions for sociology should be concerned with "ways in which human beings construct order across their social situations, rather than concentrating so exclusively on descriptions of single situations . . ." (Douglas, 1970:12).

Both "sides" may have to admit that social interaction contains components of both paradigms (e.g., Goldthorpe, 1973). It may be that the construction of realities may be more influenced by power relations, socialization processes, and class structures than by the creative interpretation of the actors engaged in interaction (Dreitzel, 1970:xvi). Indeed the task must be to assess the relative contributions of these formulations rather than to say glibly that normative and interpretive coexist.

If one accepts this convergence hypothesis that we have put forth, then why all the fuss? Doesn't the argument collapse, i.e., can't one equate the typification brought to the interaction with the norms and value-orientations that Parsons provides? We do feel that an important difference has been pointed out by Wilson and that these two perspectives do not converge on this point. The fundamental difference lies in the way the question of social order is handled. (For a comparison of how the order question is handled by Parsons and by Garfinkel, see Cicourel, 1964: Chapter 9.)

The normative framework would explain the order in interaction sequences in the following manner. Actors bring common expectations (institutionalized norms) to the interaction—social order results because actors attempt to fulfill these *imported* expectations and judge their own as well as alter's performance with reference to how one should ideally behave. For Parsons, social order results from socialization into common value-orientations which produces an internalization of rules. These rules become a need-disposition of the actor's personality. The actor also wishes to avoid negative sanctions from alter for violations of these standards; this instrumental concern is a second "guarantee" of order. Order is assured through the "double binding" of the rules through internalization and instrumental concerns (Parsons, 1951:36–38).

We have suggested that the basic assumptions of the normative paradigm produce a highly deterministic view of man. While this view is consistent with the dictates of a positivistic approach to human behavior, it may be far removed from the reality of everyday life. The twin dangers of assuming away too much and of "loading" (usually unconsciously) the questions posed to produce results consistent with our model must be recognized. Alfred Schutz suggests that the models which social scientists create may be mere toys, specifically lifeless puppets which can do no other than the master commands.

> The relationship between the social scientist and the puppet he has created reflects to a certain extent an age-old problem of theology and metaphysics, that of the relationship between God and his creatures. The puppet exists and acts merely by the grace of the scientist; it cannot act otherwise than according to the purpose which the scientist's wisdom has determined it to carry out. Nevertheless, it is supposed to act as if it were not determined but could determine itself. A total harmony has been pre-established between the determined consciousness bestowed upon the puppet and the pre-constituted environment within which it is supposed to act freely, to make rational choices and decisions. This harmony is possible only because both, the puppet and its reduced environment, are the creation of the scientist. And by keeping to the principles which guided him, the scientist succeeds, indeed, in discovering within the universe, thus created, the perfect harmony established by himself. (Schutz, 1963:346)

The interpretive paradigm, on the other hand, sees social order as a product of tentative role taking and imputation, the documentary interpretation of actions, situational factors, etc.—in short, order is negotiated and emergent:

> Thus out of a mutual process of defining and redefining the relevant or 'meaningful' elements of situations, something like a social structure, however unstable, gradually emerges. (Dreitzel, 1970:xi–xii)

Social order is an accomplishment of the participants from *within* the interaction (rather than imposed from without as Parson suggests). This endogeneous locus of social order radically alters the types of questions posed about the influence of norms and conceptualizations about norm violations. It makes the question of social order problematic and requires an examination of the process by which actors construct social reality in the everyday life. The most suggestive answers to this question are found in the scattered writings of Harold Garfinkel and other ethnomethodologists, and also in the work of symbolic interactionists. The implications of these two approaches for the definition of norms and values, as well as suggestions for handling deviance, will be presented in detail in the next chapter. Following this discussion we will outline in Chapter III the present writings on labeling theory and suggest how the implications of ethnomethodology might alter extant formulations.

Notes

1. David Matza (1969), in tracing the historical development of the sociology of deviance, shows that much of the early research on deviance in the Chicago School was primarily interpretive. (An example would be Whyte's classic, *Street Corner Society.*) Others in this tradition tend to ignore interpretive aspects. For example, Shaw and McKay (1942) ignore, by taking for granted, the interpretive definitional processes and resultant data loss underlying their measure of delinquency—juvenile court records. Our point is that most studies of deviance accept the basic assumptions of the normative paradigm, whether or not they are seen as structural-functionalist in approach. Our goal is not to present the historical development of the sociology of deviance, but to clarify and define the largely hidden assumptions made by researchers on the subject. (For detailed discussion of historical trends, see Taylor, *et al.*, 1973, and Matza, 1969. For a discussion of the influence of structural-functionalism on sociology, see Gouldner, 1970.)

2. There is a very large literature in sociology which suggests that incompatibility of various statuses may produce strain which results in deviance. There have been studies on the relationship of status inconsistency to suicide, prejudice, authoritarian attitudes, voting patterns, etc. However, the sociologist usually *assumes that the inconsistency* in status (e.g., education, income, social class) is *perceived* by the actor and second that the inconsistency is *salient* to him. Sociologists have treated status as a structural variable, and have not been concerned with measuring how the actor feels about the problem. This probably accounts for the concept's low explanatory power. (For criticisms of this research, and the implicit assumptions of status inconsistency theories, see Stehr, 1968. For a general review of this literature, see Meyers and Hammond, 1971.)

3. Challenges to the dominant positivistic approach to sociology are evident in Douglas' *Understanding Everyday Life* (1970); Matza's *Delinquency and Drift* (1964) and *Becoming Deviant* (1969); and Lyman and Scott, *A Sociology of the Absurd* (1970).

References

Ball, Donald W.
  1970   "The problematics of respectability." In J. D. Douglas (ed.),
          Deviance and Respectability. New York: Basic Books.

Berger, Peter L., and H. Kellner
  1970   "Marriage and the construction of reality." In H. P. Dreitzel
          (ed.), *Recent Sociology Number Two.* New York: Macmillan.

Berger, Peter L., and Thomas Luckmann
  1966   *The Social Construction of Reality.* New York: Doubleday.

Blum, Alan F., and Peter McHugh
  1971   "The social ascription of motives." *American Sociological Re-
          view* 36 (February):98–109.

Catton, William R., Jr.
  1966   *From Animistic to Naturalistic Sociology.* New York:
          McGraw-Hill.

Cicourel, Aaron V.
  1964   *Method and Measurement in Sociology.* New York: Free
          Press.
  1970   "Basic and normative rules in the negotiation of status and
          role." In H. P. Dreitzel (ed.), *Recent Sociology Number Two.*
          New York: Macmillan.

Davis, Kingsley
  1949   *Human Society.* New York: Macmillan.

Denzin, Norman K.
  1970   "Rules of conduct and the study of deviant behavior: some
          notes on the social relationship." In J. D. Douglas (ed.), *Devi-
          ance and Respectability.* New York: Basic Books.

Douglas, Jack D.
  1970   *Understanding Everyday Life.* Chicago: Aldine.

Dreitzel, Hans P.
  1970   *Recent Sociology Number Two.* New York: Macmillan.

Garfinkel, Harold
  1963   "A conception of, and experiments with, 'trust' as a condition
          of stable concerted actions." In O. J. Harvey (ed.), *Motivation
          and Social Interaction.* New York: Ronald Press.

The Creation of Deviance

1967   *Studies in Ethnomethodology.* Englewood Cliffs, New Jersey: Prentice-Hall.

Goldthorpe, John H.
1973   "A revolution in sociology?" *Sociology* 7 (September):449–62.

Gouldner, Alvin W.
1970   *The Coming Crisis of Western Sociology.* New York: Basic Books.

Horton, John
1966   "Order and conflict theories of social problems as competing ideologies." *American Journal of Sociology* 71 (May):701–713.

Lyman, Stanford M., and Marvin B. Scott
1970   *A Sociology of the Absurd.* New York: Appleton-Century-Crofts.

Matza, David
1964   *Delinquency and Drift.* New York: John Wiley and Sons.
1969   *Becoming Deviant.* Englewood Cliffs, New Jersey: Prentice-Hall.

Meyers, John W., and Phillip E. Hammond
1971   "Forms of status inconsistency." *Social Forces* 50 (September):91–101.

Parsons, Talcott
1951   *The Social System.* New York: Free Press.

Schutz, Alfred
1963   "Common-sense and scientific interpretation of human action." In Maurice Natanson (ed.), *Philosophy of the Social Sciences.* New York: Random House.

Shaw, Clifford R., and Henry D. McKay
1942   *Juvenile Delinquency and Urban Areas.* Chicago: University of Chicago Press.

Stehr, Nico
1968   "Status consistency: the theoretical concept and its empirical referent." *Pacific Sociological Review* 11 (Fall):95–99.

Taylor, Ian, Paul Walton, and Jock Young
1973   *The New Criminology: For a Social Theory of Deviance.* London: Routledge and Kegan Paul.

Turner, Ralph
1962   "Role-taking: process versus conformity." In Arnold M. Rose (ed.), *Human Behavior and Social Process.* Boston: Houghton Mifflin.
1970   *Family Interaction.* New York: John Wiley and Sons.

Westley, William A.
1953   "Violence and the police." *American Journal of Sociology* 59 (July):34–41

Whyte, William F.
   1943   *Street Corner Society.* Chicago: University of Chicago Press.
Wilson, Thomas P.
   1970   "Conceptions of interaction and forms of sociological explana-
            tion." *American Sociological Review* 35 (August):697–710.
Wrong, Dennis H.
   1961   "The oversocialized conception of man in modern sociology."
            American Sociological Review 26 (April):183–93
Zimmerman, Don H.
   1969   "Some issues in labeling theory." A paper read at the Pacific
            Sociological Association Meetings in Seattle, Washington
            (April).

Chapter II

Recognition, Interpretation and Application of Rules

The Ethnomethodological Proposal on Norms

Examples of Rules-in-Use

Types and Sources of Norms

"... a psychiatrist told me that stripping i moral and not normal, but I think I go straightened out, but it took a long time."

(professional stripper)

Any book dealing with deviant behavior must come to terms with the concept of "norm." As with many of the central concepts of sociology, there is much debate over definition and usage (e.g., Blake and Davis, 1964). Norms have traditionally been defined as "institutionalized expectations—that is, expectations which are shared and recognized as legitimate within a social system" (Cohen, 1959:462). Since the way we handle the definition of "norms" structures the types of questions posed in the research strategies utilized to study deviance, we will devote some time to this topic.

We will for the present suggest that norms do involve commonly held expectations. While the phrase "commonly held expectations" usually refers to behavioral expectations, we will also include expectations of *attributes* of individuals. Consequently, one may be deviant either for what he does or for how he appears. These components are reflected in Goffman's general identity norm. Goffman suggests the only completely unblushing male in America is a "young, married, white, urban, northern, heterosexual Protestant father of college education, fully employed, of good complexion, weight, and height, and a recent record in sports" (1963:129.) Due to their "minority" status, there are presumably no unblushing females. "Violations" of the general identity norm are, of course, rampant in our society, and the study of such violations may be both unmanageable and meaningless. However, we accept Goffman's position that attributes can be the basis for assignment of deviance, and thus the areas of blindness, physical handicaps, racial membership, and illness may be included under the topic of deviance. The problem is compounded because deviance may be assigned and reactions occur

---

Source: Quoted by Charles H. McCaghy and James K. Skipper, Jr., "Stripping: anatomy of a deviant life style," in Saul D. Feldman and Gerald W. Thielbar, *Life Styles: Diversity in American Society.* Boston: Little, Brown, Inc., 1972, p. 369.

because of a mixture of behavior and attributes. An example is the legendary Southern justice (by no means restricted to the South), where both offense and race of the offender affect attribution and reaction, producing a double standard of law enforcement. (We draw out some of the implications of this compounding of behavior and attributes in Chapter V.)

One reason Goffman describes the general identity norm is to suggest how the value system of a society in part determines the expectations held for its members. This relationship of values and expectations is documented in a classic article by Kingsley Davis (1938). Davis shows that the values fostered by the Protestant Ethic (e.g., individualism, rationality, and utilitarianism) were reflected in the mental hygiene movement which originated in the first decade of this century. The characteristics of good mental health, and conversely the symptoms of mental disturbance, are a direct product of the Protestant Ethic and the open class ideology of American society. Since this ethic stressed individual initiative and hard work, those who appeared uncertain about an occupational goal or who did not seem to be getting on with utilitarian activities were seen as possessing symptoms of mental illness or maladjustment. The impact of the Protestant Ethic can be seen today in the treatment of hippies and street people as deviants by society.

Davis' work set the tone for much of what followed in terms of a structural-functionalist—i.e., normative paradigm—approach to the study of values, norms, and deviance. Values were assumed to be consensually agreed upon and hence nonproblematic. Norms came to be seen as abstract rules which were widely known and accepted as guides to behavior. This led to the convention of taking the topic of norms as a given, as more or less constant across situations. As a result, the focus of inquiry was on "Why do some people violate these norms?" (cf. Douglas, 1970a). The answers proffered did not recognize the possible variability or situatedness of the rules themselves. Ethnomethodologists more than other sociologists have attempted to address these unanswered questions about norms.

The Ethnomethodological Proposal on Norms

A central concern of ethnomethodology (and one of the reasons it differs radically from conventional sociology)[1] has been studying and understanding the "practical and enforced character" of norms.

Their concern with social order is with the questions of how order is recognized, created, and accomplished for all practical purposes by interactants in an encounter. Instead of taking norms and role expectations as general guides for behavior (as in the normative paradigm), they wish to study how people justify *rules-in-use*. It is the position of Garfinkel, Cicourel and others that norms do not guide behavior as much as they provide people with after-the-fact justifications and explanations for behavior which occurs. Thus "social norms . . . are abstractions made by the sociologist and documented by common-sense knowledge he has of them" based on observations, respondents' after-the-fact reporting, etc. (Cicourel, 1964:202–203). What is needed are studies dealing with how actors recognize and respond to common expectations:

> An empirical issue which sociology has barely touched is how the actor manages the discrepancies between the formally stated or written rules, his expectations of what is expected or appropriate, and the practical and enforced character of both the stated and unstated rules. (Cicourel, 1964:203)

In the normative paradigm, norms presumably govern, guide, and direct human behavior (Cicourel, 1970a). These norms are brought to the encounter, they are known by each interactant, and they produce orderly exchanges: social order is imported and nonproblematic. Thus, norms and value orientations have been available in traditional sociological inquiries as a *resource* for "scientific analysis and explanation of regularities in social life" (Zimmerman and Wieder, 1970:288.) The radical suggestion of ethnomethodology is that concepts used as resources by sociologists be treated as *topics*, as phenomena for investigation in their own right (cf. Zimmerman and Pollner, 1970). The resultant research strategy is entirely different than the "prevailing proposal" of the normative paradigm:

> A leading policy of ethnomethodological studies is to *refuse serious consideration to the prevailing proposal* that efficiency, efficacy, effectiveness, intelligibility, consistency, planfulness, typicality, uniformity, reproducibility, of activities—i.e., that rational properties of practical activities—*be assessed, recognized, categorized, described* by *using a rule or standard obtained outside actual settings* within which such properties are used, produced, and talked about by settings' members. All procedures whereby logical and methodological properties of the practices and results of inquiries are assessed in

> their general characteristics by rule are of interest as
> *phenomena* for ethnomethodological study but not
> otherwise. (Garfinkel, 1967:33. Emphasis added.)

The ethnomethodological strategy provides for a wide range of questions usually glossed or ignored by traditional sociological inquiries. It also prescribes a radical way of looking at social order as well as extant research results. The new topic of study

> would consist not in the social order as ordinarily
> conceived, but rather in the ways in which members
> assemble particular scenes so as to provide for one
> another evidences of a social order as ordinarily con-
> ceived. . . . Thus, instead of treating statistical rates as
> representations of trends, processes, and factual
> states of the society, one would ask how members
> manage to assemble those statistics, and how they
> use, read, and rely on those statistics as indications of
> the states of affairs they are taken to depict. (Zim-
> merman and Pollner, 1970:83)

So the ethnomethodologist is concerned with questions such as: How is social order created and sustained by members of an encounter? How are events made to appear connected and orderly? How are members going about the task of investigating the scene of their actions such that they see and report patterning and structure in those scenes? (Zimmerman and Wieder, 1970:290). Thus the focus of study is not the content of a member's everyday activity but the means by which members manage to produce and sustain a sense of social structure in their everyday rounds (Dreitzel, 1970: xv). Oversimplifying, the question is not what a person does, but how he goes about giving the impression that he is doing something.[2] Therefore, the rates of deviant behavior produced by social-control agencies or by sociological studies are not of interest to the ethnomethodologist as sources of substantive information. Ethnomethodologists choose rather to answer the questions: How are rates constructed? and How do they come to be taken as real?

The works of ethnomethodologists have import for our discussions of norms and role taking in that they try to illustrate that rules-in-use is a more productive tack than traditional definitions and measurements of norms. Norms are seen as playing an entirely different role in influencing behavior: they are used to "bounce off" interpretations and produce justifications of why something occurred after the fact. Thus, it is hypothesized:

> The ways that members employ rules requires that
> they continually develop what a rule means when

> they come to treat actual cases and when they find
> that they must defend the rationality of their choices.
> By invoking rules and elaborating their sense for spe-
> cific cases, members are able to describe their own
> courses of action as rational, coherent, precedented,
> and the like, 'for all practical purposes.' The work of
> making and accepting such descriptions of conduct
> makes social settings appear as orderly for the partic-
> ipants, and it is this *sense and appearance* of order
> that rules in use, in fact, provide and that ethnome-
> thodologists, in fact, study. (Zimmerman and
> Wieder, 1970:292)

This continual development of what the rule means through an elaboration of their "sense for specific cases" is taken as an accomplishment of members' "practices of investigating and reporting on their
own affairs"(Zimmerman and Wieder, 1970:293). The ethnomethodological concern with order is "specifically and only with *how* it
is being made visible, hence 'created' for practical action, through
these practices" (Zimmerman and Wieder, 1970:293) Garfinkel
(1967) has delineated a number of these practices which include ad
hocing, documentary interpretation, making account-able, and others to be discussed below.

What is important to recall at present are the implications of this
work for the study of norms: the ethnomethodological perspective
suggests that the recognition and application of rules are ongoing
accomplishments of members' activities. Norms are subject to situational and contextual factors in their application and interpretation.
Social order is created within the interaction sequence rather than
imported from without. Members seek to make their actions appear
rational given the conditions of the situation or context. Members
may be held account-able for their actions by others (e.g., other
members of group, superiors in bureaucracy, alter in dyad, or others).
Rules-in-use are dependent upon documentary interpretation for
their meanings. All these factors can be seen as potential determinants of rules and norms in social behavior. Since these factors influence how rules are applied, they can be seen as influencing what is
recognized, defined, and labeled deviant or rule-violating behavior.
Thus our theory of deviance will have to take into account the rules-
in-use aspects of social interaction.

Examples of rules-in-use

If we adopt the ethnomethodological proposal to treat norms as
rules-in-use, as topics for investigation rather than resources to explain patterns of behavior, what are the implications? The major
requirement is that we treat norms, rules, classification systems, cod-

ing schemes, symptoms of pathology, diagnostic labels, indeed all phenomena, as the "accomplishment of the accounting practices through which and by which" these phenomena are described and explained by one member or another (Zimmerman and Wieder, 1970:293). The implication is that we systematically study how rules and laws are recognized, interpreted, and applied in everyday activities. Studies might focus on the reactions of a wife to her husband's excessive drinking, a social worker's reaction to applications for AFDC payments, a cop's interpretation and application of the law on the beat, a judge's response in a juvenile hearing or a psychiatrist's interpretation of Rorschach test results. Whatever the setting, the topic remains the same: how rules, categories, labels are applied as practical activities of members involved such that their decisions appear rational, just, normal, expected, etc., to those around them. Some of the ethnomethodological inquiries designed to address these questions can now be reviewed in order to learn something about rules-in-use. The following hypotheses involving rule recognition, interpretation, and application are suggested.

> 1. *Behavior is evaluated in terms of the intended product of the use of the rule rather than as strict rule following.*

Don Zimmerman (1969a,b, 1970) has studied the work of receptionists in a large public welfare agency where one concern was the use of rules for assigning applicants to intake workers for processing. Organizationally, the receptionist's task was to assign prospective applicants to intake workers—i.e., social workers who would record background information and establish eligibility for welfare payments. The formal assignment rule was simply to assign applicants on a first come, first served basis in serial order to a list of intake workers on the job that day. Zimmerman, as a participant observer, recorded the activities of the receptionist under various conditions. When the orderly flow of cases was disrupted—usually because one case took an inordinate amount of time for an intake worker—the receptionist would shift the order of assignments so that clients waiting for some time would not see later arrivals being processed ahead of them. Thus the receptionist occasionally violated the assignment rule. It is not the rule violation per se that we are interested in, but the apparent reasons for the change. Zimmerman suggests that

> receptionists were attentive to the appearance of that orderly flow as the intended product of the use of the rule. They understood the rule in that way. . . .

> These alterations of the rule in the course of using it were nevertheless counted as compliance with the rule. (Zimmerman and Wieder, 1970:291–92)

In this case, those using a rule determined its intended meaning—i.e., an interpretation of what it should accomplish, rationality in the goal-directed sense—and receptionists violated the rule based on this interpretation. Here the receptionist interpreted the rule as intending an orderly flow. The original intent (bureaucratic rationale) of the rule might have been to equalize the caseload for the intake workers, or to reduce feelings of inequality of assignments by intake workers. An interesting conclusion, which poses a question for any attempt to explain patterned actions by reference to normative influences, is stated by Zimmerman:

> It would seem that the notion of action in accord with a rule is a matter not of compliance or noncompliance per se, but of the various ways in which persons *satisfy* themselves and others concerning what is or is not 'reasonable' compliance in particular situations. (Zimmerman and Wieder, 1970:292)

This type of rule violation has been termed "competent rule use" to reflect the innovative aspects of rule use. Concern with avoiding trouble and providing for the smooth and efficient operation of the processing function influenced the receptionist's decision. One might say this is a trivial rule in the sense that changing it is really inconsequential. However, this rule "violation" was potentially costly to the receptionist (and thus not a trivial matter to her) in at least two ways. First, her alteration of the rule leaves her open to requests by others to change it in other ways at other times. (Any parent can attest to the dangers of this policy.) Second, if she happened to have very strict, ritualistic superiors, she might have been open to censure from them for not going "by the book." Note that competent rule use is often used to excuse or justify a particular rule violation. We would expect that studies of accounts offered for rule violations would include many appeals to competent rule use (Scott and Lyman, 1968).

Studies of norms and, relatedly, studies of norm violations should include the aspects of intended meaning assigned by the rule-user. This intended meaning is probably a central factor in many of the informal norms that develop in bureaucracies to cut red tape and proceed with the realistic demands of the task at hand.

*2. Rule or category application may depend on
perceptions of fair play or distributive justice
held by the appliers.*

David Sudnow (1965) in a study of a Public Defender Office examined the procedures used in plea-bargaining—persuading a defendant to plead guilty to a lesser charge in order to avoid lengthy trials.
The members of the P.D. office worked with the District Attorney
to insure the success of this bargaining procedure in as many cases
as possible. Decisions as to what reduced charge to use in this bargaining procedure were based on the following "principle" which
involved two factors:

> The reduction of offense X to Y must be of such a
> character that the new sentence will depart from the
> anticipated sentence for the original charge to such
> a degree that the defendant is likely to plead guilty
> to the new charge and, at the same time, not so great
> that the defendant does not 'get his due.' (Sudnow,
> 1965:165)

The first factor—assuring a guilty plea—is related to the intended
meaning assigned by officers in the Defender's Office to the criminal
charges. The intended goal was to assure a conviction, thereby easily
disposing of the case by avoiding a lengthy trial. Criminal charges
were seen as tools to ensure convictions rather than descriptions of
what really happened in the case—the original intent of criminal
charges.

The second aspect involved in this "principle" was the decision by
the processing functionaries that the defendant "get his due." Those
charged with applying the laws did not do so in accord with procedural law, but altered the charge to fit their personal feelings of what
the defendant deserved, based on the rather stereotyped details of
the case. Implicit here is the working assumption of the P.D. office
that all individuals charged with crimes had committed them (Sudnow, 1965:167). Decisions as to which statute is officially invoked—
i.e., entered in the charge—involve, in part, the concept of distributive justice (Homans, 1961), although in a slightly different sense than
Homans' usage.[3] Here the accused is not entering into the negotiation of distributive justice, but has these judgments made for him by
the social-control agents. These proceedings are not conducive to
feelings of justice on the part of the accused. (The influence of the
injustice on the deviant's behavior will be discussed in a later chapter.)

3. *Rules or categories may be applied based on preferable predicted outcomes of such applications.*

Closely related to Sudnow's work, Daniels' study (1970) of the construction and application of military psychiatric diagnoses suggests that the category applied to rule violations by military psychiatrists has great impact on the patients' future in the army. The doctors involved in the diagnoses were well aware of the implications of their decisions for the type of discharge and possible disability benefits which usually follow. Although the doctor's diagnosis was not based wholly on these concerns, Daniels reports that the psychiatrists did take these factors into account in their category placement of behavioral problems (this task being facilitated by the inherent ambiguity and overlap of symptoms for various psychiatric labels.) Another strategy utilized by military psychiatrists to influence potential outcomes of a diagnosis was to declare that the problem existed prior to entry into the service. Similarly, transferring patients to another hospital (in another jurisdiction) also provided a means of controlling discharge outcomes (Daniels, 1970:193).

4. *Rules involve an* "et cetera" *property.*

Garfinkel (1963:199) states: "I have been unable to find any game whose acknowledged rules are sufficient to cover all the problematical possibilities that may arise" in the playing of the game. Social rules even more so than game rules have unstated terms, open-ended features, contingencies not covered, etc. All forms of norms involve an *et cetera* clause as a basic characteristic of the phenomena:

> Apparently no matter how specific the terms of common understandings may be—a contract may be considered the prototype—they attain the status of an agreement for persons only insofar as the stipulated conditions carry along an unspoken but understood *et cetera* clause. (Garfinkel, 1964:247)

Indeed, Garfinkel (1964:248) suggests that the "heart of the reconstruction [of the problem of social order as it is currently formulated in sociological theory] is the empirical problem of demonstrating the definitive features of '*et cetera*' thinking."

Et cetera thinking, then, is the process of deciding what the rule means, what is implied when contingencies arise which were not anticipated in the law or contract; common-sense understandings of justice and fair play would probably surface to explicate the "meaning," "intent," or the "spirit" of the law or rule (which, it would be argued following the *et cetera* notion, had existed all along). An example would be the reaction by Congress to the Laos invasion in February, 1971—i.e., the use of American support troops, air power, and logistic support for the South Vietnamese Army. Although the action did not "officially" violate the Cooper-Church Amendment, it was seen as violating the spirit or intent of that law as understood in Congress and the country (Newsweek, Feb. 8, 1971:18–19).

Not only does the *et cetera* clause apply to an extension of an existing agreement implied in a rule or law, it may also be seen as promoting agreements or invoking rules which had not been stated or agreed to previously. Garfinkel provides an example through his favored technique of demonstration. The "experimenter" engages a "victim" in a conversation. After an extended period, the experimenter opens his jacket to reveal a tape recorder stating that the conversation has been recorded. The victim claims a breach of the expectancy that the conversation was "between us," i.e., private.

> The fact that the conversation was revealed to have been recorded motivated new possibilities which the parties then sought to bring under the jurisdiction of an agreement that they had never specifically mentioned, and that indeed did not previously exist. The conversation, now seen to have been recorded, thereby acquired fresh and problematic import in view of unknown uses to which it might be turned. An agreed privacy was thereupon treated as though it had operated all along. (Garfinkel, 1964:249)

Et cetera work by members may occur at various levels of society. It is found in informal interaction settings as well as formal societal proceedings—e.g., courts. The work of the Supreme Court can be seen as settling *et cetera* disputes on various laws based on the Court's reading and interpretation of the Constitution.

The *et cetera* property is omnipresent for all norms because of the impossibility of covering all possible contingencies (Garfinkel, 1967:4–7). Attempts at scientific descriptions have a similar feature: "to any description of a concrete object (or event, or course of action, etc.), however long, the researcher must add an *et cetera* clause to permit the description to brought to a close" (Sacks, 1963:10). Thus, descriptions, norms, category systems, and other phenomena are seen as indexical expressions (context-specific) rather than objective expressions or literal descriptions (abstractions, context-free description). It is in this sense that sociological descriptions, social norms, etc., are never complete or static. The recognition of this fact and the resultant radical alternative investigation strategy provides the demarcation of ethnomethodology and sociology (Garfinkel and Sacks, 1970).

It is in these unspecified areas which surround norms and rules that the *et cetera* work must be done. Very little empirical work has been done on this topic. One could hypothesize that perceptions of distributive justice, reciprocity, and other factors probably contribute to decisions of what a rule implies but does not cover, what the spirit of the law imparts, etc. Systematic study of these operations should provide evidence of the "practical and enforced" nature of rules (e.g., Johnson, 1972).

> 5. *Rules are recognized, understood, and applied by the documentary method of interpretation.*

The study of the recognition and application of rules demands, according to the ethnomethodological proposal, that the processes of documentary interpretation be examined as the "method that members use in discovering and portraying orderly and connected events" (Zimmerman and Wieder, 1970:294). This interpretation takes place for rules which do cover the situation as well as when *et cetera* work is required to specify the rule's meaning not covered in the fine print. The process is clearest in a court of law where evidence is presented, mitigating circumstances are considered, the doctrine of the reasonable man is applied: all involve attempts to apply a general rule to a given incident at a unique time and place under specific conditions. The jury must decide the degree of guilt or, in terms of the documentary method, the correspondence of event and pattern. But recall this is a mutual or two-way determination: the event implies a pattern and the pattern informs the event (see Chapter I above). The jurors learn not only the facts of the case, but are also instructed by the judge's instructions to the jury, counsels' remarks, etc., as to what the law intends. Also, the facts presented inform jurors (rule appliers) what the abstract legal categories mean. In this sense, the law is never applied with complete objectivity.

A good example of this mutual determination of pattern and event is the jury's problem of "documenting" criminal responsibility when "not guilty by reason of insanity" is pleaded as a defense. Under the 1954 Durham Rule, juries are charged with determining the existence of mental illness at the time of the alleged incident. The decision as to mental illness should be ideally based on evidence which is *independent* of the act—i.e., the irrational act itself should not be used as evidence for the assertion and proof of insanity at the time of the act (e.g., Blum, 1970). However, in actual practice, the jurors understand the concept of "mentally ill" by reference to a range of irrational acts. The act under consideration informs the juror's conceptions of how people behave when mentally ill and vice versa (see Szasz, 1963:128–37, for a critique of the Durham Rule.)

In a similar sense, the presumption of innocence is almost impossible to maintain when the accused enters the courtroom in prison denims and handcuffs, flanked by two armed guards. The general sentiment is "If he didn't do anything wrong, he wouldn't be in this situation." The rich have a better chance of conveying innocence than the indigent defendant who cannot afford bail or a private attorney. The rich do not come to the court directly from jail; they can better manage their impressions of innocence.

The same process of mutual determination of event and rule occurs in a more discrete way in everyday life. A study by Wieder of the inmate code as recognized and interpreted in a halfway house has specified how residents' *talk is heard as rules* by both observers and staff; thus

> accounts of a set of rules that halfway house residents were seen to follow were obtained by taking fragments of resident talk and elaborating those fragments by hearing them as rules. Hearing talk as rules involved the search for resident behavior that would have been produced if that talk was a statement of a rule. In the process of searching for behaviors that would fulfill the possible rule, diverse behaviors obtained their sense as the same kind of behavior. (Zimmerman and Wieder, 1970:293–94)

The documentary work involved in seeing talk as rules is a relatively unexplored area of study. Research such as Wieder's would provide information on how informal norms emerge, how new members are socialized into the workings of the group, how norms are recognized and, relatedly, how norm violations are perceived (see Wieder, 1974). In this manner, the study of language and its relationship to the activity of rule use is seen as a productive avenue to approach the question of the extent to which rules are the result of "the rational accountability of practical actions as an ongoing, practical accomplishment" (Garfinkel, 1967:4).

Treating rules as products of documentary interpretation implies the following:

a. Rule use depends on taken-for-granted, unstated understandings which are filled in by rule users. This fleshing-in of rules involves the *et cetera* property as well as other factors (Cicourel, 1970a).

b. Rule use is contextually determined. How the rule is applied depends on the situation which gives the rule its intended meaning (Garfinkel, 1967: Douglas, 1970c; Cicourel, 1970b).

c. Rules are open to reinterpretation and retrospective evaluation based on future contingencies. Thus, rules are dynamic rather than static, developed rather than given. Consequently, rules "can be retrospectively reread to find out in light of present practical circumstances what the (rule) 'really' consisted of 'in the first place' and 'all along' " (Garfinkel, 1964:248).

Other characteristics of rules-in-use will be outlined in future chapters. In summary, it can be said that taking the ethnomethodological proposal seriously demands a reworking of the traditional approach to norms. Norms are not assumed to be trans-situationally generalized guidelines to behavior which produce patterned action. Rather norms provide a set of boundaries which aid in recognition and interpretation of expected behaviors via the documentary method. Consequently, the question of whether our society is best characterized by a consensus or conflict model, whether society is seen as homogeneous or pluralistic is not immediately crucial (Douglas, 1970a). The ethnomethodological proposal to treat resource as topic suggests that regardless of the source, the norms and rules of society are subject to the artful practices of interpreting, accounting, and making an accomplished sense of these rules. It is through the study of the documentary method and rules-in-use that we can explain patterned behaviors which occur—not by their theoretical imposition (Douglas, 1970c).

Types and
Sources of Norms

The concept of rules-in-use outlined above alters our view of types of norms. Some of the rules which impinge upon human actors can be termed *civil-legal rules.* These are regulations in written form which specify conduct of individuals vis-a-vis organizations—e.g., legal statutes, company work rules, bureaucractic regulations, student conduct codes, etc. When these formal rules are applied in specific situations, they are often significantly changed. These cases of specific application soon produce a set of informal rules which emerge out of conflict with formal norms. These informal norms are built on instances of rules-in-use which provide expectations of behavior. Examples of informal norms would be rules which evolve in work groups to limit output (Homans, 1950), rules prescribing shortcuts in bureaucracies (Blau, 1955), rules for informal handling of criminal cases through "plea-copping" (Blumberg, 1967), and others. Informal norms are knowable in the sense that they are salient and readily verbalizable upon questioning of group members. Conversations, gestures, innuendo, are possible sources of knowledge on rules-in-use aspects of civil-legal rules.

A second area of norms involves interactional encounters; rules in this area have been termed *polite-interactional rules* (Denzin, 1970). The polite-interactional order is best characterized by the types of questions posed in Goffman's work: studies of violations of ceremonial rules, or rules of civil propriety, deference and demeanor, which are involved in face-to-face interaction (see Goffman, 1971). Topics of study include "the structure and function of situational properties and . . . [norms] governing the acquaintanceship process, body idiom, visual interaction, face work, and so on" (Denzin, 1970:124). These rules may exist in written form (Amy Vanderbilt, guides to teenage dating, sex manuals, etc.), but they are usually verbally transmitted. Polite-interactional rules are also subject to the rules-in-use phenomenon. These rules are often significantly altered when there is a relatively long-term relationship between interactants—e.g., between husband-wife, employer-employee, and where the relationships have an extensive past.[4] The relationship means that many of these polite-interactional rules can be violated, yet not seen as violations.

A third type of norm which has not been dealt with extensively by sociologists will be termed *"constitutive rules"* (Garfinkel, 1963). These rules are not codified or documented in writing, nor are they readily verbalizable or recognized in the sense of informal norms. These rules are the taken-for-granted conditions or *background expectancies* which are tacitly understood, but routinely ignored in everyday life; these rules are recognized only in their breach. To demonstrate the taken-for-granted nature of many activities, Garfinkel (1964:247) instructed his students to engage someone in a conversation and at some time during the encounter to move within two or three inches of the "victim's" nose. The students reported that interaction broke down, that the move had sexual connotations for both student and "victim" and that there were especially strong reactions by "victims" in the same-sex dyads. This norm of personal space—specifically, distance in conversations—is a constitutive rule.

Another constitutive rule could be termed an involvement norm—i.e., people are expected to look at another when engaged in conversation, to appear to be involved and interested in what the other person says, etc. Those who stare off into space, appear withdrawn, or seem as if "being away" (Scheff, 1966:35), are usually seen as "dumb," strange, or mentally ill.

There does not appear to be an equivalent rules-in-use type to apply to constitutive rules—i.e., background expectancies. At the same time, these violations are likely to produce a recognition that something is definitely wrong (although participants may be at a loss as to what). If certain constitutive rules or background expectancies are violated with great frequency, the underlying rule is likely to be made explicit and propagated to others, at which point it becomes a polite-interactional rule.

Our reasons for delineating these three forms of rules: civil-legal, polite-interactional, and constitutive (or background expectancy) are the following: first, we wish to indicate the extent to which our behavior is bounded—that is to say, surrounded, not necessarily determined—by many expectations at these three different levels. In order to understand the forms of deviance in any society, we must be cognizant of rule "violations" at all three levels. Second, some action may involve the simultaneous violation of rules at all three levels. For example, one of Garfinkel's demonstrations involved testing the "single price" norm—the idea that generally people are expected to pay the sticker price for a store item (1964). His students were instructed to select some merchandise, go to the checkout stand and offer to pay the clerk ten percent less than the indicated price for the item. This act violated a background expectancy (you pay the price the tag indicates) and polite-interactional rules (one does not argue in public; one does not hold up others in a public line, etc.). Moreover, one might be technically violating some civil-legal rule while engaged in this form of "shopping" (swindle-fraud, shoplifting, con game, disturbing the peace). Any attempt to explain why certain behaviors are recognized and reacted to as deviance must consider this possible "overlap." Third, we note that rules are not sharply delineated, nor strictly applied (as our earlier discussion of competent rule use pointed out); both civil-legal and polite-interaction rules may be in a formal (written) form or an informal (verbalized) form, where the latter is probably indicative of rules-in-use, a sedimentation of competent rule use. Background expectancies are inadvertently communicated (tacit understandings) and seem to lack the formal-informal aspect.[5] Fourth, traditional work on deviance has focused almost exclusively at the civil-legal level. We suggest that to locate and adequately study deviance, all three must be included, which leads to the following conclusion:

> We must return to the mundane and routine forms of behavior to establish a solidly grounded theory of deviance. . . . The rationale for this position derives from the fact that only a small percentage of any population ever comes to the attention of formal social control agencies. . . . In short, a complete theory of deviance must account for misconduct that does not come to the attention of broader agencies of social control. (Denzin, 1970:121)

In summary, we have tried to suggest that "finding" deviance in society demands some attention to the idea of rules-in-use. Specification of deviance by reference to violations of abstract norms imposed from outside the social setting of rule use is a vacuous process—far removed from the reality of the phenomena. Participants in an incident are seen as determining first whether a given action is competent rule use. Is the behavior vis-a-vis the rule seen as appropriate given the *intended meaning* assigned to the rule by members involved in the incident? Most studies of deviance have ignored the rules-in-use problem. For example, examine any self-report survey of delinquency (e.g., Short and Nye, 1958). It will contain questions such as: "Have you ever taken something worth between $2 and $50 in the past year? If so, how often?" Respondents are asked for reports of behaviors without reference to the context or the setting of the action. No attempt is usually made to ascertain whether the respondent felt the act was deviant or wrong, or whether witnesses to the event (confederates or bystanders) felt it was deviant. A second general type of context-free question involves studies of institutionalized norms where standard procedure is to have samples of citizens evaluate various norms (e.g., Rossi, *et al.,* 1974). They may be asked for collective evaluations of the relative seriousness of norm violations. Again the norms are responded to in a context-free manner (sociologists may try to build various contingencies into their questions, but the traditional survey procedure prohibits extensive gathering of data on rules-in-use, on the *et cetera* aspect of all rules, the negotiated character of the expectations). Our point is that both types of questions are far removed from the reality of the everyday world. For either type of question to be realistic, we would have to interview the "taker" and the "taken," and somehow observe what happened in the incident in question. What were the respective meanings assigned by violator and victim? How serious did each feel the incident was (assuming it was recognized as deviant)? Thus, the boy who said he had taken something may have been referring to "borrowing" $5 with no intent to return from his mother's purse. The mother, knowing of the incident, saw it as nothing unusual.

We grant that the kind of information we suggest as necessary to study deviant phenomena is difficult to obtain (i.e., a recording of the episode, with later reactions of parties to the setting—perhaps best recorded by a video tape of the encounter); however, this difficulty is only part of the reason for few studies of this form appearing in the literature. A major reason, as suggested previously, is that the normative perspective has not made these questions salient.[6]

One final comment about the implications of rules-in-use criterion for the study of norms. This applies to the relationship of rules and morality. Norms are seen as having an "oughtness" or moral sense (Gibbs 1966). We would agree, but given the cautions of the rules-in-use criterion, the moral sense is seen as situated morality rather than an abstract, general morality (Douglas, 1970b). Failure to conform to rules-in-use can be seen as negative reflection on the moral character of the rule-breaker. Consequently, decisions to sanction may be based on moral grounds, but morality as it is applied by participants in a specific incident.

Once we have established what the rules-in-use are for a given situation, then the question of violations of these rules becomes meaningful. We then may ask traditional questions such as: Is anything done to try to sanction the behavior? Are specific reactions forthcoming which are designed to reduce these activities? We can, at the same time, ask if these sanctioning attempts produce the desired result—i.e., is the behavior reduced, does the actor reform? The impact of sanctioning attempts on the future occurrence of the behavior is a central question which labeling theory attempts to answer.

Notes

1. For an introduction to the recurrent debate over whether ethnomethodology is a form of sociology—i.e., asking the same question or something uniquely different —see Denzin's (1969) essay, which attempts to integrate ethnomethodology and symbolic interactionism, and the response by Zimmerman and Wieder in Douglas (1970c), and the Goldthorpe-Benson exchange (Goldthorpe, 1973, 1974; Benson, 1974).

2. Ethnomethodologists have been criticized for neglecting the substantive aspects of behavior. Dreitzel (1970:xv) says that as "long as sociological analysis is confined to the study of the reality construction procedures, while leaving the *existence* of the constructed reality to one side, it remains within the limits of the phenomenological analysis of consciousness." Since we will attempt to apply work in ethnomethodology to the substantive problems of recognition and reactions to deviance, we are presenting a "vulgarized" view of ethnomethodology. While anticipating criticism from some in the area, we offer no apology. Instead, we note that there has been disagreement among writers of this school as to what ethnomethodology really is; see Denzin, 1969; Zimmerman and Wieder's reply to Denzin (in Douglas, 1970c); and the comments in the first footnote of Blum and McHugh (1971:98–99).

3. Agents in the public defender's office compared each particular case to a typified version of normal cases of this type, drawing decisions as to what a defendant should receive in terms of offense charged and resultant punishment. Homans speaks of comparison and evaluation between two persons: "a man in an exchange relation with another will expect the profits of each to be directly proportional to his investments, and when each is being rewarded by some third party, he will expect the third party to maintain this relationship between the two of them" (1961:244). Nothing in Homans' treatment of distributive justice would preclude possible reference of comparison to some typified, unspecified other—the sense David Sudnow seems to use.

4. Denzin's typology of norms made a distinction between polite-interactional and relational rules. We do not feel they are different types, but that the latter is simply an example of rules-in-use of politeness norms (cf. Denzin, 1970).

5. Background expectancies, by definition, lack written sources; they are known in their breach (Garfinkel, 1964).

6. We do not deny the legitimacy of gathering data on collective evaluations or collective expectations, provided we do not ask too much of these data. We suggest that if the goal is to predict reactions—i.e. attempts at negative sanctions—our best information lies in the setting of the violation. This is especially true in the area of criminal law violations (see Black and Reiss, 1970:69).

References

Benson, Doug
1974   "A revolution in sociology." *Sociology* 8 (January):125–29.
Black, Donald J., and Albert J. Reiss, Jr.
1970   "Police control of juveniles." *American Sociological Review* 35 (February):63–77.
Blake, Judith, and Kingsley Davis
1964   "Norms, values and sanctions." In R. E. L. Faris (ed.), *Handbook of Modern Sociology.* Chicago: Rand McNally.
Blau, Peter M.
1955   *The Dynamics of Bureaucracy.* Chicago: University of Chicago Press.
Blum, Alan F.
1970   "The sociology of mental illness." In J. D. Douglas (ed.), *Deviance and Respectability.* New York: Basic Books.
Blum, Alan F., and Peter McHugh
1971   "The social ascription of motives." *American Sociological Review* 36 (February):89–109.
Blumberg, Abraham S.
1967   *Criminal Justice.* Chicago: Quadrangle Books.
Cicourel, Aaron V.
1964   *Method and Measurement in Sociology.* New York: Free Press.
1970a   "Basic and normative rules in the negotiation of status and role." In H. P. Dreitzel (ed.), *Recent Sociology Number Two.* New York: Macmillan.
1970b   "The acquisition of social structure: toward a developmental sociology of language and meaning." In J. D. Douglas (ed.), *Understanding Everyday Life.* Chicago: Aldine.
Cohen, Albert K.
1959   "The study of social disorganization and deviant behavior." In Robert K. Merton, et al. (eds.), *Sociology Today,* Volume II. New York: Harper and Row.
Daniels, Arlene K.
1970   "The social construction of military psychiatric diagnoses." In H. P. Dreitzel (ed.), *Recent Sociology Number Two.* New York: Macmillan.

Davis, Kingsley
    1938   "Mental hygiene and the class structure." *Psychiatry* 1 (February):55–65.

Denzin, Norman K.
    1969   "Symbolic interactionism and ethnomethodology: a proposed synthesis." *American Sociological Review* 34 (December):922–34.

    1970   "Rules of conduct and the study of deviant behavior: some notes on the social relationship." In J. D. Douglas (ed.), *Deviance and Respectability*. New York: Basic Books.

Douglas, Jack D.
    1970a   "Deviance and order in a pluralistic society." In J. C. McKinney and E. A. Tiryakian (eds.), *Theoretical Sociology*. New York: Appleton-Century-Crofts.

    1970b   *Deviance and Respectability*. New York: Basic Books.

    1970c   *Understanding Everyday Life*. Chicago: Aldine.

Dreitzel, Hans P.
    1970   *Recent Sociology Number Two*. New York: Macmillan.

Garfinkel, Harold
    1963   "A conception of, and experiments with, 'trust' as a condition of stable concerted actions." In O. J. Harvey (ed.), *Motivation and Social Interaction*. New York: Ronald Press.

    1964   "Studies of the routine grounds of everyday activities." *Social Problems* 11 (Winter):225–50.

    1967   *Studies in Ethnomethodology*. Englewood Cliffs, New Jersey: Prentice-Hall.

Garfinkel, Harold, and Harvey Sacks
    1970   "On formal structures of practical actions." In J. C. McKinney and E. A. Tiryakian (eds.), *Theoretical Sociology*. New York: Appleton-Century-Crofts.

Gibbs, Jack P.
    1966   "Sanctions." *Social Problems* 13 (Fall):147–59.

Goffman, Erving
    1963   *Stigma: Notes on the Management of Spoiled Identity*. Englewood Cliffs, New Jersey: Prentice-Hall.

    1971   *Relations in Public*. New York: Basic Books.

Goldthorpe, John H.
    1973   "A revolution in sociology?" *Sociology* 7 (September):449–62.

    1974   "A rejoinder to Benson." *Sociology* 8 (January):131–33.

Homans, George C.
    1950   *The Human Group*. New York: Harcourt.

    1961   *Social Behavior: Its Elementary Forms*. New York: Harcourt.

Johnson, John M.
    1972   "The practical uses of rules." In R. A. Scott and J. D. Douglas

(eds.), *Theoretical Perspectives on Deviance*. New York: Basic Books.

Rossi, Peter H., Emily Waite, Christine E. Bose, and Richard E. Berk
  1974   "The seriousness of crime: normative structure and individual differences." *American Sociological Review* 39 (April):224–37.

Sacks, Harvey
  1963   "Sociological description." *Berkeley Journal of Sociology* 8:1–16.

Scheff, Thomas J.
  1966   *Being Mentally Ill*. Chicago: Aldine.

Scott, Marvin B., and Stanford M. Lyman
  1968   "Accounts." *American Sociological Review* 33 (February):46–61.

Short, James, F., Jr., and F. Ivan Nye
  1958   "Extent of unrecorded delinquency, tentative conclusions." *Journal of Criminal Law, Criminology, and Police Science* 49 (November–December):296–302.

Sudnow, David
  1965   "Normal crimes: sociological features of the penal code in a public defender office." *Social Problems* 12 (Winter):255–76.

Szasz, Thomas S.
  1963   *Law, Liberty, and Psychiatry*. New York: Macmillan.

Wieder, D. Lawrence
  1974   *Language and Social Reality: The Case of Telling the Convict Code*. The Hague: Mouton.

Zimmerman, Don H.
  1969a   "Record-keeping and the intake process in a public welfare agency." In Stanton Wheeler (ed.), *On Record*. New York: Russell Sage Foundation.

  1969b   "Tasks and troubles: the practical bases of work activites in a public assistance organization." In Donald Hanson (ed.), *Explorations in Sociology and Counseling*. Boston: Houghton Mifflin.

  1970   "The practicalities of rule use." In J. D. Douglas (ed.), *Understanding Everyday Life*. Chicago: Aldine.

Zimmerman, Don H., and Melvin Pollner
  1970   "The everyday world as a phenomenon." In Harold B. Pepinsky (ed.), *People and Information*. New York: Pergamon Press. (Also in J. D. Douglas (ed.), *Understanding Everyday Life*. Chicago: Aldine.)

Zimmerman, Don H., and D. Lawrence Wieder
  1970   "Ethnomethodology and the problem of order: comment on Denzin." In J. D. Douglas (ed.), *Understanding Everyday Life*. Chicago: Aldine.

Chapter

III

A Labeling Theory Approach to Deviant Behavior

The person becomes the thing he is described as being. Nor does it seem to matter whether the valuation is made by those who would punish or by those who would reform. The parents or the policeman, the older brother or the court, the probation officer or the juvenile institution, in so far as they rest upon the thing complained of, rest upon a false ground. Their very enthusiasm defeats their aim. The harder they work to reform the evil, the greater the evil grows under their hands.

Frank Tannenbaum

This chapter will deal with three related topics. First we will briefly outline extant labeling theory formulations. The major implications of this perspective and questions which it does not address or cannot answer will be delineated. Next we will present a review of the major criticisms leveled against this framework. Finally, we will present a revision of labeling theory taking into account the interpretive perspective and suggest the implications of the work of ethnomethodologists and symbolic interactionists to such a revision.

Background

The basic elements of labeling theory—variously termed the "societal reactions approach" and the "interactionist perspective"—must be gleaned from many sources, primarily the work of Becker, Lemert, and Scheff.[1] The labeling perspective is best characterized as a theory of deviant roles rather than a theory of the deviant act. The latter type of theories is concerned with explaining the initial occurrence and distribution of deviance in society (etiology and epidemiology). Labeling theory addresses the question: given that some people violate rules, which individuals continue to engage in deviance so that their activity can be characterized as a role or career of deviance? Theoretical explanations of act and role need not be in conflict; indeed they should be complementary.

Source: Frank Tannenbaum, *Crime and the Community* (New York: Columbia University Press, 1938), p. 20.

A boldly drawn and somewhat oversimplified view of the labeling perspective appeared in 1938 in the writings of Frank Tannenbaum. He was discussing the impact of police intervention in the play of children and suggested that handling neighborhood disturbances by youth through arrest resulted in a "dramatization of the evil" which had a negative affect:

> The process of making the criminal, therefore, is a process of tagging, defining, identifying, segregating, describing, emphasizing, making conscious and self-conscious; it becomes a way of stimulating, suggesting, emphasizing, and evoking the very traits complained of. . . . The person becomes the thing he is described as being. (Tannenbaum, 1938:19–20)

While Tannenbaum mentioned the potential impact of social reaction in the first chapter of his criminology text, he did not develop the implications of this statement. The next systematic treatment of reactions to deviance appeared in 1951 in Edwin Lemert's book, *Social Pathology,* which despite its misleading title remains one of the best sources of information on the acquisition of deviant careers. Talcott Parsons' *The Social System,* which appeared in the same year, also presents an extended discussion of the role of alter's reactions to ego's deviant actions. But it was not until the 1960s that labeling theory gained prominence as an explanation of continuing involvements in deviant activities.

Howard Becker expanded upon Tannenbaum's suggestion that the process of tagging and defining was crucial to the understanding of deviance. Becker's point was that deviance is a social product:

> *Social groups create deviance by making the rules whose infractions constitute deviance,* and by applying those rules to particular people and labeling them as outsiders. From this point of view, deviance is *not* a quality of the act the person commits, but rather a consequence of the application by others of rules and sanctions to an "offender." The deviant is one to whom that label has successfully been applied: deviant behavior is behavior that people so label. (1963:9. Emphasis in the original.)

Becker is referring to the role of rule creation and reaction in the "generation" of deviance. He is not saying that the rule creation produces the behavior initially, but rather that societal actions—i.e., definition of rules and reaction to those who violate the rules—produce a social fact, deviance.

Envision a primitive society where extreme violations of interactional rules are seen as signification of a link to the gods. The violator is seen as a prophet whose strange actions provide clues to the primitive religion. These prophets are consequently given high status in the tribe. Subsequently, this primitive society acquires a team of Christian missionaries and medical personnel. Through the civilizing process of Christianization, the natives are taught about false gods, and are told that the prophet's behavior is due to a sickness of the mind. The prophet's role is devalued. The missionaries as moral entrepreneurs have redefined the rule-violating behavior as mental illness and the prophet is stigmatized for his new disease and for the evilness of his past role—representative of a false god. It is important to note that the behavior of the prophet has not changed. *This is one sense in which groups create deviance.* (See Szasz, 1970, for an account of the historical redefinition of behavior once labeled witchcraft to activity indicative of mental illness.)

Becker retains a distinction between rule breaking and deviance. Deviance is simply rule breaking that has been publicly recognized and reacted to in some way. By combining information on rule breaking and public perceptions of this activity, Becker (1963:20) generates the following typology.

	Obedient Behavior	Rule-breaking Behavior
Perceived as deviant	FALSELY ACCUSED	PURE DEVIANT
Not perceived as deviant	CONFORMING	SECRET DEVIANT

Of special interest to labeling theory are the categories of "falsely accused" and "secret deviant." If societal reaction is as potentially powerful as Tannenbaum suggests, then we would predict that the falsely accused may take up the activity for which he is being punished (punished via gossip, reputation, innuendo, etc.). For example, take a teenage boy who is of slight build, with effeminate mannerisms including a rather high-pitched voice. As a result of these characteristics, others see him as "swish" and consequently he may be excluded from many heterosexual situations. Other boys will not ask him to double-date with them because they fear he does not like girls. Girls avoid him because of his reputation and the potential gossip which might ensue after a date. These reactions, based on an erroneous perception of the facts, may close off virtually all heterosexual outlets —leaving the only sexual release that with other males who have been drawn to him by his reputation. Since experimentation is restricted to homosexual contacts, he may learn to enjoy them and continue to engage in these activities.

This is a classic example of W. I. Thomas' dictum: "If men define situations as real, they are real in their consequences" (1928:572).

The self-fulfilling prophecy is central to labeling theory. In the case of the falsely accused, deviance may be embarked upon due to the self-fulfilling aspects of the perceptions and reactions of others. *Thus, a second sense in which deviance may be created:* reactions produce the behavior complained of, which had not existed before the reaction.

The secret deviant presents a greater challenge to labeling theory. If reactions are so crucial to patterns of rule breaking, how does one reconcile repetition of behavior in the absence of public recognition and reaction? It is not clear from Becker's discussion whether the secret deviant is simply someone who has never been officially detected, or someone whose rule breaking is totally hidden such that no reaction occurs. Since most rule violations have some visibility (exceptions might be masturbation or solitary shoplifting), Becker may have been referring to official reactions. If so, there may be two reasons for the continued deviance by the secret deviant. First, his action may be maintained by informal (unofficial) reactions of friends and acquaintances. A second possibility is that the individual takes the role of others and *anticipates* what the reactions might be, and thus may self-label his activities. Since these anticipations of reaction are present, no action is completely hidden (from the violator's perspective).

In summary, Becker does not suggest that rule violations cannot occur without reactions (secret deviant) but rather points up the importance of social reactions in "stimulating, suggesting, emphasizing and evoking the very traits complained of" (Tannenbaum, 1938:19). Critics who argue that Becker's definition of deviance is incomplete and misleading have failed to recognize the distinction of secret deviant and falsely accused. (See criticism number 2, page 52.)

Since social reactions to violations are seen as a potential contribution to patterns of violations, the labeling perspective recommends a shift of focus from the condemned to the condemners: "the critical variable in the study of deviance is the social *audience* rather than individual *person,* since it is the audience which eventually decides whether or not any given action or actions will become a visible case of deviation" (Erikson, 1962:308. Emphasis in original). This change in focus opens up a whole new set of questions which are usually not systematically treated in theories of deviance: what are the processes whereby laws and norms are created and applied by society? What is the role of moral entrepreneurs and self-interested regulatory agencies in imposing special moral and legal standards on certain groups? How do social control agencies expand their definitions of deviance and how do they acquire definitional and behavioral control over persons in society? Concern with these questions has been termed the "social definition" question of deviance (Akers, 1968). We will treat these questions in the second half of the book.

Perhaps the major contribution of labeling theory is to raise for empirical examination the proposition suggested by Tannenbaum over thirty years ago—mainly that official reactions to rule violations have the unanticipated effect of increasing the probability of future deviance: "the person becomes the thing he is described as being." Implicit here is the assumption that the reaction changes the definition of the situation for the accused; he suddenly is confronted with a redefinition of the act and the significance of it by various authorities and experts. Lemert feels that one incident and subsequent reaction is not sufficient. Rather, there will probably be a series of actions, reactions, and counter-actions, where the rule-breaker tries to denounce the reaction, to deflect the label. The accused will (in most cases) attempt to justify his actions through excuses and accounts, and his close friends may deny or normalize the rule violations. But, at some point, a crisis period is reached, and there is a "strengthening of the deviant conduct as a reaction to the stigmatizing and penalties" of the official intervention (Lemert, 1951:77). So rule breaking which began initially because of social strain, differential association, failure of social controls, or situational factors—what Lemert terms "primary deviation"—now, through societal reaction, gets organized into a social role. As long as the accused can ignore or defuse the reactions from control agents, his deviation will remain primary. However, once the accused "begins to employ his deviant behavior, or a role based on it, as a means of defense, attack, or adjustment to the overt and covert problems created by the consequent societal reaction to him, his deviation is secondary" (Lemert, 1951:76).

There has been some misinterpretation of the concept of secondary deviance. What the concept means is that regardless of the initial cause of the rule violations, they are now being maintained primarily by societal reactions. We have a new set of independent variables which has displaced the initial cause. What secondary deviance does not mean is that there is an automatic acquisition of a deviant role. Lemert states that there is a reorganization of former roles, but it may simply be

> The adoption of another normal role in which the tendencies previously defined as 'pathological' are given a more acceptable social expression. The other general possibility is the assumption of a deviant role, if such exists; or, more rarely, the person may orga-

> nize an aberrant sect or group in which he creates a
> special role of his own. (Lemert, 1951:76)

The following example will illustrate this important point. John is an undergraduate at a large university who (for whatever reason) violates many interactional rules. His unpredictable antics produce informal sanctions from his peers and professors. John is seen as weird, strange, or bizarre. John may respond—defend, attack, or adjust—in order to reduce the negative reactions he encounters. One possible response would be to change his major from engineering to drama, where his actions are more tolerated and indeed may be taken as signs of genius (reorganization into another normal role). A second possibility is that John could drop out of school, head for the west coast, and eventually found a religious cult in the Sierras where his bizarre behavior could be seen as a religious manifestation (development of a new role). A third outcome might be that John's behavior came to the attention of the university psychiatrist and John is referred to an outpatient clinic for help. Through this experience, John accepts the proffered role of mental illness (response is acceptance of deviant role). Unfortunately, Lemert does not provide much guidance in predicting which outcome is likely to occur given negative sanctions. We need information about the types of roles and labels available in a given society, the opportunities for taking up these roles as a response to societal reaction, and the role of the individual in selection of a response role—i.e., does he choose the role, is it selected for him by others, or is it largely situationally determined?

Another implication of the labeling perspective is that official reactions are the most likely to produce a change in the accused. It is hypothesized by Scheff and others that the *public* application of a label may produce a change in role organization and also a change in self-concept. Scheff is quite explicit on this.

> In the crisis situation occurring when a residual rule-
> breaker is publicly labeled, the deviant is highly sug-
> gestible, and may accept the proffered role of the
> insane as the only alternative. . . . The rule-breaker is
> sensitive to the cues provided by these others and
> begins to think of himself in terms of the stereotyped
> role. (1966a:88)

This relatively untested assumption that official reactions in public settings have a greater impact on secondary deviance than do informal reactions by friends and strangers is surprising when one considers that most of the theorists in this area come from the symbolic interactionist school.[2] This focus of official reactions may be due in part to the difficulty of observing and classifying informal reactions. It is obvious that both informal as well as formal reactions may produce a deviant career. What is needed is more information about how these two levels interact in their effect on the accused. What is required is some examination of the labels used by laymen and those used by social control agents. Also the impact of the official labeling process on supporters of the deviant is crucial to specifying this interaction. It may be that official processing produces a redefinition of the actor in the eyes of his supporters which thereby increases the probability of identity change for the accused (Garfinkel, 1956). He cannot easily maintain a nondeviant identity given no support from significant others in his life (Goffman, 1961).

As we suggested earlier, the labeling approach portrays deviance as a social construction which is achieved through a *process* of infractions and reactions. There is no clear-cut point at which conformity ends and deviance begins. Rather, we are all rule violators—at different stages in a deviant career if you will—yet most of us will not enter a deviant career. Consequently, the idea that deviants can be differentiated by various factors (a view required by positivistic sociologists) may be out of step with reality (Matza, 1964). There are a number of reasons why sociologists have adopted a dichotomous view of conformity-deviance. First, many researchers have adopted the agency definitions of deviance which, by and large, tend to be dichotomies: mentally ill or well, guilty or not guilty (at best guilty, not guilty by reason of insanity, innocent). Since sociologists have relied heavily on official rates of deviance for developing and testing theories, a relatively static view of deviance has evolved. Another reason for the neglect of process, with the concomitant need to reject dichotomous definitions, is the inability of structural-functionalist and other normative paradigms to reflect process (cf. Cohen, 1965). Also, the reliance on survey methods and correlational statistical analyses as the major tools of research (rather than participant observation) has prevented an adequate assessment of processual factors. The blame lies mainly with the failure to develop process in our theories. We have the techniques—analytic induction, longitudinal studies, experimental methods, path analysis—which can reflect process. The absence of this element from the literature represents a failure by the sociologist to be true to the phenomena under study (cf. Matza, 1969).

Becker (1963:23) recommends sequential models as a means of reflecting the developmental aspects of deviance. Since "all causes do not operate at the same time . . . , we need a model which takes into account the fact that patterns of behavior develop in orderly sequence." Treating deviance as a process demands a change in our theoretical models (a change which has been delayed because of the dominance of the normative paradigm in sociology—see Chapter I) and in our procedures for gathering data on deviance. Becker recommends the concept of "career" to reflect the developmental aspects, Goffman discusses the "moral career" of the mental patient, while others use the idea of a deviant role.

In addition to process, two more important determinants of future deviance are the awareness of the *situation* and the *responses of observers.* When deviance is seen as a process, the negotiated aspects of recognition and reaction are open for investigation (cf. Scheff, 1968). The situation or context in which the negotiations are played out and the role of the reactors both contribute to the outcome. The focus on process implies a change in the unit of analysis. The actor alone is no longer the center of concern, but rather the situation: actor, reactor, and context must be studied simultaneously. The change has been recognized in studies of schizophrenia within families (Laing and Esterson, 1964; Lennard and Bernstein, 1969), where the family rather than the deviant member is the unit of analysis.

Since deviance is embedded in various settings and reactions of others, our intervention attempts which focus entirely on the rule breaker may be doomed to failure. As noted above, labeling theory suggests that any intervention program may have unanticipated negative consequences. Indeed, the policy implications of labeling theory are tempting in their simplicity. Implicit in most writings is a solution which was baldly proposed over thirty years ago:

> The way out is through a refusal to dramatize the evil. The less said about it the better. (Tannenbaum, 1938:20)

Scheff (1966a) also states that most residual rule breaking (violations of interactional norms) is of transitory significance unless formally reacted to in some way. Such a radical solution demands our research attention.

Criticisms of
Labeling Theory

Before going into specific criticisms which have been leveled against labeling theory, let us briefly discuss two recurrent questions which arise for virtually any sociological formulation. First, the perennial question, is it a theory? Gibbs (1966a:52) suggests that the labeling framework is a conception rather than a theory productive of hypotheses: "since a conception precedes substantive theory, it would be unrealistic to demand testable empirical propositions at this stage." Presumably, conceptions are too general or contain contradictory statements, such that propositions are problematic. Denzin suggests that labeling theory does have propositions—e.g., Scheff's nine propositions on mental illness (see 1966a:40–101)—and thus "stands above a taxonomy because its propositions summarize and propose explanations for vast amounts of data. It is not a theory, however, because the propositions are not systematically derived in deductive fashion" (1970b:67).

Labeling theory is being criticized for the lack of systematization and formalization, which if strictly applied, would remove many of the so-called theories from sociology. It is not the criticism "it's not a theory" which is problematic—we do not subscribe to the school of thought which demands axiomatic theory. Rather, we see the problem as a failure to "ground" much of the writings in empirical work. We propose that labeling theory can be generated from, and grounded in, much of the empirical work of ethnomethodology and symbolic interaction to a greater extent than is presently found. Following Glaser and Strauss, we will be utilizing a discussional form of theory formulation. This form, termed "grounded theory," places a "high emphasis on *theory as process:* that is, theory as an ever-developing entity, not a perfected product. . . . The discussional form . . . allows it to become quite rich, complex, and dense, and makes its fit and relevance easy to comprehend" (Glaser and Strauss, 1967:32). We feel that this strategy is warranted at this stage of development. Since most of the empirical work on labeling theory has been done in the last five years, placing the formulation in deductive form might prematurely "freeze" the theory, making its expansion and revision difficult. We agree that "the form in which a theory is presented does not make it a theory; it is a theory because it explains or predicts something" (Glaser and Strauss, 1967:31).

A second common charge brought against a theory is the lack of empirical support. While some research has been done, the relative youth of the theory has precluded extensive work. Also, those interpreting and testing labeling theory have focused primarily on the impact of official reactions. There is a large amount of research in social psychology on informal reactions to rule violations which could be brought to bear on the theory. Part of our task is to bring these secondary studies to light and revise the theory when the evidence is not supportive. Let us now turn to more specific criticisms of labeling theory as a first step in our presentation of the theory, slightly revised, in the last part of this chapter.

> *1. "It is not at all clear whether Becker is pursuing a theory about deviant behavior or a theory about reactions to deviation. If it is the latter, then his focus on deviants rather than reactors is puzzling." (Gibbs, 1966a:51)*

Granted, there is some confusion about what is to be explained—deviant behavior or reaction of the social audience—but the problem is not irreconcilable. The key concept is "reaction," which has two distinct meanings in this context. First, we can study why behaviors are selected out for some official intervention by society. Here the question of the *origins* of social policy includes the role of the general public, special interest groups, moral entrepreneurs, and extant social control bureaucracies in the formulation of legal definitions of deviance (cf. Becker, 1963). A second meaning of studying reactions is to focus on the *application* of existing legal definitions.[3] Who gets selected from the potential pool of rule breakers for specialized treatment? How are informal reactions shaped by the existence of formal norms? If Gibbs meant that the focus on deviants will tell us little about the origins of rules, he may be correct.[4]

However, it is Becker's major point that the study of the application of legal definitions and the behavior of the deviant are necessarily integrally related. One cannot have an "either-or" situation as Gibbs seems to imply. The labeling perspective should account for both the infraction and the reaction (application of legal and other definitions) simultaneously. Unfortunately, much of what passes for labeling theory work does not follow Becker's recommendation. As stated earlier, what is required is the analysis of infraction-reaction *settings* rather than a methodological isolation of the rule breaker from context and witnesses. As we will suggest shortly, the theory must differentiate the recognition of rule violations and the types of reactions which follow. Indeed, many acts may be recognized as rule breaking, but no official reaction occurs, as studies of police discretion aptly testify (cf. Bittner, 1967; Black and Reiss, 1970; Black, 1970). Failure to distinguish recognition and make reaction an empirical question is related to the following recurrent criticism.

> *2. "From the viewpoint of Becker, Erikson and Kitsuse . . . deviant behavior . . . is defined in terms of reactions to it." (Gibbs, 1966a:53)*

The major problem here is semantics. Gibbs overlooks Becker's distinction between rule breaker and deviant. Thus, Gibbs' example—

if a person engages in adultery and is not caught, there is no deviance —is a misplaced criticism of Becker's position. It is simply rule breaking rather than deviance. Notice that both "sides" have adopted a normative view of deviance: Gibbs feels that deviance occurs without reaction—i.e., that deviance "somehow has an objective reality apart from the socially organized conceptions that define it" (Schur, 1969:316). Thus, Gibbs asserts the existence of transsituational deviance—an action is deviant regardless of context. Becker must engage in similar reasoning in his secret deviant category (hidden rule violations). The idea common to both is that individuals (sociological observers or laymen) can determine what constitutes a secret deviant and thereby "presupposes that one knows what constitutes deviance," independent of context[5] (Douglas, 1971:146). Using a strictly interpretive framework, deviance would be that which is recognized (and it may or may not be reacted to) by participants in the interaction sequence. Consequently, we agree with Gibbs that reactions alone cannot define deviance, but disagree with his conclusion that norms (collective evaluations or collective expectations) can be used to "find" deviance. We feel the discovery must occur within the interaction setting.

Implicit in our position is the assumption that studies of collective evaluations (stated by samples of the society) about the norms and rule breakings can have little meaning when gathered independently of the situation in which the event occurs and is interpreted by witnesses. Indeed, in a recent paper, Gibbs implies this very position when he questions the ability of surveys of collective evaluations and expectations to mirror the many contingencies which may enter into any given deviant episode (Gibbs, 1972).

Some might feel this is a very trivial point, merely sociological "nit-picking." However, the point has great impact on the approach taken to studies of deviance in terms of questions posed, variables tested, and results obtained. The normative paradigm often results in the sociologist *imposing* a normative framework upon a setting. Two examples of the problem are evident in work on delinquency: Walter Miller (1958) observed the street-corner behavior of lower-class boys in an urban area. He made the error of assuming that the most typical behaviors (most often observed) were the most highly valued by these boys. After inferring values from behavior, he then turned around to use this value framework—which he termed focal concerns of the lower-class culture—to explain the street behavior. Albert Cohen (1955) made a similar mistake in studying the same phenomenon. He characterized delinquent gang behaviors as negativistic and nonutilitarian, failing to realize that the sociologist using a Mertonian model might have a very different conception of utility than delinquent boys. Thus, the boy's vandalism and fighting, which appeared nonutilitarian and irrational to Cohen, may have been very utilitarian to status and reputation among his delinquent peers (Douglas, 1967:239–40). Cohen apparently saw this error because his later work discusses deviance designed to signify a certain identity when he introduces the concept of role-expressive actions (1966:99). These errors which inadvertently sneak into studies of deviance serve as a reminder that the phenomena under study must be treated as problematic—i.e., as a topic for investigation rather than as a legislated resource.

> 3. "But the label does not create the behavior in the first place" (Akers, 1968:464). Gibbs (1966a) also criticizes the labeling approach for failing to address the etiology question.

Proponents agree that the theory is limited in scope. Scheff states that residual rule breaking arises from many diverse sources (organic, psychological, external stress, and violational acts of innovation or defiance), generally granting that the initial cause of the action is *not* of interest to the labeling theorist. Most advocates say that the theory is only an attempt to explain career deviance—i.e., how people move from primary to secondary deviance. At the extreme, one might deny the importance of the initial cause by reasoning that these causal factors are randomly distributed and that patterns of rule violation *appear* only through societal reactions which lead to role placement (Zimmerman, 1969). Although few would actively argue this position, it is implied by the underlying logic of the theory.

Many reasons may be cited for a focus on secondary rather than primary deviance. Scheff suggests unlabeled and unreacted-to rule violations tend to be of transitory significance. Lemert and others argue that rule breaking which becomes highly organized is potentially more costly to society. Reactions may force "systematic deviation"—i.e., patterns of deviance which are supported by subcultures, and common rationalizations and life style (Lemert, 1951). By creating deviant careers, society guarantees that certain individuals will continue to violate rules; such activity may be very costly in terms of money, harm to victims, or self-harm to the deviant—e.g., drug addicts, professional thieves. Career deviants also require more attention from control and treatment agencies.

Another reason for the seeming lack of concern with questions of etiology is the large amount of work which has been done in this area. In the areas of criminal behavior and physical illness, there has been great stress on initial causes, with a relative failure to "recognize the other task of studying the way conceptions of deviance are developed and the consequences of the application of such conceptions" (Freidson, 1970:213). Medical sociology has come to stress studies of the social aspects of disease: cultural variations in the perception and reporting of pain, behavioral patterns that surround types of illness, the social obligations of the sick role, and others (Freidson, 1970). Consequently, the relative absence of work on questions posed by labeling theory, compared to the attention received by etiological questions, is often seen as justification for dismissing this recurrent criticism.

Another tack which has not been systematically developed is to suggest that labeling theory *can* account for the initiation of certain types of rule breaking. Becker's "falsely accused" may be propelled into the suggested pattern by reaction alone via the self-fulfilling prophecy. Anticipated reactions and self-labeling may also initiate or sustain untoward activities in the absence of any "outside" reaction. Thus, "the mere knowledge of potential negative evaluations of his acts may still influence the actor's behavior and his self-conceptions" (Schur, 1969:317). Self-labeling may occur when the actor learns to use the categorization system of professional agencies. This is closely related to a fourth criticism.

> 4. *"The process of developing deviance seems all societal response and no deviant stimulus" (Bordua, 1967:48). Gibbs also states that the features of deviance are located external to the actor* (1966a; also, Akers, 1968).

Many labeling formulations do present a passive view of the actor, one who often appears as an innocent victim of high-handed labeling by power groups in society. Indeed, the actor may play an active role in the labeling process in a number of ways. First, certain individuals may seek out certain labels in order to promote a particular self-image. Telling off the police and subsequent arrest are often sources of "rep" in delinquent gangs (Werthman and Piliavin, 1967). In other instances, a specific label may be chosen over a more stigmatic classification, as in the case of the child molester who pleads guilty to assault to increase his chances of an early parole and to reduce the rejection of his fellow inmates who go hard on sex criminals. The heavy drinker may support a medical label in hopes of avoiding the revolving door policy of legal handling of drunks (only to find himself in a treatment facility with an indeterminate sentence). The hypochondriac seeks sympathy by adopting a sick role.

The deviant may also be active in the sense of seeking out help because of self-diagnosis and self-referral (Lorber, 1967). As noted above, the deviant may learn the professional category systems of psychiatrists in order to gain prestige, to be "in" with the latest in psychiatric analysis. Scheff refers to these individuals as a psychiatric public—i.e., individuals who "take for granted the reality, and secondarily the respectability of mental illness" (Scheff, 1966b:120). The diffusion of professional labels to laymen must be part of the study of the impact of intervention on the acquisition of a deviant role. (We will take this up in detail in Chapter IX).

The opposite of the label seeker is the individual who plays an active role in his rejection of the label and subsequent reaction. The protestations of an innocent man brought before a commitment board by conspiring relatives come to be viewed as symptoms of mental illness. The more he tries to dispell these assertions, the more irrational he becomes, thereby sealing his doom. The topic of the perceptions of injustice and its impact on processing agency success will be detailed in Chapter X.

> 5. *The labeling perspective "locates the fate of the deviant, indeed his very development, in the acts of the reactors" (Bordua, 1967:153).*

Although similar to the previous point, the emphasis here is on "taking sides." Bordua suggests that labeling theory often becomes identified with an underdog ideology. Consequently, the theory has appeal to radical sociologists who use it to point up the evils of the system. Because of this orientation, critics argue that biased studies are produced which ignore the success of intervention while stressing the injustices and failures of the policies. Becker (1964) argues that the underdog perspective—i.e., being on the side of the deviant —is warranted because most research is from the perspective of the controllers. Since research is often financed by the power groups in a society to study the disenfranchised, and since many assume that those in power then monopolize this information for control purposes, the labeling formulation is popular among anti-establishment sociologists. The potential policy implications also appeal to the rhetoric of the new left (cf. Gouldner, 1970).

While the perspective of labeling theory may appeal to radical groups, this is not to say that the establishment may not have some interest in the answers to questions posed by this framework. In light of the great cost to society of intervention programs such as welfare, correctional projects, etc., it is important that the effects of these policies be examined. We are concerned more with the evaluation of intervention and control programs than with the political motives for such investigation. Political motives become important when they prohibit an objective analysis of the topic (cf. Gouldner, 1968).

There is another side to this criticism of extant labeling formulations—i.e., they are not political enough. To understand this critique, we return to our earlier distinction between "origins" and "application" questions. Gouldner (1968) and Liazos (1972) state that most investigations of labeling theory ideas do not address the crucial question of *political power* in the designation of deviant behavior. In other words, the focus has been on rule application to the exclusion of origins of laws and other rules in society. Gouldner is succinct in the charge:

> Becker's argument is essentially a critique of the caretaking organizations, and in particular of the *low level* officialdom that manages them. It is not a critique of the social institutions that engender suffering or of the high level officialdom that shapes the character of caretaking establishments. (1968:107)

This, then, is not so much a critique of what has been done, but an appeal to study the more macro-level questions often ignored in labeling researches.[6] We need more studies such as Platt's (1969) delineation of the origins of the juvenile court, Chambliss' (1969) analysis of vagrancy laws, Duster's (1970) treatment of drug legislation, Erikson's (1966) work on crime waves in Puritan New England, and Becker's (1963) own description of marihuana legislation. The challenge is to show the interrelationships between labeling on the societal level and the more micro, interactional level.

There have been a number of reasons suggested for this "imbalance" (see Gouldner, 1968; Platt, 1974). It is probably easier to acquire funding and get access to do research for investigations aimed at lower-level decision makers. For example, would the Law Enforcement Assistance Administration fund a study of itself? Would it give access to researchers funded by other sources? Another possibility is that sociologists, steeped in a largely normative paradigm tradition, may assume away many of these basic questions. Regardless of the reason, we would disagree with one critic's proposed remedy:

> We should not study only, or predominantly, the popular and dramatic forms of "deviance." Indeed we should banish the concept of "deviance" and speak of oppression, conflict, persecution, and suffering. (Liazos, 1972:119)

Rather, both questions must be pursued; to do otherwise would be to ignore the ubiquitous nature of labeling and its effects on the creation of deviance.

> 6. The labeling perspective does not account for the "positive aspects"—i.e., deterrent aspects—of societal reactions (Bordua, 1967:154; also Gibbs, 1966a:50).

It is necessary to modify the present theory in order to account for the deterrent effect of some intervention; although recidivism is high, it is not total; many people "go straight" after a brush with the law or function effectively after psychiatric treatment. The theory must specify the conditions which produce a reduction in future behavior; why are some intervention programs successful and others not? In answering these questions, we may bring aspects of traditional theories of deviance to bear and thereby achieve an integration of theories of the deviant act and the labeling perspective.

In summary, some of the criticisms of labeling theory have been misguided, based partly on semantic differences but also on a failure to distinguish the social construction of reality and the actual event. Other criticisms, such as a lack of concern with primary deviance and a removal of the deviant actor from the formula are accurate criticisms of current work. Still others remain valid criticisms only if labeling theory stays within the traditional confines of the normative paradigm. The theory takes on a new look when formulated within the interpretive perspective.

Before presenting this new look in the final section of this chapter, let us review the implicit points made in our reaction to the criticisms of labeling theory. Our defense of the theory provides a forewarning of the approach we shall shortly outline in detail. Our discussion has implied the following:

1. Deviance must be studied as activities grounded in specific situations and contexts.
2. The unit of analysis should be the rule-breaking actor, potential reactor(s), and the setting of the infraction—rather than the rule breaker alone.
3. Recognition that rule breaking is occurring grows out of an interaction sequence where some degree of negotiation is present. An actor's behavior is open to redefinition at any time (via the documentary method).
4. Recognition and possible reaction must be separated. Recognition can occur without reaction; indeed much deviance is normalized or denied.

5. Consequently, recognition, rather than reaction, must be our indicator of deviant behavior.[7]
6. Deviance must be conceptualized as a continuum, not a static dichotomy, thereby being true to the nature of the phenomenon. Deviance is an attribute bestowed on an actor by others via their assignment of meaning and pattern to witnessed events or reports of events.

Labeling Theory
Revised

At this point, let us anticipate some objections to our own position which could be raised by other sociologists. First, the definition of deviance which has been implicit in our first few chapters must be made explicit. Deviance is that phenomenon which is perceived (i.e., recognized) as violating expectations held by participants to an event. Deviance is that which is seen as unexpected, out-of-place, strange, out of the ordinary—given the definition of the situation held by the witnesses to the event which includes contextually shared meanings of expected, in-place, not strange, ordinary.

Our definition makes both *actions* and *attributes* topics of investigation, since either may be a source of recognition—i.e., the blind, the crippled, the deformed, as well as minority races may be seen as "out of the ordinary," not living up to expectations in various situations (cf. Goffman, 1963). At the same time, actions or attributes above and beyond situational expectations are "out of the ordinary." Consequently, we agree with Lemert (1951:24) that the "behavior of the genius, the motion-picture star, the exceptionally beautiful woman, and the renowned athlete should lend itself to the same systematic analysis as that which is applied to the criminal, the pauper, or the sex delinquent." Both of these "sets" are *recognized* as out of the ordinary, as either failing to achieve some expected state or living up to it too well (negative and positive deviance, respectively).[8]

Our situationally tied definitions of both norms and deviance are likely to encounter an objection from those preferring the normative perspective. The charge might be "rampant relativism"—an objection on the grounds of the indeterminacy which this model injects into human behavior. Gibbs (1972:46) suggests that the emphasis on meaning and definitions of the situation inherent in our position would lead down the "road to nominalism and on to solipsism." He

says that "if an act is deviant only when it is perceived as such by the
participants (that is, particular individuals) the social quality of deviation is negated" (Gibbs, 1972:47). On the contrary, we feel that a
particularistic approach to deviance and norms *stresses* the social
quality of deviation—i.e., the deviation is the result of a negotiation
process involving actor, reactor(s), and the setting or context of occurrence. Definitions of deviance are emergent products of an interpretive process. Gibbs apparently intends a different meaning by
"social"—perhaps transsituational. However, to assert—putting it
bluntly—that deviance is what participants in a setting say it is, that
deviance is in the eye of the beholder, does not rule out the possibility that similarities in recognition of deviance exist across situations
(e.g., Matza, 1969:12).

We agree that knowledge of rules and norms helps to structure and
make sensible our environment. As we suggested at the end of the
first chapter, there is a convergence of the normative and interpretive paradigms which must be taken into account. As Zimmerman
states, "for members of society, including sociologists, the various
elements of the normative-structural conceptual apparatus are available in some form as features of everyday scenes, and appear as more
or less stable across situations. That is, norms, rules, behaviors, etc.,
while they might pose particular problems on given occasions, are
not systematically problematic, and indeed are a major resource for
members in describing and explaining, and thereby making observable, the features of their everyday circumstances" (Zimmerman,
1969:16. Emphasis added). Hence, we do not deny the existence of
norms, but feel that they are often imposed on the phenomena by
anthropologists and sociologists (e.g., Miller) and present an oversocialized view of man (Wrong, 1961). We have suggested previously
that norms provide very broad and ambiguous guidelines, boundaries for the outer limits of negotiation, structures which act as back-
boards for bouncing off interpretations of behavior—i.e., competent
rule use and rule breaking (Douglas, 1971). To some extent, the
concept of norm has become reified. Norms "should be taken for
what they are: convenient ways of summarizing the tendencies of
human beings in their various roles to respond in a similar fashion in
social situations" (Lemert, 1951:31).

Through the study of various situations, we hope to find similarities
in the ways acts and events are recognized and reacted to, but this
is not to say the regularities are the result of strict rule following—
i.e., normatively determined from outside the situation. We feel that
the man on the street encounters the same problem as the sociologist. He has to make gross predictions about how others are going to

act in various situations. His general "feel" for norms and roles helps him somewhat in this task. However, at any given time or place, the man's predictions may not fit (he encounters the exception rather than the rule). At these times, he will be called upon to pay closer attention to the interpreting of the setting, to a re-establishment of trust through negotiation, and at times a redefining of identities (Denzin, 1970a; Turner, 1970). The sociologist, as long as he stays on the level of predicting rates rather than individual actions, does not have to worry about such unpleasantness; the sociologist can avoid a direct encounter with his "unexplained variance," while the man on the street cannot.

Our definition of deviance appears ambiguous since no transsituational claims (deviant in all situations) can be made. This is an attempt to mirror the definitional framework which would be used by the man on the street, an attempt to stay close to the nature of the phenomena. Our position is reflected by David Matza:

> Such uncertainty [in the definition of deviance] is troublesome for those who abhor sloppiness, but, in truth, the difficulty resides in the nature of society not in the conception of deviation. Cultural definitions, especially in contemporary society, tend toward ambiguity. . . .
>
> Whether the phenomenon personified, say, by a waitress in topless attire is deviant is a question that will yield a clear-cut answer if our conception of deviation is sufficiently rigorous and operational. But the clear-cut yes or no will be gained only by suppressing, and thus denying, the patient ambiguity of this novel phenomenon and the easily observable tentative, vacillating, and shifting response to it. (1969:11)

In taking such a position, we are simply noting that "[s]hift, ambiguity, and pluralism are implicated in the very idea of deviation. . . . The uncertainty cannot be liquidated; it can only be observed and reported" (Matza, 1969:12).

To recapitulate, deviance involves actions or attributes which are recognized as violating expectations held by participants to an event. We are departing from the predominant policy of requiring a reaction (attempt to negatively sanction)[9] to take place to delineate deviance (e.g., Kitsuse, 1964; Clinard, 1968:28). With this definition in mind, we now turn to the central concepts in extant labeling formulations: *labels* and *reactions.* Labeling theorists often use the terms "reaction" and "labeling" interchangeably. The confusion is understandable in part because a label may be a reaction. Name calling may be one response to untoward behavior in that it may be an insult to the receiver, or because it makes his reputation open to question, or causes him some embarrassment, or perhaps all three. Labels can be reactions—i.e., negative sanctions—in another sense: labels may take on a reality of their own, above and beyond the event which the label originally stood for. Thus, calling someone an alcoholic may lead to self-fulfilling consequences. People come to see others through labels, rather than as unique individuals (especially when the label refers to something they do not completely understand— e.g., mental illness or alcoholism). Since negative labels may be difficult to dispel, they may be a constant source of "reaction," usually termed "stigma."

It is necessary to define label and reaction independently and treat their interrelation as problematic, open to question. Reaction as used here refers to an attempt to *negatively sanction* the author of an action (cf. Gibbs, 1966b). Informal reactions may be a slap, a raised eyebrow, sarcastic comments, innuendo, jokes, or exclusion, to name a few. The very term "re-action" implies a response to some event; consequently, it is meaningless to classify a slap or a frown as an attempt to negatively sanction outside of the situation in which it occurs. For example, suppose you see a faculty member walk out the door of the faculty meeting room alone. This behavior—leave-taking —cannot be assigned a meaning without some information. Unless you were in the meeting or could hear through the door, you would not know if the leave-taking was: (a) an attempt to sanction the chairman for failure to follow Robert's Rules of Order, (b) a response to a request for a pot of coffee, (c) a response to prior commitments made to pick up the kids after their music lesson, or (d) simply a response to the call of nature. Thus, informal reactions cannot be easily delineated without reference to the "situatedness" of the response. In our example, the leave-taker is indeed responding to various stimuli (reacting to them), but only the first response would be classified as a reaction as we use the term—i.e., an attempt to negatively sanction.

A similar problem occurs when formal sanctions indicate reactions. Although official rates of agencies are often used to stand for the extent of criminal actions in a community, there is a great deal of "slippage" between act and charge. Learning that someone is charged with petty theft tells us nothing of the act which led to this charge. As we shall argue extensively later, the behavior of the accused is only part (at times a relatively small part) of the constituted charge made by the agency. The individual who appeared in the records as charged with petty theft may have "copped" a plea, having been guilty of grand theft. The prostitute may have been arrested for vagrancy (when the local ordinance against prostitution was declared unconstitutional) which leads to the ironic act of arresting her for "not working, not having a visible means of support" while she is "at work." At times, the charge may reflect the opposite of the behavior which actually occured—e.g., Sudnow found that drunks were routinely charged with disturbing the peace, when in fact many were quite civil or completely passive (Sudnow, 1965). Similarly, diagnostic placement by psychiatrists may reflect the social class of the patient or the auspices under which he comes to the attention of the psychiatrist—i.e., voluntary referral or involuntary commitment (Freidson, 1966; Haney and Michielutte, 1968). Diagnosis of physical illness may also be influenced by such extraneous variables (Friedson, 1970).

Consequently, using official rates of reaction to estimate the parameters of deviant behavior in a community is in error for at least two major reasons: first, the rates are biased in that they are not an accurate sample of the amount or types of deviance occurring (due to unreported and undetected acts), and second, the acts which do become known to the agents are not accurately reflected in the charges made, or in the diagnostic category assigned (cf. Kitsuse and Cicourel, 1963).

Given the problems of specifying reactions, labeling also presents difficulties. Labeling can be defined as simply the process of placing some act or event into a larger category as a means of classification. (We are divorcing it from reaction and treating it as central to recognition). Labeling as a phenomenon occurs daily in all settings. We type or label actions in order to understand them (Strauss, 1959). We place the diverse events encountered in our daily round into patterns via the documentary method described earlier and these patterns receive distinctive names or labels. The work of the scientist is an exercise in labeling when he is engaged in theory construction or when he is charged with the task of generalizing from vast amounts of data. The scientist uses theory and statistics to manage and interpret his work. The man on the street carries out a similar classification ritual in order to make sense of his environment. His classifications are not arrived at in the meticulous manner of the researcher; rather his sampling and hypothesis testing continue only as far as necessary to complete his daily round. In this sense, the categorizations of the layman are guided by "common sense rationalities" rather than scientific ones (Garfinkel, 1967: 262–83).

Since labeling is omnipresent, it is potentially trivial; everything is labeled—there are positive, negative, and neutral labels. The idea of labeling can be rescued from the charge of triviality by treating it within an ethnomethodological framework—i.e., by treating the phenomenon of labeling as a topic of investigation in its own right. As seen from our review of past formulations, labeling theorists have not systematically addressed the question of how labels are formed, recognized, and imputed as practical accomplishments of everyday activities. As Blum suggests, labeling theorists do not describe the labeling process, but affirm that the process exists and focus on its negative consequences; there has been little work on the "socially organized character of the labeling process itself. The question, then, is how to transform the labeling process into an observable phenomenon to extract the rules that organize its assembly" (Blum, 1970:39). In short, how is the labeling or categorization of everyday life accomplished?

If the reader accepts all or even part of what we have proposed to this point, he may be inclined to throw up his hands and say: How can we study norms or deviance since everything seems so patternless and relative? Are not the definitions of norms and deviance so broad as to be meaningless? Is the goal of science—prediction and explanation of patterns of events—to be abandoned? We think not. We do not agree with the usual response to an omnibus definition of deviance—"the forms of misbehavior . . . are so varied as to rule out any single explanation of them, however complex that formulation" (Gibbons and Jones, 1971:33). We feel that regardless of the form of norm violation—"cheating, unfairness, crime, sneakiness, malingering, cutting corners, immorality, dishonesty, betrayal, graft, corruption, wickedness and sin" (Cohen, 1966:1)—*the same process of recognition* of norm violations, definitions of intent imputed to actor (i.e., labeling), *and subsequent reactions* to rule violations (i.e., negative sanctions) is involved for each type. This process involves these steps:

1. *Observation.* The act is monitored in some way so that its occurrence is known.
2. *Recognition.* The act is seen as a rule violation—i.e., a violation of rules-in-use. (Implied here is a recognition of what the rules are.)
3. *Imputed Cause.* The act is categorized as accidental, not really intended, or intentional by the observer.
4. *Motive.* The question of the motive or intention of the actor is considered in evaluation of behavior (Blum and McHugh, 1971). Motives are related stereotypically to roles. Accounts may be

offered by the actor as evidence of motive (Scott and Lyman, 1968).

5. *Potential Reactions.* The observer (witness to rule violation) rehearses possible reactions to act and actor based on situational factors, normalization and denial attempts, typifications of role suggested by motive imputation, rules in use, and other factors.

6. *Reaction Is Chosen.* Reaction which is chosen among the alternatives possible is determined in part by the background and training of the reactor—especially if he or she is a social-control agent (Scheff, 1967), organizational categories available for use (Garfinkel, 1967; Douglas, 1971), existing precedents which are invoked by analogous reasoning (Douglas, 1970: chapter 1), societal expectations as to appropriate sanctions and prescribed reactors (Gibbs, 1966b), and other factors (Clark and Gibbs, 1965).

7. *Impact of Reactions.* What is the potential influence of reactions on the actor's future behavior, on perceptions of opportunities to conform or deviate, and on personal identity? Concern here will be with delineating the conditions (factors in 1–6 above as well as others) which produce movement into a deviant career. (Notice that extant labeling formulations have focused on these questions to the relative exclusion of others. In later chapters, we shall address these issues, recognizing that steps 1–6 may occur at the official, interpersonal, or intrapersonal level.)

We suggest that this sequential model is utilized in recognition and reactions to all forms of rule violations, from formal norms to constitutive rules, from the civil-legal area to the polite-interactional. The sequential model is seen in operation in institutional settings such as trials or commitment hearings where the process is quite overt and visible. It also occurs in reactions to polite-interactional rules where the process may be played out informally in a dyadic relationship.

In sum, the first part of the model deals with questions of how deviance is recognized and how actors are placed into categories— i.e., how labeling is accomplished (steps 1–4). A second set of questions involves the decision to react and the selection of negative sanctions (steps 5 and 6). Finally the model poses questions of the impact of the reaction on future behavior and identity (step 7). We will provide a detailed description of the initial steps in this model in the next chapter when we look at recognition and informal reactions to alcoholism, mental illness, and other forms of deviance.

Notes

1. In addition to Howard Becker (1963, 1964), Edwin Lemert (1951, 1972), and Thomas Scheff (1966a, 1968), we must include Erikson (1962, 1966), Goffman (1963), Kitsuse (1964), Matza (1969), Lofland (1969), and most recently Douglas (1971) and Schur (1971). These works will be referred to in the next two chapters. Thomas Scheff, in *Being Mentally Ill*, presents a very explicit formulation of labeling theory in nine propositions (1966a:40–101).

2. It is surprising, because the focus of the Symbolic Interactionist School, since the early work of Cooley and Mead, has been on the power of the primary group and informal reactions to modify and shape human behavior.

3. These two components of the social definition question are related to the level of sociological analysis. The origins question requires a macro-level analysis as evidenced in the work of Quinney (1970), Turk (1966), and other conflict theorists. The "application" question generally portends a micro-level analysis of interactional settings (e.g., Cicourel, 1968). One direction which labeling theory could move, then, would be toward conceptions which attempt to tie these levels together (see Taylor, *et al.*, 1973).

4. Singling out Howard Becker for this criticism is unfortunate since his book, *Outsiders*, does focus on the origins question by looking at the reactors (1963: Chapters 7 and 8).

5. Becker, writing ten years later on the problems with the obedient—rule-breaking dichotomy, states: "I think it better to describe that dimension as the commission or noncommission of a given act. Ordinarily, of course, we study those acts that others are likely to define as deviant. . . . Thus, we may be interested in whether a person smokes marihuana, or engages in homosexual acts in public toilets, in part because these acts are likely to be defined as deviant when discovered" (1973:180–81). For a more detailed discussion of this problem, see Katz (1972).

6. Gouldner uses this critique to distinguish radical and liberal sociologists: " . . . I think that radical sociologists differ from liberals in that, while they take the standpoint of the underdog, they apply it to the study of overdogs. Radical sociologists want to study 'power elites,' the leaders, or masters, of men; liberal sociologists focus their efforts upon underdogs and victims and their immediate bureaucratic caretakers" (1968:111).

7. Gibbs (1966a) notes that the problem with using reactions as an indicator of deviance is that reactions may not occur; or if they do, we have the problem of deciding what a reaction is, how strong it must be to qualify as such, etc. For example, Kitsuse (1964) found that students could recognize homosexuals, but that reactions did not occur or were "generally mild." Consequently, we will use recognition as our indicator of deviance and leave the question of attempts at negative sanctions open to empirical question instead of definitional legislation.

8. For both positive and negative deviance, we are concerned with this question: do reactions force a change in the behavior? Most studies have focused on the reasons for negative deviance (failing to live up to expectations) and the impact of negative

sanctions on this failure. An equally interesting question is: do those who exceed expectations in a positive direction also experience negative reactions, and do they subsequently act so as to be seen as more normal or ordinary? Does the straight-A student respond to appellations such as "brown noser," "apple polisher," or "teacher's pet" by occasionally throwing an exam and getting a C to show he is human? Does the famous movie starlet seek a normal life, but find these activities blocked for her (and subsequently commit suicide because her life seems empty)? The labeling perspective makes the study of positive deviance possible, and theoretically links it to the more standard investigation of negative deviance.

9. Howard Becker, often interpreted as one who requires reaction to specify deviance, has stated that the proper study of this phenomenon would include all four cells of his typology (presented earlier) (1973: 180). Edwin Schur, in searching for a definition, includes reaction: "Human behavior is deviant *to the extent* that it comes to be viewed as involving a *personally discreditable* departure from a group's normative expectations, *and* it *elicits* interpersonal or collective reactions that serve to 'isolate,' 'treat,' 'correct,' or 'punish' *individuals* engaged in such behavior" (1971:24). However, he then introduces the term "extent of deviantness" to argue that recognition alone may signal deviance in the absence of reaction: "A normative breach that could be ['reacted to' (read recognized)] but is not condemned or punished . . . is clearly less deviant than it would be if negative sanctions were actually applied" (Schur, 1971:24). See note 7 above.

References

Akers, Ronald L.
  1968   "Problems in the sociology of deviance: social definitions and behavior." *Social Forces* 46 (June):455–65.
Becker, Howard S.
  1963   *Outsiders: Studies in the Sociology of Deviance.* New York: Free Press.
  1964   *The Other Side.* New York: Free Press.
  1973   "Labeling theory reconsidered." Pp. 177–208 in *Outsiders* (revised edition). New York: Free Press.
Bittner, Egon
  1967   "The police on skid-row: a study of peace-keeping." *American Sociological Review* 32 (October):699–715.
Black, Donald J.
  1970   "Production of crime rates." *American Sociological Review* 35 (August):733–48.
Black, Donald J., and Albert J. Reiss, Jr.
  1970   "Police control of juveniles." *American Sociological Review* 35 (February):63–77.
Blum, Alan F.
  1970   "The sociology of mental illness." In J. D. Douglas (ed.), *Deviance and Respectability.* New York: Basic Books.
Blum, Alan F., and Peter McHugh
  1971   "The social ascription of motives." *American Sociological Review* 36 (February):98–109.
Bordua, David J.
  1967   "Recent trends: deviant behavior and social control." *Annals* 369 (January):149–63.
Chambliss, William J.
  1969   *Crime and the Legal Process.* New York: McGraw-Hill.
Cicourel, Aaron V.
  1968   *The Social Organization of Juvenile Justice.* New York: John Wiley and Sons.
Clark, Alexander L., and Jack P. Gibbs
  1965   "Social control: a reformulation." *Social Problems* 12 (Spring):398–415.

68

Clinard, Marshall B.
1968   *Sociology of Deviant Behavior.* 3rd ed. New York: Holt, Rinehart and Winston.

Cohen, Albert K.
1955   *Delinquent Boys.* New York: Free Press.
1965   "The sociology of the deviant act: anomie theory and beyond." *American Sociological Review* 30 (February):5–14.
1966   *Deviance and Control.* Englewood Cliffs, N.J.: Prentice-Hall.

Denzin, Norman K.
1970a   "Rules of conduct and the study of deviant behavior: some notes on the social relationship." In J. D. Douglas (ed.), *Deviance and Respectability.* New York: Basic Books.
1970b   *The Research Act.* Chicago: Aldine.

Douglas, Jack D.
1967   *The Social Meaning of Suicide.* Princeton, N. J.: Princeton University Press.
1970   *Deviance and Respectability.* New York: Basic Books.
1971   *American Social Order.* New York: Free Press.

Duster, Troy
1970   *The Legislation of Morality.* New York: Free Press.

Erikson, Kai T.
1962   "Notes on the sociology of deviance." *Social Problems* 9 (Spring):307–314.
1966   *Wayward Puritans.* New York: John Wiley and Sons.

Freidson, Eliot
1966   "Disability as social deviance." In Marvin B. Sussman (ed.), *Sociology and Rehabilitation.* Published by the American Sociological Association.
1970   *Profession of Medicine.* New York: Dodd, Mead and Company.

Garfinkel, Harold
1956   "Conditions of successful degradation ceremonies." *American Journal of Sociology* 61 (March):420–24.
1967   *Studies in Ethnomethodology.* Englewood Cliffs, N.J.: Prentice-Hall.

Gibbons, Don C., and Joseph F. Jones
1971   "Some critical notes on current definitions of deviance." *Pacific Sociological Review* 14 (January):20–37.

Gibbs, Jack P.
1966a   "Conceptions of deviant behavior: the old and the new." *Pacific Sociological Review* 9 (Spring):9–14. (Reprinted in Lefton, et. al., *Approaches to Deviance.* New York: Appleton-Century-Crofts, 1968, pp. 44–55.)
1966b   "Sanctions." *Social Problems* 13 (Fall):147–59.

1972   "Issues in defining deviant behavior." In Robert A. Scott and
         J. D. Douglas (eds.), *Theoretical Perspectives on Deviance.*
         New York: Basic Books.

Glaser, Barney G., and Anselm L. Strauss
1967   *The Discovery of Grounded Theory.* Chicago: Aldine.

Goffman, Erving
1961   *Asylums.* New York: Doubleday.
1963   *Stigma.* Englewood Cliffs, N.J.: Prentice-Hall.

Gouldner, Alvin W.
1968   "The sociologist as partisan: sociology and the welfare state."
         American Sociologist 3 (May):103–116.

1970   *The Coming Crisis of Western Sociology.* New York: Basic
         Books.

Haney, C. Allen, and Robert Michielutte
1968   "Selective factors operating in adjudication of incompe-
         tency." *Journal of Health and Social Behavior* 9 (Septem-
         ber):233–42.

Homans, George C.
1950   *The Human Group.* New York: Harcourt.
1961   *Social Behavior: Its Elementary Forms.* New York: Harcourt.

Katz, Jack
1972   "Deviance, charisma, and rule-defined behavior." *Social
         Problems* 20 (Fall):186–202.

Kitsuse, John I.
1964   "Societal reaction to deviant behavior: problems of theory
         and method." In Howard S. Becker (ed.), *The Other Side.*
         New York: Free Press.

Kitsuse, John I., and Aaron V. Cicourel
1963   "A note on the official use of statistics." *Social Problems* 11
         (Fall):131–39.

Laing, R. D., and A. Esterson
1964   *Sanity, Madness and the Family.* London: Tavistock.

Lemert, Edwin M.
1951   *Social Pathology.* New York: McGraw-Hill.
1972   *Human Deviance, Social Problems and Social Control.* 2nd
         ed. Englewood Cliffs, N.J.: Prentice-Hall.

Lennard, Henry L., and Arnold Bernstein
1969   *Patterns of Human Interaction.* San Francisco: Jossey-Bass.

Liazos, Alexander
1972   "The poverty of the sociology of deviance: nuts, sluts and
         preverts." *Social Problems* 20 (Summer):103–120.

Lofland, John
1969   *Deviance and Identity.* Englewood Cliffs, New Jersey: Pren-
         tice-Hall.

Lorber, Judith
1967   "Deviance as performance: the case of illness." *Social Problems* 14 (Winter):302–310.

Matza, David
1964   *Delinquency and Drift.* New York: John Wiley and Sons.
1969   *Becoming Deviant.* Englewood Cliffs, New Jersey: Prentice-Hall.

Miller, Walter B.
1958   "Lower class culture as a generating milieu of gang delinquency." *Journal of Social Issues* 14 (1958):5–19.

Parsons, Talcott
1951   *The Social System.* New York: Free Press.

Platt, Anthony M.
1969   *The Child Savers: The Invention of Delinquency.* Chicago: University of Chicago Press.

1974   "The triumph of benevolence: the origins of the juvenile justice system in the United States." Pp. 356–89 in R. Quinney (ed.), *Criminal Justice in America.* Boston: Little, Brown.

Quinney, Richard
1970   *The Social Reality of Crime.* Boston: Little, Brown.

Scheff, Thomas J.
1966a   *Being Mentally Ill.* Chicago: Aldine.

1966b   "Users and non-users of a student psychiatric clinic." *Journal of Health and Human Behavior* 7 (Summer):114–21.

1967   *Mental Illness and Social Processes.* New York: Harper and Row.

1968   "Negotiating reality: notes on power in the assessment of responsibility." *Social Problems* 16 (Summer):3–17.

Schur, Edwin M.
1969   "Reactions to deviance: a critical assessment." *American Journal of Sociology* 75 (November):309–322.

1971   *Labeling Deviant Behavior.* New York: Harper and Row.

Scott, Marvin B., and Stanford M. Lyman
1968   "Accounts." *American Sociological Review* 33 (February):46–61.

Strauss, Anselm L.
1959   *Mirrors and Masks: The Search for Identity.* New York: Free Press.

Szasz, Thomas S.
1970   *The Manufacture of Madness.* New York: Harper and Row.

Tannenbaum, Frank
1938   *Crime and the Community.* Boston: Ginn.

Taylor, Ian, Paul Walton, and Jock Young
  1973   *The New Criminology: For a Social Theory of Deviance.* London: Routledge and Kegan Paul.
Thomas, W. I.
  1928   *The Child in America.* New York: Knopf.
Turk, Austin T.
  1966   "Conflict and criminality." *American Sociological Review* 31 (June):338–52.
Turner, Ralph H.
  1970   *Family Interaction.* New York: John Wiley and Sons.
Werthman, Carl, and Irving Piliavin
  1967   "Gang members and the police." In D. J. Bordua (ed.), *The Police.* New York: John Wiley and Sons.
Wrong, Dennis H.
  1961   "The oversocialized conception of man in modern sociology." *American Sociological Review* 26 (April):183–93.
Zimmerman, Don H.
  1969   "Some issues in labeling theory." A paper read at the Pacific Sociological Association Meetings in Seattle, Washington (April).

Chapter

IV

Recognition and Reactions to Deviance

"As a matter of routine," I said to them politely, "would you mind showing me some identification." The one with the moustache shook some more, and he and thugface looked toward the tall one, and he pulled a wallet from his pocket with only four of the dozen plastic compartments occupied. None of them contained credit cards. Cops can't afford credit cards. I didn't like it. I looked toward Aurora, who was staring at the tall man's feet.

I followed her gaze. Rubber soles! The sure mark of a policeman. The cop followed our eyes, too, and knew that we knew. The bluff was up. . . .

Xaviera Hollander

The creation of deviance, according to extant societal reaction or labeling theories, lies in the official social-control machinery of a society. In our description of this approach in the last chapter, we criticized it for not actually focusing on the *labeling process*. Exactly what are the dynamics of the application of deviant labels to varied behavioral activities? We now try to describe this process. It is seen as a series of steps which involve (a) viewing a behavior (visibility), (b) recognizing it as deviant, which entails (c) the process of applying typifications of deviance to specific acts, (d) the attribution of intent to the actor to determine the "degree" of deviance, and finally (e) a decision on the transgressor's true nature—is he essentially deviant? We see this as a sequential process (although this order of effects may not always hold) which characterizes the everyday imputations and evaluations of behavior. Thus, ordinary citizens in their daily rounds come upon situations which are "out of the ordinary," where some decision is then required—i.e., the event must be categorized. This informal process involves imputation, negotiation, reinterpretation (documentary method): in short, all the elements of the interpretive view. The dynamics of the creation of deviance are thus found in the everyday behaviors of everyday people—an area largely unexplored by past labeling frameworks. The process at this informal level is similar to (but less visible than) the formal labeling process found in large control agencies. Our topic for the moment is the former; the latter is described in Chapter VII. This chapter, then, will describe

Source: Xaviera Hollander, *The Happy Hooker* (New York: Dell Publishing Company, 1972), p. 6.

the perceptual aspects of deviance recognition at the informal level (steps 1–4 at the end of the previous chapter). Whether reaction occurs, given recognition, is discussed in Chapter V.

Visibility

Setting aside for the moment the question of possible self-labeling by the secret deviant, visibility of behavior is the first step in labeling and subsequent reactions to deviance. Visibility can be defined as the probability that an event will be encountered either directly (observed by a witness) or indirectly (written or verbal reports by others). What is visible may be an instance of rule-violating behavior, or in the case of the falsely accused, behaviors or attributes which are putatively associated with some form of deviance. An example of the latter would be cases when dress or mannerisms produce a label such as "homosexual" or "whore" in the absence of any direct or indirect evidence of behaviors of alleged sexual waywardness.

Self-reported studies of deviant behavior indicate that virtually everyone commits acts for which they could be publicly labeled. However, most rule breaking is not detected, not made visible to others (Erickson and Empey, 1963). Thus, it may be more accurate to speak of variations in the visibility of rule violations than to suggest that some people are rule breakers and others are not. Stated differently, most of us have been secret rule breakers and vary only in that we have not had our behavior observed (or, as we shall argue later, observed but not recognized as deviant). Indeed, one could turn the question about and ask why, if everyone has a history of rule violations to various degrees, are not more persons engaged in ongoing deviant careers? In short, why so much nondeviance?[1]

While many factors are involved, some people are susceptible to labeling because their activities are more likely to be monitored in some way. It is therefore important to understand some of the structural aspects of visibility. One of the structural limitations upon visibility of events is the concept of private and public places. The law distinguishes public and private places by curtailing surveillance by authorities in the latter (Stinchcombe, 1964). The invisibility of behavior carried out behind bedroom doors, in private offices, and in homes is guaranteed by architectural and legal enclosure. Officially, search warrants are required to enter these private areas.[2] In addition to legal protection, the boundaries of private places are respected and entrance governed by polite-interactional rules. Thus, private places, even when accessible, are not easily encroached upon by those who do not belong—e.g., a student knocking on the open door of a professor.

Behaviors in public are by definition more visible. Since entrance to public places does not have to be justified by citizens or control agents, the probability of observation is greater. However, there are a number of public, yet semiprivate, places where observation by others is unlikely. Examples would be private areas on public transport such as restrooms in planes or trains, or the corridors of high-rise public housing units.

> The elevators and corridors of public housing projects are, in a sense, streets. . . . These interior streets, although completely accessible to public use, are closed to public view and they thus lack the checks and inhibitions exerted by eye-policed city streets. (Jacobs, quoted in Lofland, 1969:66–67)

Mainly in response to the crimes which occur in these semiprivate places, the emphasis has been on structural designs which increase visibility. Sidewalks receive better lighting, shrubs and bushes are removed from park walkways, etc. Visibility may also be increased by electronic means: metal detection devices installed at airports to detect weapons, electronically monitored identification tags or badges to restrict admittance to "public" places such as political conventions, closed-circuit monitoring of hallways and elevators in apartment buildings, are examples. Even large outdoor areas are not exempt. Closed-circuit television coverage of activities in Times Square is now being developed which would bring a large public area under surveillance. In addition, in-person observation may be invoked in public places, such as plain-clothes policemen in public restrooms; or the presence of observers may be implied as in a sign posted in the changing room of a Minneapolis men's store: "This Area is Under Observation by a Male Employee."

Certain people spend more of their time in public places, thereby increasing visibility of behavior. The urban poor are more likely to be in public places due to overcrowding and inadequate housing. One observer describes the public nature of ghetto life in south Chicago.

> During the summer months the streets in the Addams area are thronged with children, young adults, and old people. Street life is especially active in the afternoon after school or work. . . . On warm nights there is hardly a stoop, corner, alley, or doorway that

> has not been staked out by some of its regular habitues. The adults get the door stoops. The young girls stay close by, just out of earshot. The small children are given the run of the sidewalks in front of their mothers. The unmarried males are relegated to whatever little nooks or crannies are left. (Suttles, 1968:74)

Because of the limitations on private places for urban poor, their behaviors are highly visible to outsiders compared to other social classes.[3] Gambling in middle class areas is likely to be in the privacy of the home, while in crowded slum areas, gambling is likely to be carried out in alleys and vacant lots. Visibility of adolescent activities varies by social class for a number of reasons. Delinquent groups in middle-class areas have access to their parents' cars. This provides both privacy and mobility so that delinquent acts can be carried out in distant communities, thereby lowering local visibility of actions. The lower-class youth usually does not have access to the family automobile, so activities are more restricted to their neighborhood (Chambliss and Seideman, 1971). Probably the most blatant difference in social class visibility involves drinking behaviors. The rich indulge themselves in private clubs, exclusive restaurants and bars, or at home. The urban poor are more visible to police and the public, so they are more susceptible to arrest for being drunk and disorderly, or disturbing the peace.

The placement of witnesses influences the extent of visibility of various behaviors. Patrol patterns of the police determine to some extent the distribution and size of city crime rates by focusing attention on certain areas of the city. Placing more police in high crime areas helps to assure that they will remain high crime areas. Some cities have high delinquency rates in part because they have larger juvenile bureaus within the police department (Cicourel, 1968). Devoting more men to observation and recording of juvenile offenses creates more official delinquent crime. Similarly, some stores may have higher shoplifting rates because they have more floor detectives or better electronic surveillance. If stores in lower-class areas have more detectives, shoplifting rates may be artificially higher than in suburban areas where shoplifting goes undetected.

The addition of experts at various gate-keeping positions automatically results in greater discovery of deviance, or traits thought indicative of deviance. Thus, highly trained, psychiatrically oriented school counselors use more tests and rating scales on school children today then ever before, thereby finding more problems in need of correction. Although certain forms of testing, such as intelligence tests have been attacked as culturally biased and removed from some schools, they are usually replaced by "less objectionable" tests which produce differentiation. The point is that testing has become increasingly popular while little concern is shown for the labeling aspects of the test results as they affect high school tracking systems, college entrance, career placement (rather than selection), or job opportunities (Cicourel and Kitsuse, 1963).

Visibility is also affected by the extent of contact with public control bureaucracies. Those having greater contact with public agencies such as state unemployment departments, welfare departments, and public housing agencies are leading very public lives. A recent study found that 40 percent of the statutory rape cases which became known to a juvenile bureau in a large California city were referrals from welfare agencies. These cases were discovered during routine investigations of eligibility for AFDC payments. These "victims" were encouraged to cooperate with police efforts to prosecute offenders to assure welfare eligibility (Skolnick and Woodworth, 1967). This is an example of secondary visibility. Behavior is serendipitously found by one social-control agency and then referred to an agency with appropriate jurisdiction and expertise. Secondary visibility increases as persons have contact with greater numbers of control agencies.

Secondary visibility also increases with the availability of technology for information sharing between agencies. Recent developments in the computer industry help to provide the finger-tip information across agencies that maximizes information sharing. Technological advances permit national data banks to be established, and information sharing via pooled computer usage assures the quick dissemination of information (see Miller, 1971; Wheeler, 1969). One computer company has been working on a laser storage technique which would permit the recording and retrieval, on one 4,500-foot computer tape, of the equivalent of twelve printed pages of material on each person in the United States. As Orwell predicted, technology threatens to make various control agencies omnipresent in the lives of citizens, drastically reducing the amount of private (invisible) behaviors.

Summing up, the poor are more susceptible to discovery of rule-violating behaviors because they are more likely to spend their daily round in public places, thereby making their behavior more visible to witnesses; the poor are less likely to enjoy mobility and access to private places such as country clubs, restaurants, and cocktail lounges and are simultaneously more closely watched—e.g., greater police surveillance in lower-class areas. Because they are more likely to have contacts with control agencies propagated by the welfare state, they are subject to secondary visibility. These visibility differentials partly account for the overrepresentation of the poor and disadvantaged in social-control agencies. Sociologists relying on these agency-generated populations of deviants for their samples have, for years, been misled into believing that deviance was a lower-class phenomenon (Kitsuse and Cicourel, 1963). Because the behaviors of the middle and upper classes have been less visible, it has been assumed that little or no deviance originates in these groups.[4]

Recognition

Recognition is the process of organizing a number of events into some pattern which permits an understanding of what the event means, such that the action is accounted for by the observer. This matching of event and pattern is achieved by the documentary method of interpretation. Recall our earlier example of the recognition problems encountered by the woman with the black purse at the bus stop. New events kept suggesting different patterns or labels, so what actually happened was continually open to redefinition. However, the woman had a stock of knowledge about social types, roles, and labels which she could use to interpret and place diverse events. Consequently, understanding the concept of recognition requires an examination of how labels and patterns are acquired by members of society, and how they are then used in "doing recognition."

Socialization can be seen as a process of acquiring roles, patterns, or labels for various activities.[5] Children learn the role of father, mother, etc., within the family through modeling and imitation. Children's literature provides information on the role of policemen, firemen, and other occupations. Also, children's activities often center around role playing where the themes of doctor-nurse, father-mother, and other roles are in evidence. However, many of these roles are very general, providing little information about what the role incumbent is actually like. Thus, we learn rather stereotyped views of various roles, especially when first-hand experience is not available. For example, the policeman is depicted in the child's world as someone who helps lost boys find their homes, rescues helpless animals from dangerous situations, and protects people from evil vandals and thieves. The child learns only at a later time that these idealistic characteristics of the police role do not accurately describe police work.

Since conventional roles are more explicitly taught and because people have greater contact with others in these roles, the stereotypes of conventional occupations may be revised.[6] Deviant roles, on the other hand, are usually not formally taught during socialization. Rather, these roles are learned indirectly; and, since the folk knowledge about deviance is seldom revised by first-hand experience, these views remain highly stereotyped. In some cases, our knowledge of a behavior must develop in an informational vacuum. John Gagnon, in speaking of the acquisition of sexual identities in children, states that the nonlabeling of genitalia and acts of excretion "leaves the child without a vocabulary with which to describe his physical and psychic (sexual) experiences. This specific absence of terminology has two major consequences. The first is the tendency for fantasy to overrun the sexual life of the child. . . . [The second] is the tendency for unsatisfied curiosity of children to lead them directly into sexual play" (Gagnon, 1967:32–33). A failure to adequately label and explain other taboo behaviors may also lead to a fascination and searching out of more information on the deviant behavior. Where direct information is lacking, stereotypic knowledge often arises to take its place.

A second characteristic of the indirect knowledge of deviant phenomena is the overwhelming negative components which are communicated to the exclusion of any possible positive qualities. The onesidedness of the information helps to build the view that those who commit deviant acts are basically evil—i.e., that their essential character is bad. When our experiential distance from a phenomenon is high, there is a tendency to dichotomize, to see the phenomenon as good or evil, black or white. Consequently, deviance is often seen as a characteristic or attribute of the violating individual rather than as a variation on a continuum of potential behaviors (see McIntosh, 1968). The result is a tendency to see deviance as the activities of special "kinds of people" rather than as activities to be seen in relation to conforming behaviors (Cohen, 1966). Thus, we have deviance taking on the role of a master status, such that all other statuses are subordinate to it (Becker, 1963). The actor becomes known by his rule violations and little else.

But how do the stereotypes of those engaging in deviant behavior form? The question demands two answers. The first must deal with the general process of typification, of which stereotyping is but a part; the second must address the content of these typifications: how and why do the stereotypes develop in specific ways? First, typification must be defined.

Typifications are descriptions drawn from a common stock of knowledge which serve as short-hand notation for various phenomena. Typifications are thus simplified, standardized categories or labels, used to place other people or things. Berger and Luckmann (1966:30–31) note: "The reality of everyday life contains typificatory schemes in terms of which others are apprehended and 'dealt with' in face-to-face encounters." Typifications are inter-subjective, thereby allowing us to bring experiences under "broad categories which impart meaning to events." The typifications produced in everyday interactions allow the summarization of our constantly unique subjective experiences into objective—i.e., externalizable—descriptions which are less bounded by time and space. The objectification is necessary because of the impossibility of relating all subjective experiences—selection and summarization must result. In any recalling or retelling of a subjective experience, some sedimentation results; this sedimentation of basic core meanings becomes objectified—i.e., intersubjectively agreed upon. This is achieved through the use of labels or language categories which anonymize experience. Thus, typification, "perceiving the world and structuring it by means of categorical types" (McKinney, 1970:243), is a characteristic of all human perception. These categorical types vary in their accuracy,[7] and this variation may have implications for the way observers react to a witnessed event.

Sources of Typifications of Deviance and Deviants

One of the major sources of typifications of deviant behavior is everyday words and phrases. Holden Caulfield's favorite statement, "It's colder than a witch's tit" not only says something about the weather, but imparts a characterization of the physiological and personality aspects of those who practice witchcraft. Cliches such as "poor but virtuous" imply a certain view of the poor as immoral and untrustworthy. Douglas (1970:7) notes that the phrase " 'poor *but* virtuous' involves the presumption that one must normally (in the abstract) expect the poor to be wicked, since this 'but' implies a contradiction of normal expectation." The analysis of cliches would seem to provide a fertile source of typifications of both conventional and deviant behavior.

This phenomenon is perhaps most easily seen in the area of mental illness. Thomas Scheff suggests that the images of how the mentally ill look and act are transmitted inadvertently in everyday jokes and slang. Phrases such as "Don't be an idiot!", "Stop acting like a moron," "What are you, crazy or something?" are commonly used without thought of their stereotypic aspects. Verbal and written jokes about the mentally ill, or about asylums, help communicate three themes: (a) that the mentally ill look and act different, (b) that mental illness is basically incurable, and (c) that the insane are a fundamentally different class of human being (Scheff, 1966a:77). Because of the permeation of our everyday language with these jokes and cliches, public stereotypes of mental illness as well as other forms of deviance are extremely difficult to change.

A second source of typified images of mental illness, and other forms of deviant behavior, is the mass media. Radio, television, and newspaper accounts of criminal action often mention histories of mental disorder, or that the suspect was a "former mental patient." Scheff says that this selective reporting contributes to these three basic themes because readers do not hear from these same sources about the positive aspects of former mental patients, nor do they count the incidents reported where no history of mental illness was found. Indeed, Scheff states that the proportion of former mental patients involved in crime is lower than the rate for the general population. In addition to news coverage, mass media presentations of deviance in movies, short stories or novels, as well as in television programming, may provide stereotypes of deviant activities and actors. The limitations of television programming demand that the deviant be portrayed as basically evil, and that he be caught or punished. Such characterizations serve to promote the image of all deviants as inept evil-doers with no socially redeeming value. In this sense, Senator Pastore and the F.C.C. have played an important role in the forms which television stereotyping takes.[8] Of course, typification and stereotyping are not restricted to deviant activities, but may apply to whole groups. Smith (1970) found that television programming has much influence on public stereotypes of adolescents in England.

A third potential source of typifications of deviants are public education campaigns designed to make the public aware of certain social problems. These prevention-education efforts may strengthen the view that "symptoms" are easily recognized and should be the basis for referrals to professionals. The mental hygiene movement is an example of a large public educational effort to inform laymen of psychiatric symptomatology (Davis, 1938; Sarbin, 1969; Sarbin and Mancuso, 1970). The mental health movement, through its emphasis on the illness metaphor, locates the reasons for mental illness within the individual, and neglects the possible environmental reasons for the "problems in living" (Davis, 1938:60). Thomas Szasz and others have argued the inappropriateness of this metaphor and its resultant emphasis (Szasz, 1963; Ellis, 1967).

Public education campaigns often use scare tactics, generally through a one-sided presentation of the problem. Recent one-minute spots on drug addiction tend to highlight the negative aspects of drug use without reference to possible compensating points (e.g., mind expanding consciousness, greater sensitivity and awareness, ritual or religious use of drugs for meditation, and others). Televised educational commercials depicting the problem of alcoholism may generate, due to time requirements, a highly exaggerated picture of the alcoholic as someone who always has a drink in his hand. This stereotyped depiction may lead the family of a problem drinker to reject the possibility that his or her behavior may indicate alcoholism. A study of wives' reactions to husbands' drinking concluded:

> The inaccuracies of the cultural stereotype of the alcoholic—particularly that he is in a constant state of inebriation—also contributes to the family's rejection of the idea of alcoholism, as the husband seems to demonstrate from time to time that he can control his drinking. (Jackson, 1968:56)

In addition to generally well-intended educational campaigns, a fourth source of typification of deviant behavior is the activities of moral crusaders and moral entrepreneurs attached to zealous social-control bureaucracies (Dixon, 1968). In the case of social-control agencies, these entrepreneurial efforts seek to strengthen the organization's definitional claim to a certain form of deviance, to justify the agency's existence and continued funding, and also to legitimate periodic crack-downs on proposed vices.

Edwin Schur (1965) has documented the steps taken by the Narcotics Division of the Treasury Department (later to become the Federal Bureau of Narcotics) to gain control over the enforcement of narcotics use. While narcotics use was originally defined as a medical problem, eventually "through a combination of restrictive regulations, attention only to favorable court decisions, and harrassment, [this bureau] effectively and severely limited the freedom of medical practitioners to treat addict-patients as they see fit" (Schur, 1965:130). The shift from medical control to control through criminal statutes was facilitated by promotion of a dope-fiend image of the user "which depicted the drug addict as a degenerate and vicious criminal much given to violent crimes and sex orgies" (Schur,

1965:120). Dissemination of such stereotypes facilitated further legislation to strengthen the FBN's definitional control of drug use and
traffic (Duster, 1970). Howard Becker (1963:135–46) describes how
a similar propaganda program was launched by this bureau to bring
marihuana use under its control. The stereotyped views of the marihuana user, built through selected horror stories released by the
FBN's to the press, and the extant dope-fiend image of the hard
narcotic user generated the mistaken belief that marihuana was a
hard narcotic. This affected public awareness which was then called
upon to justify the Marihuana Tax Act of 1937.

Only in the late 1960s was the dope-fiend image completely ex-
ploded as myth. Research forced a recognition that marihuana and
other hallucinogens could not be equated with hard narcotics (a
realization reflected in the recent name change of F.B.N. to Bureau
of Narcotic and Dangerous Drugs).[9] It is ironic that the dope-fiend
image, which served the FBN so well in their initial definitional
control, public legitimation, and funding, has come back to haunt
their control efforts, making citizen respect for drug laws and their
enforcers open to question. This general process of entrepreneurial
work will be detailed in Chapter VI.

Diffusion of diagnostic categories and labels may occur in more
indirect ways via public educational programs or campaigns, and by
the popularity of certain categorical systems in some social groups.
It has become fashionable in upper-class circles to speak of psychiatric analysis or therapy (Scheff, 1966b). (The popularity and faddish-
ness of various therapies are reflected in discussions by television and
movie personalities on late-night talk shows.) Self-diagnosis becomes
fashionable and reality is seen through the new labels and categories
provided by therapist. This diffusion is not restricted to the upper
class, although it is perhaps greatest there. For example, students
who take an abnormal psychology course find themselves perceiving
their friends and themselves quite differently as a result.

A major influence on the public typification of deviants and their
activities are the official labeling ceremonies denoting the assignment of stigmatizing labels. Garfinkel (1956) says that these status
degradation ceremonies, to be successful, must create social types.
Therefore trials, juvenile hearings, commitment proceedings and
other official "induction" ceremonies must typify deviant *event* and
perpetrator:

> 1. Both event and perpetrator must be removed
> from the realm of their everyday character and
> made to stand as "out of the ordinary."

2. Both event and perpetrator must be placed
within a scheme of preferences. . . . The preferences
must not be for event A over event B, but for event
of *type A* over *type B*. The same typing must be
accomplished for the perpetrator. . . . The unique,
never recurring character of the event or perpetrator should be lost. (Garfinkel, 1956:422)

The socially orchestrated typifications to which Garfinkel refers
serve to legitimize and compliment the conforming witnesses, who,
because of the typification, see little similarity between their position
and that of the accused. These ceremonies contribute to the dichotomous conception of deviance alluded to earlier, and show that the
accused are fundamentally different than the righteous, and therefore deserving of their fate. The ceremony produces a greater social
distance between accused and righteous. The resulting depersonalization permits a wide range of punishments to be inflicted in the
name of reform.[10]

Even when official public degradation ceremonies are not involved, typifications derive from the ways in which remedial agencies perceive and handle their clientele. Robert Scott (1969) notes
that implicit assumptions about helplessness, inability to function,
and dependency are evident in the way agencies for the blind treat
their clientele. The agency shapes the image of the deviant and
indirectly the views of his family and supporters. Scott notes that
these expectations "embody a kind of putative identity that the expert has constructed for the person who comes to him for help. This
putative identity is manifested as the expert's expectations for the
clients' self-attitudes and behavior" (1970:257). These expectations
become part of the typifications characterizing the deviant, which
diffuse to laymen. As such, they give shape to the image of deviant
role utilized in doing recognition.

One final source of typification, often neglected for obvious reasons, is the theoretical formulations on deviant behavior derived by
social scientists (Chapman, 1968). Positivistic criminology, beginning
with the biological-natural selection theories of Cesare Lombroso,
has favored the natural science method of differentiation. Since Lombroso, criminologists have sought biological,[11] constitutional, or so-
ciocultural variables which would differentiate the criminal and
non-criminal—the implicit assumption being that criminals were
fundamentally different from the law-abiding citizen (Matza, 1964).
Matza notes that positivistic criminology "revolted against the assumption of the general similarity between criminal and conventional persons implicit in classical theory" (1964:11).

These positivistic theories and the research results which have been generated become sources of typification[12] (which may or may not be stereotyped). Thus, Jensen's recent work on racial differences in IQ may promote typifications (or reinforce existing ones) that blacks are slow, lazy, and fundamentally different from whites (Jensen, 1969). Delinquency researchers using court statistics may generate the impression that delinquents are primarily from broken homes. This information is disseminated via teaching, as well as professional journals and books, to students and practitioners, and eventually to the general public. These theorizations and findings may influence the professional control agents such that the predictions are fulfilled. In an interesting study, Stanton Wheeler and his associates (1968) found that juvenile court judges who read social science journals were more likely to impose harsher sanctions for delinquents brought before them than judges not familiar with the research literature. Perhaps these judges were more cognizant of factors which the research literature suggested as etiologically related to delinquency. This may have led to differential reaction by "informed" judges for juveniles from broken homes. (Unfortunately Wheeler's work does not examine the content of research read and types of disposition.)

The Process of
Labeling

We noted in Chapter III that extant labeling formulations do not address the basic process of labeling—i.e., the pairing of events and labels. How do typifications about behaviors get called up by unique and diverse events such that deviance is recognized? Harvey Sacks (1972a) suggests that words and actions become combined through the pairing of events (items) and "devices." Devices here are categories present in the common culture. Sacks gives an example:

> The baby cried.
> The mommy picked it up. (Cicourel, 1970:163–66)

Most people reading or hearing these two sentences would assume that the woman picking up the baby was its mother. (She need not be.) This is because the item "baby" is associated with the device "family" and, similarly, "mommy" is associated with "family." Notice two things: first, the item "baby" may correspond to a number of devices—i.e., family, immaturity ("don't act like a baby"), helplessness ("the baby cried since no one fed it"), and others. However, the appearance of two items evoked the typification or device of "family." While many devices could have been used (e.g., "emergency," where mommy was a helper and baby simply a person in distress), the situation at hand suggested family and this led to a misreading of the situation—the mommy was not the mother of the baby in question. This tendency to use the device suggested by the first item to classify the second—through a signaled device—is termed the "consistency rule" by Sacks. Second, we note that items are typically associated with devices and this sets the stage for the classification of the second item (mommy as the child's mother). The typification of "family" led to a misreading of the situation. The consistency is rendered via the typification, which is almost a background expectancy—i.e., a tacit, taken-for-granted relationship. We are surprised when this consistency is not rendered (Garfinkel, 1964).

The consistency rule, the idea that one informational item guides the placement of the second informational item via a device or category, often blocks our perceptions of various items due to the taken-for-granted nature of the device. Consider the following riddle. A father takes his son for a ride in a new sports car. In demonstrating its cornering ability, the father loses control of his new car and it rolls down an embankment. The crash kills the father and seriously injures his son. The boy is rushed to a nearby hospital for emergency surgery. The surgeon on call walks into the room, sees the boy and says, "I can't operate, that's my son!" How can this be?

The answer , of course, is that the surgeon is the boy's *mother*. The role of surgeon is stereotypically associated with the device male, as is the term father. The use of the consistency rule creates the riddle—the boy cannot have two fathers. Thus, proffered answers usually attempt to neutralize the inconsistency—e.g., the driver was the boy's step-father upon divorce and his natural father was the surgeon. The riddle demonstrates how sexual, racial, or other stereotypes may render a misreading of scenes due to the erroneous leads provided by the consistency rule in category placement.

Sacks suggests a second rule guiding category placement, an "economy rule." This states that if one device is adequate for interpreting the situation, for accounting for the problem at hand, other devices (alternative explanations) need not be entertained. This refers to the premature locking in of a category based on one or two items or events. Once the device is chosen, the search for evidence is predetermined in its scope and direction, in much the same sense that the way you ask a question delimits and partially determines the answer you will receive. Douglas, in his study of a coroner's office and its classifications of death, found what he termed a "primacy effect" of the classification upon the search for evidence. The following refers to a coroner's investigation of a supposed suicide:

> It is important to note here that the deputy coroner is specifically *searching for* information about personality, emotions, actions, etc., which are seen as relevant to inferring suicide. So, for example, he is interested in whether the victim had problems, not whether the victim had exultations. Since most people have both, and since we normally expect this, it might seem strange that there is this concentration in the investigative procedure on what is "wrong" or suicide-related. . . . We seem, then, to have a *primacy effect* here: once the classification is made of suicide, the rest of the investigation becomes a search for information that demonstrates that classification to be an adequate account. (Douglas, 1971:119. Emphasis in original.)

The economy rule and the consistency rule guide the typifications assigned to witnessed events. Thus, observers "fill in" what actually happened given the items (witnessed events) and implied categories (devices) which fit the problem at hand.[13] Typifications facilitate this filling-in process and thereby allow people to "deal effectively with an environment which carries with it ambiguity and gaps in 'directions to concrete action' because the typical is rendered homogeneous, nonproblematical, and, therefore, taken for granted" (Cicourel, 1972a:255).

The Attribution Process

Doing recognition involves two additional elements. First, the *attribution of cause* to the activity must take place—i.e., what factors produced this particular behavior at this particular time? Second, observers generally want to know why the activity occurred. Our recognition of the meaning of an act involves some type of *motive assignment to the actor* by the witnesses to a social scene. Ordinarily, most behavior tends to be taken for granted, a background expectancy which is subsumed under the reciprocity of perspectives aspect of man's natural attitude toward the everyday world. However, deviance topicalizes the questions of causation and motivation for observers. The answers tendered will affect what the witnesses do about a particular behavior—whether they reinforce it, ignore it, or seek to punish or reform it.[14]

The tendency to assign motives and dispositional states to behavior is almost automatic, in part because our language imports attribution. B. F. Skinner, who has done quite well by ignoring attributional processes of meaning, tacitly recognized this problem in remarking on the tendency of psychology students running conditioning experiments to impute dispositional states to laboratory animals. Students observing a pigeon conditioned to turn in one direction in order to secure food described the scene in attributional language: the organism was conditioned to *expect* reinforcement; the pigeon *felt* food would appear because of his actions; the pigeon walked around, *hoping* for food (Skinner, 1964, cited by Scott, 1971:29).[15] We may also impute motives and responsibility to young children before these terms have meaning to them (Cicourel, 1972b:149, 150). Another bit of evidence which suggests that imputation permeates our perceptual apparatus is the difficulty of suspending the tendency to assign responsibility. A study of juvenile bureau officers found that "the officer, in short, attributes adult basic rules to the child or juvenile when deciding the relevance of rule violations. . . . It is difficult for the officer to suspend the common-sense reasoning he uses with adult suspects" (Cicourel, 1972b:154, 155).

We begin with the question: "How do observers impute cause to witnessed events?" Events may be classified into three general types: *accidental events* where the event is seen as beyond the control of actor—e.g., breaking of a tie-rod may produce an auto accident; *forced events* where actor was under some external threat which limited his behavior choices to one action—e.g., being forced to open a safe by threat of personal violence; and *open events,* events which appear to involve a choice—the actor could have done otherwise (McHugh, 1970). The first two types involve external as opposed to internal causation. In open events, where the actor appears to make a choice, the reason for the option chosen may be perceived as external (due to environmental influences) or internal (due to some dispositional state of the actor), or a combination of external-internal. Attribution of cause to the actor is the most likely in open-choice situations.[16]

The correspondence theory of Jones and Davis (1965) delineates how attributions of internal causation are related to dispositional inferences. An action (behavior) produces an effect (pain, joy, compliance, etc.). If observers assume that (a) the actor knew the consequences of his action, and (b) he or she had the ability to carry out action, then some strong inferences of intent and disposition of the actor are made (1965:222). See the accompanying diagram.

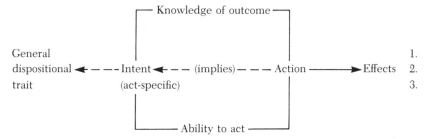

Here a correspondent inference is made from the effects of an act to the actor's basic intentions, which in turn suggest some general disposition. Thus, "behavior having the effect of dominating another person will be taken as basis for inferring the actor's intention to dominate" (Kelley, 1967:208). If observers impute that the actor had knowledge of potential effects—that most persons would say the action would be interpreted as domineering—and that the actor had a choice (he could have refrained from action), it is imputed that he intended the outcome and is, therefore, naturally dominant (disposition).

In a classic experiment, Thibaut and Riecken (1955) found that observers were more likely to attribute internal causation to explain a high-status person's compliance with a confederate's request, while low-status compliers were seen as doing so for external reasons. In regard to high-status compliers, "when we say that a person's behavior was internally caused we are saying that he behaved as he did because he wanted to, because his dispositional qualities were such that he could and wanted to perform that behavior" (Hastorf, *et al.*, 1970:74). The person of low status is *seen* as forced to comply for any number of reasons—e.g., he was coerced by a power differential, he wished to please or seek reinforcement from the requester, etc. Reasons for compliance are located outside the individual, thus little is learned of this (low-status) actor's dispositional attributes or personality traits. An example may help. The professor who accedes to the unusual request of a student is seen as doing it for internal reasons (naturally kind, likes students, true humanitarian in a world of bureaucrats, etc.), because it is not part of the role requirement. The compliance of a student to the request of a professor is seen as externally caused—a role requirement of student to comply with the mentor's requests. Thus, the low-status person is denied the opportunity to make good impressions—i.e., that he is by nature interested and motivated to comply with a request—since his action is perceived as externally motivated.[17]

On the other hand, we might speculate on attributional outcomes when high- and low-status persons do not comply. The high-status person may be seen as a noncomplier due to weak compliance pressure—i.e., the request was meaningless or not persuasive to a high-status actor (external reasons attributed for noncompliance). However, we might find that observers would assume that noncompliance of a low-status person was due to internal factors—obstinacy, open defiance, bad intentions (Hastorf, *et al.*, 1970:74). This is consistent with Hollander's (1958) studies of idiosyncrasy credit—that is, that high-status rule violators in a group are less likely to be sanctioned than middle- and low-status members: there is more tolerance of group-related rule violations. These experimental findings are suggestive of the difficulties encountered by the low-status person: he cannot win! Deviance is seen as internal—that is, due to his basic nature—and conformity is seen as externally caused, thus speaking less to his true nature.

Summing to this point, we have argued that observers' attributions of causality are internal-external; these attributions, when internal, raise the question of actor's basic nature, his dispositional traits which supposedly authored intent and action. It follows that "the fewer distinctive reasons a person might have for an action, and the less these reasons are widely shared in the culture, the more informative that action is concerning the characteristics of the person" (Kelley, 1967:208–209). The implication is clear: *we tend to read a person through his deviant acts.* By this we mean that atypical, "out-of-role" behavior is seen as providing more information about causality and, by implication, intent than typical behaviors.[18] This is true in one sense because we seldom raise the question of intent of the actor in routine, mundane activities. However, when deviance occurs (either positive or negative), we often put "why" explicitly on the interpretational agenda. In a second sense, atypical behaviors present a stimulus which demands reconciliation with our experiences—our feelings of consistency and continuity. Since we have to account for the atypical event, there is a tendency to seek to normalize it, to see it as fitting into our previous coherent field of perception. In short, we search for reasons which justify and explain the actor's atypical behavior. Usually he is quick to help us out in this search by providing excuses or justifications, but even when these are not forthcoming, we may impart reasons (causes) for the action.

A second situation where imputation of disposition is maximal is when the actor is seen as taking a great risk to carry through an action. When a person goes against the tide, thereby involving some risk, observers are more likely to see internal causation and corresponding dispositional traits as producing the action. Thus, observers of a speech given before a hostile audience impute stronger attitudes to the speaker, and see him as more sincere in his position than when he gives a speech before "fans" (Mills and Jellison, 1967).[19] To the extent deviance is seen as involving risk, this suggests a second reason why rule violations are especially informative. Deviance becomes a sort of proving ground for the essential self—as imputed by others. The delinquent who does not confess nor cooperate with the police appears by his action (because it is risky) to be highly committed to his misdeeds, and is thereby seen as essentially criminal, deserving of the strongest punishment (Emerson, 1969).

Another factor in imputational work is the degree of negative outcome which an action produces. The greater the negative outcome, the more likely observers will assign personal responsibility (internal causation) and negative dispositional attributes to the actor. Walster (1966) studied the reactions of observers (students hearing different versions of a taped description of a traffic accident) to the driver's role in the mishap. This study suggests that severe negative outcome increased correspondence of effect and dispositional trait— e.g., "the driver was hurtful." "It appears that the perceiver has an increasing need to attribute responsibility to someone as the outcome becomes more severe" (Hastorf, et al., 1970:79).

We conclude that each of us is evaluated and has our dispositional traits constituted for us through our transgressions: deviance is therefore important to everyone in that it affects how we are seen and interpreted by others (which, as we shall argue in a later chapter, may come to affect our personal view of essential self). Rule violations make people more aware of their surroundings and bring identity negotiations up front. Thus, the management and cultivation of respectability is a potential topic at any time, and one in which each of us has an interest (Ball, 1970). This alone might be reason enough to agree with Denzin's recommendation: "we must return to the mundane and routine forms of behavior to establish a solidly grounded theory of deviance" (1970:121).

Construction of an Essential Self

When internal causation is hypothesized, the question of motive arises. Observers ask: "What were his motives?" "What did he intend by his action?" When open choice is possible (responsibility), we impute reasons for the act. Through social ascription, motives become the link of action to the essential self.[20] "For any member [observer] to ascribe a motive is thus to do no less than to generate a person" (Blum and McHugh, 1971:108). The imputation of motive, with implied essential self, informs the event—i.e., it "makes activities graspable [for observers] through the formation of alter's motivated identity" (Blum and McHugh, 1971:108). Hence, doing recognition and doing motives are intimately related.

At this point we are concerned with motive in a sense which differs from traditional psychological work. We are interested in motive imputation first as a necessary component of classifying an event—i.e., as a constituent aspect of recognition. Blum and McHugh state that motive and event cannot be separated, since each depends on the other for meaning in the documentary method sense described earlier. Second, we are considering the role imputed motives play in the construction of a personal identity—an imputed essential self. In short, the "actual" motivation for an act is not at issue here, although in another chapter we will discuss how imputed motives and conceptions of essential self may come to influence behavior.

The correspondence theory of Jones and Davis suggests that as people assign causal meaning to events, dispositional traits are invoked which point to the essential nature of the individual. Thus, lay conceptions of personality are evolved by witnesses to events and imputed to the author of the event. Causation and responsibility are seen to reside in certain imputed basic traits—the essential nature of the individual. Observers thus impart essential self to others and this self serves as an organizing theme, a typification which renders situated behavior consistent and accountable.[21] There is a mutual determination (via the documentary method) of basic traits and behavior such that those violating rules (given an open event) may be seen as basically evil.[22] Since reactions to deviant acts may be greatly affected by the implications these acts have for essential self, we must examine how we sustain a belief in such overarching traits.

First, there is what might be termed a strain to consistency—inconsistent information must be reconciled to make sense of an event. We have discussed the primacy effect—that first impressions tend to color later perceptions[23]—and it may be assumed that our construction of the other person is always selective. This means that trait-imputation is rarely disconfirmed. The impression of constancy, however, obtains from another source. The simple fact that another person is physically continuous, always looks more or less the same, and has the same mannerisms, may encourage the impression that there is continuity in his behavior as well. The fact of physical con-

stancy may produce the illusion of behavioral and therefore dispositional consistency (Jones and Nesbitt, 1971:90). Another reason
behavior may appear to be consistent is that we, as observers of
others, get very biased samples of their behavior. We see them only
at certain times, and many times their behavior may be a response
to us, to our unique aspects. Thus, "one's own behavior may evoke
complementary responses in another that one then mistakenly receives as a manifestation of the other's personality" (Jones and Nesbitt, 1971:89–90). While psychologists have not found strong
evidence to support the idea that basic traits (essential self) determine behavior (Mischel, 1968), the man on the street appears to
operate from a correspondence model. Therefore, "the low empirical validity of the trait concept may be of importance only to the
psychologist. The observer, in his daily life, may achieve fairly high
predictability using trait inferences that the psychologist can show to
be erroneous" (Jones and Nesbitt, 1971:91).

Recall that atypical and socially undesirable behaviors are likely to
lead to strong attributions of disposition to the actor. Thus, deviant
activity becomes an important shaper of the perceived essential self.
Once the assignment of a person as essentially deviant is made,
deviance acts as a master status—a characteristic through which are
funneled other evaluations and behavioral reactions. The person
caught in the act of housebreaking is therefore seen by others, according to Howard Becker (1963:33), as

> A person likely to break into other houses. . . . Fur-
> ther, he is likely to commit other kinds of crimes as
> well, because he has shown himself to be a person
> without "respect for the law." Thus, apprehension
> for one deviant act exposes a person to the likelihood
> that he will be regarded as deviant or undesirable in
> other respects.

Another example is the alcoholic whose "staying dry" is seen as
merely temporary, because "once an alcoholic, always an alcoholic."[24] Such phrases only underline the common stereotypes about
the essential nature of deviant behavior. In this view, the alcoholic
remains *essentially* weak and in need of help. As we shall outline in
a later chapter, this difficulty of removing a master status and its
assumed essential nature from the actor is a major obstacle to
rehabilitation.

One reason why we assume putative deviance—i.e., that persons
deviant in one area will be deviant in others—is the imposed consistency in evaluations of behavior referred to earlier. The embezzler

is seen as one who cheats on his golf score, and probably on his wife. The unwed mother is assumed an "easy make" when, in fact, indiscriminate promiscuity was probably not responsible for the biological origin of her present master status. Again we have the difference between reality (are persons who violate rules in one area violating other types of rules?) and public perception of reality (are they seen as untrustworthy in all dimensions because they are deviant at the core—an evil essential self?).[25] A self-fulfilling prophecy may operate such that the assumed rampant deviance does indeed come about— e.g., the drunk who is seen as breaking other rules may come to do so because it is expected of him.

Deviant acts are likely to carry putative implications which combine imputational judgments to produce a verdict on the actor's essential self: "he is basically untrustworthy," "he is naturally evil." The deviant labels attached to these rule violations serve an essentializing function:

> Deviant labels are essentializing labels that carry certain implications about character that extend to all areas of personality. . . . Evidence for this is found in the tendency we have to link information about an individual's disability with other statements about him (that is, "he is a blind writer") as though the fact of his condition alerts us *to look for a special kind of personality.* (Scott, 1972:14. Emphasis added.)

One could hypothesize that when there is a lack of information about an event, due either to ignorance, superstition, or failure to get the details, we are less likely to attribute cause to the environment (external cause) and more likely to see act as the outcome of traits or essential self. Official social-control agents who do not know the accused, and who fail to get details on the incident and the background of the accused, are in a position where attribution of internal causation is maximized. Consequently, there is a built-in bias toward predicting internal reasons—usually a bad essential self—for the deviant behavior brought to the attention of social-control agents.

The Accused Deviant's
Role in Attribution

The social ascription of motives implies a negotiation between the accused and his witnesses. Let us briefly examine the actor's role in the attribution process. The actor usually does not passively accept the attribution made about his intent, but tries to shape it, to turn it away from imputations which are harmful—i.e., personal devaluation, stigma, imposition of negative sanctions, and so on. Untoward behavior is often accompanied by some form of account. Verbal accounts may take the form of excuses or justifications. In excuses, the offender admits he is wrong, but denies full responsibility, and attempts to deny that the act is indicative of his true (essential) self. Scott and Lyman (1968) cite appeals to accident, appeals to defensibility (acts out of ignorance or coercion), appeals to biological drives (deprivation-forced act, or act due to biological processes beyond conscious control—mental illness), and scapegoating (placing the blame on others for one's action). In justification, the actor accepts responsibility for the action, but argues that his act was just or right given the circumstances. Justification may be *specific*—i.e., individuals "recognize a general sense in which the act in question is impermissible, but claim that the particular occasion permits or requires the very act" (Scott and Lyman, 1968:51)—or justification may be *general*, as when actors attack the rule or the social order—e.g., political radicals. Justifications include denial of injury ("the store has shoplifting insurance"), denial of victim ("the drunk deserved to be rolled"), condemning the condemners ("the police are hypocrites, why should we be bound by their rules?"), and appeal to higher loyalties ("I had to protect my friends, didn't I?"), (Sykes and Matza, 1957). Additional justifications may be appeals to unique aspects of personal biography, what Goffman (1963) terms a "sad tale," or desire for self-fulfillment or development—e.g., using drugs for mind-expanding purposes.

In addition to linguistic displays by actor, he may initiate certain behavioral displays intended to communicate something to witnesses about motives and thereby affect their attribution process. These nonverbal "normalcy shows" have been termed "body glosses" by Erving Goffman:

> Body gloss, then, is a means by which the individual can try to free himself from what otherwise would be the undesirable characterological implications of what he finds himself doing. . . . [It is a] relatively self conscious gesticulation an individual can perform with his whole body in order to give pointed evidence concerning some passing issue at hand. . . . Here, then, we have the externalization of evidence, the lack of which might cause the individual to be ill judged. (Goffman, 1971:129, 128)

The actor, by using these behavioral displays, is trying to influence (in a favorable direction) the recognition and motive imputation made by observers. Goffman gives examples such as the individual who, upon finding he has been trying to unlock the wrong blue VW in the parking lot, will stand back, hold the key out for all to see, and shake his head in disbelief lest the owner or a police officer should happen by. Those leaving packages behind in a store may break into a mock run upon returning to give the impression of worry and concern—i.e., that forgetting the package was not a sign of true absentmindedness. (For other examples, see Goffman, 1971:129–37.)

While violations of polite interactional and background expectancy rules may produce extemporaneous behavioral displays, violators of civil-legal rules may use elaborate planning in their normalcy shows. Burglars may dress as maintainence men, drive appropriately marked vans, and carry tool kits; pickpockets may pass[26] as camera-carrying tourists in crowded tourist traps; the voyeur may develop an interest in astronomy to justify his possession of telescopic instruments, etc.

In sum, rule-violating acts may produce various types of remedial work, both verbal and behavioral displays. The event and attendant remedial work will affect how the event is classified (its recognition), as well as the motives imputed for the act. Remedial displays will also affect the observers' reactions to the rule violation in question, our next topic.

Reactions to
Rule Violations

Public reactions for rule violations may be informal negative sanctions, which would include verbal reprimands, social exclusion, expulsion from the group, avoidance of future contacts, as well as physical attempts to punish or correct the transgressor, or formal reactions, such as contacting some social-control agent in hopes of rendering correction or punishment. Public reactions may be invoked for two reasons, thereby making the transgressor open to a form of double jeopardy. The offender may be sanctioned for the act itself, or for inadequate or incomplete remedial work, or both. McHugh (1970) introduces the concept of the double deviant: the individual who violates a rule and fails to provide any remedial work. Thus, the form and content of accounts become important to a full understanding of the labeling and reaction to rule violations.

Scott and Lyman (1968:54, 57) suggest that accounts may be illegitimate ("when the gravity of the event exceeds that of the account"), may be presented in an improper linguistic style, or may be seen as unreasonable.[27] Each of us can think of instances where attempts to account for a rule violation have simply made matters worse. (This suggests that after each behavioral act which is sensed as deviant by the actor, there is an uneasy period of indecision as to whether the violator should "let it pass" or provide some remedial work.[28]) This adds a new dimension to reaction, since it is now possible to be sanctioned not for the act itself, but for failure to provide an account, or for giving an improper account.[29] We are here extending Becker's dictim that the act itself is not inherently deviant, but only when labeled and treated as deviant by a reacting population. Consequently, when reaction does occur, it may not be due to the act, but rather to an unacceptable account or behavioral display.

There is a second sense in which reaction may be unrelated to action. Since recognition and possible reaction involves a simultaneous evaluation of act and imputed motive (intent), we may have reaction without the act occurring—i.e., "an intention to deviance can be deviant, and punishment ensue, in face of behavior which is conforming. . . . Imagine the suburban wife's reaction upon discovering that her husband's fidelity is only a consequence of being unable to find an object for his promiscuous intent" (McHugh, 1970:77). This sentiment is incorporated in the civil-legal area in conspiracy statutes, where planning and intent to commit a crime, in the absense of carrying it out, is legally proscribed. When persons can be sanctioned for intent (which must be imputed), the range of reaction is large indeed. This may be seen in recent conspiracy trials of political radicals—see Chapter XI. Add to this the other bases of societal response to behavior, and the unpredictability of reaction is evident (producing problems for the accused deviant and the social scientist). In the next chapter we try to specify factors which affect audience decisions on sanctioning initiation—a crucial step in the creation of deviance.

Notes

1. Why conformity, given past deviance? This issue produces some intriguing questions: How do individuals shield or neutralize transgressions so as to maintain their respectability? How do people deflect negative labels so they have little impact? How might positive labels acquired in socialization negate the influence of negative or devalued labels such that conformity is more likely to occur?

2. The practice of bugging rooms and tapping phones has made private areas more public by overcoming architectural barriers to visibility. Current legal battles over these invasion practices, which were provided for in the 1968 Omnibus Crime Bill, will determine the extent to which private places are legally guaranteed. The Watergate scandal has shown that certain government officials are willing to make any private place quite public. For an excellent discussion of the invasion of privacy problems, see Miller, 1971.

3. While the poor lead very public lives, the rich are almost invisible if they choose to be. The strategies of traveling incognito, using doubles, and buying silence and privacy should be similar for millionaires such as Howard Hughes and for professional criminals who rely on invisibility to a great extent.

4. One method of breaking through this visibility barrier has been self-reported studies of juvenile delinquency. These studies generally show very little difference in delinquency involvement by social class. See Akers, 1964; Hirschi, 1969; Gold, 1970; Williams and Gold, 1972. For an exception, see Clark and Wenninger, 1962. Caution must be exercised here since we have few self reports on adult behavior. Also, care must be taken to distinguish frequency of delinquent acts and the type and seriousness of the acts. The evidence is mixed here too. Clark and Wenninger claim more serious acts are committed by the lower class, but a recent national sample found higher social classes engaged in more serious delinquent acts (Williams and Gold, 1972:217–18). For a review of conflicting data as to frequency and seriousness of self-reported delinquency and social class, see Box and Ford (1971) and Bytheway and May (1971). For a thorough discussion of the adequacy of the self-report technique as an indicator of hidden deviance, see Farrington (1973).

5. In addition to acquiring labels for others, socialization also entails the internalization of a number of labels directed toward one's self. Self-conception may be viewed in labeling terms, and the capacity to apply self-labels is an important requisite for functioning in society. Kenneth Gergen has noted that society, through its social-control agencies, demands the ability to self-label: "The computerized dating and mating systems that have recently flourished in the United States depend almost entirely on the individual's capacity to summarize his observations of himself in brief, conceptual form. Placement in almost any formal organization, whether religious or military, social service or business, depends on this same capacity. An individual who does not possess a sizable number of labels for himself has a truly difficult time in contemporary society" (Gergen, 1971:25).

6. Conventional occupations are stereotyped to some extent in terms of prestige ratings. Thielbar and Feldman (1969:68) found differential stereotyping of job and

job incumbent such that "respondents stereotyped incumbents with less intensity than they stereotyped occupations." Whether this distinction between role and role incumbent is made for deviant occupations is an empirical question which remains to be answered.

7. Typification is a general term referring to (a) the act of categorical placement, and (b) the content of the summarial images of the types. In regard to the latter, typifications may be accurate or stereotyped. Typifications of the latter form would fit Secord and Backman's definition of stereotypes: "The categorization of persons, a consensus on attributed traits, and a discrepancy between attributed traits and actual traits" (1964:67). The third characteristic should be treated as an empirical question rather than definitionally legislated; since all typifications (abstraction via categorical types) involve a molesting of the unique phenomenon, one should speak of the degree of discrepancy involved in any observation.

8. There are some attempts being made to reduce the stereotyping problem by presenting more realistic and unique views of certain forms of deviant behavior in television programming. A recent television movie dealing with adult homosexuality was reviewed by various homophile organizations prior to its release.

9. More recently (1973), the name has been changed to Drug Enforcement Administration reflecting a further consolidation of drug control agencies. Name changing is a reliable indication of bureaucratic entrepreneurial work; we would predict a cabinet-level office for drug surveillance and enforcement if present entrepreneurial trends continue.

10. Similarly, the enemy in wartime receive general labels and nicknames which makes it easier for soldiers to engage in destruction. Labeling the enemy "Gook," "Nip," "Charley," or other appellations facilitates their elimination. The atrocity stories attributed to the enemy also serve to show they are basically evil and deserve their fate. On the other hand, the evil of the enemy justifies our entering war, and the act establishes our righteousness.

11. It should be noted that all biological theories of deviance are not dead. Recent work on the XYY chromosome syndrome and violent crimes, on hormonal imbalances and sexual deviance, and certain chemical deficiencies and mental illness again raise the possibility of trait differentiation. Assuming for the moment that research does support some of these biological factors as determinants of behavior, this does not provide a complete explanation. Since these behaviors must be filtered through various cultural definitions and societal reactions which influence the final presentation of the behaviors, there cannot be a completely biological explanation of crime or deviance. We do agree that deviants are "fundamentally different," but only in that their behaviors have been reacted to by society; in other words, differentiation is in the reaction, not in the type of person committing the act or in any predetermining trait tending to commission of a deviant act (cf. Sarbin and Miller, 1970).

12. Alfred Schutz (1963) stated that social scientists are engaged in typifications of the second order—i.e., designing and testing abstract categorical systems to order the typifications of the layman (first-order typifications). The typifications of the scientist are generally arrived at through a more logically rigorous analysis than first-order typifications used by the man in the street, prompting Garfinkel (following Schutz) to distinguish scientific rationalities and common-sense rationalities, respectively (cf. Garfinkel, 1967:262–83). Ethnomethodologists argue that the proper focus of social science is the first-order typifications of common sense. Consequently, the folk classification systems of the laymen—i.e., language—are often the focus of ethnomethodological investigations (e.g., Sudnow, 1972).

13. "Thus, typification depends upon my problem at hand for the definition and solution of which the type has been formed" (Schutz, 1963:243). For a theoretical discussion of the use of the consistency rule by police and other professional searchers, see Sacks, 1972b.

14. We are dealing here with the question of *attributed* causation and *imputed* motives, rather than causation in the etiological sense (what factors "really" produced the behavior) or motives in the sense of internal needs or driving forces. We make no claims at this point about the correspondence of imputed causation with either the "actual" causes of behavior or with the actor's view of what caused the behavior. We simply note that these three aspects of cause—intersubjective, objective, and subjective—are important distinctions, yet relatively few empirical studies have attempted to assess the possible interrelationships. We shall deal with actor's attribution of cause and motive in a later chapter on self-labeling.

15. Skinner was more interested in a disposition-free description of the pigeon's behavior—e.g., a certain action *produced* a food pellet. The fact that our tendencies to impute motive to animals—especially pets—and to some inanimate objects —e.g., our cars—suggests that dispositional inferences from the activities of other human beings are commonplace.

16. Two qualifications must be entered: first, we note that the man on the street as observer is functioning much as the social scientist. He is imputing cause to understand and explain behaviors around him (as well as his own behavior). Phenomenologically, he is not as rigorous as the social scientist and is generally operating on common-sense rationalities rather than scientific ones (Garfinkel, 1967:262–83). Second, most of one's daily round does not involve causal analysis in any strong sense; that is, most of our encountered social scenes do not raise the question of "what caused it to happen?" When the environment can no longer be trusted (see Garfinkel, 1963), questions of causation and responsibility come to the forefront of our interactional work. That is why studies of the accounting practices used when disruptions—deviance—are encountered are salient to our knowledge of recognition and labeling processes.

17. This raises an interesting question. How do individuals in certain roles show their positive qualities as unique? How does the physician or the priest let others know of their positive attributes if these are seen as externally produced "in-role" behaviors? Those occupying very positive roles may have problems establishing a unique identity—dispositional characteristics—in the minds of others.

18. Experimental evidence suggests that unfavorable information about someone is given greater weight in imputation and evaluation than is favorable information (see Rickey, *et al.*, 1967).

19. This is one reason politicians gain credibility by speaking in the camp of the enemy—e.g., a campaigning President Nixon speaking before Meany's labor union and candidate McGovern speaking before stockbrokers on Wall Street.

20. "The observer assumes, then, that the agent shows in the event (uses the event as) one possible method of identifying himself through his action as a particular type of person" (Blum and McHugh, 1971:107). Correspondence and attribution theory, discussed earlier, are the basis of the motive imputation process.

21. "[T]he imputation of a substantial [i.e., essential] self to a particular person is the result of a long process of imputations of situated selves that are implicitly seen to involve the various characteristics of the substantial self that is then imputed *in an all or nothing way*" (Douglas, 1967:282. Emphasis added). Generally we would predict fewer situated selves would be required to arrive at the essential self if the situations involve deviant rather than typical behaviors.

22. For a discussion of the assumption that evil causes evil, and that deviance is the result of evil "kinds of people," see Albert Cohen's discussion of this alleged correlation (1966).

23. Harold Kelley's classic warm-cold experiment shows how important traits are in affecting reactions to behavior. Kelley (1950) had students listen to a guest speaker who was described beforehand by a number of adjectives. The adjectives were identical, except that some groups were told the speaker was a rather *warm* person—industrious, critical, practical and determined; in other groups he was

described as a rather *cold* person—industrious, critical, etc. The speaker and speech were similar for all groups. Students, in open-ended evaluations after the speech, reacted more negatively to the speaker when the speaker was described as cold; also, students were less likely to engage in discussions after the speech when the speaker was termed cold rather than warm.

24. This dictim is supported by Alcoholics Anonymous (A.A.) and is seen as a necessary step in rehabilitation. Notice that an alcoholic taking the cure through A.A. may have his or her success interpreted as due to external reasons (external causation due to threat of arrest if relapse occurs, informal peer pressure, etc.) rather than internal cause. In this way, observers manage to hold on to their conception of the alcoholic as essentially deviant: "He is a drunkard, and will always be one." See further discussion in Chapter XI.

25. We know of no thorough and explicit research directed at the question of putative deviant, although Lemert introduced the term in 1951. Given the concept of master status, labels can be seen as ideal types surrounded by stereotypes—one which involves other areas of deviant activities. Simmons' studies of stereotyping of various deviant labels are tangentially related (1965, 1969). There are also implications of master-status imputation in the interpretation of a deviant's biography to produce consistency; see the discussion of biography building in Chapter VII.

26. When behavioral displays are pre-planned, we can speak of covering and passing techniques; see Goffman's *Stigma*, 1963.

27. "The incapacity to invoke situationally appropriate accounts—i.e., accounts that are anchored to the background expectancies of the situation—will often be taken as a sign of mental illness." It has been suggested that schizophrenics "are individuals who construct overly elaborate accounts . . . the paranoid husband accounts for his frenzied state by relating that his wife went shopping—and, to him, going shopping constitutes the most opportune occasion to secretly rendezvous with a lover" (Scott and Lyman, 1968:53). There is another sense in which accounts may be unreasonable. One may encounter cases where individuals provide excuses or justifications for normal—i.e., acceptable and expected—behavior. Unreasonable accounts, because they are uncalled for, may produce labels of weak self-esteem, reality disorientation, and perhaps certain mental illness categorizations.

28. The absence of remedial work is then open for interpretation. Does failure to give an account mean the actor does not recognize his error, or is it a case of open flouting of the rule?

29. At times, it may be best to provide no account at all. Mileski, in her study of sentencings for public drunkenness, found that individuals who offered excuses after pleading guilty were given harsher punishments than those pleading guilty and offering no account (Mileski, 1971:508).

References

Akers, Ronald L.
1964   "Socio-economic status and delinquent behavior: a retest."
        Journal of Research in Crime and Delinquency 1 (January):38–46.
Ball, Donald W.
1970   "The problematics of respectability." In Jack D. Douglas (ed.),
        Deviance and Respectability. New York: Basic Books.
Becker, Howard S.
1963   *Outsiders: Studies in the Sociology of Deviance.* New York:
        Free Press.
Berger, Peter L., and Thomas Luckmann
1966   *The Social Construction of Reality.* New York: Doubleday
        Anchor.
Blum, Alan, and Peter McHugh
1971   "The social ascription of motive." *American Sociological Review* 36 (February):98–109.
Box, Steven, and Julienne Ford
1971   "The facts don't fit: on the relationship between social class
        and criminal behaviour." *The Sociological Review* 19 (February):31–52.
Bytheway, W. R., and D. R. May
1971   "On fitting the 'facts' of social class and criminal behaviour: a
        rejoinder to Box and Ford." *The Sociological Review* 19 (November):585–607.
Chambliss, William J., and Robert B. Seideman
1971   *Law, Order and Power.* Reading, Massachusetts: Addison-
        Wesley.
Chapman, Dennis
1968   *Sociology and the Stereotype of the Criminal.* London: Tavistock Publications.
Cicourel, Aaron V.
1968   *The Social Organization of Juvenile Justice.* New York: John
        Wiley and Sons.
1970   "The acquisition of social structure: toward a developmental
        sociology of language and meaning." In Jack D. Douglas (ed.),
        Understanding Everyday Life. Chicago: Aldine.

1972a "Basic and normative rules in the negotiation of status and role." In David Sudnow (ed.), *Studies in Social Interaction.* New York: Free Press.

1972b "Delinquency and the attribution of responsibility." In R. Scott and J. Douglas (eds.), *Theoretical Perspectives on Deviance.* New York: Basic Books.

Cicourel, Aaron V., and John Kitsuse
1963 *The Educational Decision-Makers.* Indianapolis: Bobbs-Merrill.

Clark, John P., and Eugene P. Wenninger
1962 "Socio-economic class and area as correlates of illegal behavior among juveniles." *American Sociological Review* 27 (December):826–43.

Cohen, Albert K.
1966 *Deviance and Control.* Englewood Cliffs, New Jersey: Prentice-Hall.

Davis, Kingsley
1938 "Mental hygiene and the class structure." *Psychiatry* 1 (February):55–65.

Denzin, Norman K.
1970 "Rules of conduct and the study of deviant behavior: some notes on social relationships." In Jack D. Douglas (ed.), *Deviance and Respectability.* New York: Basic Books.

Dixon, Donald T.
1968 "Bureaucracy and morality: an organizational perspective on a moral crusade." *Social Problems* 16 (Fall):143–56.

Douglas, Jack D.
1967 *The Social Meaning of Suicide.* Princeton, New Jersey: Princeton University Press.

1970 *Deviance and Respectability.* New York: Basic Books.

1971 *American Social Order.* New York: Free Press.

Duster, Troy
1970 *The Legislation of Morality.* New York: Free Press.

Ellis, Albert
1967 "Should some people be labeled mentally ill?" *Journal of Consulting Psychology* 31:435–53.

Emerson, Robert
1969 *Judging Delinquents.* Chicago: Aldine.

Erickson, Maynard L., and LaMar T. Empey
1963 "Court records, undetected delinquency and decision-making." *Journal of Criminal Law, Criminology and Police Science* 54 (December):456–69.

Farrington, David P.
1973 "Self reports of deviant behavior: predictive and stable?" *Journal of Criminal Law and Criminology* 64 (March):99–110.

Gagnon, John H.
  1967   "Sexuality and sexual learning in the child." In John H. Gag-
           non and William Simon (eds.), *Sexual Deviance.* New York:
           Harper and Row.
Garfinkel, Harold
  1956   "Conditions of successful degradation ceremonies." *American
           Journal of Sociology* 61 (March):420–24.
  1963   "A conception of, and experiment with, 'trust' as a condition
           of stable concerted action." In O. J. Harvey (ed.), *Motivation
           and Social Interaction.* New York: Ronald Press.
  1964   "Studies of the routine grounds of everyday activities." *Social
           Problems* 11 (Winter):225–50.
  1967   *Studies in Ethnomethodology.* Englewood Cliffs, New Jersey:
           Prentice-Hall.
Gergen, Kenneth J.
  1971   *The Concept of Self.* New York: Holt, Rinehart and Winston.
Goffman, Erving
  1963   *Stigma.* Englewood Cliffs, New Jersey: Prentice-Hall.
  1971   *Relations in Public.* New York: Basic Books.
Gold, Martin
  1970   *Delinquent Behavior in an American City.* Belmont, Califor-
           nia: Brooks/Cole.
Hastorf, Albert H., David J. Schneider, and Judith Polefka
  1970   *Person Perception.* Reading, Massachusetts: Addison-Wesley.
Hirschi, Travis
  1969   *Causes of Delinquency.* Berkeley: University of California
           Press.
Hollander, Edwin P.
  1958   "Conformity, status and idiosyncrasy credit." *Psychological
           Review* 65: 117–27.
Jackson, Joan K.
  1968   "The adjustment of the family to the crisis of alcoholism." In
           Earl Rubington and Martin S. Weinberg (eds.), *Deviance: The
           Interactionist Perspective.* New York: Macmillan.
Jensen, Arthur
  1969   "Reducing the heredity-environment uncertainty: a reply."
           Harvard Educational Review 39 (Summer):449–83.
Jones, Edward E., and Keith E. Davis
  1965   "From acts to dispositions: the attribution process in person
           perception." In Leonard Berkowitz (ed.), *Advances in Experi-
           mental Social Psychology: Vol. 2.* New York: Academic Press.
Jones, Edward E., and Richard E. Nisbett
  1971   "The actor and the observer: divergent perceptions of the

causes of behavior." In E. E. Jones, et al., *Attribution.* Morristown, New Jersey: General Learning Press.

Kelley, Harold H.
1950   "The warm-cold variable in first impressions of persons." *Journal of Personality* 18:431–39.
1967   "Attribution theory in social psychology." *Nebraska Symposium on Motivation* 14:192–241.

Kitsuse, John I., and Aaron V. Cicourel
1963   "A note on the uses of official statistics." *Social Problems 12* (Fall):131–39.

Lemert, Edwin
1951   *Social Pathology.* New York: McGraw-Hill.

Lofland, John
1969   *Deviance and Identity.* Englewood Cliffs, New Jersey: Prentice-Hall.

McHugh, Peter
1970   "A common-sense conception of deviance." In Jack D. Douglas (ed.), *Deviance and Respectability.* New York: Basic Books.

McIntosh, Mary
1968   "The homosexual role." *Social Problems* 16 (Fall):182–92.

McKinney, John C.
1970   "Sociological theory and the process of typification." In John C. McKinney and Edward A. Tiryakian (eds.), *Theoretical Sociology.* New York: Appleton-Century-Crofts.

Matza, David
1964   *Delinquency and Drift.* New York: John Wiley and Sons.
1969   *Becoming Deviant.* Englewood Cliffs, New Jersey: Prentice-Hall.

Mileski, Maureen
1971   "Courtroom encounters: an observation study of a lower criminal court." *Law and Society Review* 5 (May):473–538.

Miller, Arthur R.
1971   *Assault on Privacy.* New York: New American Library.

Mills, Judson, and Jerald M. Jellison
1967   "Effect on opinion change of how desirable the communicator is to the audience the communicator addressed." *Journal of Personality and Social Psychology* 47:728–31.

Mischel, Walter
1968   *Personality and Assessment.* New York: John Wiley and Sons.

Rickey, Marjorie H., Lucille McClelland, and A. M. Skimkunas
1967   "Relative influence of positive and negative information in

impression formation and persistence." *Journal of Personality and Social Psychology* 46:322–27.

Sacks, Harvey
1972a   "An initial investigation of usability of conversational data for doing sociology." In David Sudnow (ed.), *Studies in Social Interaction*. New York: Free Press.
1972b   "Notes on police assessment of moral character." In David Sudnow (ed.), *Studies in Social Interaction*. New York: Free Press.

Sarbin, Theodore R.
1969   "The scientific status of the mental illness metaphor." In S. C. Plog and R. B. Edgerton (eds.), *Changing Perspectives in Mental Illness*. New York: Holt, Rinehart and Winston.

Sarbin, Theodore R., and James C. Mancuso
1970   "Failure of a moral enterprise: attitudes of the public toward mental illness." *Journal of Consulting and Clinical Psychology* 35:159–73.

Sarbin, Theodore R., and J. Miller
1970   "Demonism revisited: the XYY chromosomal anomaly." *Issues in Criminology* 5 (Summer):195–207.

Schur, Edwin M.
1965   *Crimes Without Victims*. Englewood Cliffs, New Jersey: Prentice-Hall.

Scheff, Thomas J.
1966a   *Being Mentally Ill*. Chicago: Aldine.
1966b   "Users and non-users of a student psychiatric clinic." *Journal of Health and Human Behavior* 7 (Summer):114–21.

Schutz, Alfred
1963   "Concept and theory formation in the social sciences." Reprinted in Maurice Natanson (ed.), *Philosophy of the Social Sciences*. New York: Random House.

Scott, John F.
1971   *Internalization of Norms*. Englewood Cliffs, New Jersey: Prentice-Hall.

Scott, Marvin B., and Stanford M. Lyman
1968   "Accounts." *American Sociological Review* 33 (February):46–62.

Scott, Robert A.
1969   *The Making of Blind Men*. New York: Russell Sage Foundation.
1970   "The construction of conceptions of stigma by professional experts." In Jack D. Douglas (ed.), *Deviance and Respectability*. New York: Basic Books.
1972   "A proposed framework for analyzing deviance as a property of social order." In R. A. Scott and Jack D. Douglas

(eds.), *Theoretical Perspectives on Deviance.* New York: Basic Books.

Secord, Paul F., and Carl W. Backman
1964   *Social Psychology.* New York: McGraw-Hill.

Simmons, J. L.
1965   "Public stereotypes of deviants." *Social Problems* 13 (Fall):223–32.

1969   *Deviants.* Berkeley: Glendessary.

Skolnick, Jerome H., and J. Richard Woodworth
1967   "Bureaucracy, information and social control: a study of a morals detail." In David J. Bordua (ed.), *The Police.* New York: John Wiley and Sons.

Smith, David M.
1970   "A study of stereotyping." *The Sociological Review* 18 (July):197–212.

Stinchcombe, Arthur L.
1964   "Institutions of privacy in the determination of police administrative practice." *American Journal of Sociology* 69 (September):150–60.

Sudnow, David
1972   *Studies in Social Interaction.* New York: Free Press.

Suttles, Gerald D.
1968   *The Social Order of the Slum.* Chicago: University of Chicago Press.

Sykes, Gresham M., and David Matza
1957   "Techniques of neutralization: a theory of delinquency." *American Sociological Review* 22 (December):664–70.

Szasz, Thomas
1963   *Law, Liberty and Psychiatry.* New York: Macmillan.

Thibaut, John W., and Henry W. Riecken
1955   "Some determinants and consequences of the perception of social causality." *Journal of Personality* 24:113–33.

Thielbar, Gerald W., and Saul D. Feldman
1969   "Occupational stereotypes and prestige." *Social Forces* 48 (September):64–72.

Walster, Elaine
1966   "The assignment of responsibility for an accident." *Journal of Personality and Social Psychology* 5:508–516.

Wheeler, Stanton
1968   *Controlling Delinquents.* New York: John Wiley and Sons.

1969   *On Record.* New York: Russell Sage Foundation.

Williams, Jay R., and Martin Gold
1972   "From delinquent behavior to official delinquency." *Social Problems* 20 (Fall):209–229.

Chapter V

Conditions of Referral to Special Agencies

Nothing Unusual Is Happening
Decisions to Seek Professional Help
Converting the Nonbeliever
Referral Systems: Lay and Professional

"You oughta have your head examined!"

Anyone

In this chapter, we shall examine the conditions which produce a negative reaction to behaviors—a sanctioning attempt—given that a rule violation has occurred (or is alleged to have occurred) and has been recognized. We begin with a general question: why are certain behaviors the object of reactions? Next, we delineate reasons for reaction and suggest a general tendency not to sanction such behavior—a nonreaction bias.[1] Our focus is on the interactional setting of sanctioning initiation because we wish to show the negotiated aspects of the reaction process and to indicate the extent to which others generate a deviant career for some rule breakers and not for others. We concur with John Kitsuse:

> A sociological theory of deviance *must focus specifically on the interactions* which not only define the behavior as deviant but also *organize and activate the application of sanctions* by individuals, groups and agencies. (1962:256. Emphasis added)

Our concern will therefore be with variables affecting decisions to move from informal sanctioning to formal sanctioning agents or agencies. When and how do citizens come under the purview of professional controllers?

First, what are people getting so upset about—why are certain behaviors negatively sanctioned? The following reaction dimensions suggest themes which underpin societal sanctioning:

1. *Perceived threat* of an act: the threat may be against personal safety (crimes against person), to property and other valued goods (crimes against property), of self-harm (laws prohibiting suicide; statutes requiring crash helmets for motorcyclists), or to the values or moral structure of society (crimes without victims).

111

2. *Natural repulsiveness* of an act: behaviors are seen as unnatural and repulsive upon mental rehearsal of the act—e.g., incest, necrophilia, masochism, and sadism. Homosexuality and prostitution may be placed here by some.

3. *Unpredictability* of action: violations of background expectancies and polite-interactional rules make it difficult for others to predict actors' responses; an element of uncertainty is interjected into the situation. Mental illness and public drunkenness may be sanctioned for this reason.

4. *Uneasiness* in relating to certain individuals: persons are "ill at ease" because of the demands that the physically handicapped, the blind, the retarded may place upon them. Discomfort due to potential embarrassment to the normal person—the danger of being called upon to help or offering to help at inappropriate times and having help rejected—may produce reaction.[2]

5. *Ignorance* of the behavior: failure to comprehend the act or understand the reasons for a behavior may lead to rejection. For example, historically the mentally ill and feeble minded were locked away out of ignorance; today, reactions to witchcraft and homosexuality may also be produced by ignorance of the phenomena.

6. *Rationality* of the act: rational actions are less likely to be sanctioned than irrational, non-goal-directed acts. Thus, occupational and corporate crime is less severely sanctioned than seemingly senseless acts such as vandalism.

7. *Political intentionality* of act: what did the actor intend by his action? was he attacking the basic moral and political structure (nonconformity) or was it for personal gain (aberrant behavior)? Violations of rules for political ends may be more severely dealt with by the state than acts directed at personal gain.

8. *Perceived need for help* as indicated by action: Reaction based on benevolent concern for actor; he is treated or helped "for his own good."

9. *Protection* of certain segments of society: pornography laws assume that certain people need protection, especially the young. Also, delinquent status clauses which prohibit association with "vicious and immoral persons" are a legal mechanism of protection.

Notice from this admittedly incomplete list that behaviors and individuals with certain attributes may be the reasons for the reaction. Note also that these are not mutually exclusive and that one action may simultaneously violate a number of these dimensions—

e.g., homosexual acts may be reacted to because of perceived moral threat, repulsiveness, ignorance, or the need for help and protection. Indeed, we might hypothesize that those behaviors or attributes which are seen as violating a greater number of reactional themes are more likely to be sanctioned than those violating fewer dimensions.[3]

In speaking of reasons for reactions, the distinction between attributes and behavior is important. Our definition of deviance (Chapter III) included both attributes—e.g., physical handicaps, racial membership—and rule-violating behaviors. In a social setting, a person may be informally sanctioned because of an attribute; this response occurs because the person is seen as falling short of (or exceeding), general expectations (what Goffman termed a general identity norm). For example, the blind may be systematically rejected because the audience assumes they would not enjoy a movie or a football game, or "not fit in" in some other way. Generally, for attributes, the element of responsibility is absent—i.e., the blind are not rejected for their blindness in the same sense a person is rejected for violating behavioral expectations given a choice (open event; see discussion in Chapter IV). Since it is a condition, the question of responsibility does not arise—e.g., he did not will, nor have control over his blindness, racial membership, etc. (An exception would be stigmatized conditions or illnesses where responsibility is implied—e.g., having V.D. or becoming blind through personal carelessness.) For this reason, we speak of conformance, not compliance (Goffman, 1963:128). The person with a slight limp is more in conformance with mobility expectations than is the paraplegic. However, the element of responsibility can be applied to attributes if we recognize that certain behavioral expectations attend a condition or attribute. As Goffman has noted, the stigmatized are expected to accept their condition and make life easy for those normals encountered in the daily round (see note 2 at the end of the chapter). If the person violates these expectations, we can speak of responsibility; the person, thus, becomes open to negative sanctions on two grounds—for being a cripple and for not accepting the role and acting appropriately. For tribal stigma (attribute of racial membership), the person may be negatively sanctioned because he is black (lack of conformance), and because he doesn't stay in his place, as indicated by the derogatory term "uppity nigger" (lack of compliance). In this way, the individual with devalued attributes is also open to the possibility of being a "double deviant": for his condition and for his behavior toward it. See our discussion of the double deviant at end of Chapter IV and McHugh, 1970.

Nothing Unusual
Is Happening

Witnesses and victims, when confronted with rule violations, short-comings in attributes, or abnormal events, often adopt a "nothing unusual is happening" stance (Emerson, 1970). Individuals are apparently quite adept at imposing order on disorder, explaining away anomalies which are encountered in the daily round.[4] The process used to normalize and deny rule violations will be discussed in detail below. It may be useful, first, to offer some general comments on why deviance is not reacted to in most cases.

First, we note the effect of cultural dictates or guidelines on who sanctions and when. Children in American society are taught not to reveal others' transgressions. "Don't squeal" or "don't tattle" are admonitions regularly encountered. Extollment of the virtues of noninvolvement—e.g., "mind your own business"—as well as pronouncements of the value of loyalty to one's group may also produce a nonsanctioning bias: "one does not look for trouble and should not do anything if it is encountered." Moral and religious systems deal with themes of repentance and offer a "second chance," so much so that initial rule violations are expected to be ignored. Children and adults also learn that socially appropriate reactors exist which are charged with sanctioning duties. Children are instructed not to correct their playmates, but rather to let the appropriate parent do it. Later, it is learned that professionals exist to deal with many problems. Therefore, laymen may not take a role in initiating sanctioning. "Knowledge of the existence of specialized occupations and professions to deal with deviance leads them [witnesses] to conclude that the classification of the behavior as deviant is outside their span of competence" (Roman and Trice, 1971:3). If the transgressions occur within a family, cultural dictates of family self-sufficiency and independence are likely to preclude official reaction by family members (Jackson, 1968).

These cultural expectations which develop have been termed "reactive norms." "There are two facets of a reactive norm: (1) a prescription of what should be done in the way of reacting to deviant behavior, and (2) an identification of the appropriate reactor, meaning a designation of status occupants who should react when a given deviant act occurs" (Gibbs, 1966:154). We propose that expectations of reactions are quite ambiguous[5] and this uncertainty complicates the decision to initiate sanctions. This complication obviates a reaction in many situations.

A second factor which reduces sanctioning initiation is simple embarrassment. There are a number of reasons for this reaction. The inherent ambiguity and *et cetera* aspects of rules and the competent-rule-use idea of negotiated meaning combine to make designations of violations and violators risky. The imputer will have to show a rule was really broken and that it was a clear-cut case (not accident or coercion); otherwise, the sanctioning attempt may be discredited. The probability of reaction will therefore be affected by extent of familiarity with rules in the setting (novices in a setting are likely to let anything pass) and perceptions of degree of consensus on the rule in question. If a reactor perceives dissensus, we would expect him to refrain from a sanctioning attempt.

Embarrassment may result because of what the sanctioning initiation implies about the reactor. Those who apply labels through accusation run the risk of having the label turned back upon them, what Roman and Trice term the "boomerang effect":

> The original label need not be the same as the one returned; in fact, it appears that many career deviants with the label "paranoid" may have begun their careers with over-sensitivity to the behavior of their fellows, accompanied by cavalier administration of labels. (Roman and Trice, 1971:8)

The initiator of the sanction at times, then, runs the risk of being the object of sanctions by others.

In addition to embarrassment, no reaction may occur because of possible imputations about the reactor's causal role in the activity. Thus, victim-precipitated crimes are not likely to be reported to the police. Police often drop assault charges because the victim does not wish to press the matter—often for fear of self-implication (Black, 1970). The wife of the alcoholic may feel she will be blamed for her husband's drinking episodes. This self-implication may involve the charge of failing to act when the problem started or harboring a deviant who should have been referred to professionals. "Thus, a supervisor who initially tolerates a drinking employee in hopes he will 'shape up' eventually finds himself forced to cover-up the facts of the employee's deviance to protect his own reputation as supervisor" (Roman and Trice, 1971:10).

The failure to act immediately builds a demand to continue to treat the situation as if "nothing unusual is happening." This has been found in experimental work on bystander intervention in emergency situations. Upon encountering a potential emergency, a person may honestly be undecided; however, "the longer he waits in indecision, the harder it is for him subsequently to intervene" (Latane and Darley, 1970:122).[6] Since rule violations are generally ambiguous situations, and because rule violations are usually interspersed with conforming behavior (Emerson, 1970:220; Roman and Trice, 1971:3), immediate reaction is not likely. This inaction seems to commit the potential sanctioner to further nonintervention to appear consistent, or to avoid charges of covering for the deviant.

At times, reasons for nonreaction may be benevolent. Witnesses may refrain from labeling and officially sanctioning because it would seem unfair or cruel to do so (Trice, 1965). "Nothing unusual is happening" may be situationally constructed to protect individuals from certain official controls. Thus, police report using discretion to avoid arresting juveniles in part because they feel official reaction does more harm than good (Piliavin and Briar, 1964). At other times, the interest in protection may be wider; if the violator is very important to the group, his rule breaking is likely to be tolerated (Alvarez, 1968). Labeling and rejection may disrupt group equilibrium, so transgressions may be overlooked. At times, the deviant is a valuable group asset: he may play the mascot or group fool, a role which provides a scapegoat for group hostility (Daniels and Daniels, 1964; Daniels, 1970). Similarly, a schizophrenic family member may be harbored and protected because he is an outlet for the hostility of other family members (Vogel and Bell, 1960). Thus, "the effect of the interaction between deviant and attackers often tends to stabilize the group, maintain cohesiveness, and divert attention from underlying problems" (Daniels, 1970:249).

Another reason for nonreaction may be found when there are many witnesses to an event. How can we account for the "nothing unusual is happening" stance in the following case?

> On a March night in 1964, Kitty Genovese was set upon by a maniac as she came home from work at 3 A.M. Thirty-eight of her Kew Gardens neighbors came to their windows when she cried out in terror —none came to her assistance. Even though her assailant took over half an hour to murder her, no one even so much as called the police. (Latane and Darley, 1969:244)

This famous case has produced much research on bystander apathy. One reason for lack of action, given multiple witnesses, is the diffusion of responsibility that occurs. Individuals feel less called upon to react when in groups than when alone or with a friend (Latane and Darley, 1970:38, 88). Another possibility which compounds the responsibility argument (or lack of it in this case), is that each witness may have felt that others must surely be calling the police, so the witness can justify his own inaction (if each felt this, then the event would never be reported—a case of pluralistic ignorance).

Finally, reaction may be precluded due to the cost incurred by the sanctioner. Studies of victims of criminal acts report that less than 50 percent of victimization incidents are reported to the police (Biderman, et al., 1967; Ennis, 1967; Hawkins, 1973). Reasons given for nonreporting often refer to costs of sanctioning. In one study (Hawkins, 1973:441–42), about one-third of the nonreporting victims took a fatalistic outlook, saying that little or nothing could be accomplished by reporting the victimization: they saw little payoff in sanctioning initiation. Another one-third saw reporting as having direct costs—the trouble of filling out police complaint forms and cooperating with the investigation, plus anticipation of time and wages lost due to court appearances. In sex offenses, the stigma involved and the potential abuse encountered in prosecuting the case—e.g., rape cases where victim's moral and sexual history are central elements —make sanctioning very costly.[7]

The obverse of the above conditions should produce sanctioning initiation. If nonintervention dictates are absent or neutralized, if embarrassment or self-implication can be avoided,[8] if the sanctioning activity is not costly, if it is felt the reaction might do some good (restitution) or that it could help the offender (rehabilitation), if the rules are clear-cut and agreed upon, and if members are expendable (not a group resource), the probability of reaction should be high. Many of these factors are beyond the control of the rule breaker. In this sense, the status of the deviant can be considered an ascribed as well as achieved one. Yet, with the exception of the "falsely accused," the rule breaker's actions do influence sanctioning initiations against him. The simple volume of rule breaking and its seriousness may produce a reaction (e.g., Terry, 1967). As noted earlier, failure to provide accounts or the presentation of inadequate remedial work may also precipitate a reaction. At times, the rule breaker may take an active part in his own reaction. This is the case in so-called voluntary referrals to control agencies. We now turn to a discussion of the interpersonal dynamics leading the rule breaker in this and other situations to seek professional help.

Decisions to Seek
Professional Help

How does a particular individual in a particular social setting come
to a decision to seek professional help? For the most part, our concern here will be with such decisions in the case of psychiatric deviance alone. The lawbreaker ordinarily establishes professional help
contacts at the bidding of some official agent, not out of personal
choice; he is therefore of lesser interest in the context of "seeking"
help.[9] We are mainly concerned with help-seeking where the accused actor seeks aid or tacitly accepts the help of others in referring
the problem to a professional control agent. This is of interest to the
labeling perspective, since the actor takes part in his own sanctioning
initiation. Through interaction with others, the individual self-labels
his actions as indicative of some deviant role. In a sense, the person
seeking voluntary help may be further into the deviant role provided
for him than the individual who resists intervention. He has placed
himself in that role *by his own actions,* a fact which may have
implications for his identity. This pre-agency labeling has been neglected by previous labeling formulations which have focused mainly
on the role of formal reactions—official agency contact and experience—in accounting for the generation of the deviant career.

Very few people seek formal psychiatric help as the result of an
entirely personal decision. Rather, they solicit and/or receive consultation from other laymen. Several elements of the source and nature
of that consultation can be specified. The most vivid example of the
influence of favorable information and publicity is to be found in a
group that Charles Kadushin calls "The Friends and Supporters of
Psychotherapy" (abbreviated simply as the Friends). Kadushin's
book, *Why People Go to Psychiatrists* (1969), is limited to a consideration of psychiatric *clinic* users in one urban center and gives some
indication of a normative bias.[10] But the probability remains that
"the Friends" is a national phenomenon and that membership accounts for a great amount and a special type of psychiatric decision
making. Kadushin (1969:59) suggests that membership ". . . tells us
more about the decision process than does any other variable . . ." in
his particular study.

In summary description, a member of the Friends is a person who:
(1) is culturally sophisticated, (2) is knowledgeable about psychotherapy, (3) has previously been in therapy, (4) has friends who have gone
to psychiatrists, (5) asks those friends for psychiatric referral information, (6) has told friends about his current clinic contact, and (7)

knows others with similar psychological problems or complaints. The chief consequence of all this is the development of an ongoing, self-perpetuating assemblage of psychiatric clientele. These individuals favor a certain clinic sub-type (private psychoanalytic) and tend to present a characteristic cluster of "presenting problems" (sexual, evaluative, and interpersonal) as they commence psychiatric treatment (Kadushin, 1969:100). Thus, membership in a particular social circle is accompanied by similarity of psychiatric views, values, and perceived problems, leads to supportive interactions which are solicited *by* the "candidate," and culminates in high, continuing utilization of psychiatric clinic facilities.[11]

Other investigators note the same phenomenon under other descriptive headings. Scheff, in particular, suggests the existence of a "psychiatric following" or "psychiatric public," defined as ". . . *that segment of the population which takes for granted the REALITY, and secondarily, the respectability of mental illness*" (Scheff, 1966b:120. Emphasis in original). The author feels, consistent with our analysis, that these are the people who have been affected most strongly by the mental health movement and that this factor best accounts for clinic usage patterns observed in his research. Freidson's (1961) notion of a "lay referral system" that accounts for a public's choice of nonpsychiatric physicians also has a bearing on this point.

The social context surrounding the Friends offers a type of encouragement and support that may well account for a significant portion of psychiatric clinic clientele, as Kadushin demonstrates for his New York City sample. But what kinds of factors then account for the remainder of clinic users, for hospitalized patients, and for those engaging in private psychotherapy?

To begin with the latter, it is extremely difficult to gather any kind of data on this psychiatric subtype. The norm of doctor-patient confidentiality extends even to disclosure of names, to say nothing of social characteristics and sociological analysis of life styles and decision-making processes. This is quite unlike the situation prevailing in public clinic and hospital facilities, where confidentiality is still assured, but where pertinent research is tolerated or even encouraged.

It is quite likely that Kadushin's "Friends Theory" applies to the private patient audience with even greater strength than it applies to clinic customers. This reasoning is based upon an economic reality: it takes a lot of money to be able to sustain an extended private psychotherapeutic relationship. Money, as a fairly reliable social class indicator, directs us to place these subjects in an upper-class position. It is in that class segment that we tend to find the higher levels of "cultural sophistication" characteristic of the Friends. We also have hints that psychiatry may be used as a conspicuous-consumption, prestige-conferring item at higher class levels, which suggests a strong element of "psychiatric sophistication." We end up, then, picturing a group of subjects who look like members of the Friends and can be expected to act in accordance with the principles that apply to the Friends. These individuals, it can be assumed, simply have the finances that allow them to opt for the private route rather than the clinic setting. All this being the case, if we should find upper-class members in any setting *other than* that of private psychotherapy, we would have indirect reason to believe that something other than the theory of Friends accounts for their presence there.

What are some of those other avenues to formal psychiatric treatment? Drawing from Kadushin again, we note three distinctions important to the remainder of this section: (1) members of the Friends versus nonmembers, (2) conversations used for purposes of social support versus purposes of social control, and (3) solicited advice versus unsolicited advice. We have noted that membership, social support, and solicited advice occur together so as to account for one client contingent. By the same token, nonmembership clusters together with exposure to unsolicited advice which is directed toward social control. Furthermore, this three-fold combination seems to be most characteristic of client applicants who live at home with relatives rather than independently. We are inextricably drawn to the family and the dynamics occurring within it as we search for further explanations pertinent to the use of formal social control agencies.

Let us briefly cite one obvious possibility, so that we may than concentrate on more prevalent patterns. In delimiting his research sample, Kadushin points out that ". . . a person entering outpatient treatment is rarely forced into treatment, in contrast to the fate of many mental hospital patients" (Kadushin, 1969:293). While "railroading" a family member into an unwanted, unneeded hospitalization can and does occur, there is no conceivable way of ever learning to what extent this takes place, since no one guilty of such an act is ever likely to confess to it. We can only assume (and hope) that Hollywoodish victimization plots apply to no more than a handful of cases.[12] It is still well worth noting, however, that involuntary commitment (whether it involves railroading or not) exists mainly by virtue of a society's acceptance of psychiatric interpretations and responses to the point that it *insists* upon treatment and feels righteous about it in the bargain.[13]

We can conceive of the aforementioned "psychiatric public" as lying at one end of a continuum of psychiatric knowledgeability. At the opposite extreme, we find a segment of the population with *no* familiarity with, or appreciation of, psychiatric theories, interpretations, or processes. This is the low-social-class, low-education contingent of a society such as ours. Furthermore, since this contingent exists as a distinct subculture, it can be expected to follow its own distinct set of values, including definitions of what constitutes abnormal, unacceptable behavior. In general, one would predict more tolerance by the lower class of behavior that the middle class calls "deviant" (e.g., Mercer, 1965; Farrell and Morrione, 1972). The anticipated result of this combination of circumstances is that the "nonpsychiatric public" will generally not consider psychiatric interpretations and responses until an individual's behavior seems *grossly* abnormal. At that point, financial limitations see to it that some public agency takes over and begins to feed the case through the channels of the therapeutic state. We should, then, be able to note definite social class discrepancies in diagnosis and treatment; these *have*, in fact, been identified in studies such as the Hollingshead and Redlich classic (1958; also Gove and Howell, 1974; Routh and King, 1972).

One confirmation of the above conceptualization is to be found in an intriguing piece of research presented by Dohrenwend and Chin-Shong. These investigators found a much broader tolerance[14] of deviance among their "cross-sectional" (lower-class) sample than among a "leadership" sample (1967:425). This was as expected. But the next stage of the study divulged a finding of considerable interest: once having identified a behavior as deviant, the lower-class respondent was much more punitive and unaccepting in his recommendation of what actions should follow. There is less stress on the usefulness of a community outpatient clinic, for example, and more willingness to have the deviant carted off to a state mental hospital (Dohrenwend and Chin-Shong, 1967).

This study suggests that people at all class levels do, indeed, have conceptions of mental illness. At the same time, these conceptions vary markedly, as do responses to perceived mental illness. It is impossible from the data in this study to tell what knowledge these lower-class subjects had of available community psychiatric facilities; we suggest that such knowledge was probably minimal. If so, that fact may go a long way toward explaining the "popularity" of a state mental hospital. An illustration:

1. Person X is a member of the nonpsychiatric public. As part of that membership:

a. X regards only extreme behavioral abnormalities as constituting "craziness," and
b. X feels that "if you're crazy, you belong in the state hospital,"
   partly because that seems appropriate, but partly because
c. X is not aware of alternative treatment facilities.
2. Person X tolerates his spouse's behavior until it reaches an extreme state of abnormality.
3. X's spouse is removed to the state hospital since
   a. the behavior has progressed to a point beyond managability in
      an outpatient setting, and
   b. X cannot afford private hospitalization.

Thus far, we have noted the presence of both a "psychiatric public" and a "nonpsychiatric public." The former in a sense *overuses*
psychotherapists and their facilities by regarding them nonchalantly
as a sort of fashion item. The latter group, on the other hand, may
be regarded as *underusers* in that available facilities are sometimes
bypassed until it is too late for them to be of benefit. It is now
necessary to recognize a third group lying between the two extremes
of our awareness continuum. This group neither seeks nor rejects
psychiatry automatically. Its members are aware of, but not overim-
pressed by, psychiatric theory and therapy. They neither embrace
nor reject the notion of mental illness. But the question is: how *does*
a member of this largest public segment of all decide that a psychiatric problem exists and that something formal should be done about
it?

Converting the
Nonbeliever

Again, we must start with the initial recognition of some behavior as
being "deviant." Mental illness never exists until someone calls it by
that name, but potentially "deviant" behavior exists at all times and
in all places. Let us focus chiefly on the spouse relationship here, and
let us further specify the wife as the "healthy" party and the husband
as "mentally ill." Observe carefully that in many cases we could
reverse this role allocation *without even altering the behavioral
characteristics* of the two individuals (e.g., Laing and Esterson, 1964).
This points up the double-edged advantage often accruing to the
labeler: the labelee becomes suspect just by virtue of having been
labeled, while the labeler gains credibility for having the courage

and insight to deal with a touchy situation. It matters not whether a husband's depression is a direct result of cruel, "insane" acts on the part of the wife: if *she* says that *he* is the crazy one, who (often including the psychiatrist) is likely to test the assertion, let alone challenge it?[15] This phenomenon is illustrated beautifully in a recent film by Kenneth Loach entitled *Family Life* (previously titled *Wednesday's Child* when presented at the New York Film Festival). Another medium which effectively conveys the message is the poetry of R. D. Laing (1970).

Observe also that the deviant behavior in question can be "new" behavior unlike any the husband has ever displayed before, or it can be familiar behavior that is freshly perceived or evaluated by the wife. This point is worth mentioning since most people presume the former to be the universal case. It is quite possible, however, that the wife has read or heard something that puts a new slant on behaviors she has accepted comfortably for years. Changes in her own self-image, value system, associates, or goals may also be accountable for her coming to see things in a different way.[16] These possibilities again underscore the importance of value systems in determining deviance and casting appropriate labels.

To simplify matters now, let us assume that the husband is showing *new* behaviors that *seem abnormal* and that *make others uncomfortable*. Few wives would rush for the aid of a psychiatrist at the first sign of such behavior any more than they rush for the family doctor at the first sign of most organic symptoms. Instead, the behavior will be tolerated in one way or another and for a variable period of time. Yarrow and coauthors, in one of the very few studies of its kind, list four distinct forms of defense against the recognition of mental illness within the family (Yarrow, *et al.*, 1955). *Normalization* involves justifying a behavior by convincing oneself that many healthy people do the same thing. One tries to talk oneself out of the deviance suspicions that develop: "it isn't deviant after all." A slightly different tactic operates with *attenuation*, where the behavior is acknowledged as undesirable but "explained away" so that it need not be taken seriously—e.g., "it's just a little quirk that is sure to go away in a short time." A third defense is known as *balancing*. Here, a spouse places emphasis on the "normal" behaviors that still occur rather than on the questionable behavior. By "balancing" the two sets of behaviors, a semblance of general normality is constructed. Finally, simple *denial* may be expressed—either denial that the behavior is really undesirable or denial that it has even occurred at all.

All of these perceptual devices result in the maintenance of at least a facade of routine family relationships. They thereby forestall the application of a "mental illness" label and, of course, forestall psychiatric contact as well. The length of time that any defense is maintained depends on a number of prior conditions, value sets, etc. Basically, there is the simple matter of how much of the disruptive behavior can be tolerated. This directs us to the notion of "thresholds"—i.e., breaking points. For some individuals, the threshold of intolerance will *never* be reached: extreme disruption of the status quo by the spouse is successfully and perpetually "defended away." Thus, one husband may never be defined as mentally ill, at least as long as he avoids apprehension on criminal charges. Consequently, he avoids stereotyped processing by social control agencies (to be discussed later) and public stigma as well. Meanwhile, another husband who exhibits far less bizarre behavior may have a wife with a much lower threshold. Her defense system may falter early in the game, so that the husband soon finds himself labeled and treated. As Erving Goffman says, ". . . the claims and actions of the ill person are not necessarily bizarre in themselves, merely bizarre when coming from the particular patient addressing himself to his particular family" (Goffman, 1969:373).

One piece of evidence that this sort of discrepancy can have extremely serious consequences comes from a rather disturbing study reported by Derek Phillips (1963). In investigating social rejection of the mentally ill, Phillips presented a group of respondents with a set of personal descriptions varying in both the severity of behavior of a hypothetical individual and the type of "help-source" consulted by that individual. Two of the twenty-five possible combinations (the two of particular interest to us) were: (a) a person described as having severe withdrawal and adjustment problems, but who had not received help, and (b) a description of a normal individual who had consulted a psychiatrist.[17] In a highly significant finding, Phillips' respondents *rejected the normal individual more strongly than the severely disturbed person* (Phillips, p. 71 in Scheff, 1967). Perhaps needless to say, the normal was rejected even more strongly when described as having spent some time in a mental hospital.

It is impossible to provide clear specifications for exactly where each person's threshold will lie, but a few guidelines can be suggested. For one thing, a defense system may be prolonged far beyond a spouse's expected threshold of tolerance because of a fear of personal culpability (Yarrow, *et al.*, 1955:22). In other words, a wife who perceives that she may be involved in the creation of the husband's "condition" may be correspondingly unwilling to admit to the *existence* of a condition. Any admission runs the risk of engendering accusations toward *her* and, perhaps, the risk of requiring her own involvement in subsequent treatment procedures. One possibility, of course, is the development of a vicious cycle: the worse the behavior becomes, the less the wife can afford to acknowledge it because the worse it seems to make *her* appear. Thus, an "identification threshold" for such an individual will be a joint function of growing disruptions emanating from the spouse and reevaluation of one's own responsibility.

Social placement in the household may itself be an influencing factor in determining when this threshold is reached. We suggest the term "centrality" as a reference to the importance any given family member has for the functioning of the total family unit. In general, due to the "male breadwinner" base of the majority of American families and the economic necessities of survival, the husband-father occupies a position of highest centrality on a strictly instrumental scale. That is, the family will be in deep financial trouble if he loses his job and adequate paychecks stop flowing in. Because of this centrality, abnormal behavior will be met with early and long-lasting defense systems, particularly those of normalization and attenuation. Only when the behavior becomes severely disruptive will it eventuate in labeling as mental illness by family members. And this decision point, more than coincidentally, may come only after an employer has terminated the husband's job, thereby terminating his base of centrality in the family (e.g., Jackson, 1968).

The wife-mother in our typical family has her own position of high centrality. In Balesian terms, she is the socioemotional center of the household. With the husband off at work all day serving his instrumental functions, she almost automatically becomes the central provider of comfort, emotional support, expressions of love and concern, etc. It may well be that most families can no more afford to lose their "socioemotional leader" than the "instrumental leader." But they may feel more able to construct socioemotional *substitutes* than instrumental ones,[18] or they may feel less threatened by the socioemotional loss, whether that is a realistic response or not. (It *is* a less visible function.) Whatever the case, it is essential to further recognize that "abnormal behavior" on the part of the wife-mother stands a higher likelihood of detracting from her centrality base itself. Her behaviors will be *seen as* abnormal *because* they diminish her provision of love, understanding, care, etc. This is *not* the case with the husband; in fact, it is almost a precise opposite. Whereas he can be a complete bastard at home and still bring in the paycheck, she cannot be a complete bitch without jeopardizing her basic family role.[19] The upshot of all this is that the husband can be expected to offer fewer, less enduring defenses against the recognition and eventual treatment of his wife's "mental illness." We suggest, as a possibility open to empirical test, that "centrality" and its consequences may account for the high proportion of females under psychiatric treatment in ways well beyond any supposed greater tendency toward illness on their part (cf. Gove and Howell, 1974, and Rushing, 1971).

The centrality notion can also be applied to other household members. Very briefly, for example, an adolescent and an aging grandparent residing in the home might find that they share something in this respect. Let us imagine that both are engaging in "unusual" behaviors. Both lack the centrality of function to the family that the marital pair possesses, so we might anticipate quick and easy labeling. But we might anticipate incorrectly, for both individuals also occupy age brackets characterized by a sort of "normality of deviance." The grandparent's behavior may be written off as acceptable, predictable "eccentricity"—"after all, what can you expect from an old man?" The society provides generous license for unorthodox behaviors on the part of those who have become functionally unimportant and who are seldom in a position to "do any damage." At the same time, the adolescent is granted similar license, but under a different rationale: the natural, explorative restlessness of youth.

There is another side to this coin, of course, as evidenced by the number of elder citizens occupying chronic patient status in mental hospitals. If the central characters in the household have no desire to harbor and enfold a silly old grandparent and prefer to "put him out to pasture," community acceptance of psychiatry provides a relatively straightforward, unquestioned set of commitment proceedings. The adolescent's behavior may also reach levels of family intolerability, but the response in this case is more likely to involve legal control channels than psychiatric ones—e.g., "incorrigible youth."

In contrast to both the grandparent and the adolescent, note the likely reaction to a much younger child's behavioral abnormalities. Again, in the context of family survival needs, the child holds a position of low centrality. But this time there is no social license (explanation, rationale) to support bizarre behaviors. So if they occur, they will more quickly be perceived as having "something wrong," and a medical/psychiatric explanation and treatment will be sought. The parents can, of course, be expected to defend against recognition of illness in standard ways, but low centrality determines that the defense system will be correspondingly weaker and shorter-term. When long-term defenses *are* observed, it may often be the case that the child's centrality has risen beyond its expected, customary level—e.g., a mother who clings desparately to her child while her marriage crumbles around her.

This last example directs us to the observation that something more than personal defense systems is involved in accounting for movement from the informal problem stage to the formal system. Namely, patterns of abnormality in the behavior of one or more of the family members may themselves be functional in some way to the family unit. Indeed, several sociological theories of the etiology of severe mental illness utilize a "family balance" notion in explaining symptom development.[20] A family which has developed a comfortable balance for itself may not wish to destroy that balance by pinpointing a given member as "ill" and risking its own disruption when treatment brings about behavioral modifications. It is this theme that Sampson, Messinger, and Towne (1962) employ in suggesting that "defenses against recognition" do not tell us enough. These authors stress the "accommodation patterns" that families construct for themselves in a sort of unconscious effort to remain intact. They then propose that hospitalization (of the individual who has been "ill" throughout the accommodation phase) occurs only when the accommodation pattern fails to work any longer.[21]

Although the rule breaker's activities may occasionally be functional for the family, in most cases the rule breaker simply creates problems for the family and threatens its reputation and place. The violator's actions may unwittingly produce a spiral of interactional circles such that the family has no choice but betrayal:

> The more trouble at home, the greater the need to move into the lives of friends; the more this is done, the more the second circle will close itself off by virtue of being overtaxed; the more this occurs, the more fully does the patient take flight into unsuitable alliances and vicarious ones. Further, what remains of an inner circle tends to be alienated by what the patient attempts in the next concentric ring. (Goffman, 1969: 377–78)

These threats to the family will push it toward the reaction threshold. Family members may be driven to outside sources for advice; often they will seek sources who have had similar experiences.[22]

In this outward turning, Kadushin's "Friends and Supporters of Psychotherapy" are not to be forgotten: there are those who embrace psychiatric interpretations and responses as willingly as others reject them. We have little evidence (Kadushin's sample being as urban-regionally biased as it is) on the relative prevalence of this psychiatric segment or any other. It is reasonable to expect, however, a growing shift from denial to endorsement, in keeping with the expansion of the psychiatric public.[23] This being the case, a growing number of family systems will be characterized by dissent over attribution of mental illness and the steps to be taken in response to it. Where a family constitutes a built-in set of Friends and Supporters we find one form of agreement, and where all are antagonistic to psychiatry we find another. But what of the social processes characteristic of others' acceptance and subject's rejection of the mental illness decision—e.g., where the family members discussed above have crossed their threshold? Finally, then, what of the quite tenable situation wherein an individual defines *himself* as mentally ill while the other family members reject that interpretation?

Our best empirical leads again come from Kadushin, who reports that 80–90 percent of his sample engaged in conversations about their problems with others before seeking admission to a psychiatric clinic. Of these, some 20 percent received *only unsolicited* comments, 40 percent received only solicited comments, and the remaining 40 percent received both types. Stated differently, 60 percent of the sample were subjected *at some time* to comments they did not seek out and 80 percent at some time requested comments. There are two important points here. First, "social control of the applicant by others is an extremely important factor in bringing some persons to psychotherapy" (Kadushin, 1969:75). Indeed, it would seem to be extremely important in bringing the vast majority! In short, one is quite unlikely to reach a psychiatric setting independent of social influence. This should come as no great surprise, since attribution of mental illness is totally dependent upon evaluation of behavior in a social context. Secondly, conversation with others may be sufficient, in and of itself, to initiate a psychiatric sequence exclusive of "objective pathology."

This latter possibility brings us back to our central focus. Our interpretation is in agreement with Kadushin's own conclusion that we are directed ". . . to two opposing hypotheses: either a *high or* a *low* predisposition to recognize problems leads to conversations with laymen about one's problems" (Kadushin, 1969:177–78. Emphasis added.). High predisposition leads to *solicited* comments, which generally provide a function of social *support*. If the others involved are members of the Friends, early psychiatric visitation is predictable. If they are not, social support can easily take the form of attempts to convince the individual that he is *not* mentally ill and should stop thinking such things. Low predisposition, when accompanied by "weird" or "nuisance" behavior, leads to *unsolicited* comments, which generally provide a function of social control. The subject may be barraged with nothing but unsolicited comments which (a) continue indefinitely without having any effect, (b) cease when they are seen to fall on deaf ears or when the behavior comes to be accepted as a permanent eccentricity, or (c) actually precipitate a psychiatric contact. The latter may be with or without the subject's own recognition of a potential psychiatric problem. At one extreme, he may "voluntarily" initiate contact just to bring an end to the verbal harassment he experiences, perhaps even with the goal of disproving his detractors—e.g., "I'll have the last laugh when the experts say there's nothing wrong with me." At the other extreme, the subject may become so sensitive to the thrust of the unsolicited commentary that he comes to acknowledge tacitly that perhaps something *is* wrong; he need not be personally active in the communication system in order to undergo attitude change.

Finally, and in a great many cases, initial unsolicited comments can be expected to lead the subject into active solicitation of further comments, from the same individual(s) or from others. For example, an offhand comment by one spouse to the other may lead the subject to a series of requests for further information feedback, beginning with "what do you mean by that?", progressing to "how do you interpret it and feel about it?", and culminating in "what should I do about it?" Conversely, solicited comments may free the other party to submit unsolicited remarks, evaluations, and suggestions. This sort of interaction no doubt underlies the 40 percent of Kadushin's respondents who reported having received both solicited and unsolicited comments. Whatever the particular circumstances, sequences, and dynamics of the decision to seek help, that decision will be maximized over times past as a direct function of the proliferation of deviance definitions and the high visibility of controlling social agencies, as will be detailed in the next chapter.

Referral Systems:
Lay and Professional

Not all help-seeking decisions, of course, are family-based. Those who live alone or with non-relatives are not thereby rendered immune to deviant careers. The preceding section focused on the family because *most* of us live in family groupings and *most* psychiatric treatment decisions are strongly dependent upon the subtle and not-so-subtle interpersonal transactions that occur among family members (see Goffman, 1969). But even when the treatment consideration does have its origin in the family, the ultimate decision may involve a broader social network which functions as a lay referral system.

The concept of the "lay referral system" has its origin in the work of Eliot Freidson, who first emphasized the importance of the social network in medical decision making (Freidson, 1961). For those in family settings, the system ordinarily begins in that setting. And it very often terminates there when a spouse or parent either rejects the medical complaint as being insignificant or insists upon immediate professional attention. In indeterminate cases ("Maybe you're sick, but I'm not sure"), laymen are commonly brought into the picture just as they are at an even earlier juncture for the non-family-based decisions.

Freidson finds that the nature of the problem is a key variable in the solicitation of lay opinion even in the household setting—e.g., husband and wife are more likely to openly discuss backaches and colds than menstrual irregularities and impotence. Lack of discussion within the family, however, does not preclude use of a lay referral system outside the family. Indeed, a wife may consult female associates about a menstrual difficulty long before the husband is made aware of the problem, just as the husband may feel more relaxed talking to "the boys" about his sexual difficulties. Shifting our attention to the context of potential psychiatric illness, we become attuned to the probable significance of the lay referral system in view of the stigma and discomfort that may attenuate intrafamily consideration. We suggest the following:

1. Utilization of the lay referral system will be dependent upon the extent (number of contacts) of the individual's social network. At one extreme, the successful hermit (although "abnormal" and "weird" in the eyes of many) will not worry about his "condition" or have any contact with others who might worry about it and contribute suggestions. As a direct consequence of lack of social contact, any chance of psychiatric conceptualization or professional contact is eliminated. At the other extreme, the person with a large number of social contacts has automatic access to a referral system and will use it as such if other conditions warrant.
2. Either very close or very distant acquaintances are candidates for a given individual's referral system; "medium" acquaintances are not. The factor of social distance is not so contradictory and indeterminate as Kadushin suggests.[24] It is simply that two separate avenues of consultation and referral may be available simultaneously. The pre-patient may solicit or receive observations and

suggestions from a distant contact, both parties feeling free to engage in the exchange because of the protection of social distance and impersonality. The *same* pre-patient may *also* seek or receive information comfortably from a very close friend, the openness in this case stemming from the trust and concern implicit in the friendship bond. It is only the individual who stands midway between the passing acquaintance and the friend who is effectively ruled out of the referral system—e.g., the neighbor to whom one nods a greeting twice a week or the uninteresting work associate. These are neither far enough "away" to be rendered "safe" via impersonality of contact nor close enough to warrant assumptions of trust and confidentiality.

3. The stigma that the individual attaches to mental illness (or perceives that those in his social network attach to it) will be a factor in determining his use of a lay referral system. Recall that 10–20 percent of Kadushin's respondents reported having had *no* conversations with others about their condition. It is highly probable that many of these self-referrals involved perceptions of embarrassment, shame, or simply an unwillingness to burden others with one's own difficulties. On the other hand, the Friends and Supporters of Psychotherapy constitute a ready-made and easily available lay referral system, with psychiatric conditions regarded as a sort of "in thing" and perhaps even as prestige items. Some potential lay referrants will customarily be bypassed just on the chance that they *might* not be sympathetic and supportive. An employer may be a knowledgeable reference source and may meet criteria of "safe" social distance. Yet, the pre-patient employee may decline the use of the employer's wisdom for fear of losing his job "should the truth be found out."

In summary, a lay referral system is there to be used by almost every individual who might perceive the need for one. And evidence suggests that the vast majority of both medical and psychiatric pre-patients do experience a series of lay consultations. Whether a system is utilized at all and, if so, which particular individuals are selected, appears to be a combined function of (a) extent of the individual's social network, (b) intensity of social relationships, and (c) perceived stigma.

The lay referral system does not necessarily lead the subject directly to a psychiatrist, clinic, or hospital. For that matter, as indicated earlier, it can lead in an entirely opposite direction (i.e., to passive acceptance), if respondents fail to confirm the existence of a legitimate problem. Very often, however, the lay system propels the subject into another phase of contact that may be designated the *professional* referral system. The members of this system are those professionals who are ordinarily not accredited psychotherapists but whose work role *is taken* to include functions of listening to personal problems, interpreting, and providing counsel and support. Specifically, we include in this category physicians (nonpsychiatric), clergymen, and social workers, with our attention herein to be focused upon the first two.[25] Still other settings and occupational specialists display referral functions of a sort that place them midway between the lay and professional referral systems. Elaine Cumming, for example, characterizes school counseling services, lawyers, and employment services (along with clergymen) as "articulating" structures and agents. They "articulate" by occasionally providing indirect, dispatching routes into the formal control system. They also add complexities to the problem of inter-agency territory, referral, and exchange, the chief focus of Cumming's work and a topic we shall address in a later chapter (Cumming, 1968, especially Part II, pp. 177—240).

The individual who is hesitant to divulge his problems to friends and acquaintances (or the individual who is declined support but still persists) may make his own way to the professional referral system. He regards it as an appropriate, safe, and helpful source of advice and assistance. He can get some feedback from qualified professionals, he can get it within the protection of a relationship guaranteeing confidentiality; and, with any luck, the problem can be handled effectively without the necessity of proceeding further—i.e., to explicitly psychiatric settings. When lay consultation *does* take place, the consultant will often encourage entry into the professional referral system for the same kinds of reasons. Basically, it is easier for the individual and more protective of the relationship to say "have you discussed it with your doctor?" or "why don't you talk with your minister (priest, rabbi, etc.)?" than to say "you'd better see a psychiatrist!" In this way, the friend, relative, or acquaintance can confirm recognition of a problem and encourage therapeutic counsel without risking antagonism, rejection, or personal entanglement. Furthermore, the layman may honestly perceive that physicians or clergymen are appropriate and suitable choices; or, at least, that they *might* be able to take care of the problem.

The act of referral—whether to an inappropriate or appropriate source—is important in its implication for violator and witnesses alike, because it conveys a certain seriousness and legitimacy to the problem. After all, one does not refer minor cases! The initial act of referral is in one sense an admission of defeat on the part of the supporters of the deviant. It is no longer possible to normalize or deny the problem; it is now seen as "out of control." The referral also becomes an instant explanation of why the supporters have been unable to help the rule violator. The problem was beyond control— a job for a professional.

In addition to the change in attitude of supporters (and perhaps the deviant himself), the fate of the "case" once it is in the hands of physician or clergyman is subject to a whole new set of variables. Of Kadushin's respondents, for example, 70 percent of *hospital* psychiatric clinic applicants had previously consulted physicians, whereas less than half of the applicants to other types of clinic had done so. Similarly, ". . . over one-third of those applying to a religio-psychiatric clinic had consulted a clergyman" (Kadushin, 1969:313). This pattern reflects what may be a phenomenon not only of deviance processing but of human behavior in general: a consultant offers advice and recommends further procedures that are in greatest harmony with his own value set. Thus, those whose professional referral system contact has been a physician are most likely to be *directed toward* a hospital-based clinic, those who have consulted a clergyman are most likely to be *directed toward* the religio-psychiatric clinic, etc. Such range of choice, of course, applies only in large urban centers. In smaller communities, where facilities may be limited to private psychiatrists and/or to a single mental health clinic at the most, the question is reduced from one involving choice of particular agency to one of any endorsement at all. The nonpsychiatric professional who rejects the basic legitimacy of psychiatry (and there are many) may do whatever he can to keep the case out of psychiatric "territory" by attempting to handle the problem himself or by downplaying its importance.[26] If a physician does see a need for psychiatric referral, his own training and ideology influences his choice of psychiatric treatment style. Bynder, for example, presented a sample of physicians with the task of indicating their response to a hypothetical psychotic episode occurring within their own family. In listing referral choice, only 62 percent chose a psychiatrist at all. By psychiatric subtype, only 16 percent chose an "analytic-psychologic" psychiatrist, whereas 42 percent picked a psychiatrist characterized as "directive-organic." Bynder accounts for this disparity in terms of the physician's view that analytic-psychologic psychiatry finds "part of its source and inspiration in the social sciences" rather than in medicine (Bynder, 1965:85).

On the other side of the coin, evidence suggests that psychiatrists and psychiatric agencies themselves bear a major share of the responsibility for the level of effectiveness of the professional referral system. They do this (perhaps largely unknowingly) through a very simple omission: failure to report the progress of the cases referred to them. Eugene Piedmont, after observing that there is a general reluctance on the part of clergymen and general practitioners to deal with the plethora of emotional problems that are brought to them, accounts for their paradoxically low rate of psychiatric referrals in terms of "reciprocity failures" (Piedmont, 1968). Summarizing key sections of Piedmont's findings, general practitioners averaged 2.7 referrals per *month* of 211.9 patients seen per week. Those figures yield a referral rate of roughly 0.3 percent compared with estimates of "primarily mental problems" in general practitioner's caseloads that run as high as 75 percent. Clergy averaged 1.9 referrals monthly of 7.3 parishioners seen per week—a rate of 6.5 percent, compared with estimates of a 33 percent emotional problem caseload. Referral rate for both professional types, then, is substantially below rates predictable on the basis of the nature of the problem—dramatically so for both, but astonishingly so for GPs. Next, of those responding to the relevant questionnaire item, 56.7 percent of the GPs and 73.7 percent of the clergy indicate that they receive reports on the progress of their referrals (a) only on the occasion of marked change, (b) only if they request it, or (c) no more than once per year or once in all. Following this lead, Piedmont asked his respondents whether they would anticipate more referrals if, in the future, they were to receive more frequent, more regular, and better reports back about their patients. Although the responses to this item yielded a variety of intriguing complexities (particularly in the case of GPs), the general expectation was that referrals would increase markedly if this "reciprocity" on the part of the psychiatrist were itself to rise.

For our purposes, the Piedmont study suggests that a given professional's standing impression of the legitimacy and value of psychiatry is not the only factor involved in determining a subject's movement to psychiatric agencies and agents. In addition, a tacit exchange process is presumed to exist by those doing the referring: in exchange for referrals, they expect (for a variety of reasons) informational feedback. The feedback in question here involves general information such as whether the person referred actually went to the agency, whether the case was accepted or passed on, etc., and does not refer to details of the case which would be protected by rules of professional confidentiality. Failure to provide such feedback is regarded as a violation of the implicit exchange agreement, leading to a corresponding cutback in their part of the relationship. Such changing impressions may then, of course, be incorporated into the professional's image of psychiatry, thus further affecting his willingness to cooperate.

Despite all the restrictions upon maximal referral to control agency settings, the fact remains that ever greater numbers of people find themselves involved with such settings. Thanks to a psychiatric public and the "Friends," whose informal recruiting tactics have worked, such proliferation *has* occurred. Indeed, the small proportion of cases referred onward by professionals such as physicians and clergymen still constitutes a sizeable increase over the numbers referred in the past.[27] That people bring their emotional problems to any professional at all attests to the role which organizational recruitment, stereotyping, and proliferation of popularized deviance definitions play in the creation of deviance—our next topic.

Notes

1. There is little debate over one point in the sociology of deviance: most deviance is not officially reacted to by society. Self-reported delinquency investigations, victim surveys, community studies of physical and mental illness epidemiology show that a high volume of activity occurs which could be officially labeled deviant, but goes undetected or is known yet not referred to control agencies. The labeling perspective raises the question, why so *little* official deviance? rather than, why so *much* crime, delinquency or mental illness?

2. Goffman suggests that the stigmatized are told by normals to adjust to their handicap which means "the unfairness and pain of having to carry a stigma will never be presented to them [normals]; it means that normals will not have to admit to themselves how limited their tactfulness and tolerance is; and it means that normals can remain relatively uncontaminated by intimate contact with the stigmatized, relatively unthreatened in their identity beliefs" (1963:121). For an excellent discussion of a case in point, see Fred Davis's description of deviance disavowal among the handicapped (1961).

3. This must be immediately qualified since not all dimensions are equal. It is generally assumed that threat of personal violence is most important, yet at times concern with property may take precedence—e.g., directives to shoot looters on sight.

4. In a set of ingenious experiments, Peter McHugh investigated the circumstances surrounding construction of a "nothing unusual is happening" definition of the situation. Subjects were told they were testing a new form of nondirective psychotherapy. They were instructed to describe their problems, and then pose a series of ten questions which could be answered yes or no by the therapist. Communication was through a microphone so that the therapist was not seen by subjects. Each person was told to verbalize his or her thoughts after each yes or no response and then formulate the next question. Unknown to the subjects, yes or no responses were random, meaning that many of the responses were senseless or inconsistent with previous answers. McHugh was interested in the constructive processes elicited from an imposed disorderly situation. What is remarkable is that a majority of subjects made it through all ten questions without questioning the situation; they saw it as a technique designed to help them. They were able to impose an order upon the random responses (McHugh, 1968:83–126, especially p. 104).

5. Albert Cohen, who takes a normative paradigm approach to norms, also recognizes the potential ambiguity in reactive norms: "Responses to deviance can no more be left normatively unregulated than deviance itself. Whose business it is to intervene, at what point, and what he may or may not do is defined by a normatively established division of labor. In short, for any given role—parent, priest, psychiatrist, neighbor, policeman, judge—the norms prescribe, *with varying degrees of definiteness*, what they are supposed to do and how they are supposed to do it when other persons, in specified roles, misbehave" (Cohen, 1965:9. Emphasis added). What we have said about norms and competent rule use in earlier chapters also applies to reactive norms—i.e., they are negotiated, open-ended, and problematic, therefore ambiguous.

136

6. After a number of experiments, these researchers conclude: "Subjects in our experiments responded early or not at all. Over 90 percent of all subjects who responded, responded within the first half of the relatively short time available to them" (Latane and Darley, 1970:122). It is difficult to break out of the initial definition of the situation (primacy effect)—e.g., initially silent students find it increasingly difficult to raise questions as the course passes on in time.

7. Victim compensation plans may increase the payoff for the victim and should therefore increase reporting of crimes against person. Those insured against property crimes are required by companies to report victimization to the police in order for claims to be processed.

8. An example of this is the practice of setting up procedures for receiving anonymous tips, which found its widest application in the Heroin Hotline, a toll-free Washington number where tips on pushers and distributors could be recorded. This program was abandoned when it was discovered that its cost was exceeding its payoff in terms of arrests and convictions. Somewhat more successful are locally-based monetary rewards which are offered for information on crimes "leading to the indictment and conviction of the perpetrators." Potential respondents have become aware of the selection process in the criminal justice system, such that more recent rewards have not demanded conviction as a condition for payoff.

9. There are of course various degrees of voluntariness in psychiatric help seeking. In the hospitalization of mental disorders, one study outlined three conditions of entrance: voluntary, non-protested, and compulsory. In compulsory commitment the "patient at one stage or another, or in all stages, expresses reluctance or resistance to hospitalization" (Rock, et al., 1968:33). Under each of these legal-organizational headings, there would be great variation in degree of willingness actually possessed by the rule breakers.

10. E.g., "*After all, the persons in our sample are deviants,* and as such are likely to provoke the reactions of others" (Kadushin, 1969:175. Emphasis added.).

11. Mental health publicity campaigns have, to a great extent, succeeded in making psychiatric care not only acceptable, but in some ways and to some people even prestigious. (For evidence on this point, see Dohrenwend and Chin-Shong, 1967:421–22). This is not to say there is no longer any stigma attached to being a mental patient. Even amongst the psychiatrically informed, there is a vast difference between a weekly session with a fashionable "right" psychoanalyst and an extended stay in a mental hospital. However, increasing public awareness and acceptance of mental problems acts as a backdrop to "help seeking." We will discuss the role control agencies play in generating community acceptance of mental illness and intervention in a later chapter.

12. And if a patient complains about having been institutionalized unjustly, his accusation is often taken as evidence of "paranoia"—"proof" that his hospitalization is legitimate. (See Rushing, 1971: 524 for a note on railroading.)

13. Community acceptance of psychiatry (psychiatric public), plus ambiguity of symptoms and resulting diagnosis, make the despicable act of "railroading" one which could be easily justified. Consequently, guilt and the urge to confess would be low —the colluders may come to believe they did the right thing, albeit for the wrong reasons. We shall examine the role which control agencies play in producing support for psychiatry and the resultant therapeutic state in Chapter VI.

14. In this study, there is a critical distinction implicit in the term "tolerance." The authors essentially use tolerance in two senses. The first might be termed "tolerance by default": behaviors are tolerated because they are not seen as serious, or as mental illness (not recognized as deviant). Respondents were asked to judge six behavioral descriptions of fictitious persons. The lower-class, cross-sectional sample rated fewer cases as signifying mental illness (pp. 423–25). This is due to a lower level of sophistication and knowledge of psychiatric labels and symptoms among the lower-class respondents than was true of the leadership (i.e., high-

138   The Creation of Deviance

status) sample—evidence for the point made here. It is important to recognize a
second meaning of tolerance; it might be termed "reaction severity." Given that
a behavior is seen as mental illness, what do respondents say should be done? The
more severe the reaction prescribed, the greater the intolerance. The researchers
found lower-class respondents were more likely to recommend mental hospitalization, while the leadership sample was more likely to recommend out-patient
treatment. The problem here is that the hospital response by the lower-class
respondents may have been due to lack of information about alternative treatment facilities (p. 429). If true, the sociologist who imputes intolerance to the
hospitalization recommendation may be in error. Other indicators, such as social
distance scales, should be used; Dohrenwend and Chin-Shong did find more intolerance among their lower-class sample when this indicator was used (1967:430).
In passing, it should be noted that other studies indicate greater acceptance
(tolerance) of certain deviant behavior patterns in the lower-class cultural milieu
than in the middle class—e.g., Mercer's work on mental retardation found lower-
class families more likely to accept a retarded child in their family, while middle-
class families preferred continued hospitalization (1965).

15. The success of the accusation depends in part on the relative power of the accuser
and the person accused. Thus, in a family, a member with very little power—e.g.,
a child—is likely to be placed in the deviant role when in fact most of the members
are acting abnormally (Vogel and Bell, 1960). This does not negate the "boomerang effect" described earlier, but suggests those in power may be relatively immune from it. Note also that the illness model used by most psychiatrists, which
locates the problem within the person rather than in primary interaction networks, gives the accuser the advantage and reduces the risk of the turning back
of labels upon the sanctioner.

16. For example, some married women coming in contact with the ideology of wom-
en's liberation are suddenly realizing that they have been living with a male
chauvinist for years. As a result, surprised husbands are being accused of conspira-
torially motivated deviant activities heretofore taken for granted as within the
role of "head of the household."

17. The reader's appreciation of the findings will be enhanced by noting the whole-
some character of the "normal person" as described to respondents: "Here is a
description of a man. Imagine that he is a respectable person living in your
neighborhood. He is happy and cheerful, has a good enough job, and is fairly well
satisfied with it. He is always busy and has quite a few friends who think he is easy
to get along with most of the time. Within the next few months he plans to marry
a nice young woman he is engaged to" (Scheff, 1967:311, n22).

18. This idea finds support in a study of family reactions to mental illness of the wife.
Sampson, et al., (1962) found that a wife's residual rule violations were less tolerated, and more likely to be officially referred, when an extended family was
present. If the wife's mother or mother-in-law was available to come into the
family to help with the problem (and the housework), she often provided the
socioemotional substitute and thereby enhanced the daughter's entry into official
treatment channels.

19. One explanation for greater incidence of "actual" mental illness in women (especially married women) than men is that the latter have two or more major roles,
while the female is generally relegated to one, family-tied role. This means that
the male having problems in one role area can switch his interest and time to
another, or balance "losses" in one against "gains" in the other. The woman does
not have this advantage, thus the greater suspectibility to mental illness (Gove and
Tutor, 1973; also Chesler, 1972:39). Women's liberation, to the extent it brings
about changes in sex roles, may reduce this problem; also, role changes may mean
greater sharing of instrumental and socioemotional functions, to some extent
dissipating the differential in reaction.

20. For example, see several articles under the heading of "Family Dynamics" in Don D. Jackson (ed.), *The Etiology of Schizophrenia*, New York: Basic Books, 1960.

21. While this approach extends our understanding a bit further, it still offers no explanation of precisely *what* terminates the accommodation pattern any more than Yarrow, *et al.*, explain the ultimate breakdown of a defense system. We are left, perhaps unavoidably, with no satisfactory accounting of what determines that an individual can be perceived as sane at one moment and mentally ill at the next. Nevertheless, the factors presented thus far, together with the "threshold" notion, take us a considerable distance toward the understanding we seek.

22. We predict that those with previous experience are likely to recommend appropriate professional help sources. In Phillips' study cited earlier, he found that those respondents having first-hand experiences with someone termed mentally ill did not reject those who had problems and sought professional help. As we shall see shortly, friends without this experience are likely to suggest "inappropriate" help sources such as an M.D. or clergyman.

23. Even when family members are not pro-psychiatry, there is a built-in demand that the rule breaker, once labeled, act in terms of that label. If the member acting mentally ill "reverses his behavior and becomes more collected, the [family members] must try to get him to admit that he has been ill, else his present saneness will raise doubts about their motivation and their relationship to him. For these reasons, admission of insanity has to be sought" (Goffman, 1969:374).

24. "The greater the distance, the easier it is for one to tell another that the latter has problems, for the adviser is not intimately involved and has greater objectivity. At the same time, intimacy also produces interaction, if only for the reason that another person is available" (Kadushin, 1969:178). (Cf. Scheff, 1966a:96, 123).

25. There are several other possible inclusions, but we prefer to regard them as part of the *lay* referral system. The often-cited bartender, with crying towel in hand, provides one example. It may well be true that bartenders throughout the land are obliged to listen to countless tales of woe and to respond as sensibly and comfortingly as they can. But bartenders receive no formal training in this regard, do not seem to be particularly effective at it, and prefer to regard themselves (as do most of their customers) as dispensers of drink rather than of psychological cure.

26. This response varies enormously according to severity of symptoms. The most recalcitrant internal medicine specialist still makes quick use of psychiatric consultation when he encounters a patient who (a) has attempted suicide or (b) exhibits "bizarre," disruptive behaviors. See: Meyer and Mendelson, 1960; Tiedeman, 1968.

27. At the same time, it seems from these studies of referrals that physicians and clergymen may have a greater role in the neutralization of deviance than previously expected; these relatively nonstigmatized professions may serve as a buffer which keeps many individuals from more bureaucratized social-control agencies. Future research might focus on some of the denial and normalization techniques used by these "first-line" referral agents.

References

Alvarez, Rodolfo
    1968   "Informal reactions to deviance in simulated work organiza-
            tions: a laboratory experiment. *American Sociological Review*
            33 (December):895–912.

Biderman, Albert D., Louis A. Johnson, Jennie McIntyre, and Adrianne W.
Weir
    1967   *Report on a Pilot Study in the District of Columbia on Victim-*
            ization and Attitudes Toward Law Enforcement. Washing-
            ton, D.C.: U.S. Government Printing Office.

Black, Donald J.
    1970   "Production of crime rates." *American Sociological Review*
            35 (August):733–48.

Bynder, Herbert
    1965   "Physicians choose psychiatrists: medical social structure and
            patterns of choice." *Journal of Health and Human Behavior*
            6 (Summer):83–91.

Chesler, Phyllis
    1972   *Women and Madness.* New York: Doubleday.

Cohen, Albert
    1965   "The sociology of the deviant act: anomie theory and
            beyond." *American Sociological Review* 30 (February):5–14.

Cumming, Elaine
    1968   *Systems of Social Regulation.* New York: Atherton Press.

Daniels, Arlene Kaplan
    1970   "Development of the scapegoat in sensitivity training ses-
            sions." In Tamotsu Shibutani (ed.), *Human Nature and Collec-*
            tive Behavior. Englewood Cliffs, New Jersey: Prentice-Hall.

Daniels, Arlene Kaplan, and Richard R. Daniels
    1964   "The social function of the career fool." *Psychiatry* 27 (Au-
            gust):219–29.

Davis, Fred
    1961   "Deviance disavowal: the management of strained interac-
            tion by the visibly handicapped." *Social Problems* 9
            (Fall):120–32.

Dohrenwend, Bruce P., and Edwin Chin-Shong
  1967   "Social status and attitudes toward psychological disorder: the problem of tolerance of deviance." *American Sociological Review* 32 (June):417–33.

Emerson, Joan P.
  1970   " 'Nothing unusual is happening.' " In Tamotsu Shibutani (ed.), *Human Nature and Collective Behavior.* Englewood Cliffs, New Jersey: Prentice-Hall.

Ennis, Philip H.
  1967   *Criminal Victimization in the United States: A Report of a National Survey.* Washington, D.C.: U.S. Government Printing Office.

Farrell, Ronald A., and Thomas J. Morrione
  1972   "Social interaction and stereotypic responses to homosexuals." Paper presented at American Sociological Association meeting. New Orleans, Louisiana.

Freidson, Eliot
  1961   *Patients' Views of Medical Practice.* New York: Russell Sage Foundation.

Gibbs, Jack P.
  1966   "Sanctions." *Social Problems* 13 (Fall):147–59.

Goffman, Erving
  1963   *Stigma: Notes on the Management of Spoiled Identity.* Englewood Cliffs, New Jersey: Prentice-Hall.
  1969   "The insanity of place." *Psychiatry* 32 (November):357–88.

Gove, Walter R., and Patrick Howell
  1974   "Individual resources and mental hospitalization: a comparison and evaluation of the societal reaction and psychiatric perspectives." *American Sociological Review* 39 (February):86–100.

Gove, Walter R., and Jeannette F. Tutor
  1973   "Adult sex roles and mental illness." *American Journal of Sociology* 78 (January):812–35.

Hawkins, Richard
  1973   "Who called the cops?: decisions to report criminal victimization." *Law and Society Review* 7 (Spring):427–44.

Hollingshead, August B., and Fredrick C. Redlich
  1958   *Social Class and Mental Illness.* New York: John Wiley and Sons.

Jackson, Don D.
  1960   *The Etiology of Schizophrenia.* New York: Basic Books.

Jackson, Joan K.
  1968   "The adjustment of the family to the crisis of alcoholism." Reprinted in Earl Rubington and Martin S. Weinberg (eds.),

Deviance: The Interactionist Perspective. New York: Macmillan.

Kadushin, Charles
    1969   *Why People Go to Psychiatrists.* New York: Atherton Press.

Kitsuse, John I.
    1962   "Societal reaction to deviant behavior." *Social Problems* 9 (Winter):247–56.

Laing, R. D.
    1970   *Knots.* New York: Pantheon.

Laing, R. D., and A. Esterson
    1964   *Sanity, Madness and the Family.* London: Tavistock.

Latane, Bibb, and John M. Darley
    1969   "Bystander 'apathy'." *American Scientist* 57:244–68.
    1970   *The unresponsive bystander: why doesn't he help?* New York: Appleton-Century-Crofts.

McHugh, Peter
    1968   *Defining the Situation.* Indianapolis: Bobbs-Merrill.
    1970   "A common-sense conception of deviance." In J. D. Douglas (ed.), *Deviance and Respectability.* New York: Basic Books.

Mercer, Jane R.
    1965   "Social system perspective and clinical perspective: frames of reference for understanding career patterns of persons labelled mentally retarded." *Social Problems* 13 (Summer):18–34.

Meyer, Eugene, and Myer Mendelson
    1960   "The psychiatric consultation in post-graduate medical teaching." *Journal of Nervous and Mental Diseases* 130:78–81.

Phillips, Derek
    1963   "Rejection: a possible consequence of seeking help for mental disorders." *American Sociological Review* 28 (December):963–72. Reprinted in Thomas J. Scheff (ed.), *Mental Illness and Social Processes.* New York: Harper and Row (1967).

Piedmont, Eugene B.
    1968   "Referrals and reciprocity: psychiatrists, general practitioners, and clergymen." *Journal of Health and Social Behavior* 9 (March):29–41.

Piliavin, Irving, and Scott Briar
    1964   "Police encounters with juveniles." *American Journal of Sociology* 70 (September):204–214.

Rock, Ronald S., Marcus A. Jacobson, and Richard M. Janopaul
    1968   *Hospitalization and Discharge of the Mentally Ill.* Chicago: University of Chicago Press.

Roman, Paul M., and Harrison M. Trice
    1971   "Normalization: a neglected complement to labeling theory."

Paper presented at American Sociological Association meeting. Denver, Colorado.

Routh, Donald K., and Keith M. King
1972 "Social class bias in clinical judgment." *Journal of Consulting and Clinical Psychology* 72:202–207.

Rushing, William
1971 "Individual resources: societal reactions and hospital commitment." *American Journal of Sociology* 77 (November):511–26.

Sampson, Harold, Sheldon L. Messinger, and Robert D. Towne
1962 "Family processes and becoming a mental patient." *American Journal of Sociology* 68 (July):88–96.

Scheff, Thomas
1966a *Being Mentally Ill.* Chicago: Aldine.

1966b "Users and non-users of a student psychiatric clinic." *Journal of Health and Human Behavior* 7 (Summer):114–21.

1967 *Mental Illness and Social Processes.* New York: Harper and Row.

Terry, Robert M.
1967 "The screening of juvenile offenders." *Journal of Criminal Law, Criminology and Police Science* 58 (June):173–81.

Tiedeman, Gary H.
1968 *Psychiatric Consultation in a Medical Setting: Intraprofessional Differentials and Resolutions.* Unpublished Dissertation. University of North Carolina.

Trice, Harrison M.
1965 "The reactions of supervisors to emotionally disturbed employees." *Journal of Occupational Medicine* 7 (June):177–83.

Vogel, Ezra F., and Norman W. Bell
1960 "The emotionally disturbed child as family scapegoat." In N. W. Bell and E. F. Vogel (eds.), *The Family.* New York: Free Press.

Yarrow, Mirian R., Charlotte G. Schwartz, Harriet S. Murphy, and Leila C. Deasy
1955 "The psychological meaning of mental illness in the family." *Journal of Social Issues* 11:12–24.

Chapter VI

Controlling
Deviance Is
Big Business

Proliferation of Definitions of Deviance and
  Social-Control Agencies
"Recruiting" Tactics
Control Over Definitions of Deviance
Special Interests and the Recruiting of Deviants
Moral Entrepreneurs

One must distinguish an unconscious tendency in a homosexual direction, which may be quite manifest to other people—at least to psychiatrists—and yet unknown to the possessor, from a conscious desire and preference for homosexual contact.

Karl Menninger

Picture two contrasting societies. In one, there is little or no conscious concept of deviance. At the most, the members of this society develop a notion of what behaviors are detrimental to their own survival and they commence to deal with these behaviors in an informal, unstructured, rather spontaneous way. If someone kills (unless, of course, he has killed an enemy), he is killed. If someone steals, he is beaten. If someone refuses to work, he is ostracized. There are no laws, no police, and no social-control agencies.

In the other society, we find published lists of inappropriate, unacceptable behaviors. Any individual who publicly exhibits one of these behaviors is summarily reported to a particular control agency, sometimes as the result of surveillance by agency authorities but frequently by his acquaintances, friends, and even family members. The villain's subsequent fate is totally at the determination of the control agency. He may be imprisoned, hospitalized, fined, or dismissed according to the interpretations, definitions, and reactions of the control agents.

Neither of these descriptions accurately portrays the means by which deviance is generally handled today. Yet, if forced to match current U.S. society to one of the two, we would have to choose the second description. Industrialized, complex societies are closer to the image of a formalistic social-control system than to that of the informal system. Yet informal systems do not disappear; rather they are significantly affected by the actions of the formal control agencies.

Source: Karl Menninger, *The Vital Balance.* New York: The Viking Press, Inc., 1963, p. 196.

Before we try to specify how this occurs, and consequently "who gets to do what to whom," let us examine the types of agencies involved in the "doing."

American society, like most advanced, industrialized societies, has three broad spheres of formal social control: the legal system, the therapeutic-health system, and the social welfare system. In a sense they all compete for social-control clientele, so some general comment on each is in order. Nicholas Kittrie compares the therapeutic and welfare state:

> The therapeutic state differs from its more estab-
> lished sister, the public welfare state, in that the lat-
> ter offers its services to the voluntary recipient while
> the former seeks to impose its "beneficial" services
> compulsorily (since the recipient is held to be incom-
> petent). Under the public welfare, the citizen is
> faced, at least theoretically, with the final choice ei-
> ther to accept or reject the offered public assistance
> and any concomitant governmental scrutiny and de-
> mands, but the state's therapeutic function is often
> authoritarian and may be exercised on a deviant indi-
> vidual for the asserted public interest with little or no
> consideration of his own choice. (Kittrie, 1971:41)

The therapeutic approach is characterized by its concern with the prevention of deviance rather than reactions and potential deterrence. The therapeutic state thus seeks to prevent deviant behavior before it occurs, while the criminal law has been largely a reactive mechanism (although general deterrence is claimed for it). The therapeutic approach is seen as effective because of a central assumption of the therapeutic agent that most deviant behavior is the result of compulsive actions by the offender (cf. Murphy, 1969). Compulsive behavior is nondeterrable; consequently, unsolicited societal intervention before the act is justified to prevent harm to society. The therapeutic state thus becomes highly authoritarian, although it is represented as a "service to society."

Thus, the state is protected by a panel of scientific experts who make decisions about who qualifies for preventive detention or an indeterminant sentence so that unconscious and unrecognized problems can be treated. The danger, of course, is that moral and political problems are soon generalized into this medical model, due in part to the propaganda appeal of providing help for a "health" problem. Since the definitional boundaries of the therapeutic state are quite porous, one outcome has been an increase in the types of deviance seen as medical problems. This shift in the handling of deviance is, in part, the result of our failure to deal effectively with many forms of deviance through the criminal law. Kittrie comments that

> ... The therapeutic state has become the receiving ground for past mistakes of criminal law, when society finally repents of its error but is not yet willing to tolerate the offensive activity, even though it is not particularly harmful. Many of the activities of the mentally ill which result in commitment are of this ilk. Similarly, this is the direction that the movement for treating alcoholics is taking. In addition, once the therapeutic model is established, it is particularly easy for it to accommodate within its sanctions forms of behavior which otherwise would be left unsanctioned by the criminal law. (Kittrie, 1971:383–84)

The potential for expansion of definitions of deviance and realms of social control are definite characteristics of the therapeutic state.

Proliferation of Definitions of Deviance and Social-Control Agencies

There is a man named Garrett Trapnell who boasts what must be one of the strangest careers of deviance ever reported. After being apprehended on charges of armed robbery during his teens, Trapnell's lawyer offered him the option of prison sentence or mental hospitalization. Trapnell chose the latter and spent most of his time reading " 'more damned books on psychiatry and psychology than probably any psychology student will in any school in the world' " (*Time,* January 29, 1973:20). Subsequent to his discharge, Trapnell renewed what was to be a lengthy career of lucrative armed robbery marked by numerous arrests and convictions but by not one single day spent in prison. How is that possible? Because every time he is brought to trial, Trapnell pleads "not guilty by reason of insanity," maintaining that he cannot be held responsible for acts perpetrated by his evil alter-ego (known as Gregg Ross). He is hence committed to a hospital, from which he escapes to take up more robbery until the next arrest begins the cycle again. At this writing, Trapnell awaits a trial for an abortive skyjacking attempt which he claims, of course, to have been masterminded by Gregg Ross.[1]

Trapnell's career can be accounted for in terms of what Kittrie describes as a movement from criminal law to the therapeutic state

(Kittrie, 1971). What was once regarded as a reprehensible act against society and met with punishment is now seen as requiring treatment. There are not very many Garrett Trapnells around (at least not yet), but the fact that there is even one suggests that societal reactions have undergone significant change. How and why has that change transpired?

Kittrie's chief explanatory tool (and a highly effective one) is summarized in the phrase: "the divestment of criminal justice"—i.e., the criminal law's "relinquishing of its jurisdiction over many of its traditional subjects and areas" (Kittrie, 1971:4). This divestment helps to contribute to the fact that "for every criminal sent to prison, more than four persons are subjected to noncriminal incarceration" (Kittrie, 1971:7). Something has clearly led society to remove "criminal" behaviors of the past from the sanctions of criminal law. Have we become more humane, more tolerant of deviant conduct? That is unlikely, at least to the extent that it could be taken to account for the current state of affairs. For a more effective answer, we must take note of the role that has been played by none other than the social sciences themselves.

One of the identifying characteristics of the social sciences is the stress they place on environmental determinants of behavior. While important genetic influences obviously exist, the social scientist stresses the tremendous complex of societal forces outside the individual that mold and shape the person. Thus, the sociologist talks of normative systems, institutions, role expectations, primary groups, subcultures, etc.—not of chromosomes and genes. In other words (and this is the key that unlocks the subsequent process), every individual is (1) malleable and (2) not "personally responsible" for all personal feelings, attitudes, and behaviors. This being the case, the individual is presumed to be open to continuous environmental shaping, including those stimuli received after having committed some deviant act.

In a society where the individual is held directly accountable for personal actions, we have a supportive base for social-control policies of retribution, punishment, and custodial confinement. But in a society where there is a consensus (by those who make the decisions, at any rate) that one is shaped by environmental circumstances, it must be regarded as senseless to punish or confine an "innocent victim of the surroundings." On the contrary, what is called for is *therapy* and *rehabilitation.*

It is important that we avoid misinterpretation on this point. The social sciences are not directly responsible for the creation of deviants. They do, however, help create "deviance" as a concept. Theories are then constructed about how the deviance comes about. These diverse theories share an emphasis on the forces of environment and, conversely, an implicit emphasis on the relative innocence of the deviant. This kind of "environmental determinism" is notable as the main theme of contemporary sociology and is a dominant current in this very volume. The emphasis is valid, honest, and exciting. But it has also had the effect of underwriting the development of an expanded set of social-control agencies. This it has done by its direct support of the divestment of criminal justice and the movement to a therapeutic state.

It is more than a simple coincidence that psychiatry experienced its rapid expansion and growth in acceptability during the same time period that the social sciences have come into vogue. Without elaborating in detail, it should be noted that twentieth-century psychiatry has borrowed heavily from the social sciences in revising its strong Freudian emphasis on the way to becoming a standard part of contemporary man's vocabulary and world view. In this sense, psychiatry's contribution to a therapeutic state duplicates that which we have already cited in regarding the social sciences. But psychiatry and its related social science, psychology, have made special, additional contributions to the proliferation of *definitions* of deviance. This has been accomplished via the development of a lengthy and impressive categorical listing of mental illness syndromes, begun by Emil Kraepelin in the mid-nineteenth century but expanded and refined ever since. Some of these categories do nothing more than provide new names for behaviors already accepted as deviant—e.g., discrete subtypings of what used to be grouped under the heading of "the insane." Others simply move a deviant behavior into psychiatric territory—e.g., alcoholism.[2] But a major subset of labels and categories carve out *new* forms of deviance—undetected, undiscussed, and *untreated* prior to the psychiatric era. Under this heading fall most of the various neuroses, character disorders, psychopathologies, and sociopathologies. With more deviant labels to attach to people, we would naturally expect to find more deviants and more agencies specifically established for the purpose of controlling that deviance. Such has been the case.

Next, we turn to the roles of conformity and prevailing conceptions of morality. It is a commonplace assertion that an expanding middle-class in an industrializing society develops a clearly delimited set of behavioral norms. It seeks to impose these norms upon the total society as constituting "right," "healthy," and "proper" behaviors. Furthermore, through its significant abilities at structuring the society in its own terms, this segment succeeds in creating the appropri-

ate agents and agencies for handling behaviors that fall outside the
normative bounds.[3] Thus, the alcoholic, the derelict, the street
fighter, the truant, the petty thief, and the eccentric living in a
frontier society will have their predictable problems of social adaptation, but will undergo no *formal* labeling procedures and little, if
any, control at the hands of specified agencies. The same individuals,
in a contemporary setting, find themselves categorized and treated
in accordance with established normative guidelines. At least in part,
this is as a direct result of the "normative narrowing"[4] that has taken
place (even while greater diversity of behavior is also observable, and
with nominal societal support of its legitimacy).

So far, we have stressed "proliferation factors" that may seem to
explain more about psychiatric deviance than about criminal deviance. In terms of Kittrie's divestment of criminal justice idea, however, the two realms have become almost inseparable. (The case of
Garrett Trapnell attests to this quite dramatically.) We should not be
confused, therefore, into thinking that fewer acts are thought of as
being criminal or unlawful. On the contrary, definitions of deviance
have proliferated under the specifically "criminal" heading as well.[5]
Trapnell's crime of skyjacking is an excellent example of one source
of new definitions: the society and its technology. As new technological developments make new behaviors available (e.g., inexpensive jet
air travel) and as people develop techniques for disrupting the new
behaviors, society reacts by constructing a new deviant category and
a new set of control agents (e.g., "sky marshalls" and baggage inspec-
tors).

We have already alluded to the passing of the frontier format. This,
too, has a part in proliferation, especially as it is tied to the increasing
urbanization and sophistication of a society. As people begin to live
closely together, interdependent upon one another for long periods
of time, a desire for quieter, more stable conditions appears to set in.
Boisterous and violent behaviors become more and more intrusive,
so new laws are established to protect persons and property from
such offensive activities. The end effect of the typical urban experience is that large police forces exist, in substantial visibility, for the
purpose of enforcing law. Not only does this social-control agency
proliferate in total size and in number of branches, but the definitions of deviance proliferate as well, to include such "new" offenses
as noise ordinance violations and traffic violations. Furthermore, the
police force is susceptible to the Parkinson's Laws that affect any
bureaucracy: it mushrooms internally in size and complexity. Few
elements of this diverse range of proliferation would occur were it
not for the general societal patterns of urbanization and population
increase.

Returning to the models of two contrasting societies presented earlier in this chapter, it can be suggested that current U.S. society could be placed somewhere between the two extremes. We talk a great deal about the importance of rehabilitation and therapy, but we also seem to think that a good many crooks and loonies should "get theirs" because of acts or behaviors for which we still insist upon holding them personally accountable. The result of such inconsistency can be a distortion of stated therapeutic goals whereby repression operates more comfortably than ever before from within a cloak of therapy. In other words, we may simply find "the old intolerance coupled with a new willingness to resort to pseudoscience for more effective societal controls" (Kittrie, 1971:248).

Perhaps nowhere do all of these factors of proliferation converge as convincingly as in the community mental health system, where "all one needs to do to be included as a deviant ... is to have a 'problem'—either self- or other-defined" (Dinitz and Beran, 1971:101). As for those whose behavior has become or is becoming "decriminalized":

> These deviants have no sure way of knowing if they will be labeled criminal, insane, or with a problem in living; if they will be acted on by police officers, psychiatrists, or social workers; or if they will be sentenced to a prison, committed to a state hospital, or enrolled in an encounter group." (Dinitz and Beran, 1971:104)

We now turn to the role played by the control agencies and professionals in the proliferation of deviance creation.

"Recruiting" Tactics

The word "recruiting" may convey an immediate image of the U.S. Army and its attempts to entice throngs of able-bodied young men into voluntary military service. The Army's publicity campaigns, in order to interest those who might not otherwise aspire to military careers, omit reference to negative considerations and emphasize the advantages of a life as a professional soldier. Posters, pamphlets, and mass-media blurbs feature the lures of free international travel, twenty-year retirement, specialized job training, unquestioned patriotism, and exotic romances rather than scenes of carnage, devastation, and Veterans' Administration hospital amputee wards. Other

kinds of organizations require volunteer participants in order to ensure their survival, and they may advertise in similar ways and with
similar positive emphases—e.g., businesses, private schools, clubs.

Social-control agencies also require subjects in order to exist (as we
shall stress in the next chapter). To the extent that a publicity effort
like the "mental health campaign" succeeds, by broadening and
destigmatizing the concept of mental illness, in sensitizing people to
"enlist" themselves voluntarily, we find a rough parallel to the U.S.
Army example. But that expansion of scope falls more properly in our
"proliferation" discussion than under the more specific notion of
recruiting. Beyond that, most social-control agencies are precluded
from advertising directly for clients, both because they are often
governmentally associated and because so many of their subjects are
there only involuntarily; one just does not say "commit a crime,"
"develop a mental illness," or "become destitute," so that "we may
be of service to you."

Still, recruiting tactics exist and are in prevalent use. In general,
two broad recruitment processes may be noted. The agency may
engage in indirect recruitment (which *may* include straightforward
advertising techniques, in the case of private facilities), targeting not
upon the eventual client himself but upon referral sources. Or, the
agency may have to do nothing more than sit back and let others do
the recruiting for it. The latter approach has a special appeal, since
it eliminates charges of vested interest, allows the agency to concentrate its resources and attention upon internal matters, and fosters
the premises of the normative approach with which so many of us
seem to be most comfortable. A number of factors affecting recruitment of either type must now be discussed.

Control Over
Definitions of Deviance

Perhaps the most efficient means of recruiting subjects is to maintain
direct control over the definitions of deviance that eventually channel people into agency settings.[6] In comparing criminal and psychiatric deviance, psychiatric agents maintain a marked advantage here.
For example, even though a particular policeman may be violently
opposed to the act of abortion, there is nothing he can legitimately
do to a qualified practitioner as long as the law approves abortion.
The policeman is dependent upon statements of law established by
others for guidelines as to what he can treat as deviance. The psychia-

trist, on the other hand, is directly dependent upon no one for his determination of what constitutes a case of mental illness. If he says it is, at least within his sphere, it *is*. If he says it is not, at least within his sphere, it *is not*. True, policeman and psychiatrist are alike in that both may *dis*regard behavior that *does* qualify as deviance. But this is a matter of discretion, not of definition. Only the psychiatrist has relatively free reign to do the opposite—i.e., to treat behavior as deviance that does *not* objectively qualify as such.[7]

The criminal-psychiatric contrast can be illustrated in another way as follows. Most of us, technically speaking, owe the society up to several years of imprisonment on the basis of undetected or unenforced violation of laws that prohibit littering, jaywalking, spitting on the sidewalk, loitering, a long list of traffic offenses, etc. None of us will ever serve those sentences, despite our guilt, and there is probably not a law enforcement officer in the country who would argue that we *should* serve them. Meanwhile, a study known as the Midtown Manhattan study concluded that some 23.4 percent of its sample belonged in a mental health category it termed "Impaired," while 18.5 percent were clearly and totally "Well." This left 58.1 percent with either "Mild Symptom Formation" or "Moderate Symptom Formation" (Srole, *et al.*, 1968:75).

Without further elaboration, it is to be observed that psychiatrists are more effectively able to argue that 23 percent of the population require treatment for *assumed* misbehavior than are police able to argue that 99 percent of the population require incarceration for *acknowledged* misbehavior. If the reader requires any "proof," one has simply to note the lack of public outcry against the psychiatric claim and then to imagine the protests if all of us were instructed to pack up our bags and head for the nearest detention center.

In addition, however, the Midtown Manhattan statistics have been grossly misused, and *still* without public complaint. In one author's personal experience, several respected psychiatrists in one major metropolitan center have publicly misquoted the study as finding that 80 percent (sic) of the American public are mentally ill and require psychiatric care. In fact, although only 18.5 percent were typed as "Well," the appropriate emphasis is upon a 23 percent "help-needing" segment, not 80 percent—i.e., 77 percent. Furthermore, the statistics (1) apply to only the 20–59 age range, (2) are based upon the most highly urbanized sector of the most highly urbanized city in the country, and (3) are derived from a set of assumptions and categorization criteria developed by a particular research team.

This sort of control over definitions of deviance is implicit in the movement toward a "therapeutic state" and, more specifically, in the "mental health campaign." The key question is, what makes it possible? How is it that psychiatry is able to assume such control? One answer, with more substance to it than there might seem, is simply that very few have registered any complaints. With silence easily interpreted as tacit endorsement (a psychiatric variation of the "silent majority" on the political scene), definitional control and expansion continues. But *why* have so few registered complaint? At least three explanations suggest themselves: (1) the ambiguity of psychiatric terminology, (2) the unique character of medical authority, and (3) a version of the "It Can't Happen Here" phenomenon.

"Mental illness" differs from all other illness in that it refers not to organic malfunctioning but to *behavior*.[8] When a physician diagnoses an organic ailment, he tries to base his decision upon objective characteristics that indicate departure from a state of bodily health —e.g., fever, elevated blood pressure, lesions, growths, abnormal cell count. Similarly, when a psychiatrist (or lesser psychiatric agent) diagnoses a psychiatric ailment, he purports to indicate a departure from a state of mental health. But his decision has an inherent *subjective* base because of its linkage to behavior rather than to physiological malfunctioning. Thus, the psychiatric decision constitutes a more obvious value judgment (Davis, 1938; Szasz, 1970a:25–48).

Public conceptions of what is illness and what is not show wide variation in both the physical and the mental illness contexts (Koos, 1954; Hollingshead and Redlich, 1958; Star, 1955). As David Mechanic puts it,

> social values play an essential part in medical determinations and in the provision of medical care. Much of medical practice involves attempts at helping people to conform more adequately to social rather than physical standards. (Mechanic, 1968:20)

But it is of special importance to the creation of deviance that the chance of "expert" disagreement on the diagnosis befitting a given set of conditions *jumps markedly* in the shift from organic to mental disorders. This disagreement exists in "mental illness" decisions precisely because the "normality" or "acceptability" of all behavior is open to interpretation (see Mechanic, 1968:100–107 for review of reliability studies of psychiatric diagnosis). A psychiatrist, having judged that a set of presenting characteristics constitutes socially unacceptable behavior in his opinion, is then able to "biography build" as a means of determining level of severity. He may then choose from a broad set of abstractly defined labels the one that he prefers (e.g., schizophrenic reaction, acute undifferentiated type). A

second psychiatrist may decide upon equivalent severity but a different label (e.g., schizophrenic reaction, paranoid type), a third on
differing severity *and* label (e.g., depressive reaction), a fourth on
normality, etc.[9] Thus, labels are attached with a facility that is unavailable to the decision maker who looks to hard criteria and hard
evidence that would permit only a narrow range of available options.

Most mental illness diagnostic categories are encumbered with
such vague, subjective, and broad placement criteria that diagnostic
"errors" are rendered a near impossibility. In general, what is diagnosed as condition X comes to be regarded as condition X, whether
or not ample objective evidence supports the diagnosis. Few challenge the decision for the same self-evident reasons that few challenge a move in any other game without rules. There *are* no rules
of evidence comparable to those found in a court of law. Since this
condition largely accounts for the lack of challenge from *within* the
profession, it is understandable that no challenge intrudes from without; the layman is unattuned to the subtleties of diagnostic process
and regards it as simply another element of the mysterious aura of
modern medicine.

One of the most recent empirical demonstrations of psychiatric
control over definitions of deviance via ambiguity (and one of the
most vivid ever reported) comes from a study carried out by D. L.
Rosenhan (1973). Stanford professor Rosenhan and a varied group of
seven colleagues posed as "pseudo-patients" seeking admission to
twelve separate psychiatric hospitals which varied in approach, region, funding, etc. In admission interviews, each pseudopatient presented himself honestly and without contrivance—with one
exception: he reported that he had been hearing voices. *Immediately*
upon admission, the simulation of this symptom was ended and the
individual proceeded to work toward the earliest possible discharge
by convincing the staff of his sanity. The results of this fabrication
were startling, to say the least. (1) Every pseudopatient was admitted,
(2) all but one were diagnosed as schizophrenic, (3) the length of
hospitalization averaged nineteen days and ranged from seven to
fifty-two days, and (4) all were described at discharge as evidencing
schizophrenia "in remission." Rosenhan says, "As far as I can determine, diagnoses were in no way affected by the relative health of the
circumstances of a pseudopatient's life. Rather, the reverse occurred:
the perception of his circumstances was shaped entirely by the diagnosis" (Rosenhan, 1973:253).

The same article reports the results of a related experiment that
further confirms the ambiguity of psychiatric definitions. In this case,
the dubious staff members of yet another psychiatric hospital in

effect challenged Rosenhan to slip a pseudopatient by them without detection. It was agreed that one or more such patients would attempt admission over a specified three-month period. Of 193 patients admitted, "forty-one patients were alleged, with high confidence, to be pseudopatients by at least one member of the staff" (Rosenhan, 1973:252). In reality, *no* pseudopatients had made admission attempts. The importance of this finding is its demonstration "that the tendency to designate sane people as insane can be reversed when the stakes (in this case, prestige and diagnostic acumen) are high" (*Ibid.*).

Braginsky and Braginsky provide additional evidence descriptive of psychiatrists' control over definitions, even though their main theme is quite distinct from our own (Braginsky, Braginsky, and Ring, 1969; Braginsky and Braginsky, 1973). They reject the credibility of the labeling approach along with that of the traditional medical model, arguing instead that many chronic mental patients choose and perpetuate their own hospitalization. The mental hospital is viewed as a "last resort" (with intentional double meaning), the patients having not been able to find any equally contented and secure life style in the outside world. What is of chief interest to us is the contention that much of this is made possible by psychiatry's unstinting willingness to confirm a state of mental illness (particularly schizophrenia) on the basis of questionable evidence, or even no evidence at all. In the authors' words, "the hospital and its formal function are a fiction maintained by the staff and the outside world" (Braginsky and Braginsky, 1973:30).

Turning now to the character of medical authority, it is to be suggested that no other professional commands the unquestioning respect and acceptance that the physician does. Patients may argue with their doctors, but the arguments are usually over billing procedures, scheduling arrangements, and other such incidentals—*not* over diagnosis. Even when the patient does reject a diagnosis, the customary response is not argumentation but simply change of physicians. After all, one's doctor has spent all those tedious years in specialized training to acquire a wealth of understanding of the body and its workings. Other professionals devote comparable time periods to their own specialized training, of course, but the mysteries of the human organism seem to generate some special kind of sanctity that does not apply to other experts. If the lawyer says it's embezzlement, or homicide, or even medical malpractice, a court will determine whether it is or not. If the doctor says it's an ulcer, it *is* an ulcer. If he says it's rheumatoid arthritis, it *is* rheumatoid arthritis. And if he says it's schizophrenia, or obsessive-compulsive neurosis, or involutional melancholia, it must *be*. But whereas the ulcer and the arthritis *are* probably there and can be substantiated by others, the psychiatric syndrome has inherently fewer strict guidelines for consensual identification. In this way, ambiguity and the authority image combine to facilitate psychiatric definitions free from restriction or challenge.

The "It Can't Happen Here" phenomenon is usually applied to those naive citizens of a democratic nation who blithely assume that the danger of totalitarian tactics is an absurd thought when applied to their own open form of government (e.g., Gross, 1974). This feeling is evident in the perspective that "good," "normal" people generally take toward deviance or other social problems. For example, the cigarette smoker continues his habit with the thought that cancer only happens to *other* people. The couple continues to reproduce children on the grounds that overpopulation only need concern those in remote places like India and Latin America. Closer to our context, the law-abiding citizen supports restrictive law-and-order provisions because they could never possibly interfere with *his* freedoms. Similarly, there is no need even to keep oneself informed as to the nature of psychiatric definitions and decision making. It is enough to know that the crazies and loonies and nervous breakdowns are being controlled, since that sort of thing happens to other weirdos. "It can't happen here"—i.e., "to *me.*" The indirect consequence of such an attitude, taken together with the functions of ambiguity and medical authority, is to grant license for continuing control over definitions of deviance and for bureaucratic recruitment of clientele.

An example of how "it could happen here" is the Hutschnecker Plan, a scheme devised by Arnold Hutschnecker, M.D., a specialist in psychotherapy but not a board-certified psychiatrist. His plan, which was submitted to HEW in 1970, called for massive administration of psychological tests to school children between ages of six and eight to detect potential mental disturbances or a propensity for antisocial behavior. Based on test results, children would be helped to adjust in federally supported day care centers, older children would attend after-school clinics to receive constructive counseling, and the more seriously antisocial would be sent to special camps for incorrigible teenagers.

When the Hutschnecker plan was discovered and publicized by the press, the author was reportedly stunned at negative Congressional reaction. "My premise is that we vaccinate children to prevent physical disease, why not provide psychological tests and treatment to prevent the problem of crime?" (*Newsweek*, 1970:76). Indeed

Hutschnecker saw the major problem as one of implementation, *Newsweek* reports:

> The main problem, as Hutschnecker sees it, is devising tests that can be given on a massive scale. A conventional battery of personality tests, including the Rorschach inkblot test, takes several hours and can cost as much as $150, obviously making them impractical for his purpose. Currently, Hutschnecker is studying a simple 'value profile' . . . which, he believes, can accurately detect antisocial tendencies by a child's reactions to a set of eighteen pictures. The test can be given in a few minutes and the results analyzed by a computer. (Newsweek, 1970:76)

Such a program would permit the testing of all school children in two to three months at minimal cost. The fact that this plan was officially under consideration by HEW, even though Secretary Finch in 1970 said it would not be pursued further *for the moment* (Newsweek, 1970:77), suggests "it can happen here." Mass labeling programs such as this one are real possibilities given the general level of acceptance of psychiatric intervention and widespread belief in the accuracy and reliability of psychological testing.

Special Interests and the Recruiting of Deviants

While bureaucratic "definition controllers" account for the greatest share of social-control recruiting tactics, special-interest groups, as well as individuals with special interests in mind, also serve as occasional "recruiters." Three types of special interest will be noted and briefly discussed: political, personal gain, and private agency economic interests.

The Thomas Eagleton affair of the 1972 Presidential campaign did not result in anyone's hospitalization; on the contrary, it centered around a vice-presidential candidate who had successfully *completed* psychiatric treatment some years in the past. Nevertheless, it serves as a case in point of the role played by political vested-interest groups (however unintentionally) in social-control recruitment. Just as Barry Goldwater's election failure in 1964 was partially conditioned by widespread allegations that he was some kind of clinical paranoid lunatic, so George McGovern's defeat was influenced by the public's dismay at his having the poor taste to select a running mate of Eagleton's psychiatric ilk. Those who develop and perpetuate such negative imagery have an obvious special interest to serve: the worse the opposition party candidates can be made to look, the better one's own chances become. In a subtle way, however, the consequences extend beyond the political short run.

It would not seem that those who castigated Goldwater and Eagleton actually sought to have them committed for psychiatric care. Rather, the attempt was solely to create such public doubt that effective functioning in office would become an impossibility. But the *latent* effect of such campaigns is not to sensitize the audience to the weaknesses of the man but to *sensitize it to the psychiatric perspective in general.* The audience becomes increasingly accepting of the premise that psychiatric considerations exist, that they are important, and that they should be applied in evaluating political candidates. Having expanded their awareness in this way, it follows that the outlook will also be applied to lesser candidates, business associates, neighbors, friends, and relatives.

Similar points apply to the criminal context. If a political rival can be shown to be demonstrably criminal in his behavior, one's own position is clearly enhanced. The history of electoral politics is replete with examples wherein an incumbent's reelection chances plummet downward when a hint of graft, other criminal conduct, or plain old lack of ethics is substantiated. The Watergate affair was the most explosive case in point in the early 1970s. Again, those bringing the accusations may often be much more interested in furthering their own careers than in bringing formal charges, but the latent sensitizing effect is still there.[10]

Recruitment based on personal gain takes us to the realm of the stereotypical "railroading" job so often depicted in television dramas and grade B movies. Although the number of fictional portrayals may exceed the number of actual incidents, it is conceivable that a group of relatives may find it expeditious to have rich old Uncle Charlie tucked away through commitment proceedings, or that a husband may free up his social life by committing a wife who refuses to grant a divorce. Vested interest is clear-cut in these examples, and the reader can readily construct additional scenarios. The victim in such cases may often be guiltless, but nevertheless finds himself or herself "recruited" into the control network with the assistance of superficial commitment hearings and overzealous diagnosticians. The criminal may also enter the criminal justice system at the behest of others— e.g., a crime may go undetected if not for an "informer" who "squeals" out of personal socioeconomic motivations or on behalf of another who seeks to curtail the range or intensity of a rival's criminal activity.

Certain private social-control agencies must recruit deviants so that facilities can operate in the black. An example is private psychiatric hospitals which recruit clientele overtly through publicity directed at psychiatrists. The following samples are taken from advertisements appearing in major psychiatry journals in the years 1932, 1938, and 1972; they demonstrate that while some of the content has changed in forty years, substance has not.

> Homelike environment with ideal surroundings in a beautiful hill country provide a restorative influence. (*American Journal of Psychiatry* 89, November, 1932:ii)

> Modern hospital facilities combined with the delightful environment of home for the care of convalescent, rest, nervous, habit (sic) and selected mental patients. The two mansion houses and several cottages situated on the beautiful grounds have the appointments and atmosphere of comfort, culture and refinement. The hydrotherapy department is equipped for giving Scotch Douche, continuous tubs, cabinet baths and colonic irrigations. . . . Rates are from fifty dollars ($50.00) to one hundred dollars ($100.00) a week. . . . Physicians referring patients are invited to retain them in charge. (*AJP* 95, November, 1938:vi)

> Full cooperation with referring physicians. . . . Lower Rates. (*AJP* 95, November, 1938:vi)

> Psychiatric experience has shown that mental cases do much better in hospitals than at home for the reason that, since the patient cannot think for himself and the relatives are usually too distressed to think wisely, the decision lies with the doctor. . . . Mental and nervous diseases cannot and should not be closely associated with general hospital cases. . . . Physicians are invited to write concerning their psychiatric problems. List of hospitals comprising the Association furnished on request. (*AJP* 95, November, 1938:vii)

> Eleven buildings on fifty acres of high woodland, especially designed and built for the care and treatment of nervous cases. . . . Separate cottage for sports, bowling, squash, etc. (*AJP* 95, November, 1938:x)

Work in the out-of-doors is a distinct part of the treatment. The Institution has its own truck farm, dairy and poultry yard. An illustrated booklet will be sent upon request. (*AJP* 95, November, 1938: inside back cover)

Masseuse . . . Miniature Golf . . . Ethical Standards. . . . Rates from $7.50 a day. . . . (*AJP* 95, November, 1938: back cover)

Located 30 miles north of Boston on 130 acres, set among peaceful meadows bordering a quiet lake and wooded hill, Baldpate presents a relaxing atmosphere to the problem-beset patient. . . . Single rooms with and without bath, shared accommodations, and cottages are available. Most major health insurance plans acceptable. (*AJP* 129, July, 1972:15)

Beautiful country estate of 140 acres, pool, gym, farm, shop, modern physical plant. (*American Journal of Orthopsychiatry* 42, January, 1972:189)

A fully carpeted hospital: featuring private and semi-private rooms in colorful decor; adjacent baths, color television and individual phones available; comfortable day rooms. (*American Journal of Psychiatry* 129, July, 1972:31)

Such advertising messages do not (and ethically *could* not) say, "find more people mentally ill and send them to us." But, by promoting their various attractions, facilities, and ideologies in this way, they provide the psychiatrists who read the journals with an awareness of a wide range of formal treatment centers. Awareness, in turn, promotes utilization, just as advertising facilitates adoption of a commercial product whose manufacturers seek to develop "brand name" status for it.

Moral Entrepreneurs

Those guardians of norms who seek to determine the thresholds of impermissibility fall under the heading of "moral entrepreneurs," a terminology initiated by Howard Becker in his widely-cited book, *Outsiders* (1963). Becker distinguishes between two types of moral entrepreneurs: rule *makers* and rule *enforcers*. Up to this point, we have been concerned with documenting the role of rule enforcers in the creation of deviance through various avenues of recruitment. We note in passing that at the bureaucratic level, rule making and rule enforcement or application often come to one and the same. When a police officer makes a decision to arrest,[11] he is in a narrow sense making the rule which he is enforcing (Black, 1971). At a broader level, this fact is reflected in the legal realists' position that law is made by the courts, as well as by the legislature.[12] As we noted above, the distinction in rule making and enforcement is even more blurred in the case of psychiatric diagnoses and treatment. In what is perhaps a historical analog, similar blurring occurred in the witch hunts of an earlier time. It has been shown that the rate of witchcraft was determined almost exclusively by the legal system within which this deviance was handled. (See Currie, 1968, for differences in English and European legal systems which produced much higher rates of witchcraft on the Continent; also, Szasz, 1970b, and Katz, 1972.)

We now turn to the question of rule creation at the broader societal level. What are the processes involved in the formation of civil-legal norms? A complete answer to this question would take us beyond the scope of this book; however, we shall indicate some factors involved in the creation of deviance in its purest form: the origins of rules. Richard Quinney (1969, 1970) has proposed an interest-group theory of law formation. Of concern here are his first two propositions:

1. "Crime is a definition of human conduct that is created by authorized agents in a politically organized society" (1970:15). Consistent with Becker (1963) and Turk (1969), crime is seen as an ascribed status.
2. "Criminal definitions describe behaviors that conflict with the interests of the segments of society that have power to shape public policy" (1970:16).

Those groups in power will seek to solidify their position, and their view of social order by criminalizing those activities (and individuals) defined as a threat to that order. Hence, Quinney asserts that "the greater the conflict in interests between the segments of a society, the greater the probability that the power segments will formulate criminal definitions [directed at the less powerful groups]" (1970:17). (It might be argued that power groups may also utilize other legal controls—e.g., civil law—to enforce their views; Quinney, however, restricts his discussion to criminal law.) He then goes on to state that interest groups and power differentials condition the application[13] of the law, such that powerless groups are more open to application of criminal labels (1970:18–25). Implicit here is the assumption that those in power are less likely to have their behavior criminalized through law formulation, and are unlikely to experience criminal-law applications. The fact that white-collar crimes and crimes against the people are usually ignored, or handled through civil law and administrative boards rather than criminal law is evidence for this assertion (Clinard and Quinney, 1973; Schur, 1969).

The question of rule origins requires, in Quinney's view, a description of the special-interest groups which affect legislation, a focus on a conflict model of law origins rather than a consensus model (see Chambliss and Seidman, 1971; Miller, 1973), and an understanding of the relationship between capitalism and formation (and application) of criminal law. To this end, he recommends the recognition and acceptance of the following assumptions:

1. American society is based on an advanced capitalist economy.
2. The state is organized to serve the interests of the dominant economic class, the capitalist ruling class.
3. Criminal law is an instrument of the state and ruling class to maintain and perpetuate the existing social and economic order.
4. Crime control in capitalist society is accomplished through a variety of institutions and agencies established and administered by a governmental elite, representing ruling class interests, for the purpose of establishing domestic order.
5. The contradictions of advanced capitalism—the disjunction between existence and essence—require that the subordinate classes remain oppressed by whatever means necessary, especially through the coercion and violence of the legal system.
6. Only with the collapse of capitalist society and the creation of a new society, based on socialist principles, will there be a solution to the crime problem. (Quinney, 1974b:24)

The clear implication is that the ruling class controls virtually all the rule-creation, decision-making machinery within society and operates it exclusively in their best interest.[14] Quinney states his case more strongly elsewhere:

> The legal system provides the mechanism for the forceful and violent control of the rest of the population. In the course of battle, the agents of the law

(police, prosecutors, judges, and so on) serve as the
military force for the protection of domestic order.
. . . In other words, the military abroad and law enforcement at home are two sides of the same phenomenon: the preservation of the interests of the
ruling class. (1974a:136, 138)

We wish to examine here his assertion that criminal law flows from
"a governmental elite, representing ruling class interests." What is
the evidence?

First, we note that a large bulk of extant criminal law can be
directly traced to the interests of the ruling class. Chambliss describes how vagrancy laws were produced in the fourteenth century
by the economic demands of a labor shortage—"these statutes were
designed for one express purpose: to force laborers (whether personally free or unfree) to accept employment at a low wage in order to
insure the landowner an adequate supply of labor at a price he could
afford to pay" (1969:54). Laws involving crimes against property
were established by the mercantile and propertied classes (e.g., Hall,
1969). Nelson (1974) argues that the criminal law was used in Puritan
New England prior to the Revolutionary War to preserve morality
and attacks on religion; after the war, control shifted to protection
of property. Erikson (1966) also documents the rule-enforcement
powers of the religious leaders of the Puritan colonies: their role in
preserving the established religious beliefs was manifest in crime
waves which corresponded to threats to the community. On the
question of enforcement, it appears that fear of riots by the "dangerous classes"—the poor and unpropertied—was a major impetus to
the establishment of an organized urban police force (Bordua and
Reiss, 1967:282; Silver, 1967). In sum, there appears to be some
evidence for Quinney's assertions (see Quinney, 1974c, for other
evidence).

There is some evidence, however, that some laws evolved in the
face of relative indifference from the ruling class. Indeed, Quinney's
early work on interest groups implies that any group may gather
enough political power on one particular issue to secure legislation
of interests (1970).[15] Some legal policies do appear to be the result
of work by "moral crusaders"—individuals who seek the passage of
new laws to confirm and enforce their particular moral beliefs. Often
these crusaders sincerely feel that others (and society at large) *will
benefit* by their actions (Becker, 1963:148). These crusaders may be
influential individuals with a vision, such as those women active in
the child-saving movement (Platt, 1969),[16] or they may be representatives of social-control bureaucracies concerned with justifying in-

creased budgetary requests—e.g., the role of FBN personnel in securing legislation on marihuana (Becker, 1963; Dickson, 1968; Reasons, 1974). At other times, there do not seem to be any major interest groups involved. Duster notes that legal controls over narcotics seemed to result because the United States was out of step with other nations:

> The handful of nations represented at the first Shanghai conference [an international conference on narcotics control held in 1909] recognized the need for obtaining agreement and compliance from every nation in the world. The United States found itself in the embarrassing position of being the only major power without any control law covering distribution of medicinal narcotics within its borders. (Duster, 1970:14)

The response was the Harrison Act (1914), a revenue tax act which permitted physicians to use narcotics in the treatment of addicts. The argument that the narcotics legislation of 1914 grew out of ruling class demands is simply not convincing, given the fact that the middle and upper classes were the heaviest users at that time (Duster, 1970).[17] Another example of legislation occurring without ruling class sponsorship is the sexual psychopathy laws which arose from public demands over highly publicized sex crimes. Here, grass-roots pressure, later given direction by psychiatrists, produced a set of laws directed toward a specific behavior (Sutherland, 1950). In short, there is evidence that some criminal legislation resulted from the work of relatively small groups of citizens lacking a broad power base or from moral entrepreneurs concerned with societal moral standards. Perhaps one reason for the success of these groups was the lack of organized opposition. Becker notes that the Marihuana Tax Act of 1937 had only minor opposition from industries using hemp, but no organized group of users was present to oppose the bill (1963: 145).

There are also examples of situations where there seems to be a balance of opposing forces—i.e., interest groups both for and against a law. As an example, let us consider three distinct, contemporary illegality controversies: abortion, marihuana, and job discrimination. As corresponding crusader groups, we might cite the Right to Life Committee, the Drug Enforcement Administration (historically, the Federal Bureau of Narcotics), and the National Association for the Advancement of Colored People (NAACP). Each, on the basis of its strongly held moral principles, seeks to have certain behaviors specified as illegal. The Right to Life Committee holds that life begins at the time of conception, that the taking of any life constitutes murder, and that abortion should therefore be disallowed. The Drug Enforcement Administration contends that marihuana use precipitates a variety of personal and societal hazards and that it should therefore be disallowed. The NAACP proposes that any sort of preferential treatment on the basis of racial identity violates personal freedoms and that discrimination in hiring should therefore be disallowed.[18]

Those many readers who find themselves in agreement with one or two of the above positions but not with all three should immediately perceive that "liberal" versus "conservative" ideologies may have very little directly to do with the growth of social-control networks. There are no consistent "good guys" in that respect. I may support restrictive legislation on humanitarian grounds on one issue while you oppose it, but we may switch stances on the next issue. For, while the above-named groups go about their business, their opposites will be similarly active. The National Organization of Women (NOW) contends (on moral grounds of freedom and humanity) that a woman's body is her own concern and that the abortion laws should have been stricken from the books. The Committee for the Legalization of Marihuana argues that the drug can be used without harm and to one's betterment and that laws prohibiting possession, use, and sales should be eliminated. The John Birch Society and the Ku Klux Klan maintain that civil rights legislation is not only part of a communist conspiracy but a direct violation of a citizen's right to make independent decisions and that antidiscrimination laws are therefore unconstitutional. To the extent that the Right to Life Committee, the Narcotics Bureau, and/or the NAACP succeed in their efforts to establish legal restrictions, they succeed in establishing *new categories of deviance*. Abortionists, pot smokers, and discriminatory employers *become* criminals for the first time at the moment the relevant law goes into effect.

It must be recognized that moral entrepreneurs are expanding in number and influence.[19] Some have been established even though their goals often conflict with the interests of corporate capitalism—e.g., the Environmental Protection Agency, the Food and Drug Administration, Consumer Products Safety. Others seem directly to support the state's view of social order—e.g., Law Enforcement Assistance Administration (Gerth, 1974; Quinney, 1974c). With this expansion, a greater range of behaviors (and individuals) are brought under the auspices of social-control agencies. As these new agencies become concerned with perpetuation, the recruitment and definition-expansion processes delineated above should become apparent.

The new rules and regulations which result guarantee the continuation of the deviance creation process.

By way of summarizing this section, we assert the following: first, understanding the deviance creation process is facilitated by analyses using an interest group conception rather than the terms "ruling class" or "capitalist elites"; we see more benefit, given the evidence cited above, in the early Quinney formulation. Rules arise outside, and at times in spite of, the influence of governmental or corporate elites. Second, an attempt should be made in each case to ascertain the power base of the various entrepreneurial work—e.g., individual-directed, agency-initiated, or a conscious effort by the state to regulate behaviors. Quinney himself recognizes the need for this distinction:

> The day-to-day work of reform has [often] been undertaken by middle class urban reformers, professionals, and special interest groups. *These reformers have not simply been the lackeys of big business.* Most have been sincerely interested in relieving human misery and creating a just existence. (1974c:171. Emphasis added.)[20]

Third, there should be some specification of the objects of the rule and the intended purpose of the policy—to whom is it primarily directed? Is it directed to the "dangerous classes" or to all offenders regardless of status—e.g., early drug legislation? Such a specification of the intended objects of rule making may require an examination of the motives of the rule creators. To what extent do governmental elites conspire to repress citizens in order to insure the continuity and stability of the status quo?[21] Or, are the processes which produce rules at the societal level relatively uncoordinated and haphazard, but nevertheless appear as an organized repression?

A crucial question here is the extent to which actors in society *see the rule creators and enforcers as engaged in an orchestrated attempt at repressive control.* This is a question of human consciousness—i.e., how will the actor designated as deviant see and react to his criminalization through rule creation? What is required is a formulation which would describe the authors'

> degree of consciousness, bound up with men's location in a social structure of production, exchange and domination, which of itself would influence the ways in which men defined as criminal or deviant would attempt to live with their outsider's status. That is, men's reaction to labelling by the powerful would

> not be seen to be simply a cultural problem—a prob-
> lem of reacting to a legal status or a social stigma: it
> would necessarily be seen to be bound up with men's
> degree of consciousness of domination and subordi-
> nation in a wider structure of power relationships
> operating in particular types of economic context.
> (Taylor, *et al.*, 1973:220)

Those who impute a conspiracy theory to the controllers should be more likely to engage in political deviance, or otherwise organize to assert their rights;[22] (this is, of course, a version of the legitimacy of authority question, cf. Turk, 1969.) An adequate theory of deviance must link deviance creation actions on the societal level to the micro level of deviant action and social reaction.[23] Such a linkage would permit an analysis of the role which the state plays in producing the very behaviors legislated against. The state, therefore, creates deviance in two ways: by creating rules, and by providing some motivation for the violation of these rules by certain segments of the population. To form such a link between policies of the state and actions of individuals in their daily round requires studies—now largely absent within labeling formulations—of the power structure, or what Taylor, *et al.*, term the "political economy" question (1973:270; also Gouldner, 1968). However, these macro-level theories are likely to ignore the larger middle ground which lies between the state policies and individual actions (infraction and reaction)— i.e., the deviance production power of the "bureaucratic apparatus of official caretakers" (Gouldner, 1968:107).[24] The role of these low-er-level control agents in the creation of deviance is our next topic.

Notes

1. It is informative to note in the Trapnell case that an earlier jury ended hung at 11-1 in favor of conviction. The one contrary vote came from an experienced psychiatric social worker who argued that *even if Trapnell was faking insanity, the faking itself provided evidence of actual insanity!* (Logical precedent for this argument may be found in Joseph Heller's *Catch 22* (1955). One is also reminded of the Salem, Massachusetts witch hunts whereby the accused was submerged under water, proclaimed innocent of witchcraft if she drowned in the process, and promptly executed if she came up still breathing. Moral: witches have big lungs and actors are all crazy!)
2. The trend can be reversed, given persistent political pressure. The American Psychiatric Association recently removed homosexuality from its lexicon of personality abnormalities after years of debate and pressure from various homophile organizations.
3. Documentation of these influences can be seen in the temperance movement (Gusfield, 1963, 1967), in the establishment of a juvenile court system (Platt, 1969), and in drug legislation and agency expansion (Becker, 1963; Schur, 1965; Duster, 1970). Public sentiment is often shaped and harnessed by extant control agencies to expand the scope of deviance. Thus, the former Federal Bureau of Narcotics used propaganda techniques to win favorable legislation and court decisions (Schur, 1965; Dickson, 1968). The psychiatric profession was instrumental in disseminating conceptions of normality and mental health through the mental hygiene movement (Davis, 1938), and influencing the criminal law on sexual offenses such that "sexual psychopath" laws were virtually written by psychiatrists at the behest of an aroused public (Sutherland, 1950).
4. Normative narrowing refers to the reduction of tolerance limits for certain behavioral patterns. This occurs when previously unregulated activity comes under the purview of some social-control agency or expert. An example would be the normative narrowing which has occurred within the classrooms of those schools where experts on learning disabilities and psychiatric counselors are employed. The categories of hyperactivity, hyperkinetic conditions, and minimal brain dysfunction have established a narrower band of tolerated, acceptable activities. Actions previously ignored have become, often overnight, indicators of these conditions and often lead to the use of drugs to correct behavioral problems. (See Kopkind and Ridgeway, 1971, for a description of this particular phenomenon, and the role of drug company advertisements in shaping parental attitudes about tolerable child behavior.) This trend occurs against a background of greater heterogenity in the pupil population due to district consolidation, bussing, and other factors. Negative parental reactions in some areas indicate that such normative narrowing may not always have community support.
5. One of the continuing curiosities of our time is the extent to which those who cry out against rising crime rates and for more "law and order" fail to recognize that the creation of more laws in itself is directly responsible for having more crime! The simplest way to cut a city's crime rate drastically overnight is to invalidate

the morality laws that affect its citizens. In 1967, the President's Crime Commission concluded that "almost half of all arrests are on charges of drunkenness, disorderly conduct, vagrancy, gambling and minor sexual deviations" (Morris and Hawkins, 1970:4). Also, since size of police departments affects rates of officially recorded crimes, it is ironic that "law and order" fanatics insist upon greater numbers of more efficient police and then express shock when they see that the crime rate jumps to even higher levels as the result of more efficient reporting, detection, and apprehension!

6. We propose that control agencies can expand their influence by (a) developing very general definitions of deviance so that greater numbers of people are included, (b) bringing new forms of rule breaking under their umbrella of control (Freidson, 1966), and (c) getting access to a larger pool of individuals for testing or other deviance-detection procedures (Lofland, 1969).

7. Police at an individual level may, of course, "get" those who are not legally reachable. Police brutality may be legitimated by tactics such as planting a gun on the suspect—a practice which has apparently been informally instituted in some urban police departments (Stark, 1972). Frame-ups, tip-offs to underworld connections, and off-duty vigilante work are also within an individual officer's purview to help assure that justice is done. The police differ from the psychiatrist in that their high-handedness is illegal and they can be, if caught, legally sanctioned in either a criminal or civil proceeding (see Akers and Hawkins, 1975).

8. The very few psychiatric categories that pinpoint brain damage or biologically based mental retardation provide the only exception to this distinction.

9. "Schizophrenia" is a psychiatric favorite, to the point that it ranks as the "most prevalent" of all mental disorders. But, as seen by a student observer of one state mental hospital, "It is no wonder that schizophrenia is statistically the most prevalent mental disorder—if you have a big enough garbage can, you can stuff all kinds of things into it. Everyone that comes through the Admissions Ward is diagnosed as one of two things—either schizophrenic or sociopath" (Personal communication to GHT, September 29, 1972). The process of constructing a person's biography to fit the diagnostic classification is detailed in Chapter VII.

10. A number of attempts were made by numerous politicians to show that electronic eavesdropping was standard practice before Watergate. Thus, George Bush, Chairperson of the National Republican Committee, charged an investigator on Senator Ervin's Select Committee with bugging Nixon for the Democrats during the 1960 campaign. Some felt this a deliberate attempt to build a case in the media that "everyone does it," to move bugging from the unique to the typical, so that some of the heat could be removed.

11. This is not to say the police have a free hand in making the rules. They are bounded from above by department directives on discretion, requirements of evidence, and due process rules, and from below by the parameters of the enforcement situation: "What happens in an encounter may have less to do with crime and law than with the demands of the situational order, with social etiquette or pressures of group size or spacial configuration" (Black, 1971:1110). For discussion of these types of controls on the police officer in the field, see Akers and Hawkins, 1975: Part III.

12. Legal realism asserts that "judges make law rather than find it. ... The real decision [in the courts] is made first—on the basis of the judge's conceptions of justness, determined partly by his predilections, personal background and so forth —and then it is 'rationalized' in the written opinion" (Schur 1968:43). The parallel to our earlier discussion of competent rule use, and its retrospective nature, is obvious here.

13. Austin Turk's conflict theory of criminalization focuses on application questions; he tries to specify conditions under which controllers successfully criminalize "norm resisters" and where such attempts will lead to conflict. He ignores the

question of rule origins: "How authorities come to be authorities is irrelevant" (Turk, 1969:51). Quinney, on the other hand, is concerned in his most recent writings (1974c) with who comes to be in a position of authority and how they use the criminal law to stay there. For a criticism of both these conflict theories, see Taylor, *et al.*, 1973.

14. Quinney is representing one thrust of the conflict approach to the study of deviance—i.e., the role of conflict in the creation and application of rules designed to suppress the powerless groups in society. One implication following from this approach is that all crime is political crime. (See our critique of this assertion in Chapter XI.) A second thrust regards the etiology question: capitalism generates crime and other deviance. In this view, most civil-legal rule violations (and some polite-interactional and background expectancy violations usually classified as mental illness) are seen as an inevitable product of the exploitation, inequity, and injustice of the capitalistic system. This seems to be an underlying theme in the critique by Taylor, *et al.*, of extant criminological theory (1973, especially chapters 7–9; also Schur, 1969).

15. Quinney's radicalization is evident when comparing his *Social Reality of Crime* (1970) to his most recent *Critique of Legal Order* (1974). In the latter, he substitutes the term "ruling class" or "governmental elites" for the less specific and more neutral term "interest group" used in the former book. As an example of the shift in view, the index of the first book indicates that only two pages were devoted to "capitalism" and the term "ruling class" did not appear. For an autobiographical account of his metamorphosis, see his paper, "There's a lot of folks grateful to the Lone Ranger: with some notes on the rise and fall of American criminology" (1973).

16. The impetus for the child-saving movement came largely from middle- and upper-class women. Platt says the "movement attracted women from a variety of political and class backgrounds, though it was dominated by the daughters of the old landed gentry and wives of upper class nouveau riche" (1974:370). However, Platt, an advocate of the new radical criminology, seems to have reinterpreted his data in light of this perspective. He newly asserts that since these women were married to the corporate elite of society, they "were instrumental in devising new forms of social control *to protect their privileged position* in American society. The child-saving movement was not an isolated phenomenon but rather reflected massive changes in productive relationships, from laissez-faire to monopoly capitalism, and in strategies of social control from inefficient representation to welfare state benevolence" (*Ibid.*, p. 369. Emphasis added). While the latter sentence may be true, to assume that these women were consciously acting on behalf of a corporate elite seems to be imputing motives more consistent with radical criminology's demand for "demystification" than with the reality of the situation. In other words, we find in Platt (1974) and Quinney (1974c) the nucleus of a conspiracy theory of rule creation, yet the evidence is incomplete.

17. The first attempt to legislate narcotics use (specifically opium smoking) in the United States occurred in San Francisco in 1875, and was seen as "an attempt to control the Chinese immigrants, to make them conform to the 'American Way of Life' " (Parks, 1974:280). Evidence of concern for the "dangerous classes" is not apparent, however, in events leading to the first federal legislation of 1914. (Indeed, Quinney seems to recognize that the Harrison Act cannot be accounted for within his theory; see his roundabout "explanation" in 1974b:97.)

18. We note in passing that moral entrepreneurs may use the law as a means of changing public attitudes about certain behaviors or groups of individuals. Civil rights laws and open housing legislation are examples of legal attempts to force integration on the assumption that close contact will eventually reduce prejudicial attitudes (see Morroe Berger, *Equality by Statute*, 1967). The effect of legal changes on public attitudes has been investigated experimentally by Berkowitz and Walker (1967).

19. Universities become important in deviance creation since they often provide support to various moral enterprises through applied research, training of technicians and control agency personnel, and by lending an air of scientific respectability, and hence justification, for many societal control programs (Gouldner, 1968; Platt, 1974; Quinney, 1974c). This is the reason Quinney charges that criminology and sociology, as well as academia in general, serve to support and legitimate the existing social order.

20. Quinney goes on to say, rightly so, that "most reforms have accepted (and continue to accept) the structure of the capitalistic system, seeking to moderate some of its inequities and inconsistencies. What reformers fail to do is question the basic assumptions of the existing system" (1974c:171). This is one reason Richard Quinney recommends a radical challenge to the present ideology.

21. Conspiracy theory of rule creation and enforcement was given credence in the actions of the Nixon Administration to control and suppress both real and imagined enemies; the conspiracy—evident in the White House tapes—produced Watergate and its cover-up, the Ellsberg break-in (justified on grounds of national defense), creation of an enemies list, use of the IRS and other governmental agencies to manipulate and control political opponents, as well as other repressive actions. For a discussion of the problems of documenting repression, see Clements, 1974.

22. See our discussion of political deviance and the politicalization of deviants in Chapter XI.

23. The demands are great; what is required is (a) an integration of structural, societal factors with the interactional level of action-reaction, (b) a simultaneous focus on the rule breakers and the rule creators-enforcers (Becker, 1963:163), and (c) all of this situated in an historical context of a particular kind of deviant behavior. Paul Walton succinctly summarizes what would be entailed: " 'the specificity historically of that kind of behavior, the reasons for that kind of behavior, the motives of the individuals engaged in that behavior, the motives of those that bring the force of the law to bear on that behavior, and so on . . . but all situated historically, yet hanging together as a total process. It's a very heavy job. Very few pieces of research can be judged successful in these terms' " (Mintz, 1974:40).

24. Austin Turk sees this as a significant area of criminalization; "the more important proposition appears to be that criminalization of [norm] resisters will be more probable, the more offensive the prohibited attribute or act is to the first-level enforcers" (1969:65).

References

Akers, Ronald L., and Richard Hawkins
1975   *Law and Control in Society.* Englewood Cliffs, New Jersey: Prentice-Hall.

Becker, Howard
1963   *Outsiders: Studies in the Sociology of Deviance.* New York: Free Press.

Berger, Morroe
1967   *Equality by Statute.* New York: Doubleday.

Berkowitz, Leonard, and Nigel Walker
1967   "Laws and moral judgments." *Sociometry* 30 (December):410–22.

Black, Donald J.
1971   "The social organization of arrest." *Stanford Law Review* 23 (June):1087–1111.

Bordua, David J., and Albert J. Reiss, Jr.
1967   "Law enforcement." In P. Lazarsfeld, *et al.* (eds.), *The Uses of Sociology.* New York: Basic Books.

Braginsky, Benjamin M., and Dorothea D. Braginsky
1973   "Mental hospitals as resorts." *Psychology Today* 6 (March):22–34, 100.

Braginsky, Benjamin M., Dorothea D. Braginsky, and Kenneth Ring
1969   *Methods of Madness: The Mental Hospital as a Last Resort.* New York: Holt, Rinehart and Winston.

Chambliss, William J.
1969   "The law of vagrancy." In W. Chambliss (ed.), *Crime in the Legal Process.* New York: McGraw-Hill.

Chambliss, William J., and Robert Seidman
1971   *Law, Order, and Power.* Reading, Mass.: Addison-Wesley.

Clements, Joyce M.
1974   "Repression: beyond the rhetoric." In C. Reasons (ed.), *The Criminologist: Crime and the Criminal.* Pacific Palisades, Calif.: Goodyear Publishing.

Clinard, Marshall, and Richard Quinney
1973   *Criminal Behavior Systems.* (2nd ed.). New York: Holt, Rinehart and Winston.

Currie, Elliott P.
    1968   "Crimes without criminals: witchcraft and its control in
            Renaissance Europe." *Law and Society Review* 3 (August):7–
            32.
Davis, Kingsley
    1938   "Mental hygiene and the class structure." *Psychiatry* 1 (Feb-
            ruary):55–65.
Dickson, Donald T.
    1968   "Bureaucracy and morality: an organizational perspective on
            a moral crusade." *Social Problems* 16 (Fall):143–56.
Dinitz, Simon, and Nancy Beran
    1971   "Community mental health as a boundaryless and boundary-
            busting system." *Journal of Health and Social Behavior* 12
            (June):99–108.
Duster, Troy
    1970   *The Legislation of Morality.* New York: Free Press.
Erickson, Kai T.
    1966   *Wayward Puritans.* New York: John Wiley and Sons.
Freidson, Eliot
    1966   "Disability as social deviance." In Marvin B. Sussman (ed.),
            Sociology and Rehabilitation. Washington, D.C.: American
            Sociological Association.
Gerth, Jeff
    1974   "The Americanization of 1984." In R. Quinney (ed.), *Criminal
            Justice in America.* Boston: Little, Brown.
Gouldner, Alvin W.
    1968   "The sociologist as partisan: sociology and the welfare state."
            American Sociologist 3 (May):103–116.
Gross, Bertram
    1974   "Friendly fascism, a model for America." In R. Quinney (ed.),
            Criminal Justice in America. Boston: Little, Brown.
Gusfield, Joseph R.
    1963   *Symbolic Crusade.* Urbana: University of Illinois Press.
    1967   "Moral passage: the symbolic process in public designations of
            deviance." *Social Problems* 15 (Fall):175–88.
Hall, Jerome
    1969   "Theft, law and society: the Carrier's Case." In W. Chambliss
            (ed.), *Crime and the Legal Process.* New York: McGraw-
            Hill.
Heller, Joseph
    1955   *Catch 22.* New York: Simon and Schuster.
Hollingshead, August B., and Fredrick C. Redlich
    1958   *Social Class and Mental Illness.* New York: John Wiley and
            Sons.

Katz, Jack
1972   "Deviance, charisma, and rule-defined behavior." *Social Problems* 20 (Fall):186–202.

Kittrie, Nicholas N.
1971   *The Right to be Different: Deviance and Enforced Therapy.* Baltimore: Johns Hopkins.

Koos, Earl L.
1954   *The Health of Regionville.* New York: Columbia University Press.

Kopkind, Andrew, and James Ridgeway
1971   "The mental health industry: this way lies madness." *Ramparts* 9 (February):39–44.

Lofland, John
1969   *Deviance and Identity.* Englewood Cliffs, New Jersey: Prentice-Hall.

Mechanic, David
1968   *Medical Sociology: A Selective View.* New York: Free Press.

Miller, Walter B.
1973   "Ideology and criminal justice policy: some current issues." *The Journal of Criminal Law and Criminology* 64 (June):141–62.

Mintz, Robert
1974   "Interview with Ian Taylor, Paul Walton and Jock Young." *Issues in Criminology* 9 (Spring):33–53.

Morris, Norval, and Gordon Hawkins
1970   *The Honest Politician's Guide to Crime Control.* Chicago: University of Chicago Press.

Murphy, Jeffrie G.
1969   "Criminal punishment and psychiatric fallacies." *Law and Society Review* 4 (August):111–22.

Nelson, William E.
1974   "Emerging notions of modern criminal law in the Revolutionary Era: an historical perspective." Pp. 100–126 in R. Quinney (ed.), *Criminal Justice in America.* Boston: Little, Brown.

Parks, Evelyn L.
1974   "From constabulary to police society: implications for social control." In C. Reasons (ed.), *The Criminologist: Crime and the Criminal.* Pacific Palisades, Calif.: Goodyear Publishing.

Platt, Anthony M.
1969   *The Child Savers: The Invention of Delinquency.* Chicago: University of Chicago Press.

1974   "The triumph of benevolence: the origins of the juvenile justice system in the United States." In R. Quinney (ed.), *Criminal Justice in America.* Boston: Little, Brown.

Quinney, Richard
   1969   *Crime and Justice in Society.* Boston: Little, Brown.
   1970   *The Social Reality of Crime.* Boston: Little, Brown.
   1973   "There's a lot of folks grateful to the Lone Ranger: with some notes on the rise and fall of American criminology." *The Insurgent Sociologist* 4 (Fall):56–64.
   1974a   "Crime control in capitalist society." In C. Reasons (ed.), *The Criminologist: Crime and the Criminal.* Pacific Palisades, Calif.: Goodyear Publishing.
   1974b   *Criminal Justice in America.* Boston: Little, Brown.
   1974c   *Critique of Legal Order.* Boston: Little, Brown.

Reasons, Charles E.
   1974   "The 'dope' on the Bureau of Narcotics in maintaining the criminal approach to the drug problem." In C. Reasons (ed.), *The Criminologist: Crime and the Criminal.* Pacific Palisades, Calif.: Goodyear Publishing.

Rosenhan, D. L.
   1973   "On being sane in insane places." *Science* 179 (January 19): 250–58.

Schur, Edwin M.
   1965   *Crimes Without Victims.* Englewood Cliffs, N.J.: Prentice-Hall.
   1968   *Law and Society.* New York: Random House.
   1969   *Our Criminal Society.* Englewood Cliffs, N.J.: Prentice-Hall.

Silver, Allan
   1967   "The demand for order in civil society: a review of some themes in the history of urban crime, police and riots." In D. Bordua (ed.), *The Police: Six Sociological Essays.* New York: John Wiley and Sons.

Srole, Leo, Thomas S. Langer, Stanley T. Michael, Marvin K. Opler, and Thomas A. D. Rennie
   1968   *Mental Health in the Metropolis.* New York: McGraw-Hill, 1962. Pp. 68–123 excerpted in Harry Silverstein (ed.), *The Social Control of Mental Illness.* New York: Thomas Y. Crowell.

Star, Shirley A.
   1955   *The Public's Ideas About Mental Illness.* University of Chicago: National Opinion Research Center, mimeographed.

Stark, Rodney
   1972   *Police Riots.* Belmont, Calif.: Focus Books.

Sutherland, Edwin H.
   1950   "The diffusion of sexual psychopath laws." *American Journal of Sociology* 56 (September):142–48.

Szasz, Thomas S.
1970a   *Ideology and Insanity.* New York: Anchor Books.
1970b   *The Manufacture of Madness.* New York: Harper and Row.
Taylor, Ian, Paul Walton, and Jock Young
1973   *The New Criminology: For a Social Theory of Deviance.* London: Routledge and Kegan Paul.
Turk, Austin T.
1969   *Criminality and Legal Order.* Chicago: Rand McNally.

————

1970   "Dr. Hutschnecker's plan." *Newsweek* (April 20):76–77.

————

1973   "Return of Dr. Jekyll." *Time Magazine* (January 29):20.

Chapter

VII

The Creation of Deviants by Social-Control Agencies

For a successful bureaucratic adaptation, professionals need to develop a primary commitment to the larger aims or general rationale of the organization they serve. . . . And he may not feel that he is a captive of the organization as he goes about his work.

Arlene K. Daniels

Introduction:
A Case Example

Among the routinely scheduled group sessions common to many social-control agencies is a meeting variously known as the Diagnostic Conference, Screening Conference, or Intake Conference. Consistent with the theme of this book, the session might more appropriately be termed the Labeling Conference. It is here that assorted agency workers gather soon after the admission of a new client for purposes of reviewing selected client characteristics and arriving at some decision as to the nature of the stigma and the appropriate course of treatment.

Picture such a Diagnostic Conference. The setting is the inpatient service of the psychiatric facility attached to a university teaching hospital. Those in attendance include a senior staff psychiatrist, a psychiatric resident physician, two interns, a staff psychologist, a social worker, an occupational therapist, and several staff psychiatric nurses. The "new patient" in question is a twenty-year-old male first admission who has been suffering "severe bouts of anxiety and depression." He is a voluntary admission, having checked into the facility at the request of his concerned parents.

As the admitting intern concludes his presentation of the above basic details and summarizes the quite normal physiological state of

Source: Arlene K. Daniels, "The captive professional: bureaucratic limitations in the practice of military psychiatry." *Journal of Health and Social Behavior* 10 (December, 1969), p. 264.

179

the patient, a call is sent out and the patient is ushered into the room for a crucial face-to-face encounter with the staff experts-in-residence. According to participation guidelines consistent with medical staff hierarchy, the senior staff psychiatrist takes the lead in conducting the interview. Ostensibly to "break the ice," the patient is asked to tell something about himself and the difficulties he is experiencing. He responds freely, but with obvious embarrassment, emphasizing depression and lack of motivation to accomplish anything. He has no trouble fielding standard items designed to isolate the presence of potential "organic brain damage"—e.g., "who is the governor of the state?" or "start with 100 and count backwards by sevens." Moving next to the area of functional mental illness categories, the psychiatrist offers two "proverb tests": gross misinterpretation of standardized American homilies may be taken as a cue for the existence of one or another form of severe mental illness.

[*Psychiatrist*]:   "What does it mean when someone says, 'Don't cry over spilled milk'?"

[*Patient*]:   "It means that if something bad has already happened, you can't do anything about it, so you might as well not worry about it and get on with other things. You shouldn't let failures of the past ruin your future life."

[*Psychiatrist*]:   "OK. Now, what about this one? 'The golden key opens the gate of iron.'"

[*Long pause*].

[*Patient*]:   "Gee, I've never heard that one before."

[*Further pause. Total silence in the room.*]

[*Patient*]:   "I suppose it could mean that if you face a difficult prob- ˉ lem, you shouldn't give up right away. If you think about it and approach it the right way you can come up with a good solution to help you overcome it, just like a golden key can fit into the lock on a heavy iron gate and open it." (He demonstrates.)

Other staff members ask a few more questions, and the patient is dismissed from the room. It is now time to fit the pieces together and establish at least a tentative diagnostic label. The floor is open to suggestions and interpretations, but responses are slow in coming. When they do come, the early consensus is that the patient seems to be in good control, that he responded well, that minor problems of depression forecast a short hospital stay, and that perhaps this individual needn't take up any inpatient space at all. The senior psychiatrist then announces that, "We do in fact have a psychiatric casualty here, a difficult case for treatment, an individual exhibiting characteristics of possibly overt but probably latent homosexuality." On what grounds? The senior psychiatrist replies, "Did you notice his gestures when I gave him the golden key parable? He made a loop of the thumb and forefinger on one hand and inserted the forefinger of the other hand into the circle." *He* demonstrates. "A standard clue to homosexual tendencies." The resident and one intern nod their heads in understanding and agreement. The others in the room remain silent, some with mouths agape, until the social worker attempts a challenge by announcing that she has never heard of the "golden key parable" and that the patient seemed to her to have provided a cogent and sensible interpretation. She, and her potential but cautious supporters, look to the psychiatrist for his rebuttal, which consists of the proclamation that the Golden Key Proverb is a standard and accepted psychiatric device for detecting homosexual tendencies and that the social worker may be excused for not knowing such specialized information. In an attempt to strengthen his case, the psychiatrist calls upon the staff psychologist for confirmation by way of the results of the MMPI (Minnesota Multiphasic Personality Inventory) administered to the patient as part of intake procedure. The psychologist replies that certain "area profiles" are indeed consistent with a finding of homosexuality. The case is differentially diagnosed as one of "Severe Depression Marked by Homosexuality," the discussion is closed, and the next case is introduced.

The patient is at this point marked as a homosexual (at least officially) and will be treated as such for the duration of this hospitalization episode (at least officially). Unconvinced session participants may choose to disregard what they consider to be an inappropriate diagnosis when and if they can manage to do so. But other staff members may be party to only the official word or rumors thereof and will act accordingly, as may fellow patients and family members. And, upon subsequent admission to this or some other psychiatric facility, the patient's past records will declare in black and white that he was once diagnosed and treated as a depressed homosexual, thus simplifying the labeling procedure for a new set of diagnosticians. A deviant career is born.

The incident reported above is not a contrived fictional account. It is a summary of an actual Diagnostic Conference attended by one of the co-authors. It is, of course, intentionally selected because it assists in making several points. While it is certainly to be hoped that it is an extreme example, it is not the most extreme example possible, nor is it atypical of events that transpire daily in social processing agencies. Organizations, via the agents that work within them and the visible and invisible structures that enhance organizational efficiency, actively create images of deviants and of deviance. Clients who might have remained untroubled, unlabeled, and unstigmatized without contact with a given organization "become" homosexuals, or schizophrenics, or incorrigibles, or addicts, or problem learners as a result of passage through an organizational processing cycle.[1] A complete labeling formulation must explicitly consider the process and impact of category application in order to understand the dynamics of deviancy creation within social-control agencies. In this chapter, we begin such a task by examining the role of "processing stereotypes" in case disposition.

The basic assumption underlying the notion of processing stereotypes is that people utilize *categories* to shape the perceptions and interpretations of their environment and to select actions within that environment (see Chapter IV). Order enhances manageability: to the extent that we are able to observe, interpret, and understand any event or behavior, we are then prepared to categorize and label it so as to proceed more comfortably and efficiently (Klapp, 1962). Without labeling there could be no symbolic communication and no social systems.

The normative perspective accurately suggests that the label and definitions we apply have a grounding in sets of norms that prescribe role expectations for given role sets. (You and I can talk together about "crime" and "illness" without further elaboration because we share some kind of normative distinction between "crime" and "non-crime" and between "illness" and "health.") But the normative perspective, quite unnecessarily and unfortunately, suffers credibility losses when it essentially ignores standard subcultural and adult socialization notions and insists upon *universal* role prescriptions with shared meanings *across* population groups. By so doing, it does not take into account that you and I may demonstrate vastly different *background expectancies* that make for vast differences in our detailed specification of what constitutes crime and illness and why we think so. (A barroom knifefight might seem "sane" and "lawful" behavior to me; is it to you? Cheating on an exam might seem "sane" and "lawful" to the student; is it to the instructor?) Finally, the normative perspective disregards the effects that direct interaction with another individual (or knowledge of potentially extraneous characteristics about him) may have on our typing and accounting of his behavior.

The processing stereotype contention does *not* imply:

a. That all processing agents are authoritarian mandarins who receive ego-gratification by way of arbitrarily imposing their standards and powers upon masses of the unintelligensia,

b. That there are no legitimate normative standards of deviant behavior,
c. That there is no such thing as crime or illness, or
d. That all deviants are innocents who happen to have been subjected to the whims of "enforcers" and "labelers" who create them.

We *do*, however, propose:

a. That control agencies will differ in the categorical system such that a wide variety of potential fates awaits any given individual exhibiting any given set of "symptoms" (e.g., different forms of psychiatric therapies),
b. That organizational prerequisites fix and perpetuate a preexisting tendency on the part of particularistically trained agents to categorize clients, and
c. That an inevitable result is a social system wherein many of those who come to be typed as "deviant" are *created* as such through their encounters with social processing agencies.

Processing stereotypes are generated and used as a response to the demand of a bureaucratic organization on its personnel to perform efficiently, to process a large volume of cases, to reduce uncertainty and ambiguity, and to promote a smooth flow of individuals through the system. They are, therefore, to be seen as part of the informal system which supplements (and often circumvents) the norms of the formal system. For example, Arthur Niederhoffer (1967:55–94) noted that the professional ideal of police work soon gives way to the "pragmatic precinct approach" in the experience of new police cadets. Police (as well as physicians, teachers, and other control agents) often face a conflict between pressures to process large numbers of cases on one hand and expectations for carrying out the requirements of "due process" on the other (Skolnick, 1966). The dilemma of providing due process rights in a setting demanding maximization of case disposition is quite evident in our overloaded criminal court system. Blumberg (1969:225) describes how the conflict is resolved:

> A rather tenuous resolution of the dilemma has emerged in the shape of a large variety of bureaucratically ordained and controlled "work crimes," short cuts, deviations, and outright rule violations adopted as court practice in order to meet production norms. Fearfully anticipating criticism on ethical as well as legal grounds, all the significant participants in the court's social structure are bound

into an organized system of complicity. This consists of a work arrangement in which the patterned, covert, informal breaches, and evasions of "due process" are institutionalized, but are, nevertheless, denied to exist.

In these ways, the organization of social-control agencies becomes structured such that efficiency and technical proficiency are rewarded while the rights of those being processed may be simultaneously neglected (Blumberg, 1969; Skolnick, 1967; Szasz, 1961, 1963). To understand the labeling process, and its effect on the accused, we must examine the sources of these processing stereotypes.

Processing Stereotypes

The term "processing stereotype" is suggested as an analytic concept to encompass and subsume several related concepts—e.g., Sudnow's "normal crimes" and Scheff's "diagnostic stereotypes," "normal cases," and "typification" (Sudnow, 1965; Scheff, 1966). Although each of these concepts refers to the kinds of standardized, simplified categorization we have in mind, "processing stereotype" seeks to connote a broadened stress upon the importance of such standardized procedures and responses *for events that follow*—for not only diagnosis but also prognosis and treatment of individuals "passing through" social-control agencies.

Our use of the "stereotype" component of the term differs somewhat from traditional usage. A "stereotype" commonly implies *incorrect, illegitimate* application of categories and labels. Stereotyping is regarded as "bad" because it does not jibe with the objective facts of the matter. Secord and Backman (1964:67) define stereotyping in terms of three characteristics: "the categorization of persons, a consensus on attributed traits, and a discrepancy between attributed traits and actual traits." We treat the third characteristic strictly as a variable; the typing may be accurate or biased, just as it may be under a term such as "typification."

Processing stereotypes, then, are simplified images used by processing agents to categorize and order their environment. They entail the removal of, or inattention to, diverse, unique background characteristics and specific contextual factors of the rule violation; they substitute uniform background expectancies, thereby assuring that "the essential features of socially recognized 'familiar scenes' may be detected" (Garfinkel, 1967:36). These simplified images may have as their referent either (a) the "moral character" of the processee, (b) his alleged behavior, (c) the motive imputed to the processee's behaviors, (d) the background characteristics of the processee, (e) the *modus operandi* of his acts, or some combination of these factors.

Processing stereotypes are important because they make up the major interpretive resources of control agents. They come to supplant, to stand for, what really happened in the case of a rule violation. To learn the shape which deviance will take demands an explication of these categorical typifications. In the organizational creation and shaping of deviance, processing stereotypes become a major constructional tool. As we shall see, they are central to a labeling explanation of deviant behavior.

Contributing
Organizational Characteristics

All formal organizations share a threefold set of requirements, here termed *efficiency, perpetuation,* and *accountability.* In the organizational types that are of special concern here, each of these requirements contributes—both directly and indirectly and both singly and in interaction with others—to the creation of images of deviance by way of processing stereotypes. Each does so in a predominantly unformulated, latent manner rather than manifestly and intentionally. That is, organizations do not seek to be efficient, long-lasting, and accountable so that they can then create images of deviance; but images of deviance nevertheless inevitably follow the pursuit of said goals.[2]

Efficiency

In Western societies, the organization that is regarded as "best" is commonly taken to be the organization that is most efficient. The identification is not always a valid one. The human relations approach precipitated by the Mayo studies, for example, indicates that some elements of what may be seen objectively as "inefficiency" can be of vital importance to the overall effectiveness of an organization (see Madge, 1962: Chapter 6). In a somewhat different vein, there is the "too much of a good thing" phenomenon, technically known in the literature as "overbureaucratization" and also denoted by the phrase "the irrationality of rationality." Despite such bureaucratically based difficulties, efficiency continues to operate as a central feature in the establishment of organizational structures. It has its pragmatic payoff most of the time and is often *believed* to have such benefits even when it does not (exceptions are overlooked or explained away—simply another variation of the social construction of reality).

Most of the standard itemizations found in Weber's classic ideal-type listing of bureaucratic characteristics relate in one way or another to the achievement of efficiency. Two of these characteristics are particularly crucial to the theme of this chapter: (1) hierarchical structure and (2) rules and regulations.

Hierarchy:	"The principles of office hierarchy and of levels of graded authority mean a firmly ordered system of super- and subordination in which there is a supervision of the lower offices by the higher ones." (Weber, 1958:197)
Rules and regulations:	"The management of the office follows general rules, which are more or less *stable,* more or less *exhaustive,* and which *can be learned.* Knowledge of these rules represents a special technical learning which the *officials possess.*" (Weber, 1958:198. Emphasis added.)
In Sum:	"Its [bureaucracy's] specific nature ... *develops the more perfectly* the more the bureaucracy is '*dehumanized,*' the more completely it succeeds in *eliminating* from official business love, hatred, and all purely *personal, irrational* and emotional elements which escape calculation. This is the specific nature of bureaucracy and it is appraised as its *special virtue.*" (Weber, 1958:215–16. Emphasis added.)

The drive for efficiency, then, normally involves a quest for order, control, stability, predictability, objectivity, rationality, and closure. Social-control agencies, which represent one broad bureaucratic sub-type, are not immune to such proclivities (e.g., Jamison, 1969). The primary focus of their attention, however, is people and their behavior rather than hard material goods. Assuming that greater latitude exists for judging and categorizing personal behavior than for judging and categorizing a box of detergent, a social-control agency can best (or only) meet the shared organizational goal of efficiency by submitting to various assumptions, specifications, codifications, and simplifications. These actions are significantly, but not totally, fostered by the hierarchy and standardization components of efficiency-producing bureaucratic characteristics as cited above. The "golden key homosexual" scenario that opened this chapter provides a relevant case in point.

The concept of "rationality" implies accuracy, objectivity, and validity. Organizational structuring designed to increase efficiency may, indeed, increase efficiency in terms of routinization and standardization. But as they gain this element of efficiency, social-control agencies risk a loss in the accuracy, validity, and objectivity components of rationality. In methodological parlance, they move progressively toward a condition of reliability without validity; responses become quite predictable but more prone to error. Although control agencies may be charged with the task of documenting reality, in fact they are less concerned with validity (in terms of the reality of what the processee actually did) than with organizational "validity"—i.e., how accurate category placements are *vis-à-vis* the demands of the bureaucracy.[3] Organizational and professional demands are the focus of their validity checks, rather than what actually happened. For example, Douglas (1971) found that investigators for a coroner's office were not concerned with proving a death was suicide beyond a reasonable doubt, but proceeded to gather data to rule out the alternatives (natural death, accidental death, or homicide) *to the satisfaction of their superiors.* When it was discovered, often by a concerned relative of the deceased, that evidence indicated the categorization of suicide was in error, the agent would stress that he handled the case in the usual manner, and the case seemed to him typical of other cases so classified. David Sudnow (1965) also found that categorizations of cases in a public defender office were more likely to reflect agents' conceptions of typical cases than actual details of the case being processed. This produced high reliability between agents in category placement, but their reactions did not mirror reality. As hierarchies grow and become entrenched and as rules and regulations multiply and intensify, irrationality increases via oversimplification, forced categorization, and labeling. Hence, utilization of processing stereotypes is enhanced by demands for organizational efficiency. Thus, as bureaucracies develop a "special virtue" in terms of organizational efficiency, they often prevent the attainment of another special virtue—avoidance of the creation of deviance.

Perpetuation

Most organizations seek or accept growth in size; some seek stability, while very few seek reduction. Similarly, most seek expansion of scope (although reduction of scope, as a function of specialization, is more commonly sought than reduction in size). But it is a rare organization that seeks complete dissolution. When the chips are down, survival is the number one concern. Apart from the case of manipulated bankruptcy, no organization harbors a death wish, even if it *ostensibly exists for purposes of combatting an "evil"*—e.g., hospitals, prisons, criminal courts. Survival is a prime "need" for organizations just as it is for individuals.[4]

As mentioned in the last chapter, agencies may engage in various recruiting tactics to increase "clientele," as well as definitionally expand conceptions of deviance. A social-control agency can also *enhance its own survival by categorizing clients in a manner that reflects the agency's mandate: to solve problems.* In agencies of control based upon a medical model, a selection rule evolves which seems to be: *when in doubt, treat.* This selection rule seems to grow out of two basic assumptions: first, disease demands treatment, because without it the condition will recur and may be fatal; second, if a person is not ill, the treatment will not produce any lasting harm. For these reasons, it is better to err on the side of treating someone who is well than to dismiss a sick patient without treatment (Scheff, 1966:108–117). However, these two assumptions become questionable when applied to deviance. Nevertheless, the selection rule seems to operate for the mentally "ill," mentally retarded, juvenile delinquents, alcoholics, and homosexuals, to name a few. As noted earlier, these are areas of great ambiguity as to diagnosis, especially in the case of mental "illness," so the proportion of cases which are in doubt may be quite sizable. Altering the selection rule would not be in the interests of agency perpetuation.

Even given the principle of "when in doubt, treat," agencies do find clients who are clearly inappropriate for their particular services. Cases are (occasionally) referred to other agencies or returned to society; however, such actions can also be interpreted as demonstrating usefulness. Here the agency *enhances its survival by demonstrating that it has played some essential part in the control process* —e.g., diagnosis, referral, filtration.

Demonstrated usefulness may also be used as a device for fostering perpetuation in quite an opposite sense. This second usage, for lack of a succinct descriptive title, might be termed the "we're doing a good job, but not really good enough" strategy. Any given agency seeks acceptance of the idea that it is performing an essential service by fighting the particular evil associated with it. But it may also send forth occasional reminders to the effect that there are more criminals to be caught, more ignorant to be educated, more indigents to be served, or more patients to be cured. The annual budget request that asks for less operating funds for the upcoming year is an extremely rare animal, if not a mythical one. (For a description of the Federal

Narcotics Bureau's budgetary problems and subsequent action, see Dickson, 1968.)

At the same time, most agencies are careful not to overplay the "needs yet unmet" idea. For, if the public and/or the relevant authorities come to perceive that only minuscule results are being reached, the agency's functions may be terminated or shifted elsewhere. The likelihood of this outcome varies, of course, with the importance attached to eliminating the target evil. Inefficient marihuana enforcement, in the face of new medical evidence and changing public attitudes, may help to promote lackadaisical and financially reduced surveillance, whereas cutbacks in equally inefficient heroin enforcement would be far less likely.[5] Whatever the example, it is to the agency's benefit in perpetuating itself to strive for license in *carte blanche* categorization of potential clientele (Freidson, 1966).

Accountability[6]

All organizations, and *public* processing agencies in particular, are subject to examination and evaluation. Such checks usually take place in accordance with routine established schedules. At times, they may be activated in reaction to a crisis situation—e.g., the crime rate has skyrocketed, a prison riot has occurred, a potentially dangerous mental patient has escaped, students are discovered to be smoking pot in a dormitory, a budget cut necessitates a cutback of services. Of more recent vintage, audits and investigations may be initiated by organized "consumer protection" groups, *a la* Nader's Raiders.[7] At the time of such reviews, regardless of source or context, the organization is obliged to provide evidence that it is doing the job for which it exists, or at least trying as hard as possible to do so. Informal supportive testimony by organizational representatives, to be accepted by the reviewer on the basis of trust, is in almost all cases an unacceptable technique. Records and documents must be displayed as an accompaniment to official testimony, even on their own *without* personal testimony.

The impression made by the display of records and documents generally increases in effectiveness as its content includes larger amounts of esoterica via technical language.[8] The use of such language implies not only expertise but the existence of special, unique, beyond-the-call-of-duty programs. Thus, we get the following chain of events:

1. The demand for accountability increases as the organization establishes itself as being active, committed, and essential.

2. The organization can best establish itself as being active, committed, and essential by portraying itself as a unique agency providing a unique service.
3. The organization can best portray its uniqueness by reporting utilization of specialized categories of clientele, personnel, and programming.
4. Utilization of specialized categories can best be reported when organizational devices, techniques, and supporting values for ready, uncomplicated categorical placement exist—i.e., when processing stereotypes are institutionalized.

Picture two contrasting public mental hospitals faced with an annual evaluation proceeding. Imagine that both have served identical client (patient) groups. Let us call one Szasz Hospital, in honor of the author of *The Myth of Mental Illness,* and the other Processing Stereotype Hospital. Szasz Hospital renders the following summary report:

> People come here with problems of living and our untitled staff workers sit around and talk with them and try to offer what help we can.

In contrast, Processing Stereotype Hospital reports:

> We currently have 23 hebephrenic schizophrenics, 18 catatonics, 14 manic-depressive psychotics, 43 obsessive-compulsive neurotics, (etc.), being treated with psychotherapy, occupational therapy, work therapy, electroshock therapy, drug therapy, (etc.), by a staff composed of 10 psychiatrists, 4 clinical psychologists, 7 social workers, 22 registered psychiatric nurses, and 17 attendants.

Given these two statements, it is to be proposed that equally contrasting responses would be forthcoming from review boards. Szasz Hospital might well be told, in so many words: "We're wasting the taxpayers' money on you; we might as well shut you down and send everyone to their local bartenders and ministers for therapy." Processing Stereotype Hospital, on the other hand, might be told: "Great —a very impressive report. We apologize for the burden imposed by this administrative necessity and will attempt to provide additional funding for further expansion and development in support of a job well done."

Efficiency and accountability to funding sources help guarantee the perpetuation of the bureaucracy and its work. Indexing and categorizing systems which speed organizational handling of cases make these agencies more efficient. Demands for external account-ability are often satisfied by production of statistical summaries and tables. Both influences lead to a concern with information gathering —information of a highly standardized and truncated nature.[9] Con-sequently, processing stereotypes of cases evolve through the de-mand for standardized data.

> The more massive and complex the world which the bureaucracies of official morality are trying to con-trol, the simpler their pictures of that world and their practices for dealing with it have become. And, [paradoxically,] the more democratic the societies have become, the more rigid and autocratic the in-formation forming much of the foundation of the administration of justice has become. (Douglas, 1971:56)

The above paragraphs are concerned with the necessity of *external* accountability—accountability to a set of authorities *outside* the or-ganization. Aspects of *internal* accountability are also relevant to our current interests. Each employee, with the occasional exception of the chief administrator, is expected to carry out his work in accor-dance with certain organizational guidelines and expectations. In the process, he may have to submit continuing or periodic reports de-scribing his work performance—e.g., number and descriptions of cases handled, dispositions, etc. Short of such an obligation, he is at least expected to operate in a manner consistent with organizational perspectives and espoused techniques. As a means of simplifying and ordering this internal accountability, the organization provides stan-dardized report forms, checklists, manuals of operating procedures, etc. The demand for internal accountability of agents' time and en-ergy becomes a second source—along with demand to document the production of cases to external monitors—of perpetuating standard-ized forms[10] (Zimmerman, 1969b).

The Socialization Variable: Professional Ideologies

Variation in the nature (and effect) of processing stereotypes occurs as the result of professional and subprofessional training and the specific ideologies that follow from that training. On a broad level, two factors are of major importance. First, professional socialization of social-control personnel produces explicit or implicit theories of etiology which are later employed stereotypically. Physicians and psychiatrists are taught to perceive behavior in terms of a disease model, where "abnormal" behavior is seen as a manifestation of some underlying condition that must be treated (Angrist, 1966; Scheff, 1966; Mechanic, 1968; Taber, *et al.*, 1969). Judges, attorneys, and other court officials generally apply a legal model based on the premise that man possesses free will—i.e., he is free to choose between legal and illegal behaviors. Alternative models marked by recent social science emphases have not been adopted to any significant extent by processing agents, despite occasional encouragement from within the ranks (Szasz, 1963; Clark, 1970).

The medical model and, to a lesser extent, the legal model contribute to the formation and utilization of processing stereotypes in that they call for examination of the deviant act outside of the context in which it occurs.[11] Scheff notes that "psychiatric and judicial interviews shear away most of the information about the context in which the 'symptomatic' behavior occurred" (Scheff, 1966:174). Commitment hearings, for example, are routinely structured such that little background information can be presented, and that which is presented may be ignored (Scheff, 1966; Wilde, 1968). In short, use of a medical or legal model constitutes a narrowing of the range of focus which, by itself, permits various forms of typification. Processing stereotypes, as such, are put into practice when facilitative categories and labels are applied within such a non-contextual perspective (e.g., truancy, manic-depressive psychosis, possession of dangerous drugs).

A second broad-level factor flows from the above-mentioned, restrictive model aspect of professional socialization. Scheff (1967:4) notes that when diagnostic categories are learned in medical school, they are often based on extreme cases: "The tendency to use extreme examples for analytic clarity reinforces the popular stereotype of the extremeness of mental illness, and serves also to reify classifications (such as paranoid behavior, depression) in concrete disease entities." Use of extreme examples in the training process, then, leads directly to stereotyping and reification even when "unextreme" cases are encountered later in actual practice.

Freidson directs our attention to another force promoting reification which, however, comes into play for almost opposite (but still model-related) reasons. The "professional" approach includes an explicit denial of the stigma attached to deviance by the general public. For example, psychiatry's mental health campaign contains a rejection of such popular labels as "crazy," "mad," and "nuts" in deference to a view of mental illness as just another form of illness. But what the agency sees as public inattention to the seriousness or appropriate interpretation of the problem "may lead them deliberately to employ stigmatized labels as a form of public education" (Freidson, 1966:69). Hence, "neurotic" and "psychotic" may begin to displace "nerves" and "looney" but only as substitute stigma terminology which, furthermore, reflects and propels professional stereotyping and reification.

The above points imply a processing stereotype consensus among control-agency workers, which is far from the actual case. Some differentiation is common both between and, to a lesser extent, within occupational groupings in any heterogeneously staffed agency setting. Smith (1957, 1958) and Bucher and Strauss (1961) first emphasized the existence of discrete, sometimes antagonistic intra-professional segments. These segments exist as a direct consequence of professional training experiences and the accompanying emphasis on specialization. Urologist and psychiatrist, or corporation tax lawyer and criminal trial lawyer, are likely to experience quite different training emphases, work settings, colleagues, social partners, subject matters, and theories of etiology and treatment, to list just a few areas of dissimilarity. Strauss and colleagues (1964) built a theory of organizational negotiation around the necessity of smoothly resolving inter- and intra-occupational differences in orientation. Tiedeman (1968) cites segmental conflicts as a crucial background consideration in interpreting the relationship between psychiatrist and internist in the general hospital. Within the medical specialty of psychiatry, vast differences in perspective are harsh and clear-cut. The battle between Freudians, neo-Freudians, and non-Freudians has raged throughout the twentieth century and shows little sign of abating. Hollingshead and Redlich, in their familiar *Social Class and Mental Illness*, (1958), cite fundamental psychiatric distinctions in terms of "analytic and psychological orientation" versus "directive and organic orientation." Even popular works of fiction feature plot lines involving the relative benefits and effects of psychotherapeutic and strict organic perspectives (e.g., lobotomy) (Kesey, 1962; Baker, 1963).

A patient who arrives at the hospital (or private office) of Psychiatrist X will encounter a professional who identifies himself as a member of the Freudian, Sullivanian, Rogerian, organic, functional, directive, or non-directive "school" of psychiatry, to list just some of the dominant possibilities. But it is, in any case, a school, which means a perspective and, in turn, *a* particular focus. By virtue of his own set of mentors, the caseload sample he has experienced as both trainee and practitioner, and his own personal preferences, Psychiatrist X will select and emphasize some case cues over others and may be prone to using one diagnosis or set of diagnoses more than others. In the course of data collection carried out by Tiedeman in one psychiatric setting, for example, "obsessive-compulsive neurosis" was the favored diagnosis by one contingent of the psychiatric staff, while another contingent routinely opted for "transient character disorder" as a more appropriate label *for the same cases.* Each control agent uses process stereotypes in accordance with his own professional predispositions as to what factors should be taken into account and what conclusions should be drawn.[12] This applies with equal weight not only to psychiatrists, of course, but to police officials, social workers, judges, teachers, etc.

Hence, processing stereotypes can be anticipated as a common organizational feature, while specific form and content will vary across organizations, occupations, and individuals as the result of differential professional socialization.[13] To the extent that the organization controls selection of its own personnel, some consensus regarding processing stereotypes is likely to exist. This is because self-selection of employees enhances the possibility of constructed homogeneity wherein *any* given individual of the same occupational grouping (or even across groupings), having been selectively chosen, will display similar background expectancies and similar current perspectives. Except in the case of private facilities, however, social-control agencies generally are faced with "equal opportunity" personnel selection. To the extent that some objective, merit-based placement system applies (e.g., civil service test scores, educational records, outside references), organizational heterogeneity of personnel is enhanced. A client's "fate" in such a setting will depend more strongly on the particular employee contacted. Employee A may use process stereotypes in such a way as to send the client along one route while Employee B may activate a quite different (or even opposite) route.

Even in open, public agencies, the possibility of personnel heterogeneity is countered in two ways.

1. Selective employee *candidacy* may occur. Most organizations have "emphasis-and-perspective reputations" that make the rounds of job-seekers via informal communications grapevines. A potential applicant may not even offer his candidacy if he anticipates that he "might not fit." The "get tough" type cop may completely bypass the opportunity to work within a police department renowned for its leniency and human relations orientation, for example.

2. Selective *attention* to *and consideration* of applicants can take place, prevailing equal opportunity statements notwithstanding. Thus, even if a noncongruent type does apply, there are ways of bypassing him. Files may be lost or misplaced, or rejection may be made on the basis of some extraneous attribute that is nevertheless a legitimized part of employee screening—e.g., a record as an ex-con, a physical defect, etc. (e.g., Chambliss, 1972).

However, such purging of personnel is generally not required. As long as societal intervention is bureaucratized, the demands of efficiency, perpetuation, and accountability will enhance the development of processing stereotypes. We propose the following hypotheses:[14]

1. The greater the ambiguity or uncertainty as to diagnosis, the greater the probability that processing stereotypes will evolve.
2. The greater the volume of cases per control agent, the greater the probability that processing stereotypes will evolve.
3. The more organizational levels within the bureaucracy through which a diagnosis must pass, the greater the probability that processing stereotypes will evolve.
4. The greater the demand for interchangeability of agency personnel, the greater the probability that processing stereotypes will evolve.
5. The greater the demand for collective decision-making (which serves to defuse personal responsibility in cases of blatant misclassification), the greater the probability that processing stereotypes will evolve.

Application of
Processing Stereotypes

Rather than detailing each of these hypotheses, we turn to the question: how are they applied?[15] Given the presence of processing stereotypes in control bureaucracies, why are they applied to some and not to all? We predict that processing stereotypes are less likely to be applied when the rule-breaker is in a position of power, or when the case has received considerable "press." Also processing stereotypes are less likely to be applied if the deviant is represented during his agency transition. In many psychiatric and criminal cases, this representative is expressly hired to serve as a defender, spokesman, or advocate for the accused. Wenger and Fletcher (1969:69) have documented the effect of the presence of a lawyer in mental hospital commitment proceedings. Of eighty-one cases observed, 91 percent (61 of 66) of those *without* legal counsel present at the hearing were committed to the state hospital. Of the 15 subjects *with* an attorney, only 4 (26 percent) were admitted. However, when these representatives were appointed or assigned to hearings by the state, they were less likely to be effective; indeed, Scheff's research indicates that they may not take issue with official diagnoses because they are paid a flat rate—to do so would be to take a cut in pay! (1966:137). Friends or relatives may be able to perform similar services if they can locate and gain access to the relevant organizational processes and personnel—e.g., a parent protesting an examination grade. Whether amateur or professional, the "stand-in" attempts to provide information or emotional appeals designed to broaden the agent's view of the deviant and the incident so as to postpone or eliminate the stereotype.

The extent of contact between the processing agent and the deviant can affect the application of processing stereotypes. When time and contact are at a minimum, stereotypic dispositions are predicted. For example, contact may be restricted simply by structural arrangements such that some agents get little or no time to apply their expertise. Psychiatric consultants, for example, find themselves frustrated by a hospital practice termed "diagnosis by exclusion." This means that all possible psychological explanations for a medical-surgical enigma are thoroughly checked before a psychiatric interpretation is deemed credible and a consultant is requested. By definition, the typical patient is nearing the end of his hospital stay at that point. This leaves very little time to work on the case and prompts the consultant's description of himself as "someone who stands by the hospital door and tries to catch the patient on his way out." The consultant finds himself in a dilemma. On the one hand, he can construct a quick review, interpretation, and recommendation that does not satisfy him and may be inaccurate because he has not had the time he needs. If his forced conclusions prove to be erroneous, internists will become increasingly reluctant to call upon him for his services. On the other hand, he may reject the consultation request on the grounds that time is too limited for him to perform effectively, in which case the internists will later hesitate to call upon him because of the prior rejection (Tiedeman, 1968). In both situations, the patient suffers the consequences: either a rapidly constructed processing stereotype or no consultation whatsoever. If friends or legal representatives were present in the organization to make sure of adequate access time for the deviant, such problems of time and contact might be reduced.

In addition to the greater probability of discovery and utilization of detailed information in the disposition given more contact, it may mean that an agent develops a personal concern with the case.[16] As contact reduces social distance, we would expect more positive input on case decisions with increased agent-client contact. It has been shown that human beings simply seem more willing to engage in detrimental judgments and behaviors concerning other human beings when they can do so from a distance. Milgram's widely discussed experiments, for example, disclosed that most subjects were quite willing to administer electrical shocks to another human (despite screams and shouts) as long as a wall blocked the recipient from direct view. Upon removal of physical barriers to vision and contact, however, willingness to obey "shock him" instructions from the experimenter-authority dropped sharply (Milgram, 1965). "Such results suggest that the blindfolding of a condemned prisoner may have another meaning than the one usually attributed to it. It is not so much to protect the victim's feelings that a blindfold is needed but rather to protect the executioner from his surveillance" (Gamson, 1968:134). By the same token, it is suggested that agency labels are affixed with greater abandon when the recipient is not in direct view.

Implications of Category Placement

What do processing stereotypes imply for the deviant passing through control agencies? First, the use of standardized instruments to record data (demanded for internal and external accountancy) requires a very selective notation of a limited range of information. This produces an informational "funneling effect," whereby potentially relevant data are abandoned while recorded data are subject to increasing reification and typification. The inquiry on relevant data, guided by processing stereotypes, may end rather abruptly so that some questions are never posed. A study of public defenders found client interviews were "interrupted when he [public defender] had enough information to confirm his sense of the case's typicality and construct a typifying portrayal of the present defendant" (Sudnow, 1965:268). This results in category placement being prematurely locked into, such that further "search for evidence" is thereby severely delimited.[17] The assigned processing stereotype also determines the direction of the questions. Again, the public defender:

> The most important feature of the P.D.'s questioning
> is the presumption of guilt that makes his proposed
> questions legitimate and answerable at the outset. To
> pose the question "Why don't you start by telling
> where this place was that you broke into?" as a lead
> question, the P.D. takes it that the defendant is guilty
> of a crime. . . . (Sudnow, 1965:269)

Because of these inquisitional limitations, and the premature categorization, the act is never fully understood within the context in which
it occurred. Not only is actual context ignored, but many times reified
expectations of normal circumstances or typical case characteristics
become part of the bureaucratic description of "what went on"
(Cicourel, 1968; Emerson, 1969).

In addition to "loaded" questioning, label permanency increases as
the case ascends the organization's hierarchy of officials. In other
words, processing stereotypes are reified and perpetuated as a case
moves into higher organizational levels. A certain classification in-
ertia develops such that revision of initial categorization is problematic.[18]

> This is especially true of official classifications, since
> an official becomes publicly committed to a classifica-
> tion once it has been officially recorded. There is . . .
> a great deal of paper work, and embarrassment, that
> must go into filing "amended death certificates" in
> most states [for coroner officials investigating sui-
> cides]. (Douglas, 1971:114)

While it may be true that "the higher a person is in the hierarchy
(and therefore the more removed from organizational routine), the
less stereotyped are his typifications" (Scheff, 1966:184), this characteristic may be of little consequence. The higher official is generally
bound by the information supplied by lower and middle processing
agents, and unless external pressure (from the press, politicians, or
influential relatives) is applied, decisions are seldom reversed. Even
then, the external sources need evidence in order to force a reclassifi-
cation as agency chiefs are likely to remain loyal to their staff members. Examples of this are periodically found in publicity on a police
chief's handling of complaints against his officers.

Secondly, application of processing stereotypes means that extraneous variables often play an important part in agency decisions. The
stereotypes held by police officers will influence which individuals
are arrested and which are simply reprimanded and released. Decisions on arrest may be influenced by factors such as race, sex, de-

meanor, age, dress, and mannerisms, whether the person is alone or in a group at the time of the offense, the availability and wishes of the complainant, as well as the race and social class of the victim.[19] At later points in the criminal justice system, these and other factors affect dispositions: those without jobs or respectable relatives are more likely denied bond, children from broken homes are more likely to be referred to juvenile court for their offenses, etc.

Recent literature pertaining to psychiatric settings also offers abundant substantiation for the processing stereotype perspective, both implicitly and explicitly. Wilde (1968) suggests that psychiatric commitment decisions are commonly based upon extraneous interviewee characteristics rather than upon evidence confirming the presence of "commitable mental illness" characteristics. Data concerning adjudication of incompetency in the state of Florida indicate that nonlegal and nonmedical factors such as age, type of petition, and committee composition are crucial in influencing judgments (Haney and Michielutte, 1968). Patient-therapist alignment in terms of social class and of verbalization-insight abilities is a well-established predictor of selected mode of therapy (Hollingshead and Redlich, 1958; Rowden, et al., 1970; Waller, 1965). To cite one further example, Robins (1969) has provided insightful cautionary guidelines for properly distinguishing causes and consequences of behavior that is branded as psychiatric disorder (cf. Scheff and Sundstrom, 1970).

Third, the above factors may decrease the chances that public intervention attempts will be successful. If treatment or punishment is to become preventative, it should be directed toward the causes of the behavioral displays. To the extent processing stereotypes make problematic or unlikely the close analysis of a case which would permit a discovery of what is maintaining the behavior, we would expect "corrective" efforts to be ineffective and misguided. The classic example of this is in juvenile court, where the child is usually seen as unrelated to the family environment. His behavior is analyzed out of context, and he is generally taken out of the family and school and treated—again out of context. As trends toward increasing prevalence of processing stereotypes continue, we would expect that rehabilitative success would remain minimal.

Finally, all of these factors combine to increase the sense of mystification in the accused; the confusion results in part from inability to predict the factors being used to decide his fate. Realizing that the entire story of his or her deviation has not been recorded or considered, discovering that extra-legal and seemingly unrelated facts such as race, sex, age, dress, and demeanor may be central to the decision-making process, the accused may well develop a sense of injustice.

Figure 1   *Implications of category placement*

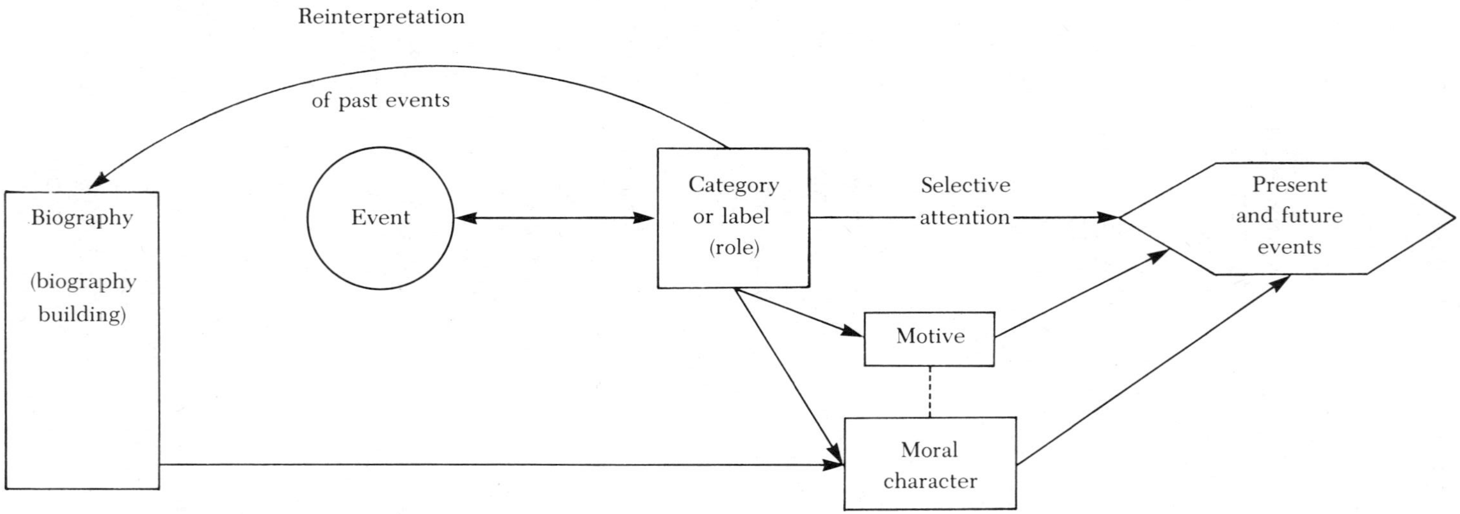

Reinterpretation

of past events

Biography
(biography
building)

Category
or label
(role)

Event

Selective
attention

Motive

Moral
character

Present
and future
events

If the sense of injustice reduces the chances of effective treatment, we see the irony of policies instituted for processing efficiency in fact working against intervention effectiveness.[20]

In previous chapters, we have shown how events imply some category or label and how these categories, in turn, inform and permit meaning to be assigned to events (documentary method of interpretation). Figure 1 summarizes some of the implications of category placement, especially when this is done within control agencies.[21] Labeling, guided by processing stereotypes, has four major implications: *biography building, assignment* of specific *motives,* imputation of essential *moral character,* and a pre-set cognitive frame for interpreting future behavioral events, producing *selective viewing.*

Biography building

This is best viewed as a reconstruction project whereby the control agent searches into the individual deviant's past for evidence to document the category or label applied. This construction of the past must, by the nature of the task, be highly selective:

> No actual biographical rendering of an individual is exhaustive. What is called biography is of necessity an extremely short and highly *selective* list of events. . . . The fact of enormous selectivity, without benefit of a sampling frame or random selection procedures, means that the biographies available on Actors are likely to be highly distorted (in the probability sense), for what is known is unlikely to depict accurately the essential features of the vast amount that is unknown. (Lofland, 1969:152)

Agent ideology or training predisposes control agents to selective categorization of the initially disclosed acts or behaviors that have brought the subject to the agency's attention. Interviewing and other forms of "subject review" are then directed toward the discovery of actual characteristics that are consistent with, and supportive of, the preexisting typification (Scheff, 1968). Those aspects of the deviant's biography consistent with the processing stereotype are focused on in the reconstruction—e.g., the arrestee *does* have a prior record, the psychiatric patient *has* had previous admissions or *does* show psychological testing results consistent with the proposed diagnosis, the poor student *has* flunked other classes. Concern is not directed toward other, broader, "irrelevant" elements of the total biography— e.g., the arrestee's family has not always been destitute, the psychiatric patient performs well in general or shows more testing results that are inconsistent with proposed diagnosis than are consistent, the poor student does a lot of squinting at the blackboard from his seat in the back of the room. And, if the subject or some other party offers these broader biographical factors anyway, they can be ignored on the familiar grounds of "irrelevance." (Dismissal as "irrelevant," unjust, and illogical as it may seem, is commonly and easily defended on the basis of specialization, expertise, and/or authority.) In short, agents go about constructing the sort of biography they want to see, which usually happens to be one that supports the agency's functions and the utilization of its facilities.

To facilitate biography building most efficiently, admission forms, interview schedules, agency records, etc., are structured in such a way as to provide desired information and avoid the extraneous. Where provision is made for more inclusive information, it is often no more than a token gesture. Tiedeman notes the usage made of the "Social History" and "Psychological History" sections of general hospital medical and surgical admission interview forms. First, only two lines of writing space are provided for each entry, in contrast to the abundant space made available for physiological commentary. Typical "Social History" entries include "Smokes two packs of cigarettes per day," "Drinks in moderation," and "Lives at home with husband and children." "Seems well oriented" often suffices as "Psychological History" (Tiedeman, 1968). Sociopsychological patient information can prove crucial to isolating a psychosomatic condition, successful preparation for surgery, or simply aiding in adjustment to the rampant impersonality of a modern hospital. However, little use—if any —can be made of these superficial data. Parallel means of organizing forms and records to facilitate biography building are to be found in other control-agency settings.

The various aspects of biography building interact progressively with one another to provide a total effect greater than and distinct from the sum of its parts. As certain images become more and more pragmatic, more restricted, and more simplified, they can receive increasing concentration, while others are dropped from consideration. Forms and records can be similarly and simultaneously tightened. In this way, selectivity that has consequences for future acts and future responses by other agents is also enhanced. In the extreme case, a single index comes to be regarded as sufficient—e.g., a *black* revolutionary militant, a *female* professional trainee, the use of a precise *gesture* in response to the Golden Key Proverb.

Biography building can be seen as involving various degrees of negotiation between deviant and control agents. The deviant has the greatest impact on the way his biography is rendered when his social status is equal to or above that of the processing agent and where agency contact is voluntary. Here, the patient-client has the greatest power. When involuntary treatment occurs, the deviant has little power, especially if defined as incompetent in some way (e.g., mental patients, juvenile delinquents). Control agents would have almost complete control of biography building in cases of suicide, where the only corrective input may be from sympathetic relatives.[22]

Biography building becomes important for the long-term component of the creation of deviance. When selective interpretations or misinterpretations pave the way for a new phase of biographical constructions, the resultant funneling effect contributes to a self-fulfilling prophecy that is central to our entire thesis. The accused is unable to escape his past (albeit highly selective) even upon leaving an agency. He may even take up the particular official biographical explanation provided, and use it to justify continued deviance (Warren and Johnson, 1972).

Motive assignment

The next two aspects are closely related: motive assignment and imputations of moral character. Motive for an infraction is often incorporated into the typification of the offense (Sudnow, 1965). Hence, the category comes to imply a typical or standard motivation for the infraction. Because perceived motivation is a crucial factor in the way a case is handled in terms of diagnosis and prognosis (Freidson, 1966), its "documentation" is critical to the forms which the deviant career will take. The particular motive assigned and the label or category invoked both affect the assignment of moral character.[23] Thus, in mental hospitals, "[a]n over-all title is given to the pathology, such as schizophrenia, psychopathic personality, etc., and this provides a new view of the patient's 'essential character'" (Goffman, 1961:375).

Moral character

To illustrate the dynamics of character assignment, we turn to a recent study of a large metropolitan juvenile court. Robert Emerson (1969), in his observations of case processing, found that three types of moral character were routinely imparted to juveniles: normal, disturbed, and criminal. We shall deal with the different clues used by police and probation officers to typify a juvenile as either normal or criminal in character. Generally, a criminal moral character is indicated by infractions which evidence (a) a high degree of commitment to illegal activity—e.g., infraction for profit rather than for fun or personal needs; (b) a willingness to cause harm or injury to the victim in carrying out illegal activity; (c) a style and techniques of sophisticated nature—e.g., special tools, or a professional *modus ope-randi.* "Normal" delinquents engaged in acts which were not extremely profitable, relatively harmless in terms of personal injury, and situationally influenced. Inferences of moral character are made from the details available on the infraction and the usual motive assigned to such infractions, as well as other behaviors—such as the strategies of the defense used by the accused in court. Emerson (1969:126) reports that delinquents who routinely appeal their conviction or sentence are seen as having a criminal moral character, since the appeal "shows the youth too knowledgeable of the technicalities and loopholes of the legal system." Even reliance upon a private defense attorney instead of the public defender may be seen as indicative of sophistication in criminal law and, consequently, immersion in a criminal way of life. Hence, the ironic outcome is that those who utilize their procedural rights to the fullest are likely to be penalized through imputation of an essential moral character demanding severe sanctions.

Selective viewing

The final influence of the category placement and attendant factors such as biography, motive, and moral character is the selective attention and selective perception of present and future behaviors. The actor is now seen through a label and his actions are therefore tinted to fit the expectations implied by the label (Payne, 1973:36).

> Although Actor may be emitting the same acts, they can take on different meanings. Instead of having imagination, he may now be a wild visionary. Instead of being optimistic, he may now be gullible. . . . As a long tradition of social psychological experimentation suggests, ambiguous situations are open to the imputation of meaning. Once imputation as a deviant begins, the inherent ambiguity of action makes possible redefinition of a wide range of Actor's conduct. This redefinition involves little or no empirical contradiction, since the empirical materials provided by persons are almost never very clear. (Lofland, 1969:148, 149)

Selective perception is especially evident in total institutions where conceivably all behavior could be monitored and recorded. What happens, in fact, is that only rule violations tend to be recorded, while conformity is often overlooked or only briefly described (Goffman, 1961; Kesey, 1962; Rosenhan, 1973).

Processing Stereotypes and
Labeling Theory

What remains to be done is to show the relationship of processing stereotypes to the labeling process experienced by the deviant. Scheff's proposition, which is the core of extant labeling theory, proposed that in the "crisis occurring when a residual rule-breaker is publicly labeled, the deviant is highly suggestible, and may accept the proffered [deviant] role . . . as the only alternative" (Scheff, 1966:88). We propose that processing stereotypes function to increase the probability that the accused will accept the proffered role.

First, the use of processing stereotypes by control agents tends to *coopt* the supporters of the deviant. Family and friends will often side with the deviant in arguing that his behavior was not that bad, neutralizing or normalizing it in some way. The supporters who share the accused deviant's definition of reality are converted to the agency's version of reality when shown how typical the case is, how similar it is to other cases routinely handled by the agency, and that the agency has successfully dealt with the type in the past. In Goffman's terms, supporters are lead through a betrayal funnel, where their help and cooperation are requested; and it is argued that it would be in the best interest of the client if they *helped* during this difficult transition period. Conversion of supporters makes the control agent's job less difficult. In the case of entering a mental hospital, control agents' actions are often two-fold:

> While a person is gradually being transformed into a patient, a next-of-relation is gradually being transformed into a guardian. With a guardian on the scene, the whole transition process can be kept tidy. . . . Some of the prepatient's abrogated civil rights can be transferred to him, thus helping to sustain the legal fiction that while the prepatient does not actually have his rights he somehow actually has not lost them. (Goffman, 1961:142)

In short, most social controllers attempt to convert the accused, as well as his supporters, to the agency definition of reality. Processing stereotypes aid in the conversion process.

The effect on the deviant of the loss of his final supporting referents is often an angry rejection of his next-of-relation. At this point, the deviant stands alone against his accusers. Following the social psychological studies of Asch and others, we would expect the deviant to come to accept the agency definition of his case—i.e., the probability of taking on the imputed role will increase. The combination of resentment over betrayal and confusion over the processing decisions (especially when there is a great distance between the details of the case and the resultant processing stereotype) should precipitate the identity crisis to which Scheff refers.

A second way in which processing stereotypes facilitate the acquisition of a deviant role is through the presentation of a *united front* to the accused. To the extent that processing stereotypes are used in case disposition, the deviant receives a unified picture of his problem. An example is found in the closed staff meetings such as the diagnostic session described at the first of this chapter. Goffman observes:

> [T]he differential image of himself that a person [i.e., inmate] usually meets from those of various levels around him comes [in the hospital staff meeting] to be [*unified behind the scenes into a common approach,*] [hence] the patient may find himself faced with a kind of collusion against him. . . . (1961:160. Emphasis added.)

Such collusion may be expanded to relatives and friends through cooptation. Both are facilitated by processing stereotypes (cf. Goffman, 1969). In this way, processing stereotypes are central to the labeling process. If the accused received very different pictures and advice from each agent within a control organization, or conflicting pictures from different agencies processing the case, we would expect a greater ability to resist the imputed label. Within an agency, the presence and application of processing stereotypes should increase the probability of the accused taking on the proffered deviant role.

Third, processing stereotypes also give the impression to the deviant that the decision in his case is a *fait accompli.* Announcement of the label by experts, at times in a public setting, suggests a consensus that strengthens the binding force of the label. The impression is that the label and its signaled "condition" are a foregone conclusion, and thereby accurate, unchangeable, and unchallengeable.[24] This perhaps accounts for the finding by Baum and Wheeler (1968) that youths being sent to a reform school by a juvenile court were not initially critical of the decision and accepted their fate. For these reasons, processing stereotypes are central to the labeling process. What happens to them and to the deviant when cases are handled by many agencies is the topic of our next chapter.

Notes

1. In accordance with the cautions cited in Chapters I–III, the reader is urged to remember what such a statement does *not* suggest. It does not suggest that the normative framework is worthless, that there is no such thing as schizophrenia or addiction, or that all agency clients are improperly and arbitrarily handled to the detriment of man and society. But the normative framework *is* misused and overused. Improper and arbitrary handling of agency clients *does* take place. The *proportion* of all cases, or of any single case, that is best understood by way of the normative "versus" the interpretive framework is a meaningless consideration. *Both* frameworks apply as part of the labeling approach proposed and subscribed to herein. If our subsequent emphasis seems one-sided, that is a consequence of the relative inattention that has thus far been directed toward the interpretive framework and associated conceptualizations.

2. Thomas Scheff states: "Just describing the structure of the normal cases [processing stereotypes] in an agency would be a major step in understanding how the organization functions" (1966:185).

3. This is of course a major reason why official rates are not valid indicators of deviant activities in society. These rates reflect the organizational demands for record-keeping and accounting for the agent's time and behavior more than what actually happened. The same validity problem is found in self-reported studies carried out by sociologists; definitions of what is deviant are imposed upon the respondent by the researchers (who freely borrow from legal descriptions of offenses). Few details are gathered on the circumstances of the act, or the respondent's definition of the action. (For an exception, see Erickson, 1971). For other examples of sociological arrogance, see Douglas, 1971: 32–39.

4. One of the most often heard pleas from police departments, court systems, public schools at all levels, and social welfare agencies is that they are overloaded with clients and cannot, therefore, do the job that is expected of them. These pleas are not meant to indicate that the work being done is substandard—only that more help is needed. We contend that, well beyond the problem of personnel shortage, the work *is* substandard in that the situation forces extensive usage of processing stereotypes. A reminder may be in order here. We do not seek to condemn individual control agents or to suggest that such agents go out of their way in a conscious attempt to stereotype clients. We are attempting only to pinpoint properties that insure that labeling *will* take place even if directly contrary to the wishes of the agent. No individual is *necessarily* at fault.

5. In one sense, heroin control policies may be too effective. The policy of paying foreign governments (e.g., Turkey) to restrict opium production has created a shortage of the opium derivative, codeine, for medical purposes.

6. As a preliminary note to this section, the reader is cautioned to distinguish between organizational "accountability" as discussed here and personal "accounting" as discussed elsewhere in this volume. The two have quite separate meanings, despite the semantic similarity.

7. While Ralph Nader has not taken on any control bureaucracies to date, there is a core of dedicated lawyers who use class action suits and other legal weapons to make mental institutions and prisons accountable for types of treatment (or lack thereof); see Ennis, 1972, Ennis and Friedman, 1973.

8. In the words of a *Time Magazine* essay, "The amount of expertise varies in inverse proportion to the number of statements understood by the General Public" (1966:14–15). In passing, we note there are many parallels between agencies accounting for their effectiveness in quantifiable terms and the sociologist, or other social scientists, accounting to granting agencies and journal editors.

9. A major contribution of ethnomethodological inquiries has been the specification of factors which get into organizational records and how these factors are selected with an eye toward organizational accountancy. (See especially Garfinkel, 1967:11–24; Cicourel, 1968; Zimmerman, 1969a, 1969b, 1970; and Douglas, 1971.)

10. It should be added, parenthetically, that demands of internal accountability of agent's time and work can produce pressures which affect the rates of officially recorded deviance. For example, policemen on traffic duty are informally expected to average a certain number of citations per day or per week. Those failing to write a certain number of tickets may be called upon to account for their inactivity in the field (Skolnick, 1966).

11. Legal "mitigating circumstances" such as self-defense and insanity do involve consideration of context to some extent.

12. For an experimental documentation of this point, see Langer and Abelson, 1974.

13. The exact form which processing stereotypes will take in an agency is affected by inter-agency and inter-professional rivalries and conflicts, which we discuss in the next chapter.

14. Some of these hypotheses are given in Scheff's discussion of diagnostic typification (1966:178–84). For evidence on hypothesis 4, see Sudnow's discussion of "station manning" (1965).

15. We are now asking another set of questions. Up to this point we have tried to show how and why processing stereotypes develop within a control agency. We are now asking for the conditions under which extant processing stereotypes will be assigned to a specific individual and his rule-breaking incident. This might be termed the *degree* of "processual stereotyping."

16. This is a standard mystery plot-line, where an honest detective becomes intrigued with a case, finds the real murderer and frees the innocently accused, all the while risking the wrath of his superiors. Professional training generally admonishes the aspirant to avoid involvement with clients. For a discussion of the modifications which occur in professional-client relationships when service is embedded in a control bureaucracy, see Daniels, 1969.

17. See our earlier discussion of "primacy effects" in Chapter IV.

18. When classification takes place in a group setting, lower officials are likely to defer to the judgments of higher authorities in the agency, as the Golden Key incident described earlier indicates.

19. See Black and Reiss, 1970; Cicourel, 1968; Emerson, 1969; Erickson, 1971; Ferdinand and Luchterhand, 1970; Piliavin and Briar, 1964.

20. The sense of injustice will be examined in detail in Chapter X.

21. The implications of category placement are similar whether done in a formal control bureaucracy or informally when one person labels another's behavior. We focus on the former, because the implications of labeling are clearer, and to an extent more exaggerated, in control bureaucracies than when carried out by the man in the street. After all, the expert should be more efficient in these things than the lay person.

22. For a detailed discussion of biography building in suicide cases, see Jack Douglas, 1971. Attributions of intent to die from biographical information have been experimentally investigated by Hood, 1970. Lofland (1969:149–52) details the role of the mass media—especially the press—in biography building.

23. This attribution process was outlined in Chapter IV.

24. Most readers will recognize that this impression of authority may be found at less formal levels of interaction. In everyday conversation the statement "You are _____" or "I think you are _____" is likely to prompt denials and rebuttals whether the remark is insulting or complimentary. But the statement "Everybody knows that you are _____" is more typically followed by a silence that implies acceptance and allows the speaker to proceed on that assumption.

References

Angrist, Shirley S.
1966   "Mental illness and deviant behavior." *The Sociological Quarterly* 7 (Fall):436–48.

Baker, Elliot
1963   *A Fine Madness.* New York: G. P. Putnam's Sons.

Baum, Martha, and Stanton Wheeler
1968   "Becoming an inmate." In S. Wheeler (ed.), *Controlling Delinquents.* New York: John Wiley and Sons.

Becker, Howard S.
1963   *Outsiders: Studies in the Sociology of Deviance.* New York: Free Press of Glencoe.

Black, Donald J., and Albert J. Reiss, Jr.
1970   "Police control of juveniles." *American Sociological Review* 35 (February):63–77.

Blumberg, Abraham S.
1969   "The practice of law as confidence game: organizational cooptation of a profession." In W. J. Chambliss (ed.), *Crime and the Legal Process.* New York: McGraw-Hill.

Bucher, Rue, and Anselm Strauss
1961   "Professions in process." *American Journal of Sociology* 66 (January):325–34.

Chambliss, Bill
1972   *Boxman: A Professional Thief's Journey.* New York: Harper Torchbook.

Cicourel, Aaron V.
1968   *The Second Organization of Juvenile Justice.* New York: John Wiley and Sons.

Clark, Ramsey
1970   *Crime in America.* New York: Simon and Schuster.

Daniels, Arlene K.
1969   "The captive professional: bureaucratic limitations in the practice of military psychiatry." *Journal of Health and Social Behavior* 10 (December):255–65.

Dickson, Donald T.
1968   "Bureaucracy and morality: an organizational perspective on a moral crusade." *Social Problems* 16 (Fall):143–56.

Douglas, Jack D.
1970   "Deviance and respectability: the social construction of moral meanings." In Jack D. Douglas (ed.), *Deviance and Respectability.* New York: Basic Books.
1971   *American Social Order.* New York: Free Press.

Emerson, Robert
1969   *Judging Delinquents: Context and Process in Juvenile Court.* Chicago: Aldine.

Ennis, Bruce J.
1972   *Prisoners of Psychiatry: Mental Patients, Psychiatrists and the Law.* New York: Harcourt.

Ennis, Bruce J., and Paul R. Friedman
1973   *Legal Rights of the Mentally Handicapped.* (3 vol.) New York: Practicing Law Institute.

Erickson, Maynard L.
1971   "The group context of delinquent behavior." *Social Problems* 19 (Summer):114–28.

Ferdinand, Theodore N., and Elmer G. Luchterhand
1970   "Inner-city youths, the police, the juvenile court, and justice." *Social Problems* 17 (Spring):510–27.

Freidson, Eliot
1966   "Disability as social deviance." In Marvin B. Sussman (ed.), *Sociology and Rehabilitation.* Washington, D.C.: American Sociological Association.

Gamson, William A.
1968   *Power and Discontent.* Homewood, Ill.: Dorsey Press.

Garfinkel, Harold
1967   *Studies in Ethnomethodology.* Englewood Cliffs, New Jersey: Prentice-Hall.

Goffman, Erving
1961   *Asylums.* New York: Doubleday.
1969   "The insanity of place." *Psychiatry* 32 (November):357–88.

Haney, C. Allen, and Robert Michielutte
1968   "Selective factors operating in the adjudication of incompetancy." *Journal of Health and Social Behavior* 9 (September):233–42.

Hollingshead, August B., and Frederick C. Redlich
1958   *Social Class and Mental Illness.* New York: John Wiley and Sons.

Hood, Ralph W., Jr.
1970   "Effects of foreknowledge of death in the assessment of intent

to die." *Journal of Consulting and Clinical Psychology* 34:129–33.

Jamison, Harold B.
1969   "On characteristics of professional organizations." *Journal of Health and Social Behavior* 10 (December):344–45.

Kesey, Ken
1962   *One Flew Over the Cuckoo's Nest.* New York: Viking.

Klapp, Orrin E.
1962   *Heroes, Villains, and Fools.* Englewood Cliffs, New Jersey: Prentice-Hall.

Langer, Ellen J., and Robert P. Abelson
1974   "A patient by any other name . . .: clinical group differences in labeling bias." *Journal of Consulting and Clinical Psychology* 42 (February):4–9.

Lefton, Mark, and William R. Rosengren
1966   "Organizations and clients: lateral and longitudinal dimensions." *American Sociological Review* 31 (December):802–810.

Lofland, John
1969   *Deviance and Identity.* Englewood Cliffs, New Jersey: Prentice-Hall.

Madge, John
1962   *The Origins of Scientific Sociology.* New York: Free Press.

Mechanic, David
1968   *Medical Sociology: A Selective View.* New York: Free Press.

Milgram, Stanley
1965   "Some conditions of obedience and disobedience to authority." *Human Relations* 18:57–76.

Niederhoffer, Arthur
1967   *Behind the Shield.* New York: Doubleday-Anchor.

Payne, William D.
1973   "Negative labels: passageways and prisons." *Crime and Delinquency* 19 (January):33–40.

Piliavin, Irving, and Scott Briar
1964   "Police encounters with juveniles." *American Journal of Sociology* 70 (September):204–214.

Robins, Lee N.
1969   "Social correlates of psychiatric disorders: can we tell causes from consequences?" *Journal of Health and Social Behavior* 10 (June):95–104.

Rosenhan, D. L.
1973   "On being sane in insane places." *Science* 179 (January 19):250–58.

Rowden, David W., Jerry B. Michel, Ronald C. Dillehay, and Harry W. Martin
1970 "Judgments about candidates for psychotherapy: the influence of social class and insight-verbal ability." *Journal of Health and Social Behavior* 11 (March):51–58.

Scheff, Thomas J.
1966 *Being Mentally Ill.* Chicago: Aldine.
1968 "Negotiating reality: notes on power in the assessment of responsibility." *Social Problems* 16 (Summer):3–17.

Scheff, Thomas J. (ed.)
1967 *Mental Illness and Social Processes.* New York: Harper and Row.

Scheff, Thomas J., and Eric Sundstrom
1970 "The stability of deviant behavior over time: a reassessment." *Journal of Health and Social Behavior* 11 (March):37–43.

Schur, Edwin M.
1965 *Crimes Without Victims.* Englewood Cliffs, New Jersey: Prentice-Hall.

Secord, Paul F., and Carl W. Backman
1964 *Social Psychology.* New York: McGraw-Hill.

Skolnick, Jerome H.
1966 *Justice Without Trial.* New York: John Wiley and Sons.
1967 "Social control in the adversary system." *Journal of Conflict Resolution* 11 (March):52–70.

Smith, Harvey L.
1955 "Psychiatry: a social institution in process." *Social Forces* 33 (May):310–16.
1957 "Psychiatry in medicine: intra- or inter-professional relationships?" *American Journal of Sociology* 63 (November):285–89.
1958 "Contingencies of professional differentiation." *American Journal of Sociology* 63 (January):410–14.

Strauss, Anselm, Leonard Schatzman, Rue Bucher, Danuta Erlich, and Melvin Sabshin
1964 *Psychiatric Ideologies and Institutions.* New York: The Free Press of Glencoe.

Sudnow, David
1965 "Normal crimes: sociological features of the penal code in a public defense office." *Social Problems* 12 (Winter):255–76.

Szasz, Thomas S.
1961 *The Myth of Mental Illness.* New York: Hoeber-Harper.
1963 *Law, Liberty and Psychiatry.* New York: Macmillan.

Taber, Merlin, Herbert C. Quay, Harold Mark, and Vicki Nealey
  1969   "Disease ideology and mental health research." *Social Problems* 16 (Winter):349–57.

Tiedeman, Gary H.
  1968   *Psychiatric Consultation in a Medical Setting: Intra-professional Differentials and Resolutions.* Unpublished Ph.D. dissertation, University of North Carolina.

Waller, Gary
  1965   *Social Class Orientations in the Initiations of Patient Careers: The Study of a Psychiatric Outpatient Department.* Unpublished M.A. thesis, University of North Carolina.

Warren, Carol A. B., and John M. Johnson
  1972   "A critique of labeling theory from the phenomenological perspective." In Robert A. Scott and Jack D. Douglas (eds.), *Theoretical Perspectives on Deviance.* New York: Basic Books.

Weber, Max
  1958   "Bureaucracy." In H. H. Gerth and C. Wright Mills (eds.), *From Max Weber: Essays in Sociology.* New York: Oxford University Press.

Wenger, Dennis, and C. Richard Fletcher
  1969   "The effect of legal counsel on admissions to a state mental hospital: a confrontation of professions." *Journal of Health and Social Behavior* 10 (March):66–72.

Wilde, William A.
  1968   "Decision-making in a psychiatric screening agency." *Journal of Health and Social Behavior* 9 (September):215–21.

Zimmerman, Don H.
  1969a   "Record-keeping and the intake process in a public welfare agency." In Stanton Wheeler (ed.), *On Record.* New York: Russell Sage Foundation.

  1969b   "Tasks and troubles: the practical bases of work activities in a public assistance organization." In Donald Hanson (ed.). *Explorations in Sociology and Counseling.* Boston: Houghton Mifflin.

  1970   "The practicalities of rule use." In J. D. Douglas (ed.), *Understanding Everyday Life.* Chicago: Aldine.

  1966   "Right you are if you say you are—obscurely." *Time Magazine* 88 (December 30):14–15.

Chapter
VIII

Inter-Agency Processing and Labeling

Expertise institutionalized into a profession is not, as much writing seems to assume, an automatically self-correcting, purely task-oriented substitute for "arbitrary" bureaucracy. The definition of the work—that is, how the client should behave and what other workers should do—is a partial expression of the hierarchy created by the office, and of the ideology stemming from the perspective of the office as well as of the purely technical character of the work itself. And when that work involves personal services of some importance to the welfare of the client, both the ideology and the technology combine to produce bureaucracy-like consequences for his fate.

Eliot Freidson

Social-control agencies have been classified as service organizations because their raw material is people rather than objects. Service organizations include schools, universities, hospitals, clinics, welfare agencies, unemployment bureaus, juvenile courts, police departments, prisons, and other people-processing institutions. To make this category more parsimonious, we can subdivide these organizations into service and control agencies. Service organizations involve voluntary symmetrical relationships between professional and client, while control agencies involve asymmetrical, usually involuntary relationships between agency and "clients."[1] In control agencies it is difficult to know for whom the services are provided. Supposedly, police work services the community and specific victims of criminal acts, but some would argue that the police serve those they process, since they are arrested from a life of crime. Police work is euphemistically seen as the first step on the road to rehabilitation, although most police work is described as more punitive than rehabilitative.

Service organizations, as opposed to economic production organizations, "are generally assumed to be more concerned with social goals and less with profit and loss" (Lefton, 1970:19). Consequently, a service ethic rather than a profit motive is generally assumed to underlie the activities of people-processing agencies. This is not to say social-control agencies are not concerned with money. Control

Source: Eliot Freidson, "Dominant professions, bureaucracy, and client services." In William R. Rosengren and Mark Lefton (eds.), *Organizations and Clients: Essays in the Sociology of Service* (Columbus, Ohio: Charles E. Merrill), 1970, p. 90.

bureaucracies must often justify their existence to legislators and others in order to receive continued support for their activities from the public. Agencies such as police departments, the Drug Enforcement Administration, the FBI, and others must show some success in their control work, while at the same time not appearing too successful. Organizationally-created statistics are used to document the extent of the problem—e.g., rising crime rates, increasing drug traffic, etc.—to legitimize requests for funds to improve and expand control procedures. At the same time, the same statistics are called upon to show that progress has been made, that the fight against crime, or the war against poverty, is being won. Control agencies must argue that past funding has produced results and that future support is still warranted.

Service organizations are unique in the sense that they process reactive objects. Patients and prisoners talk back, demand their rights, and at times demand part of the action. That clients can react to and shape the service organization while being processed opens up new and interesting problems for organizational analysis. For example, to what extent do those being processed influence their course of passage through the organization? Do the inmates really run the asylum? We would expect the negotiation power of clients to be greater in service agencies than in control agencies; but, even in the latter, the deviants may significantly affect their future. Roth found that patients committed to a TB sanitarium were instrumental in negotiating their medical discharge date (Roth, 1963). Similarly, the prisoner influences his release date by "doing good time" and impressing the parole board by taking advantage of training programs within the prison.

Lefton and Rosengren (1966) provide an analytic approach to service organizations. They suggest that such organizations can be classified in terms of each agency's concern with the client's past and future biography. Agencies vary in their concern about the time span or longitudinality of their clients. Organizational interest may range from a truncated span of time—as in a hospital emergency room or the booking room of a police department—to an almost indeterminate time span in cases of prisons and psychiatric hospitals. Organizations also hold varying degrees of interest in the client's biographical space or the "surroundings" of a client. This lateral dimension ranges from no concern about the details of the individual (e.g., emergency room, traffic court) to an extensive concern with the current social situation in which the client lives (e.g., psychiatric outpatient treatment facilities). Given the dimensions of longitudinal and lateral interest of organizations in clients, Lefton and Rosengren outline the four logical combinations. While their examples were drawn mainly from medical service organizations, the classification can also include legal control agencies, as Figure 1 indicates.

Figure 1   *Organizational interest in clients*

		Biographical interest	
		Lateral	*Longitudinal*
Type	*Examples*	*(Social space)*	*(Social time)*
I	Police departments Public defender office Adult criminal court Small claims court Jails Commitment boards Welfare agencies (agency-directed)	–	–
II	State and federal prisons Reform schools Psychiatric hospitals District attorney office Parole boards	–	+
III	Juvenile bureau Juvenile court Court psychiatric clinics Welfare agencies (client-directed)	+	–
IV	Probation department In-community treatment and prevention programs: (e.g. Provo Experiment, Synanon, etc.)	+	+

Adapted from Lefton and Rosengren, 1966:806.

It must be made clear that the types shown in Figure 1 are ideal types and that there may be variations within each of the four classes. For example, prisons and psychiatric hospitals for the criminally insane may have a longer range concern with an inmate's temporal biography than a parole board or a district attorney's office. There are also some problems of overlap between these four ideal types. For example, client-directed social workers may fit under type III, while agency-directed social workers would be more accurately character-ized by type I. Also, there would be some legitimate reasons for placing public defender's office and district attorney's office together under type I. However, the DA's office is more likely to have a vested political interest in getting a conviction, and in that sense may be oriented to the defendant's biography along a longitudinal dimension. Police might be seen as holding some longitudinal interest in suspects, but they are placed under type I because this interest is, by the nature of police work, short-lived. Police officers may follow a case to court but, after disposition, interest evaporates. These exceptions suggest that the two dimensions are best conceived as separate continua rather than dichotomies.

While any typology of service organizations contains some imprecision, the longitudinal-lateral scheme has some heuristic value in organizing a discussion of inter-agency contacts,[2] specifically the form and tone and the degree of conflict which may be generated in inter-agency exchanges. Prefatorily, there is one other distinction which will affect inter-agency contacts: sequential or simultaneous processing of cases. Some cases are processed in settings where a number of agencies and professions come together for dispositional reasons (simultaneous)—e.g., juvenile court, hospital psychiatric wards, etc. Other cases involve sequential processing, where the case is referred along a chain of agencies, where each in turn provides some input which shapes and directs case passage. Any case may involve both sequential and simultaneous agency contacts. An example would be the disruptive high school student. The case begins sequentially when school authorities refer the student to the police and the police refer the student to the juvenile court. Once in court, many of these agencies, plus some additional ones such as the probation department, may simultaneously seek a disposition. The juvenile court becomes a pivotal agency where conflicting diagnoses and dispositions are worked out. While agencies are seldom pure types, the distinction has some meaning when the topic is inter-agency conflict and its resolution.

Given these analytic distinctions as to types of control agencies, we now move to the major task of this chapter, which is to delineate the major sources of inter-agency conflict, to suggest how conflict is reduced, and to assess the resultant impact on case disposition. We also examine the possibility of the formation of inter-agency processing stereotypes and the impact this stereotyping may have on the organizational embellishment of deviant roles. We are continuing a task begun in the last chapter: to elucidate factors affecting case disposition which stem from organizational-structural variables—i.e., factors unrelated to the particular deviant act in question and the accused deviant actor. This is one sense in which social-control agencies create deviance. The limited input which the accused may have in all this and the resultant sense of injustice which may evolve will be examined in the following chapters.

Inter-Occupational Conflict in Social-Control Agencies

While there are many reasons for friction between various social-control agencies, a major source of conflict is occupational territoriality. One need not go to the extremes proposed by writers such as Robert Ardrey in *The Territorial Imperative* to find relevance for human behavior in the concept of territory. It is one thing to maintain that territorial pursuit and defense serves as a baseline for most or all social activity and quite another to argue simply that some social behaviors and outcomes may be better understood with reference to territorial contests. We suggest only the latter. We are also less concerned with physical space (although that may have some bearing on the issue of deviance imputation[3]) than with what we refer to as "occupational territory."

Any occupation is identifiable *as* that occupation because it is thought to include workers skilled in the performance of some particular set of tasks. Thus, we have no trouble recognizing that plumbers do something different than ministers do, who do something different than anthropologists do, who do something different than bartenders do, etc. In most work situations, each occupational group possesses a special skill that is not shared by any other occupation, and when a number of occupations come together within the same organization, the structure and process of the organization reflects these discrete skill areas. Such is the case in the typical production organization. At General Motors, an assembly-line worker, a research scientist, and a personnel director could not swap jobs with one another and expect any one of the three jobs to be performed effectively. For that matter, two assembly-line workers in two different parts of the plant may be trained to perform two quite different tasks. This system works satisfactorily because there is no obvious need for most of the specialized functions to overlap and reflect one another. In fact, production efficiency may reach its peak precisely when such discrete role separation approaches a maximum level. Accordingly, training and employment practices have come to support and perpetuate occupational specialization.

The range of skills and appropriate tasks attributed to a given occupation by its own members and/or by others can be referred to

as that occupation's territory. In a manner analogous to that in which
man (or animal) defends his personal physical space from attack by
others, the members of any occupational group seek to protect their
occupational territory from infringement.[4] If our hypothetical GM
research scientist, for example, were to begin expressing a desire to
involve himself in personnel decisions, the personnel director could
be expected to set up some resistance to such a move. We are not,
however, directly concerned with the territoriality and territorial
conflict involved in the production of automobiles. As long as each
worker does his prescribed duties well, the customer can anticipate
the manufacture of a quality product. What happens to the car along
the way should be unaffected by any territorial squabbles that may
happen to occur. The car cannot react. Its course on the assembly
line and into the marketplace remains much the same regardless of
territorial disagreements. The same *cannot* be said of the human
products that are dealt with in social processing agencies. For that
reason, occupational territory in such settings takes on an extra dimension and an extra importance. Organizations that deal with human beings as their "products" cannot compartmentalize their
attention to the product *without consequences for the nature of that
product.* A new automobile is unaffected by the fact that it has passed
through a variety of independent, specialized hands; a prospective
patient, criminal, student, or welfare recipient *is* affected. The individual remains a single, homogeneous entity despite any and all
efforts to fragment him into parts.

Largely as a result of this integral, continuous nature of the client,
the various specialists who staff social processing organizations may
have difficulty in establishing where A's role ends and B's begins. This
is in part because assembly-line, sequential handling may not apply.
A and B may direct their respective efforts toward the individual
relatively concurrently. The *continuing* activities of doctor, nurse,
social worker, occupational therapist, etc.—all in behalf of a single
patient—represent one case in point. It is in these simultaneous,
multiprofessional interventions where conflict over occupational territory is most visible. This is not to say that territorial conflicts do not
arise in sequential processing, but it is less visible; and, to the extent
that agencies are not mutually interdependent, it may be of little
consequence. Conflict in sequential processing is likely to occur at
transfer points, points of case passage from one agency to another;
conflict may also be manifest in a refusal to send (or accept) cases. We
will turn to conflict resolution in sequential processing later in this
chapter. For the moment, however, we are particularly concerned
with an agency in which *overlap of job function and perceived expertise* is built into the organization.

For simultaneous processing, hospital settings provide an excellent example of rampant territorial expansion, impingement, and defense. The various professions operating in a hospital must negotiate "who gets to do what" (Strauss, *et al.,* 1964). In hospitals, such negotiations are influenced, first, by a growing ideology of "holistic care" which supplements the naturally occurring overlap of interest and function (that of "providing care and treatment") by fostering increased intrastaff communication and decision making. The extreme case is that of the purportedly egalitarian "health care team." Second, changing definitions of occupational boundary lines include challenges to preexisting territorial claims. Most of these challenges (but not all) apply to occupational "ground" traditionally held by the physician. Nursing, for example, seeks to alter and improve its professional image by taking on functions of planning, coordination, and general supervision. Pharmacy, faced with the prospect of its own displacement by the drug manufacturing industry, talks of new professional involvements. One proposal is that the pharmacist become a member of the hospital's health team, utilizing his special pharmaceutical expertise to advise and monitor drug regimens and perhaps even to prescribe medications. Psychiatry "intrudes" upon general medicine (via a body of theory and findings concerning psychosomatic medicine) with the suggestion that every patient can benefit from a broadened perspective that includes psychiatric considerations. In turn, psychologist and social worker argue that their training equips them for the practice of psychotherapy (see Zander, Cohen, and Stotland, 1957). In each case, one party's occupational territory is variously threatened by another party which proposes to take over familiar tasks and *which would perform those tasks in different ways consistent with occupationally discrete training, experience, and emphases.*

From studies in a general hospital setting, Tiedeman (1969) has reported several varieties of territorial negotiation. When psychiatric residents are assigned as consultants to medical and surgical wards without an invitation from the ward physicians and with supervisory instructions to make themselves full members of the ward medical team, we have all the necessary ingredients for territorial conflict. Most ward physicians (specialists in internal medicine or surgery) are reluctant to share their prerogatives with someone they regard as an intruder. Most of the psychiatric residents, at the same time, adhere to the notion that a psychiatric perspective can benefit almost any medical-surgical case and can be crucial to some. Since the ward physician is the more powerful of the two parties in any resultant processes of negotiation, the psychiatrist must develop and apply various strategies and tactics if he hopes to make any territorial inroads.[5] Notice that two levels of negotiation may be involved in the processing of deviants. First, there is negotiation between the deviant or patient and the processors, and second, there is negotiation between various control agents as to category placement and disposition.

The significance of the psychiatric consultation example is that the interpretation applied to a given patient, the diagnostic label attached, and the treatment administered can vary significantly as a function of the psychiatrist-internist territorial exchange. Theoretically, the same patient could be regarded as having a purely organic problem at one extreme or a purely psychiatric problem at the other, with various psychosomatic interpretations lying between the two extremes. What happens to and around the patient can (and usually does) vary drastically as a result. Thus, the type of deviance "created" depends in one sense on the winner of these occupational conflicts[6] (Strauss, et al., 1964; Scott, 1970).

In addition to problems arising from professional territoriality and occupational encroachment, conflict between agencies is predicted if the agencies are divergent in their client concerns. "We would expect that a similarity in laterality or longitudinality would be likely to enhance formal collaboration while contrasting types would be inhibited in collaboration, and even experience open conflict" (Lefton and Rosengren, 1966:809–810). This would, of course, be only one of many reasons for inter-agency conflict. Stoll (1968) suggests that agencies differ in attitudes about free will versus determinism which affect their reactive stance toward deviance, with the former demanding punishment and the latter promoting disinterested rehabilitation. An example would be the conflicting demands of the police and probation officers before a juvenile court judge. Variations in operating philosophies have been cited as one reason for the failure of community delinquency prevention programs (Miller, et al., 1968). Walter Miller, in discussing conflict between concerned community agencies concludes that

> the major impediment to effectiveness in this field relates more to the nature of relations among the various concerned institutions than to a lack of knowledge as to effective procedure. Much is now known about the causes of delinquency and promising ameliorative techniques have been developed. The principal difficulty lies in the *application* of these techniques. . . .[7] (Miller, 1958:23)

Variations in training and operational philosophies foster a professional ethnocentrism which affects each professional's view of individuals working in other agencies. Studies of inter-agency esteem ratings show these ratings split along punishment-rehabilitation lines. One study found that policemen held social workers in low esteem, and social workers, in turn, held prosecuting attorneys, court officials, and the police in low regard (Haurek and Clark, 1967:54, 59). Miller also found antagonism and open hostility between social workers in a delinquency prevention project and neighborhood police (Miller, *et al.*, 1968:93–94). Another delinquency study found police and court psychiatrists holding very opposite views on delinquency causation and treatment, generating conflict (Wheeler, *et al.*, 1968:41–45).

With conflict between agencies being generated from so many sources, it is somewhat surprising that any work gets done. The conflict is overcome in large part by the inter-dependency of organizations in the processing of cases. To the extent that their operational domains overlap, we would expect greater pressure for cooperation[8] between two agencies (Thompson, 1970). Organizational demands for efficiency, as described in a previous chapter, bring about the necessity for coordination in the production of cases, which sets the stage for the development of rather complex exchange processes between control agencies. Coordination is often an uneasy peace maintained by each agency's control over resources required for efficient operation by other agencies. Let us turn to a specific example to show how exchange relationships develop in the inter-agency processing of cases.

Exchange Relationships in Juvenile Court: An Example

Problems of coordination and exchange are evident in the juvenile court, which is a lateral agency concerned with many aspects of the individual's life and character, plus the specific actions which may have led to a particular arrest. Rosengren (1970:124) sums up the major problem faced by lateral institutions such as the juvenile court:

> A broad lateral orientation normally means that the organization draws support from many different groups in the community. This is potentially a divisive pattern because it leads to competitive processes among supporters, with the organization itself as the target for manipulation and control.

Support for this assertion is found in a study of a large metropolitan juvenile court by Robert Emerson (1969). He documents the importance of the exchange process between the juvenile court and other agencies on which the court relies for its cases. The court, historically charged with a concern for the social space (laterality) of juveniles, consequently stresses many extra-legal factors in the disposition of cases (Platt, 1969). Since the range of possible information which may have a bearing on moral character is so large, the court must entertain the suggestions of many community agencies. The potential for conflict is great and it is incumbent upon the juvenile court judge to provide conflict resolution so that cases can be quickly and efficiently processed (Matza, 1964). The image Emerson builds is one of a juvenile court judge who is more or less an arbitrator of cases, coordinating and placating the demands of other agencies which have an input to the proceedings. The judge, in the process of negotiation and placation of vested-interest groups, loses much of his assumed independence.

Agency-court relations can be divided into roughly two areas based on traditional orientations to cases: enforcement and treatment. Enforcement agencies which have entry to the court include the police, the prosecutor's office, probation officers, and—to a lesser extent—schools and welfare agencies which can act as direct referral agencies to the court. The exchange process between the court and enforcement agencies can be seen in the case of the police. The conflicts which evolve between these two agencies are due in large part to the problem of the "visibility of errors" (Wheeler, *et al.*, 1968). The police feel the courts are too lenient, while the court sees the police as overly punitive; each agency sees only half of the picture:

> The police, having selected the worse [cases] to refer to court, feel that the court should validate their selection process. But the court, not being exposed to the better cases that police did not refer to them, must find their better risks from among those that come before them, and indeed commit only a small proportion of all the cases they see to correctional agencies. . . . Thus the police can make only one type of error [from the judge's standpoint], that of referring a boy to court who the judge feels should not be there. (Wheeler, *et al.*, 1968:50)

The police fail to realize that the court does not see or review informal dispositions by police officers, and the court is often not aware of the extent of police adjudication. An exception occurs when very serious cases come to the attention of the court where records show a long history of informal disposition by police. These exceptions contribute to the conflict.

This natural conflict between the court and enforcement agencies is resolved through an exchange of services. Each agency controls certain resources or rewards; and, through negotiation, a reciprocal agreement evolves which facilitates "getting the work done." Police hold power over the juvenile court through refusal to bring cases to court, or by increasing automatic referrals such that court calenders are flooded with inappropriate cases. The police are also an important link between the juvenile court and the community (Emerson, 1969:45–46). In addition, police provide needed services to the court such as special investigations in child neglect cases.

The court holds power over the police in dispositions of cases and has the right to oversee and control police activities. The court also has the power to support the legitimacy and authority of police actions and the personal integrity of the individual police officers who appear before the court (Emerson, 1969:51). With these aspects more or less explicit in the inter-agency relationships, exchanges are made[9] and standardized expectations arise which reduce conflict and facilitate coordination of effort.

The court's interaction with the second type of agency—treatment resources—is much more discretionary and negotiated in nature than are the largely unavoidable contacts with enforcement agencies (Emerson, 1969:57). Emerson found that court transactions with the child welfare department were relatively explicit and formalized. The court relied on the welfare department for help in the placement of delinquents in foster homes. The welfare department relied on the court for assistance in three areas: in emergency cases requiring immediate court action, in cases where sanctions of the court (or threat of sanctions) might resolve a family problem, and in difficult cases originally referred to the welfare department where the court could serve as a dumping ground (1969:59–72).

In contrast to relations with the welfare department, the court has a strained relationship with a Children's Mental Hospital which supposedly serves the court and the community. The conflict in the relationship is perpetuated because the juvenile court had nothing to offer the hospital in exchange for the use of psychiatric referral acceptance. Thus, the hospital could refuse to accept cases sent from the court, and the court had little recourse in the matter. Here, in spite of ideological agreement (both agencies professed a concern with rehabilitation), the lack of control over crucial hospital resources by the court meant that contacts were strained and case referrals difficult.

Territorial Conflict,
Exchange and the
Labeling Process

Professional territorial conflict has implications for processing stereotypes of cases, and thus, indirectly, will affect the labeling process,
which in turn has consequences for the acceptance or rejection of the
proffered label. We would expect the following, stated in the form
of hypotheses:
1. The greater the territorial conflict between professions in social-
   control agencies, the less likely it is that processing stereotypes
   will form in the disposition of cases.
2. The greater the territorial conflict, the lower the permanency of
   the category placement—i.e., the less likely it is that a diagnostic
   category or label will be locked in.
3. The greater the territorial conflict, the more likely it is that the
   accused deviant will resist the category placement—i.e., that the
   deviant will reject the label and corresponding deviant role.[10]
When territorial conflict between agencies (or ideological conflicts
within the same profession[11]) are overt, we expect variations in diagnosis, prognosis, and recommended treatment or punishment. These
differences may mean that very different details or aspects of a case
are selected for emphasis by the contending professions. Consequently, more of the unique aspects of the case or situation are
maintained, decreasing the probability of process stereotyping. Also,
to the degree that these conflicts produce high staff turnover, we
would expect less uniformity in case categorization and disposition
(e.g., Wolkon, *et al.*, 1971:353). This disagreement should make it
easier for the accused to resist the attributed deviant labels. If a
united front is absent, then the probability decreases that the confusion and suggestibility which occur during processing will produce
a self-concept change. Since there is not a uniform stimulus across
agencies, the deviant's definition of the situation is more easily maintained.

Also, without such a united front, the supporters of the deviant—
who may play a crucial role in getting the accused to accept the
proffered role—may be more likely to continue to deny or normalize
the rule violations in question. Their reasoning might be: "if these
experts can't agree on Bill's problem, maybe he doesn't have one."
Thus, without processing stereotypes and the resultant united front,
agency cooptation of supporters is more difficult.

We would expect, however, that the same pressures for efficiency in case disposition found within an agency (see Chapter VII) would also be found in multiagency settings. Indeed, the demand for efficiency may be greater, in that the interorganizational processing may generate rewards for effective disposition above and beyond rewards extant within each agency or profession. Scheff (1966) gives an example of multiagency processing in his observations of commitment hearings in a midwestern state. He found that psychiatrists on a commitment panel, as well as the lawyers who were appointed as guardians for those whose sanity was being determined, were both paid a flat fee per case. This form of remuneration increased the pressures to maximize case volume. As a result, there was virtually an automatic recommendation for hospitalization: 196 of 196 cases observed resulted in commitment! If either the psychiatrist or the lawyer "wished to recommend discharge, they would have to interrupt an on-going process, take the responsibility for such interruption, and build a case for discharge. Building such a case would have required considerably more time, thus severely reducing their rate of pay" (Scheff, 1966:137). Given these structural reinforcement contingencies, it is likely that processing stereotypes will flourish and facilitate (as in one court observed) hearings lasting an average of 1.6 minutes (Scheff, 1966:135). Similar organizational factors may account for the brevity of juvenile court hearings—three minutes per case in a 1959 study of Los Angeles courts (Lemert, 1967:94).

This is but one example of pressures for speed and efficiency influencing case disposition in a multiagency setting. We propose that such organizational pressures lead to negotiation and exchange processes which overcome territorial and definitional boundary disputes.[12] These negotiations themselves may be time consuming, so standardized procedures evolve to stabilize the referral and disposition process (given some interdependence and mutual need for exchange commodities between agencies). Processing stereotypes serve this standardization and facilitative function.

We see, in addition, that the form which process stereotyping will take depends on an expansion of a distinction made earlier between simultaneous and sequential processing. Following Litwak (1970), organizations which can function without prior or subsequent subject contact with other agencies can be referred to as autonomous organizations; they are conceptually distinct from interdependent organizations. Thus, interdependent organizations fit together to constitute "sequential systems," while any relationships between autonomous organizations comprise "homogeneous systems." To the extent that hospitals operate as autonomous organizations, this is

perhaps not so much due to any strictly logical artifact of their subject matter (illness) as to their obvious success at *creating* autonomy
for themselves. Freidson (1970) suggests the latter probability in his
analysis of the role of "dominant professions" (versus the role of
bureaucracy *per se*) in the construction of organizational boundaries.
He argues that physicians dominate the field of health so completely
as to be able to define, delimit, and direct most matters of organizational health care, despite the existence of clearly relevant services
and agencies outside of the medical division of labor. He then suggests that "serious problems of access to relevant care and of the
rational coordination of care are created by the barriers which the
profession creates between that segment of the division of labor it
does dominate, and that segment it does not" (Freidson, 1970:87).
Documentation for this claim lies in the marked failure of health care
agents and organizations to reciprocate referrals that come to them
from nonmedical sources—e.g., clergymen, social workers (Piedmont, 1968; Wolkon and Melzer, 1968). As we saw in the juvenile
court–children's hospital interaction outlined above, sequential, interdependent organizations have difficulty in working with autonomous organizations.

Processing stereotypes aid in this manufactured autonomy. For
example, a social worker employed by a local mental health clinic
recently complained to one of the authors that coordination was
entirely lacking between the clinic and other community agencies,
particularly those focusing on drug and alcohol problems. Any clinic
patient with drug or alcohol problems quickly came to be defined as
a "mental health case" and nothing else, purely as a function of the
perspectives of the clinic and its resultant processing stereotypes. A
subject with the identical characteristics and problems, but who
comes to the alcohol-related agency or the drug agency first, is defined in keeping with that agency's particular competence. Thus,
"the very particularism of an agency can also lead to its gaining a
virtual monopoly over dealings with people who fit its definition"
(Freidson, 1966:84). To the neutral observer, it may seem that any
two of these agencies, or all three, should be involved in the case,
with each contributing its own specialized abilities. However, the
disuse of available and potentially helpful client services that follows
from medical boundary building means that the patient becomes the
unknowing victim of a sort of professional imperialism.

It is important to recognize that organizational monopoly and
stereotyping in the above example were possible because each
agency had the initial "license" to define the case in its own terms.
The subject could be seen as either a drug problem, or an alcohol

problem, or a mental illness problem. This license is maintained because the autonomous organization may abstain from inter-agency relationships, or may fail to reciprocate interactions directed toward it from other agencies. Over time, they develop more control of intake. When this occurs, the autonomous agency is free to use process stereotypes to the extent permitted by its subject matter and its own internal structure. In short, in autonomous organizations, processing outcomes are likely to be unchallenged, which guarantees the perpetuation of an outcome uninfluenced and unchanged by subsequent processing in other agencies.

We propose that an agency's position in the sequential chain will influence its power in terms of definition and process stereotyping of cases. Our initial suggestion is that agencies which are first and last in the sequence will have stereotyping possibilities exceeding those of mid-range agencies. The advantages of the initiating end of the scale include a definitional access to the problem and a pre-setting function as to the nature of the problem, suggested diagnosis, prognosis, and the referral path which a case will be sent through. Given the initiating agency's rendering of the accused and the case, it has some assurance that its initial placement decision will be accepted and utilized by the next agency in line. While the second agency in the chain may revise the characterization to some degree, it is not likely to alter the image drastically, or to reverse it, for three reasons. First, most ordered sequences exist to begin with because they permit step-by-step progression through a cohesive whole based on common perceptions and interests. Mutually hostile or irrelevant agencies have little basis for relating to one another, especially in a formal sequence, so such sequences facilitate orderly operation. Second, each agency in a sequence has a specialized function in the sequence that builds upon what the prior agency has already completed. This may grow out of demand for coordination. Standard forms are often developed to facilitate inter-agency transfer of cases. Since these forms are one source of processing stereotypes, and since they are not likely to be challenged or altered by the accepting agency, the case classification usually stands. Thus, extension and expansion of typifications applied by prior agencies is to be expected, while drastic revision is not. This constitutes an interorganizational funneling effect and indicates that sequential inter-agency relationships strengthen, solidify, and perpetuate processing stereotypes, if territorial conflicts have been resolved or set aside. Thirdly, the initiating agency may be influenced by the second agency in line and thereby change their acceptance of cases accordingly. For example, police are reluctant to intervene in mental illness situations because they are afraid the hospital may not accept the suspect, thereby leaving them in a very difficult position (Bittner, 1967).

The processing advantages held by those agencies appearing last in a given sequence are implicit in the notion of autonomy discussed earlier. Final agencies, such as prisons, psychiatric hospitals or graduate schools, have an added element of freedom in terms of intensifying processing stereotypes, since they are not accountable to or dependent upon any other agency from the moment the subject is under their control. Whereas even the initiating agency (with all its pacesetting potential) must make some effort to substantiate its decision in anticipation of review by subsequent organizations, the terminating agency faces no such limitation. It is because of this combination of autonomy and sequential termination that two particular agencies—mental hospitals and prisons—exercise the greatest power over the deviant's identity and future opportunity structure. The ironic situation produced here is that agencies which eventually may release the deviant into society are the most powerful and unlimited in their stereotyping and disposition of cases. This contributes to the deviant's problems of reentry into the conventional society. In the remaining chapters we examine evidence on other problems which agency contact produces for the person being processed, as well as possible solutions available to the officially labeled deviant.

Notes

1. The distinction between voluntary and involuntary is difficult to delineate empirically, however. Thus, we find many individuals who are encouraged to "volunteer" for agency treatment by threat of unilateral force—e.g., addicts caught committing crimes are often given the option of "volunteering" for a drug treatment program in lieu of a jail sentence. Homosexuals are often forced into "voluntary" aversive therapy programs designed to create well-adjusted heterosexuals. Juvenile delinquents are occasionally given the option of joining one of the armed services in place of a stay in a state correctional facility. If the service-control dichotomy is faithfully applied, then public schools would be classified as control agencies, given compulsory school attendance laws, but would become service agencies in higher grades as students pass the mandatory age. To avoid such confusion, we prefer to use the terms "social-control agency" or "people-processing agency" to stand for both service and control, since we feel any agency processing people may provide both functions. We prefer to leave the question of auspices of entrance an empirical, rather than a definitional, one. For a general discussion of voluntary service agencies in American society, see Gersuny and Rosengren (1973).

2. Another scheme found in the organizational literature involves dividing agencies into "people-processing" agencies and "people-changing" agencies. The former refers to organizations which "shape a person's life by controlling his access to a wide range of social settings through the public status they confer" (Hasenfeld, 1972:256). Examples would include employment agencies, college admissions offices, credit bureaus, and diagnostic clinics. "People-changing" organizations would be mental hospitals and prisons, where behavioral change is an explicit goal. We do not see this distinction as empirically useful for two reasons. First, any social-control organization may involve elements of both—i.e., these are perhaps better seen as two functions which any agency provides rather than types of organizations, as Hasenfeld readily admits (1972:256). Second, many people-processing agencies which change status also change people—e.g., an agency which passes on a credit rating may change that consumer's behavior; or, as in some cases where the agency does not actually change status, such as the person acquitted of a crime, the agency contact may affect future behavior options. Conversely, many so-called people-changing agencies simply do not serve that function, leaving the distinction artificial at best and misleading at worst.

3. See Stanford M. Lyman and Marvin B. Scott, "Territoriality: A Neglected Sociological Dimension" (1967).

4. Protection of organizational territory and functions is provided by unions, professional associations, and societies. One example is the active role police benevolence societies and associations have taken in opposing civilian review boards, the establishment of ombudsmen systems and even police-community relations units. These are seen as threats to the autonomy of the police officer and are rejected. As other police functions are threatened, as they are now to some extent by the

rising number of private police agencies, we would expect organized opposition to result.

5. See Rushing, (1962; 1964) for similarities to the "deference behavior" exhibited by nurses in their interactions with physicians.

6. Parenthetically, the inter-agent negotiations may produce temporary role reversals. In one case observed by Tiedeman, an internist argued for a psychiatric diagnosis while the psychiatric consultant insisted upon a totally organic explanation of a patient's chronic stomach pain. We might hypothesize that the role reversal may be due, in some cases, to a recognition that knowledge of the profession involved does not cover the case, thus a desire to attribute the problem to variables outside the purview of the agent's field.

7. While we agree with Miller's major point, we do not share his optimism about etiological studies of delinquency and effective prevention. In short, if inter-agency conflict could be eliminated, programs would probably not increase drastically, or even moderately, in effectiveness. For one such attempt to apply etiological theories of delinquency to a community delinquency treatment program, see Empey and Lubeck, 1970.

8. Similarity of goals and organizational philosophies does not always guarantee cooperative relationships, since these organizations may be involved in competition over domain, as well as monetary resources to support their work (see Hasenfeld, 1971).

9. However, these negotiations and exchanges may not be evident if cases are separately analyzed. Emerson (1969:32) cautions that "to focus attention on the individual case and the negotiation processes surrounding it would lose sight of the overall patterns of negotiations in which the individual case is the basic unit. For the court is able to bargain for a certain service or advantage from an institution on behalf of one case and repay its obligation in its handling of a completely different one." Consequently, a separate case analysis approach may miss the intricacies of the exchange process. Also, the exchange may involve resources other than clients and cases—e.g., technical information, instruction for personnel, etc.—further complicating the analysis of negotiation (Levine and White, 1961). Participant observation of the type carried out by Emerson (1969), Cicourel (1968) and Matza (1964) may be the only way to tap these inter-organizational exchange patterns effectively.

10. We are ignoring for the moment the processed individual who does not resist, but rather seeks out a label. We would expect such individuals to be very "put out" with these disagreements since they delay and cloud his official labeling.

11. Conflicts over strategies of prevention and treatment exist, of course, within social-control professions. The medical profession, often considered the "prototype of professions" manifests considerable internal heterogeneity (Smith, 1958; Bucher and Strauss, 1961). Armor and Klerman (1968) review the contention that psychiatry includes three competing ideologies—somato-, psycho-, and socio-therapeutic—and confirm that the ideological differences are systematically related to psychiatric activities. In another profession, Epstein (1970) notes the absence of an integrated professional social work community. We have discussed the role which differences in professional socialization play in the labeling process within the same control bureaucracy in Chapter VII.

12. This hypothesis is based on scattered studies of the type cited in the previous paragraph, rather than on any definitive studies. These studies of inter-organizational processing stereotypes (images held in common about cases or deviants) and the mechanics of process stereotyping (applying typified images to unique cases) simply have not been done to date. Hopefully, this discussion will generate such comparative organizational research.

References

Ardrey, Robert
1966   *The Territorial Imperative.* New York: Atheneum.

Armor, David J., and Gerald L. Klerman
1968   "Psychiatric treatment orientations and professional ideology." *Journal of Health and Social Behavior* 9 (September):243–55.

Bittner, Egon
1967   "Police discretion in apprehending the mentally ill." *Social Problems* 14 (Winter):278–92.

Bucher, Rue, and Anselm Strauss
1961   "Professions in process." *American Journal of Sociology* 66 (January):325–34.

Cicourel, Aaron V.
1968   *The Social Organization of Juvenile Justice.* New York: John Wiley and Sons.

Emerson, Robert M.
1969   *Judging Delinquents: Context and Process in Juvenile Court.* Chicago: Aldine.

Empey, LaMar T., and Steven G. Lubeck
1970   *The Silverlake Experiment.* Lexington, Mass.: D.C. Heath.

Epstein, Irwin
1970   "Professionalization, professionalism, and social-worker radicalism." *Journal of Health and Social Behavior* 11 (March):67–77.

Freidson, Eliot
1966   "Disability as social deviance." In Marvin B. Sussman (ed.), *Sociology and Rehabilitation.* Washington, D.C.: American Sociological Association.

1970   "Dominant professions, bureaucracy, and client service." In William R. Rosengren and Mark Lefton (eds.), *Organizations and Clients.* Columbus, Ohio: Charles E. Merrill.

Gersuny, Carl, and William R. Rosengren
1973   *The Service Society.* Cambridge, Mass.: Schenkman.

Hasenfeld, Yeheskel
    1971   "Organizational dilemmas in innovating social services: the
            case of the community action centers." *Journal of Health and
            Social Behavior* 12 (September):208–216.
    1972   "People processing organizations: an exchange approach."
            American Sociological Review (June):256–63.
Haurek, Edward W., and John P. Clark
    1967   "Variants of integration of social control agencies." *Social
            Problems* 15 (Summer):46–60.
Lefton, Mark
    1970   "Client characteristics and structural outcomes." In William
            R. Rosengren and Mark Lefton (eds.), *Organizations and Cli-
            ents.* Columbus, Ohio: Charles E. Merrill.
Lefton, Mark, and William R. Rosengren
    1966   "Organizations and clients: lateral and longitudinal dimen-
            sions." *American Sociological Review* 31 (December):802–
            810.
Lemert, Edwin M.
    1967   "The juvenile court—quest and realities." In *Task Force Re-
            port: Juvenile Delinquency and Youth Crime.* Washington,
            D.C.: U.S. Government Printing Office.
Levine, Sol, and Paul E. White
    1961   "Exchange as a conceptual framework for the study of inter-
            organizational relationships." *Administrative Science Quar-
            terly* 5 (March):583–601.
Litwak, Eugene
    1970   "Toward the theory and practice of coordination between
            formal organizations." In William R. Rosengren and Mark
            Lefton (eds.), *Organizations and Clients.* Columbus, Ohio:
            Charles E. Merrill.
Lyman, Stanford M., and Marvin B. Scott
    1967   "Territoriality: a neglected sociological dimension." *Social
            Problems* 15 (Fall):236–48.
Matza, David
    1964   *Delinquency and Drift.* New York: John Wiley and Sons.
Miller, Walter B.
    1958   "Inter-institutional conflict as a major impediment to delin-
            quency prevention." *Human Organization* 17 (Fall):20–
            23.
Miller, Walter B., Rainer C. Baum, and Rosetta McNeil
    1968   "Delinquency prevention and organizational relations." In
            Stanton Wheeler (ed.), *Controlling Delinquents.* New York:
            John Wiley and Sons.
Piedmont, Eugene B.
    1968   "Referrals and reciprocity: psychiatrists, general practition-

ers, and clergymen." *Journal of Health and Social Behavior* 9 (March):29–41.

Platt, Anthony M.
1969   *The Child Savers.* Chicago: University of Chicago Press.

Rosengren, William R.
1970   "The careers of clients and organizations." In William R. Rosengren and Mark Lefton (eds.), *Organizations and Clients.* Columbus, Ohio: Charles E. Merrill.

Roth, Julius A.
1963   *Timetables: Structuring the Passage of Time in Hospital Treatment and Other Careers.* Indianapolis: Bobbs-Merrill.

Rushing, William A.
1962   "Social influence and the social-psychological function of deference: a study of psychiatric nursing." *Social Forces* 61 (December):142–48.

1964   *The Psychiatric Professions.* Chapel Hill, North Carolina: University of North Carolina Press.

Scheff, Thomas J.
1966   *Being Mentally Ill.* Chicago: Aldine.

Scott, Robert A.
1970   "The construction of conceptions of stigma by professional experts." In Jack D. Douglas (ed.), *Deviance and Respectability.* New York: Basic Books.

Smith, Harvey L.
1958   "Contingencies of professional differentiation." *The American Journal of Sociology* 63 (January):410–14.

Stoll, Clarice S.
1968   "Images of man and social control." *Social Forces* 47 (December):119–35.

Strauss, Anselm, Leonard Schatzman, Rue Bucher, Danuta Erlich, and Melvin Sabshin
1964   *Psychiatric Ideologies and Institutions.* New York: Free Press.

Thompson, James D.
1970   "Domains of organized action." In W. Richard Scott (ed.), *Social Processes and Social Structures.* New York: Holt, Rinehart, and Winston.

Tiedeman, Gary H.
1969   "Territoriality and collaboration in the health professions: an analysis of conflicting trends." Paper presented at annual meeting of the Pacific Sociological Association, Seattle, Washington.

Wheeler, Stanton, Edna Bonauch, M. Richard Cramer, and Irving K. Zola
1968   "Agents of delinquency control." In Stanton Wheeler (ed.), *Controlling Delinquents.* New York: John Wiley and Sons.

Wolkon, George H., and Arden E. Melzer
1968 "Disease or deviance: effects on the treatment continuum." In Mark Lefton, et al., (eds.), *Approaches to Deviance.* New York: Appleton-Century-Crofts.

Wolkon, George H., Daniel Lanier, Jr., and Sharon Moriwaki
1971 "Organizational functioning and care in a children's treatment center." *Journal of Health and Social Behavior* 12 (December):348–54.

Zander, Alvin, Arthur Cohen, and Ezra Stotland
1957 *Role Relations in the Mental Health Professions.* Ann Arbor, Michigan: Institute for Social Research, University of Michigan.

Chapter
IX

Reactions of the
Accused Deviant

*Walking into a gay bar is a momentous act in
the life history of a homosexual, because in
many cases it is the first time he publicly identifies himself as a homosexual. Of equal importance is the fact that it brings home to him the
realization that there are many other young
men like himself and, thus, that he is a member
of a community and not the isolate he had previously felt himself to be.*

Martin Hoffman

Introduction to
Labeling Effects

In delineating possible labeling effects, we must distinguish between
objective effects and *subjective effects*.[1] The former refers to objective consequences of informal or formal labeling—e.g., are people
denied job opportunities, are they reacted to differently by significant others, are they forced into deviant subcultures as a means of
attack or adjustment to the label, etc.? An example of a study dealing
with objective effects would be the Schwartz and Skolnick study
(1962) which assessed employment opportunities for those variously
labeled on the criminal charge of assault. Potential employers of an
unskilled labor position in hotel work were given one of four employment folders. Characteristics of applicants described in each folder
were identical except for experimental conditions of past labeling;
employee was described as (a) someone convicted and sentenced for
assault, (b) someone tried and acquitted on an assault charge, (c)
someone tried and acquitted but whose folder carried a letter from
the judge certifying the not guilty finding and reaffirming the legal
presumption of innocence, or (d) someone who had no mention
made of any criminal record. For each folder, twenty-five employers
were contacted; job offers were forthcoming in nine instances for "no
record" folders. This became the baseline of availability of hotel
employment. "Convicted" folders elicited only one job offer; the
accused-but-acquitted file produced three offers; and the letter-cer-
tified acquittal received six positive responses. The study indicates
that even innocent contact with criminal justice agencies may limit
objective job opportunities.

Source: Martin Hoffman, *The Gay World: Male Homosexuality and the Social Creation of Evil* (New York: Basic Books, 1968), p. 16.

Subjective effects "refer to the way in which the deviant thinks about himself and his situation, the way he now interprets the social world around him from the vantage point of his new [deviant] status" (Williams and Weinberg, 1971:11). An example, analogous to occupational opportunities, would be studies designed to assess the actor's *perception* of availability of legitimate opportunities. Such studies indicate that those with official police records are more likely to see legitimate opportunities closed than are individuals without official contacts (Short, *et al.*, 1965; Schwartz and Stryker, 1970).[2] This would seem a subjective response to objective outcomes—i.e., they realize that a criminal record makes achievement in conventional occupations more problematic. Williams and Weinberg propose the following subjective effects of labeling; actor will:

(a) be less self-accepting,
(b) be more likely to see self as abnormal or deviant,
(c) be more likely to see self as determined (mood of fatalism),
(d) develop an "uncommon knowledge of social structures," i.e., become more aware of interpretive aspects of social interaction due to need to pass or cover,
(e) feel more vulnerable in social interaction, due to possibility of "discovery,"
(f) assume less reciprocity of perspectives with normals, and
(g) develop a sense of injustice because of societal reactions. (1971:12–19)

In the following sections of this chapter, we shall try to document both objective and subjective effects of labeling. Extant labeling formulations assume *both* effects occur as seen in the concept of secondary deviance. However, if we assume for the moment that objective and subjective effects may be independent in some cases, the following possibilities arise:

Rule violation occurs and is known
Objective effects[3]

	Present	Absent
Present	Complete labeling	Imagined labeling
Subjective effects		
Absent	Naive optimism	Neutralized deviance

The minor diagonal is of greatest interest. In "naive optimism" the actor may fail to connect objective consequences such as jobs denied, friends lost, etc., with his rule violations. Or, if he does make the connection, he may engage in self-neutralization of effects so that self-evaluation and self-esteem are not affected. We would expect such rule violators would blame the system for their failures, such as problems in securing employment.[4] In the case of "imagined labeling," self-fulfilling consequences are likely. The person feels "potentially discreditable" and therefore does not act to secure a job or initiate a friendship with conventional others. Self-labeling leads to objective effects being self-imposed rather than being a result of audience exclusion or punishment. We now turn to the question of subjective consequences of labeling as it relates to questions of personal and social identity.

Personal and
Social Identity

We have been dealing with identity indirectly throughout this book, mainly with identity as imputed by audience to actor—socially constructed identity. We now turn explicitly to the topic and especially to the question: how does social identity affect personal identity, how we see ourselves?[5] It has been assumed that personal identity is changed in the labeling-reaction process and, furthermore, that this has implications for future rule breaking. There has been much confusion over what personal identity actually is, and consequently it is quite difficult to make sense of the various empirical attempts to relate identity to behavior. The following is designed to bring some clarity to the issue.

We shall speak of two components of personal identity:[6]

1. *Self-image:* how does the individual nominatively define himself? Does he conceive of himself as deviant or conventional?
2. *Self-esteem:* how does the individual *feel* about his total self as he sees it. Does he have positive or negative feelings of self-worth?

One may have positive self-esteem with either a self-image as deviant or conventional—i.e., self-image and self-esteem may vary independently.[7] However, deviance-related research on self-concept has generally *assumed* those with self-images as deviant would have corresponding negative feelings of self-esteem.

This assumption is clearest in the work of Walter Reckless and his associates—termed containment theory—where positive self-concept is seen as an insulator, an internal buffer against external forces pushing toward deviance; negative self-concept supposedly does not provide any internal containment; thus, when external bonds to society are weak, deviance would result. This framework assumed[8] that self-concept (negative or positive), which purportedly existed prior to the rule breaking, could be used to predict future rule violations and trouble with the law. In addition to mixing the dimensions of self-image and self-esteem, Reckless generally used very dubious, and at times completely erroneous, measures of self-concept, as when he used teachers' ratings of delinquency potential.[9] The theorizing of Reckless is the opposite of that proposed by labeling theorists. For Scheff, Lemert, and others, self-concept was affected by involvement in rule breaking and reactions to public labeling. Until the confusion over what is meant by self-concept (self-image or self-esteem) is removed, this disagreement over direction of effect cannot be resolved. To help clarify this problem, we examine in some detail one study which treated both aspects of what we term "personal identity."

The following study by Gary Jensen (1972) is treated at some length because it is one of the few empirical works which assesses both self-image and self-esteem for the same population. It involves a large sample of both white and black male adolescents who, in addition to identity items, provided self-reported information on the number of delinquent acts committed in the past year and the number of police contacts during that period. Official police records were obtained, so that an independent measure of police contact was available. We begin with a description of the findings on the effect of official police contacts (from police records) upon self-image— seeing self as delinquent. For white males, those who sometimes, often, or always saw themselves as delinquent were more likely to have experienced police contact during the past three years: of those with no official record, 37 percent saw themselves as delinquent; 56 percent of those with one contact, and 73 percent of those with two or more contacts saw themselves as delinquent (Jensen, 1972:90, Table 1).[10] However for black males, the extent of police contact did not greatly affect self-image as deviant; corresponding percentages were 36, 47, and 48. Regardless of the social class of black adolescents, "[c]onfrontation with a predominately white authority structure appears to be of lesser consequence for delinquent self-conceptions of blacks than whites" (Jensen, 1972:90). For whites, there was a social-class effect, such that lower-status whites were significantly more likely to see themselves as delinquent than were upper-status whites; Jensen concludes that "both upper-status white adolescents and black adolescents in general may find themselves in contexts where others neutralize or reject the label" (p. 93).

There are a number of possible explanations for the lack of effect of official records on the self-image of blacks. First, blacks may not internalize middle-class values, hence the label has less meaning, and therefore self-images are not greatly affected.[11] Second, there may be an expectation among blacks that their children will experience police contacts,[12] which then defuses the effects of the label on self-image. Gould (1969b:335) proposed that for urban black youth, "being labeled as a deviant or troublemaker is so common that it must become of little personal relevance." The fact that blacks at all age and social-class levels tend to have more negative attitudes toward the police than whites (Smith and Hawkins, 1973) means that a brush with the law may not influence self-images; the impact of evaluations of self by lower-class whites, generally more accepting of police, may be greater in terms of conceptions of delinquency, given official contact. Some have suggested that deviance may be an outgrowth of lower-class cultural expectations, and involvement in delinquent activities, as well as some trouble with the law, may be prestige-conferring (see Miller, 1958).[13] Given this greater cultural tolerance and even support for delinquent activities, it would be argued that self-definitions as deviant may not occur.[14] These various factors simply suggest the importance of the "backdrop" against which the label is applied.

Now for the second dimension of personal identity: feelings of self-worth, what we have termed self-esteem. How does the actor feel about himself—regardless of his self-classification as deviant or conventional? In other words, is there an effect upon self-esteem ratings for those with official records such that feelings of self-worth are lower? Jensen did not find any strong relationship between level of self-esteem and agency contact for either blacks or whites. When social class was controlled, he found that blacks had a positive relation of esteem to official record, but effect was negative for higher social classes (1972:95). Thus, for blacks, getting into trouble with the law may *enhance* self-esteem for those of lower status—consistent with Walter Miller's prediction. However, for middle- and upper-class black youths, "delinquency has greater negative consequences for feelings of personal worth" (p. 95). For upwardly mobile blacks, the delinquency of a family member may be particularly costly since they are trying to overcome racial stereotypes and appear respectable. Hence, delinquency and official contact seems to produce greater feelings of negative esteem for those with the highest status and stakes in conformity. When coupled with strong attachment to others, self-esteem is even more strongly affected by official contact. When conventional others are likely to react, there appears to be a greater effect of police contact on self-worth (Jensen, 1970:10); and we would expect these individuals would be more likely to reform given agency contact.

For whites in Jensen's research, self-esteem was not affected by official contact; however, a class effect was evident: as with blacks, those with higher social status were more likely to experience low self-esteem if they had a delinquency record (p. 95). The general lack of effect upon feelings of self-worth has been found in other studies of delinquents. Schwartz and Stryker (1970:77-78) found no difference in esteem ratings for those informally labeled as good and bad risks by teachers.[15] Research on homosexuals indicates they do not have low self-esteem (Weinberg, 1970; Hammersmith and Weinberg, 1973).[16] Studies have indicated that self-esteem for "normal" blacks and whites does not vary significantly, Goffman's comments on tribal stigma notwithstanding (see Rosenberg, 1965; Hartnagel, 1970; Heiss and Owens, 1972; and Yancey, et al., 1972).

What appears in the Jensen study (and others) is that self-esteem is not greatly affected by official processing. There appears to be little evidence for the labeling assertion that holding a self-image as a deviant leads to low self-esteem. Jensen found a weak correlation between self-image and self-esteem, supporting an earlier conjecture that "a delinquent self-concept is not necessarily a negative self-concept" (Tangri and Schwartz, 1967:187 in Jensen, 1972:94). While we have dealt only with Jensen's study and do not wish to generalize too far from it, we see it (and other supplemental studies cited) as suggestive of self-image and self-esteem aspects of personal identity. We see that, in the case of delinquency, labeling does not have the predicted effect upon personal identity. How can this nonsupportive finding be accounted for?

A number of rival hypotheses might be suggested. First, high tolerance may preclude a strong reaction to delinquency by society. If so, trouble with the law may not produce great effects on self-worth—which is in part a reflection of others' attitudes toward the actor (Matza and Sykes, 1961; Fisher, 1972). However, the finding of high self-esteem scores among other more stigmatized deviants—e.g., homosexuals—could not be accounted for in this manner. A second possibility is that persons cannot tolerate low self-esteem for any length of time, and thus develop a sense of worth regardless of their engagement in rule violations. Cognitive dissonance theory would suggest that individuals in less than ideal objective situations may find positive aspects. This hypothesis would predict little variation in self-esteem scores between groups, implying that when negative feelings of self-worth are discovered, they are temporary.[17]

A third, and closely related explanation, is that the person may become committed to a deviant identity, which then becomes a source of positive self-worth. This may be a commitment out of drift, where the person slowly moves into a deviant career and unperceivably adjusts and takes on a deviant identity (Davis, 1971). Or the person may be converted by a deviant subculture which is sought out because of feelings of inadequacy or failure (Lofland and Stark, 1965).[18] The development of very positive views of self-worth may be a way of adjusting to the objective consequences of labeling. Thus, prostitutes see themselves as having high self-esteem, but rate other women and men below them (Bryan, 1966).

A study of black and white gang and non-gang boys in Chicago found that gang members rate themselves somewhat lower than non-gang boys, but when measures of ideal-self and real-self rating were compared, there was no difference in the gap between them. The gang boys, then, seem to have adjusted downward their self-expectations due to delinquency reputation, but if their self-esteem was negatively affected, we would expect a greater gap between ideal and real self-ratings than would be the case for nondelinquents. This was not the case (Short and Strodtbeck, 1965:60).

Another possibility, for which there is some evidence, is that the effect of labeling on self-esteem is curvilinear. Self-esteem may be low upon initial labeling and during a change in self-image from conventional to deviant. Over time, however, as a commitment to the deviant role develops, feelings of self-worth may be reinstated. Schwartz and Stryker (1970:23–27) found that self-esteem was lower for younger boys rated as bad risks; for older bad risks, self-esteem was no different than comparable "good boy" groups. They also propose that time in the role may be related to the stability or certainty of self-esteem. Studies of homosexuals indicate a similar pattern such that older, more committed homosexuals had more stable self-conceptions (Weinberg, 1970; Hammersmith and Weinberg, 1973). Thus, the movement into the deviant role settles the identity problem, provides for more certainty of self-conceptions, and permits more positive feelings of self-worth. This is related to what labeling theory predicts as the consequence of official reaction. The accused who is stigmatized receives mixed reviews from others: some see him as deviant, others neutralize or deny the rule breaking or its implications. When responses from others are mixed or ambiguous, we expect a more negative self-esteem. Low self-esteem also makes the actor more susceptible to outside influences; he is more likely to seek social support and acceptance by others (the social identity becomes very important at this point).[19] Also, the person with temporary feelings of low self-esteem is less confident in personal opinions and, hence, more open to social influence (Gergen, 1971:65–80). Since the mixed reviews are likely to be mainly negative from conventional others, the deviant identity may become a realistic alternative. We would expect change in self-image from conventional to deviant, followed closely by building up of self-esteem after an initial sense of "worthlessness." These dynamic processes are difficult to document in the survey methodology of Jensen and other studies cited here. However, participant observation of individuals being labeled and their adjustments would be able to test this hypothesized relationship.

With the concept of "personal identity," we begin to see the active part which the accused may play in the labeling drama. Such an activation of the heretofore passive recipient of societal labels leads us to another topic, that of label-seeking as a form of adjustment to the problems—both subjective and objective—precipitated by official labeling.

Identity Through Deviance:
The Label Seekers

One of the implicit assumptions of labeling formulations is that the transgressors have internalized the conventional values held by normals. Without this assumption, there is nothing to explain! It is assumed the deviant wants to return to conventional ways, thus the deviant labels are stigmatic for him. He supposedly feels guilt and shame, and tries to cover or pass as normal.[20] If this internalization is absent, there should be few subjective labeling effects, and while objective labeling consequences may occur, there should be fewer problems of adjustment and little need to use deviance for attack or defense, drastically reducing secondary deviance aspects.[21] While we do not wish to ignore or detract from the very real problems that official intervention produces, it must be recognized that the response made by the deviant will vary depending upon his commitment (supportive, apathic, or opposed) to the conventional order.

Recognition that all individuals do not accept conventional values demands a consideration of circumstances under which persons may seek out deviant labels. This recognition provides a bridge between the labeling framework and cultural deviance theories. Walter Miller (1958), in his observations of inner-city gangs, states that some "trouble with the law" may be prestige-conferring in the lower class. Certain criminal labels may be sought as a means of achieving and maintaining status in adolescent groups. Sutherland's differential association theory implies variation in acceptance of criminal behaviors and labels. Slums may be characterized by a deprivation of positive reinforcers such that aversive stimuli (public labeling and degradation) may acquire reinforcing properties.[22]

Introducing the idea that deviant actors, or those so accused, may direct label placement removes the image of the deviant as a passive receptacle for societal labels. Labeling can be directed from below. One reason for such direction may be personal gain. Some individuals may seek a reprieve from obligations by adopting a sick role—e.g., sickness rates among students during exam periods. At other times, the sick role may be adopted to further group ends—e.g., "blue flu" among police officers collectively seeking higher pay.[23] The very fact that the illness label is sought for personal gain raises questions about all illness in terms of symptoms and motives (Szasz, 1956). Audience evaluation is likely to occur along these lines:

> If a person has no motive to be ill and has symptoms, he is clearly ill. If he has a motive and symptoms, his condition may be psychosomatic or hysterical. If he has a motive and questionable symptoms, he is open to the charge of malingering. (Lorber, 1967:305)

Thus, illness may demand a performance; those with legitimate illness, as well as those "faking it,"[24] must try to get others to see it as legitimate. (The problematics of these imputational dimensions are very salient to the student who is *actually* sick the day of an exam.)

The performance element implies that labels are actively negotiated and that individuals looking for certain diagnoses may shop around until they find a physician who legitimates their claim (Scheff, 1968). Since the sick role may be relatively nonstigmatic depending on the illness, and implies lack of responsibility (it is an accident of trauma or infection), we would expect more label seeking than would be true for more negative labels. The personal gains for embracing the sick role are temporary removal of responsibility for action and some secondary gains of sympathy and help for one's condition.[25] There may be advantages in seeking disability labels in that role expectation may change in a favorable direction for the deviant (see Haber and Smith, 1971).

Extant labeling formulations would have us believe that all labeling experiences are psychologically detrimental. This is not necessarily the case, as the above examples indicate. For example, the voluntary psychiatric patient who learns how to understand and deal with his intrapsychic problems emerges from his agency experience with a distinctly improved self-image and a more positive sense of self-worth. There may even be a sense of gratitude for having been labeled if the patient feels the labeled condition and treatment are preferable to the previous state of despair, confusion, and depression; however, these subjective gains may clash with more objective consequences of labeling—e.g., when the out-patient fails to take into account how others might react to his agency contact (Phillips, 1963).

At other times, labels might be sought based on the assumption that positive objective consequences will follow. This may be found in cases where a person learns (from members of the Friends of Psychotherapy) that status and social acceptance can be had by visits to the "right" psychiatric settings, and, therefore, voluntarily seeks the experience and the diagnostic typifications that go with it. If all goes according to plan, the subject emerges feeling better about himself *despite* his new label *because* of the gains that it facilitates. The prime risk attached to this plan of action can be termed the "more than I bargained for" phenomon, wherein the self-defined well-and-happy subject stumbles into unanticipated self-doubts and insecurities assisted by a diagnosis of notable psychiatric impairment.

Of course, the sick role is only one of many possible roles available to the individual, and there are many reasons why a deviant label may be sought. At times, we find individuals will seek labels to avoid feelings of personal failure. There is some evidence that mothers on welfare may eventually take on the sick role as a legitimate reason for their failure to find work in order to personally justify being on the dole (Cole and Lejeune, 1972:349). The student doing poorly in his academic pursuits may seek a hippie life style and attendant labels to legitimize his rejection of formal education, and his failure in it. Juveniles experiencing a series of job failures may move into a delinquency role (Empey and Lubeck, 1971). Suicide attempters may seek the label "potential suicide" as a way of securing help and sympathy for personal problems (Maris, 1971).

There are also cases of seeking a label as a means of momentarily passing, such as the stripper who wishes to avoid the amorous advances of male customers who assume sexual availability. Thus, one exotic dancer "claimed that although she did not care to engage in homosexual activities she would frequently go to a lesbian bar where she would 'have a good time and not be bothered'" (McCaghy and

Skipper, 1969:268). Here the setting was used to produce imputations of deviance (homosexuality) for secondary gains. Donald Ball has termed this taking on of false labels[26] "feigning unrespectability," and gives an example of instrumental and expressive feigning:

> In the heterosexual situation of the male hairdresser and his female patron, [the required] bodily juxtaposition is potentially sexually threatening and tension-generating. By socially withdrawing—that is, by presenting himself as other than sexually normal, as not physically attracted to women—the hairdresser taken to be homosexual minimizes the potentially disruptive, strain-provoking, sexually threatening aspects of the spatially intimate male-female, practitioner-patron dyad. He thus feigns unrespectability, misinforming his audience for instrumental purposes. More mundanely, by the way, we sometimes call the expressive-oriented feigning of unrespectability by the prosaic label of slumming. (Ball, 1970:335)

However, there are conditions where deviant labels are sought on a more permanent basis, even though sanctions are likely to occur. The label "homosexual" may be sought as a way of avoiding military service or as a reason for discharge once in the service. In the latter case, the less-than-honorable discharge means the person loses veteran's benefits and is likely to find some employment opportunities blocked.[27] Psychiatric labels may be sought in some cases to avoid prosecution on criminal charges. In each case, the expectation of personal gain,[28] as well as secondary gains of sympathy and support in the sick role situations, motivates the search for the application of the deviant label.

Another form of personal gain can be seen when label seeking occurs in order to solve personal identity problems. In some cases, the solution is actively sought. For example, for some adolescent males "the art of seduction may be cultivated not because it is an alternative means to the goal of sexual satisfaction, but because the practice of the art validates a claim to being a certain sort of person" (Cohen, 1966:102).[29] Here, deviance and its label becomes a way of proclaiming or expressing a certain kind of self or identity for the individual. Active identity seeking is likely to occur during adolescense, a traditional time of identity crisis. Reputations based on amorous exploits, fighting abilities, or conning activities are engineered to establish a specific social identity. We are speaking here of situations where the deviant identity is an end rather than a means to an end.[30] Generally, such identity searches are for personal gain in that the actor anticipates rewards or advantages will accrue. (He, of course, may be mistaken—e.g., the person who secures a psychiatric label and treatment with an indeterminate sentence in lieu of the determinate prison sentence under criminal law auspices.)

Another instance of identity seeking occurs when a deviant label is embraced as the lesser of two evils. Deviant labels were one means of resolving conflicting group loyalties for Japanese-Americans during World War II. One observer reports:

> Japanese-Americans could secure release from the troublesome obligations to the container group [American society] ... by denying *all* loyalty to the container group. By denying all loyalty, they assumed a deviant role [internee] whose costs were continued internment and eventual expatriation but whose immediate benefit was release from the specific problematic obligations. (Turner, 1972:315)

The deviant label solved an identity problem as well as producing some secondary gains—i.e., "young men became eligible for the draft when they left the centers" (Turner, 1972:313). The forced choice resolved the identity dilemma.

Another example of label seeking to resolve identity problems is the systematic or professional check forger. His occupation demands high mobility, seclusiveness (meaning close personal contacts and attachments to individuals are avoided), and the playing of multiple roles, which produces a certain identity anxiety. With increasing involvement in check passing, the forger finds it difficult to cope with the "massive personal crisis which inheres in the prolonged enactment of his spurious roles. . . . [Consequently] an impressive number engineer their own downfalls" (Lemert, 1972:171). Societal intervention solves the identity problem, removing the pseudonymity:

> Arrest immediately assigns the forger an identity, undesirable though it may be, as a jail or prison inmate. In effect he receives or chooses a *negative identity* which despite its invidious qualities, is nearest and most real to him. At this juncture he is much like the actor who prefers bad publicity to none at all, or the youth who is willing to be a scapegoat for the group rather than not be part of the group at all. (Lemert, 1972:180–81)

To summarize, label seeking for personal gain or identity reasons ranges from the feigned performances of some male hairdressers (where labels are sought in the absence of rule violations) to the forger's identity search growing out of a fear of societal reaction— "once the check forger passes a series of worthless checks, the central fact of his existence becomes the threat of arrest" (Lemert, 1972:165). Of course, label seeking may occur for other reasons. For example, it may be part of a strategy to produce social change or completely destroy the established order. The political deviant (to be discussed in a future chapter) may seek deviant appellations as a method of attacking the legitimacy of the system. Here, labels are sought out of collective, humanitarian concerns rather than for self-centered purposes (Schafer, 1971). Regardless of the reasons, there is a continuous thread woven through most of these instances of label seeking; each involves the use of deviant behavior and resultant labeling and reaction to build a specific personal identity. The deviant plays an active role. No longer the put-upon victim of labeling machinery, he is now the opportunist, an identity entrepreneur, who is more subject than object (cf. Matza, 1969). His ability to act, to choose, and to control must be recognized. This active (as opposed to merely reactive) conception of the deviant leads to the consideration of another aspect of labeling—that which is self-imposed.

On the Possibility of Self-Labeling

When self-labeling has been discussed,[31] it has generally been in the context of adjustment to official labeling and stigma. Lemert treats it in the context of secondary deviance:

> Defining one's self as deviant is instrumental in seeking out means of satisfaction and mitigating stigmatization. *The redefinition of self leads to reinterpretation of past experiences,* which in turn reduces inner tensions and conflict. (Lemert, 1972:84)

We propose that self-labeling can occur without societal reaction (informal or formal labeling as deviant). On one level, this occurs when the actor internalizes categorical systems of control agencies, anticipates what reaction of others would be if activity became known, and engages in a self-diagnosis of the problem. Such self-diagnosis usually involves a reorganization of one's biography. Such retrospective interpretation—carried out by the actor—may be facilitated by various internalized control typification systems. For instance:

> Psychoanalaysis provides for many people in our so-
> ciety a ... method of ordering the discrepant frag-
> ments of their biography in a meaningful scheme.
> This method is particularly functional in comfortable
> middle-class society, too "mature" for the coura-
> geous commitment demanded by religion or revolu-
> tion. (Berger, 1963:62)

We have outlined in a previous chapter the role of friends and supporters of psychotherapy in perpetuating this self-evaluation
schema.[32] Such self-labeling may lead to self-initiated contacts with
control agents as in most cases of physical illness and much psychiatric "illness." For other behaviors, self-labeling may lead to perpetuation of deviant behavior, in part as an adjustment to *anticipated*
reactions; here self-labeling does not lead to agency referral—it remains private. For example, studies indicate that the vast majority of
homosexuals are never subjected to public labeling (arrest or trial for
homosexual actions).[33] This datum could not be explained by a labeling formulation relying on public reactions to account for career
deviance. To use self-labeling as an explanation, the following must
be shown:

1. The person anticipated reactions of others to homosexual activity;
2. The person is concerned with this potential reaction, he passes as
   heterosexual, makes adjustments in behavior and attitude in face
   of anticipated reaction;
3. As a result of adjustments, anticipation of public censure, and
   possible change in self-attitudes, the behavior continues.
4. Also, we would have to show that other variables are not producing the relationship, or would have to document their independent effects and interactional effects with self-labeling upon
   future deviance.

The problems of measurement are significant. To test the self-labeling hypothesis, we must independently define self-labeling and the
continuing rule violations—i.e., to assume that those with deviant
careers must have previously engaged in self-labeling makes the
hypothesis tautological. Also, it must be shown that self-labeling
preceded extensive involvement in the deviant behavior. Since researchers are generally not on tap when deviant activity begins, we
rely upon actor's reports of deviant careers, often spanning a number
of years. The problems of selective perception, recall, and retrospective interpretation by the actor of his or her background further
complicate the matter.

Self-labeling assumes that the person internalizes to some degree the societal proscriptive views of the activity, that the actor experiences some guilt or uneasiness in contemplation of act, and that the actor sees the behavior as fairly universally prohibited by the community. It further assumes that the actor knows the stereotypes of the deviant role so that self-placement in the role is accomplished. As we have stressed earlier in our interpretive conception of norms, this consensus may not exist; however, actor may impute a normative consensus to others. Warren and Johnson (1972:79) deal with this apparent inconsistency:

> Homosexuality is symbolically labeled deviant. It is suggested that this is primarily so because, even in our immensely pluralistic society [homosexuality] tends to be one type of deviance condemned, at least rhetorically, by almost everyone. As a result, homosexuals appear to be largely symbolically labeled as deviants in American society. . . . "Mundane" events occur throughout the life of the (not known) homosexual that symbolically label him as deviant, by denigrating the category of which he is a member.

Examples of such denigration would be homosexuals being present when homosexual jokes are aired, or being subjected to "heterosexual talk" which cannot be ignored, or which demands participation.

The homosexual actor anticipates that sanctions will be forthcoming upon discovery of his sexual preferences. He sees a unified, negative reaction—one which empirically may not be forthcoming, as Kitsuse's (1962) study of students' reactions to homosexuals indicates. But here, as with many behaviors, action is maintained by "avoided tests."[34]

In essence, self-labeling involves the mental rehearsal of an activity and an estimation of what others will think and how they will respond. A basic tenet of Symbolic Interaction is that we take the role of the other and anticipate, in imagination, their reactions (Strauss, 1969:64–69). While we are often not aware of this rehearsal aspect in most mundane activities, it becomes salient to the actor anticipating a rule violation.[35] In this sense, there are no truly secret deviant acts, since actor goes through some anticipation of audience reaction.[36]

If this premise is accepted, self-labeling *may* be seen as a requisite for committing the initial deviant act. This line of reasoning would argue that a decision to act is predicated upon the ability to mentally rehearse the act, and to see oneself as doing the act. David Matza sees this as crucial:

> It is picturing or seeing oneself, *literally,* as the kind
> of person who might possibly do the thing. The self
> ordains itself but initially only as open [i.e., as a per-
> son who might do the thing]; ... different circum-
> stances and the affinities implicit in them result in a
> variable sense of option or closure. (1969:112. Em-
> phasis in original.)

Some will not be able to come around to a self-view as the type of person who would engage in a specific rule violation. (These individuals are deterred, which gives meaning to the term general deterrence—they exercise self-control.) For instance, individuals who cannot overcome moral apprehensiveness, or who cannot see themselves as effectively hiding the effects, are not likely to become marihuana users (Becker, 1963).

Such a rehearsal brings the actor to the invitational edge of deviance, or what Lofland (1969) terms "encapsulation." If actor comes to see himself as the type of person who might do X, there is likely to occur, simultaneously, "a constriction of the range of perceptible action alternatives and a foreshortening of the time span to which Actor refers his conduct in order to judge its propriety" (Lofland, 1969:50). What we have is a self-imposed "crisis" similar to the public crisis of official labeling which Scheff (1966) proposes for the accused deviant. Facilitants to encapsulation may occur such as extent of actor's past experiences which "allow" imaginative rehearsal of act, and extent to which others are present to provide social support.[37] For instance, there may be regular marihuana users who coach the novice in techniques of smoking, or simply on-lookers who demand some commitment to deviant action, as in the case of juveniles daring others to "do it." These factors influence the actor's decision as to "accepting the invitation" (Becker, 1967).

The self-labeling continues *during* and *after* the infraction. "The subject discovers himself in process. There is no other way. Not being preordained, the subject is fated to continuous reconsideration" (Matza, 1969:118).[38] The subject goes through his own version of documentary interpretation—the same process used by others to evaluate his behavior (see Chapters II and III). He comes to see himself as "one who could use marihuana" or "one who would throw rocks through school windows," a conversion which is facilitated by incorporated views—based mainly on stereotypes—of the particular deviant role in question (cf. Scheff, 1966:56–83). Through infraction, the actor "*makes up his mind,* literally" (Matza, 1969:122). He conceives himself in action; in the project at hand, the actor comes to reinterpret the *meaning* of his own action. Following Bem,[39] we expect that the actor uses ongoing and accomplished behaviors to document attitudes and essential self. In other words, behaviors are used to indicate what attitudes must have been present to produce the act. We see much out-of-the-ordinary behavior as having a self-conversion potential; it has a greater impact on an actor's self-evaluation than do ordinary actions. As with witnesses to an event, the author of a deviant action is likely to assign more significance to it and, hence, it comes to imply more about essential self. In short, *infraction* makes actor more conscious of *action* and increases consciousness of *self-in-action.* The actor becomes a witness to his own action, now mentally replayed and reviewed. He becomes self-conscious.[40] In other words, he pays more attention to himself in-the-action.

An example is found in the novel *In Cold Blood.* Perry Smith, during his recounting of the murder incident at the Clutter house where he and Dick Hickock were drawn by rumors of money, describes this self-consciousness:

> 'I frisked the girl's room, and I found a little purse—like a doll's purse. Inside it was a silver dollar. I dropped it somehow, and it rolled across the floor. Rolled under a chair. I had to get down on my knees. And just then it was like I was outside myself. Watching myself in some nutty movie. It made me sick. I was just disgusted. Dick, and all his talk about a rich man's safe, and here I am crawling on my belly to steal a child's silver dollar. One dollar.' (Capote, 1965:271–72)

This leads to another sense of self-consciousness: as he is paying more attention than usual to his course of action or his "project," he begins to feel that others are too. The actor becomes more acutely aware of being "watched," of the possibility that others have seen or will discover the infraction.[41] He thus develops a feeling of being constantly "on view" (Goffman, 1959). In this sense, the deviant may feel like a professional actor in a play, being on stage for both critics and audience—each producing evaluations of the performance.[42] Being "on" means the actor more closely attends to all his behaviors, leading some to propose that deviants who pass and cover become more knowledgeable of the negotiated aspects of social reality (Goffman, 1963; Williams and Weinberg, 1971).

Not only does the actor feel more closely watched, but partly as a result, he begins to question his ability to hide evidence of his act. A sense of transparency evolves when an actor feels guilt or shame for his action—i.e., when he has internalized the ban on the action

(Matza; 1969:146–55). It grows out of the feeling of being "on" which, when coupled with heightened self-awareness of the infraction, has implications for the actor's assessment of his essential self (see Messinger, *et al.*, 1970). Notice these are self-imposed components of labeling: "it is the subject who causes his own sense of transparency" (Matza, 1969:150). Under the mood of transparency, nothing is done easily. Old routines can no longer be relied upon, but demand scrutiny to assure they will be seen as routine. The deviant actor experiences a generalization effect such that all situations are transformed —he must engage in reflexive gymnastics. Matza describes the problem:

> He watches himself to be sure he behaves naturally or casually: at the precise level of involvement, with the exact wisdom and style he thinks his associates expect of him. He is engaged in a remarkable project of imitation—being himself as he thinks he is ordinarily. (*Ibid.*, p. 153)

Remarkable indeed! An extremely difficult task, one which continually reminds a person of his past infraction while simultaneously affecting feelings of essential self. Add to these mental gyrations the time devoted to formulating accounts or other remedial work which must be ready if the transparency is actualized,[43] and we begin to see that the transgressor is engaged in much self-judgment; such demanded activities escalate the self-labeling process and work to amplify the significance of the initial infraction. "Conscious of the possibility of his transparency, the subject becomes more highly attuned to his deviance, and, thus, in a phenomenological sense, one's deviance is compounded" (Taylor, *et al.*, 1973:190).

As an aside, we would expect the feelings of transparency and audience scrutiny to be present for the label seeker, but in a slightly modified sense. Here performers would monitor their actions in order to assure that the audience takes the rule violations in the intended manner. The person who malingers wants to avoid imputations of malingering during his illness performance. The political deviant who seeks a label and attendant publicity must take care that the audience sees action as an attack on the system—not the self-centered antics of a spoiled child.[44] For example, protesters must try to get audiences to define rule breaking as legitimate protest. One observer notes:

> To be credible as protestors, troublemakers must seem to constitute a major part of a group whose grievances are already well documented, who are

believed to be individually or collectively powerless to correct their grievances, and who show some signs of moral virtue that render them "deserving." (Turner, 1969:818)

We would add that protesters must not be seen as acting out of concern for personal gain. Note that each of these "requirements" of legitimate protest may be a source of the State's attack on the credibility and legitimacy of the protest.

Other factors influence self-labeling. The etiological theories held by the actor may affect self-imposed reactions to behavior. For example, homosexuals may use the latest psychological or sociological studies of etiology to explain their own behaviors and may "reconstruct their own biographies in light of them" (Warren and Johnson, 1972:79). The homosexual, without official prompting, may reconstruct his biography to account for his "condition" and may use this reconstruction to justify his continuing involvement in the deviant behavior ("sad tales").[45] The deviant actor may embrace a medical definition of his problem because to treat his behavior as a condition removes some, if not all, of his responsibility in the matter. In this way, homosexuals may "welcome and support the notion that homosexuality is a condition. For, just as the rigid categorization deters people from drifting into deviancy, so it appears to foreclose on the possibility of drifting back into normality and *thus* removes the element of anxious choice [for the deviant]" (McIntosh, 1968:184). Similarly, drug addicts may see themselves as legitimate occupants of the sick role and forego attempts to get off the drug (McAuliffe and Gordon, 1974:830–31). Likewise, the mental patient, the heavy drinker, the child with "learning disabilities," the woman who fails to achieve multiple orgasms, and others may come to see their problems as medical in nature, thereby removing responsibility from themselves (and foregoing the question "Should society be treating this as deviance?"). In these ways, theories of etiology, especially illness models, may be used in self-labeling of behaviors such that an individual resigns himself to a career of deviant activity, even without official agency contact.

In concluding this discussion of self-labeling, two important qualifications must be entered. First, self-labeling seldom occurs in a vacuum; rather, it is interwoven with public labeling, usually of an informal nature. In fact, self and public labeling may conceivably be at odds with each other:[46] the actor may self-label his behavior deviant in absence of public response, or perhaps more likely, one may hold to positive self-labels in face of public imputations of deviance (e.g., Dank, 1971). For the label seeker, the self-definition of deviance may precede the public label; for those rejecting the label, public reaction may lead to self-definitions. In the latter case, public degradation ceremonies are seen as means whereby the accused becomes convinced of his essentially deviant nature (Garfinkel, 1956; Scheff, 1966; Emerson, 1969).

A second caveat is that self-labeling does not automatically lead to deviant careers. We concur with Matza that the actor has a bounded choice both before and after the initial act. Self-labeling may indeed produce reform, and we see it as affected by many of the same variables that affect response to public labeling. We now turn to this issue of the conditions under which self or public labeling may lead to recidivism or reform.

Labeling:
Recidivism or Reform?

Labeling theory has been both praised and condemned for its anti-establishment implications. In tone, it purports that societal sanctioning of deviance has the unintended consequence of increasing future deviance rather than controlling it.[47] Perhaps the pessimism inherent in the labeling formulation has prohibited the question, "does it ever work?" from being raised. Thus, we now seriously ask, when does self or public labeling produce reform? Answers will help specify the conditions where labeling will have self-fulfilling consequences.

We begin by examining the backdrop, the gestalt against which the labeling drama is played out. One backdrop is the degree to which an individual is attached to conventional other people, and the extent to which he is committed to conventional activity.[48] We would predict that if rule violations are publicly detected, reform is likely if the offender is highly attached and committed. High-status offenders are likely to be deterred from future deviance for a number of reasons. First, initial labeling can usually be resisted due to the idiosyncratic credit available to high-status individuals; this also means that greater tolerance limits are granted to the powerful. High attachment usually means the offender will have a group of supporters who will help to neutralize the label and support future conformity. In short, labeling is not likely to have much effect in terms of objective labeling consequences. Second, while actual labeling may be weakened, the high-status offender also has more to lose:

deviance is more costly because of possible loss of position and prestige. The confrontation of a high-status deviant with the label shocks
him into a realization of these possibilities. Also, rule violations seem
highly inconsistent with past actions. The result is that the person is
subjectively affected by the deviant act and the label. He is likely to
have self-esteem reduced. This temporary reduction in feeling of
self-worth may pressure reform. Conversely, labeling for low-status
individuals—when weak on attachments and low on commitment to
the system—may produce a sense of deviant identity, which in turn
may lead to more positive self-esteem. In sum, we predict reform for
high-status individuals given informal labeling, or even less than full
public contact with official control agents. This is evident in a study
of amateur shoplifters (largely middle-class housewives). Cameron's
(1964) research concluded (while it is not true for professional shoplifters) that

> among pilferers who are apprehended and interro-
> gated by the store police but set free without formal
> charge, there is very little or no recidivism. ...
> [O]nce arrested, interrogated, and in their own per-
> spective, perhaps humiliated, pilferers apparently
> stop pilfering. The rate of recidivism is amazingly
> low. The reward of shoplifting, whatever it is, is not
> worth the cost of reputation and self-esteem. (Cam-
> eron, quoted in Chambliss, 1969:367)

Thus, for high-stake individuals, here reputable middle-class women,
relatively private labeling is likely to deter future deviance. This
suggests that the degree of "publicness" of labeling, and the extent
to which the label is disseminated to others, will increase the probability of future deviance. Thorsell and Klemke (1972:396) use this
reasoning to predict greater deterrent impact of primary group reactions, while labeling from secondary groups may force movement
into a deviant career. We add that this reform is conditional, based
upon social status.

Cameron's work also asserts that when the offender does not conceive of herself as deviant, and when no "in-group" or subcultural
support is available for the rule breaking, that recidivism is not likely
to occur. This probably accounts for the lack of stigma and lack of
labeling effects for those convicted of traffic offenses (Ross, 1961).
When these two conditions are absent, the primary group reaction
of conventional others is very significant: "lacking peer support for
the deviance in his conventional environment, any negative sanctions applied through primary relations will be more powerful; this

itself may prevent further deviance" (DeLamater, 1968:451). Under these circumstances, official and informal reactions are likely to produce reform.

Rule violations which occur during the performance of acceptable and routine activities—e.g., shopping, driving, working—may take little psychological preparation. Thus, the individual is less likely to see the activity as truly deviant, since it is not extensively planned nor does it involve behaviors outside the normal routine of the daily round. For this reason many white-collar criminals do not see themselves as "criminals."

Another backdrop is the degree of psychological commitment to an action. Where commitment is low, we predict reform upon societal reaction; where it is high, labeling may produce continuing deviance (Chambliss, 1969:368–72). Even for the same activity, some may have low commitment to the deviant act, while others have a high commitment. Studies of physician addicts indicate they often begin use of addictive drugs by viewing it as experimentation (part of their work) or because they feel they can control the addictive effects (medical training is seen as providing knowledge of how to prevent getting hooked). They do not come to see themselves as deviant, see little support for such activity among colleagues—thus, the need to keep it secret—and when caught are likely to reform (Winich, 1964). The street addict is more likely to see himself as drug dependent and to have subcultural support for his activity,[49] even though this support is often predicated upon others' desire to sell drugs or otherwise benefit from the person's continued addiction. In this example, we also have a difference in stakes in the system. The physician has much to lose, and reforms; the street addict is not likely to have much stake or status in conventional society, thus recidivism is more likely.

Somewhat related to degree of commitment to the act is the idea of overlap[50]—the view that certain deviant activities overlay with conventional activities. Thus, leisure values present in the conventional culture lead to a tolerance of certain forms of juvenile delinquency (Matza and Sykes, 1961). The business ethic legitimates to some degree various forms of occupational and corporate crime (Clinard and Quinney, 1973). This means that certain deviance—delinquency and white-collar crime—is more tolerated than other crimes. Consequently, labels applied to these activities may be less stigmatic and have fewer objective and subjective effects on the rule breaker. For example, physicians hit with malpractice suits report no negative effects, and in some cases the medical practice may improve after a suit, in part because of patient referrals from sympathetic colleagues

(Schwartz and Skolnick, 1962). A study of homosexuals discharged from the military concluded:

> For the majority of respondents, managing the stigma of their discharge did not pose insurmountable problems. This we feel is due mainly to the nature of the label itself having little influence outside of certain occupations and appearing on the official records of few of the organizations that circumscribe a person's life. (Williams and Weinberg, 1971:183)

When labeling is restricted in its dissemination, reform is more likely. At times, the secrecy may be imposed by the control agency, as in the expungement of juvenile court records, or situations may be structured so that labels remain hidden. Thus, in Sweden, the ex-convict:

> is advised to change his name and to take up residence in a community or part of the country different from the one in which his crime was committed. A job and, if necessary, living accommodations are found for him there. The only member of his new community aware of this true identity is his employer who is sworn to secrecy. (Thorsell and Klemke, 1972:399)

Consequently, we predict that when a label is hidden or can be easily removed, the probability of the person moving toward conforming behavior is greater.

Labeling effects—specifically stigma and master-status implications—may be blunted by active primary group support for the activity, but against the label. Reiss's (1961) study of delinquent gang members who hustled adult homosexuals implies that members freely engaged in homosexual acts, but were not labeled as "homosexual" by their peers: they were doing it for money. There were shared expectations that members would not enjoy the act, nor engage in it without payment. Those engaging in homosexual acts did not come to see themselves as "queer."[51] Studies of female homosexuality in prison is another sample of this phenomenon. Many women enter into a homosexual career in prison to adjust to the sex-role deprivations of the total institution, but few remain homosexual upon release (Giallombardo, 1966). Here also there is peer-group support for the behavior but against the label.

Another factor is implied by the above examples: the perceived transiency of the behavior (and consequently the labeled condition). In the case of female homosexuality in prison, both inmates and staff generally see it as temporary in nature. In delinquency, the condition is seen as a passing phase, something every boy[52] goes through, and this, combined with overlap, means that bad behaviors by males are usually tolerated. Those who go beyond the expectational duration of the activity are likely to be met with other, less transient labels, such as "ex-con" or "sociopath." Of importance here are the prognostications of the condition—where temporary causes are imputed, the behavior is more likely discounted (Friedson, 1966).

The level of self-esteem prior to the time of the deviant act can be an important backdrop to labeling. We mentioned earlier that persons with low self-esteem (not necessarily derived from involvement in deviant acts) are more susceptible to societal influence. Conversely, actors with high self-esteem and confidence in their self-definitions (self-image) as conforming may resist the impact of labeling by significant others.[53] Why might this be so? Gecas proposes two dimensions of self-esteem: power and worth. He suggests that an actor "defines himself largely in terms of the effect he has on this environment. When feelings of confidence in one's power break down it is often accompanied by serious repercussions throughout the self system" (1971:468). Those experiencing a series of failures, or who now see their lives as highly determined (mood of fatalism), are likely to have feelings of self-worth negatively affected. This makes them more susceptible to self-fulfilling consequences of informal and formal labeling—that is, candidates for a deviant career.

Another factor which conditions labeling impact is the actor's perception of the "deviant" action. If he sees it as merely "competent rule use," he may dismiss the imputations of seriousness placed on the act by others, if he is in a position of some power. Another possibility is that the deviant will convert his accusers to his view, so they do not see the action as deviant, but as acceptable under the circumstances (Turner, 1972). Under these conditions, the person is not likely to see his activities as deviant and is less likely to engage in self-labeling, guilt, or feelings of deviant personal identity. On the other hand, when the actor does see his action as wrong, then self-reaction and audience reaction increases the probability of continued involvement in the behavior. In this case, self-labeling and public labeling are working in the same direction, increasing the chances of development of a deviant self-image and future rule violations as the result of the actor's attitude toward the rule.

Finally, labeling may lead to reform simply because the opportunities to move into a deviant career are not available. Lemert (1951:81–98) speaks of external and internal limits which affect the direction which adjustments to societal reactions take. External limits refer to opportunities to enter a deviant career. Illegitimate opportunities may be open or closed such that juveniles engaging in delinquency do not automatically have the option of entering into a career in professional crime. If illegal means are open, a criminal gang is likely to form where individuals are tied into an organized adult criminal subculture where law breaking is profitable and protected by the fix. If the neighborhood lacks organized crime elements, individuals are likely to have access to conflict gangs, where fighting is a major activity, or retreatist gangs, drug-oriented subcultures often made up of those failing to get into the other two deviant subcultures (Cloward and Ohlin, 1960). In the case of mental illness careers, an external limit may be the extent to which a person has acquired indirect knowledge of the deviant role. Indeed, those who don't take on the role of "good analysand" or "good patient" may be removed from treatment agencies and denied legitimate (agency-sanctioned) mental or physical illness careers (Lorber, 1971). External limitations are more applicable to certain types of criminal behaviors than others— i.e., more to professional crime than to occasional property offenders. Other things being equal, we would expect labeling effects to have a greater impact on maintaining mental illness careers than criminal careers, since the external limitations on entrance into the latter are potentially greater.

Internal limits refer to intra-individual blockages which preclude or make more difficult involvement in a deviant career. Individuals may lack the skills or courage to initiate or continue a rule violation —i.e., a state of preparation is not achieved (Matza, 1964). Some women may be repulsed by the idea of anonymous, impersonal, economically motivated sexual acts, and therefore do not enter into prostitution, even when the opportunity arises. Fear of injection may deter some from hard narcotics use (Lemert, 1951:82). Lack of awareness of a deviant role on the part of the individual may increase the chances of reform (Dank, 1971). Also, inability to role play may preclude a career, as is the case with systematic check forgers who must be able to take on a variety of identities and roles (Lemert, 1972:153). Finally, limitations may be purely physical—such as lack of appropriate body measurements to enter the career of stripper (Skipper and McCaghy, 1970).

In summary, we have outlined some of the factors which mediate labeling effects, with specific attention to conditions under which societal reactions produce a reduction in rule breaking. As noted in Chapter III, there is another possibility lying between reform and recidivism: redirection. This adjustment "may be the adoption of another normal rule in which the tendencies previously defined as 'pathological' are given more acceptable social expression" (Lemert, 1951:76). Redirection depends on the availability of alternative, somewhat acceptable roles, knowledge of such roles, and personal resources to facilitiate their adoption. Generally, we would expect the rich to have greater access to these roles, and that is one reason why this group tends to remain out of socially disapproved roles. Again, we find the disenfranchised are less likely to have access to alternative, acceptable roles. When social class is coupled with little chance of avoiding surveillance, recognition, and reaction, we realize why the players of deviant roles are often drawn from the lower strata of society.

Notes

1. The distinction is made explicitly in a study of consequences of less-than-honorable discharge from the military service for homosexuality. In this work, Williams and Weinberg (1971:12) define objective consequences as "how the deviant acts or behaves, or what happens to him, rather than how he feels" which are subjective effects. By objective effects, we take a more limited definition treating only "what happens to him" and leaving as problematic "how the deviant acts or behaves" in response to these objective consequences. Reactions to societal labeling will, of course, involve objective and subjective aspects.

2. It should be pointed out that these studies are attempts to test strain theory, and therefore generally assert that perception of legitimate opportunities (as closed) leads to rule violations. They also propose that potential rule violators are more aware of openings in the illegitimate opportunity structure which pulls them toward illegal behavior. We see the causal direction as problematic and feel more comfortable arguing that involvement in deviance, plus informal or formal reactions, leads to changes in perceptions of these opportunity systems (see Gould, 1969a). Longitudinal or experimental analyses which would resolve this issue remain to be done.

3. "Objective effects present" means that others react differentially, close legitimate opportunities, etc. "Absent" means that persons do not discriminate toward the actor because of the rule violation.

4. If they blamed themselves, they would be likely to experience subjective effects and "move into" the Complete Labeling cell.

5. The concepts of personal identity and social identity are inextricably bound; personal identity is constructed to a great extent, as Cooley, Mead, and others have indicated, from actual or anticipated reactions of others.

6. The designation of terms is arbitrary here; in the literature, the terms self, self-concept, identity, self-image, self-evaluation, and even self-esteem are often used synonymously. Students are warned to look closely at operational indicators of terms when reading in this area.

7. These are independent to some extent because there may be many sources of self-esteem besides self-image of conventional or deviant, as we shall see later. In speaking of deviance, one important difference in personal identity and social identity is that for social identity, once an imputation of deviance is made (self-image assigned by others), there is virtually an automatic devaluation of personal worth by the audience—e.g., Simmons, 1965; 1969.

8. For a review of the work of Reckless and his students, see Reckless and Dinitz, 1967. For devastating critiques of this work, especially the operationalization of self concept, read Schwartz and Tangri, 1965; Tangri and Schwartz, 1967; Jensen, 1970.

9. Teachers were asked to rate male students as to the probability they would get in trouble with the law in the future. Reckless assumes that teachers' ratings as

"good risks" or "bad risks" were correlated with self-concept as positive or negative (see Jensen, 1970). One remarkable finding of these studies was that the teachers were fairly accurate predictors of which boys will get in trouble with the law. This may be the result of informal labeling. Following Rosenthal's work on teacher expectations, we may hypothesize that differential reactions by teachers after the ratings may have promoted behavioral problems which eventuated in trouble with the law (Rosenthal and Jacobsen, 1968). To the extent this trouble-potential dimension was not salient to teachers prior to Reckless' research, the questionnaire itself may have labeled certain students in the minds of some teachers. This is an ethical question largely unrecognized by individuals using this research procedure.

10. Self-image as deviant, given no record, could be the result of self-definitions due to hidden delinquency, or of informal reactions to known, but not officially recorded, acts. We are not arguing that official contacts are the only factor influencing self-image, but we are concerned with the relative impact of records on self-image for racial and social-class groupings.

11. Evidence on value orientations of both white and black delinquent gangs in Chicago do not support this assertion. Generally, delinquents internalize middle-class expectations and show them as value preferences (Short and Strodtbeck, 1965:60).

12. Expectations of greater susceptibility to official contact for blacks seems realistic in light of a Philadelphia study. A cohort analysis of all males born in the city in 1945, followed from age 10–18, found 28.6 percent of white males had one or more police contacts compared to 50.2 percent for nonwhites (Wolfgang, et al., 1972:244–45).

13. Walter Miller proposed a lower-class value system where activities opposite of middle-class expectations would be reinforced. Jensen's research indicates support for Miller's trouble potential among blacks, but less so among whites. It should be noted that Miller derived his cultural theory from observations in primarily black, lower-class areas of Boston.

14. There does appear to be greater tolerance of delinquency among blacks in Jensen's study than among whites; respondents were asked to rate others' evaluation of them: blacks with official police contacts were less likely to feel others saw them as delinquent than were whites with such contacts.

15. This study in the Reckless tradition speaks of self-evaluation, but of the four factors derived from a semantic differential adjective list (evaluation, activity, potency, and interpersonal quality), they focus upon "evaluation" (Schwartz and Stryker, 1970:78–79) which had factor loadings highest for these bi-polar adjectives: important-unimportant, better-worse, smart-stupid, interesting-dull, good-bad, successful-unsuccessful (p. 43). We see this as closer to what other studies describe as self-worth items, hence we treat this as a self-esteem study.

16. These two studies do not provide comparative measures of self-esteem levels for heterosexual samples, so this is only indirectly evidence for deviant identity and positive self-esteem. It is difficult to make cross-study comparisons on self-image, self-esteem, and labeling (or any other variable), because of variation in methodological procedures used to assess self-concept. Studies may use direct measures such as Rosenberg's self-esteem items (1965)—e.g., Jensen, 1970, 1972; Weinberg, 1970; Hammersmith and Weinberg, 1973. A more indirect assessment involves various forms of the semantic differential (Osgood, et al., 1957), where responses to a series of bi-polar adjectives are factor analyzed into dimensions of self-concept —e.g., Short and Strodtbeck, 1965; Sherwood, 1965, 1967; Hartnagel, 1970; Schwartz and Stryker, 1970; and Gecas, 1971, 1972. For a description of other methods of measuring self-concept, see Tucker (1966) for review of Twenty Statements Test (which involves twenty open-ended responses to the question "Who am I?") and Miyamoto and Dornbusch (1956) for still other procedures.

17. Studies of self-concept have generally ignored the question of situated identities or essential identity. If self is a product of the situation and significant others, we would expect variation across situations, such that we would expect the same person to have high self-esteem in some settings and low feelings of self-esteem in others. For an empirical attempt to assess situated self, see Mahoney, 1973.

18. Some may actively seek a deviant label to build a reputation or seek the secondary gains of the sick role. Label seeking is discussed in detail below.

19. As noted earlier, personal identity is greatly influenced by social identity—that identity assigned to actor by others. (See Miyamoto and Dornbusch, 1956, for one of many empirical documentations of this point.) We are simply asserting that when official imputations of deviance are made, the socially constructed reality becomes even more important as it affects personal identity.

20. This assumption underlies Goffman's discussion of stigma, since he deals mainly with "problems of management of spoiled identity" and only sketchily treats (in three pages) the possibility of a militant rejection of conventional society and conceptions of normality (1963:112–14).

21. "Labeling an individual whose initial socialization was into deviance, and who is thus committed to deviance as a way of life, probably has little effect on him other than to add more or less serious costs . . . primarily associated with deprivation of freedom and other unpleasant aspects of arrest and trial, or hospitalization, etc." (DeLamater, 1968:454).

22. Burgess and Akers (1966:143), in their reformulation of Sutherland's work, are quite explicit on this point: "if lawful behavior did not result in reinforcement, the strength of the behavior would be weakened, and a state of deprivation would result. This, in turn, would increase the probability that other behaviors would be emitted which are reinforced and hence would be strengthened. And, of course, these behaviors, though common to one or more groups, may be labeled deviant by the larger society. Also such behavior patterns themselves may acquire conditioned reinforcing value and, subsequently, be enforced by the members of a group by making various forms of social reinforcement, such as social approval, esteem, and status contingent upon that behavior."

23. While this is qualitatively different than the student example in that a collective action is undertaken to achieve a group goal, it is still primarily for personal gain. The "strikers" are not attacking the legitimacy of the system, simply demanding a larger share in it. Hence, we would not see it as political deviance—a topic discussed in Chapter XI.

24. "Faking it" differs for hysterical and malingering patients: "hysterical patients have no organic basis for their symptoms and findings so that in a sense, they are 'faking' their disease. The important point is that this faking is on a subconscious level and the patient is perfectly sincere in the belief that his symptoms and findings are bona fide. The malingerer is also a fake, but his dissimulation is on a conscious level and he knows perfectly well that he is 'putting it on' for a purpose" (Bowers, quoted in Lorber, 1967:308).

25. Freidson (1966:80) notes that the sick role is conditionally granted, and research indicates that certain groups are more likely to have their illness claims legitimated than others (e.g., Petroni, 1969). The sick role involves the following expectations: (1) person is excused from normal duties, (2) person has a legitimate claim to care and assistance from others, (3) person is expected to want to get well as quickly as possible, and (4) one is to seek professional help in order to recover (Parsons, 1951: chapter 10).

26. Notice that the concept of label seeking gives new meaning to Becker's typology; now the "falsely accused" seeks such a false label in the absence of rule-violating behaviors rather than having it thrust upon him. To what extent feigned actions and audience definitions may have self-fulfilling consequences in such cases as the male hairdresser remains to be studied. We would predict such consequences are

more likely where the label was sought than where it was rejected, because the person has committed himself to a consistent line of action by his own behavior. He placed his own "side bets" (see Becker, 1960).

27. All military discharge numbers have carried an embedded three-digit code which describes the circumstances of the discharge. This code was known to employees, but not to the veteran, so that some servicemen were being denied jobs even though they had an honorable discharge. In what must be termed "secret labeling," applicants were often denied employment if certain code numbers appeared. For example, one code stood for involvement in peace marches or other political causes while in the service, black-balling an applicant without his knowledge. This secret labeling has recently been discovered and a Congressional Committee has ordered the Pentagon to stop such practices.

28. We realize that unsought labeling may produce unanticipated personal gains. One study found that marital difficulties were reduced when the deviant spouse entered the institutionalized mental patient career (Sampson, *et al.*, 1961), yet few would wittingly enter such a career to save a marriage. In terms of criminal labels, the fraud involved in the Howard Hughes biography has provided Clifford Irving with material for a best seller, and Spiro Agnew appears to be launched on a writing career based on his criminal activities and resultant labels.

29. Concepts such as role-expressive and role-supportive behaviors are introduced by Cohen to rescue Mertonian strain theory. In its original form, this framework could not account for seemingly irrational, nongoal-directed behaviors. Indeed, Cohen's later writings on deviance can be seen as an attempt to bring more interpretive, processual questions to bear on what is basically a structural theory (e.g., Cohen, 1965).

30. The political deviant (Chapter XI) may seek a deviant identity as a way of raising consciousness or acquiring sympathy and support for the cause, but this is generally viewed by such persons as a means to an end.

31. The topic of self-labeling has received little detailed discussion in the literature. Rather, it is interjected as an explanation for continuing deviant activity in the absence of official labeling—e.g., "indirect or unofficial negative labeling, or the mere knowledge of potential negative evaluations of his acts, may still influence the actor's behavior and his self-conceptions" (Schur, 1969:317). Judith Lorber (1967) treats the subject, but mainly within the context of the sick role.

32. "Friends" may give direct advice upon learning of someone's behavioral problems, or may simply be a source of folk knowledge about psychotherapy which leads to self-diagnosis and self-initiated referral.

33. See Humphreys, 1970; Dank, 1971; Warren and Johnson, 1972.

34. Garfinkel, in speaking of standardization of background expectancies, states: "If upon the arousal of troubled feelings, persons avoid tinkering with these 'standardized' expectancies, the standardization could consist of an *attributed* standardization that is supported by the act that persons avoid the very situations in which they might learn about them. . . . Indeed the more important the rule, the greater is the likelihood that knowledge is based on avoided tests" (1967:70. Emphasis in original.). The deviant may likewise attribute more consensus on the rule and more propensity for sanctioning than is in fact the case.

35. Mental rehearsal is not restricted to deviance, but also applies to conventional behaviors contemplated for the first time. One need only recall the protracted internal rehearsals which precede a first date.

36. Possible exceptions would be rule violations engaged in while under the influence of drugs (drunk or high), where the actor could not recall the incident, and where no one witnessed the action.

37. See Lofland, 1969:54. Matza also asserts that contemplated actions are reviewed such that the actor sees the projected act in terms of past actions of which he is

reminded during the mental rehearsal (1969:121); and he also notes the role of peers in various reconsiderations of the doing (p. 124).

38. Matza is taking a "soft determinism" perspective here in that the actor is seen as having bounded choice at the invitational edge (e.g., 1969:122; also 1964:1–32). He implies that the choice is made evident in the doing, so that pure mental rehearsal is not likely to yield a conversion to the deviant activity; "such a yield may be regarded as light" (1969:118). In other words, pure self-labeling is not likely to produce the initial deviant act.

39. Daryl Bem (1972) has proposed that instead of conceiving attitudes as producing behavior, that behaviors occur, and these actions are used to interpret what the actor's attitude, desire, etc., *must have been* in the situation. Bem's work at the intrapersonal level seems to parallel work of attribution theorists at the interpersonal level (see Chapter IV). While witnesses seem to read an individual through his deviant acts via attributions about basic character, so too the individual makes self-attributions about essential self after the infraction. However, there are some important differences in attribution by self and others (see Bem, 1972: 40–42).

40. This is what phenomenologists refer to as an epoché—a standing outside of and observing a scene while bracketing the context of what happened. Being self-conscious in this sense may lead to other troubles. This self-consciousness may be seen as a polite-interactional rule violation because the actor focuses more attention on himself than on the conversation, thereby appearing uninvolved or aloof. "At the cost of his involvement in the prescribed focus of attention, the individual may focus his attention more than he ought upon himself—himself as someone who is faring well or badly, as someone calling forth a desirable or undesirable response from others" (Goffman, 1967:118).

41. Duvall and Wickland, (1972:218), in experimental attempts to document awareness of self-in-action, suggest that anticipation of others' evaluations leads actor to more closely monitor his action, and—by implication—he comes to see the self as vulnerable to discovery.

42. The dramaturgical model has some interesting implications for analysis of deviance. The audience at a play provide the immediate feedback on the performance similar to informal reactions to rule violations, while critics might be seen as more formal agents of control whose evaluations appear later (in the morning papers). Also, the critic seems to have more power to sanction than the audience.

43. Troubles of transparency and concern with remedial work also characterize the officially labeled deviant when he tries to return to conventional roles. He finds it necessary to anticipate knowledge of his past on the part of others, the nature of that knowledge, and whether or not informational additions or corrections are advisable. Employment and friendship contexts are both crucial in this regard— e.g., "Should my employer (or friend) know that I was a mental patient or a prison inmate, or are we both better off if he doesn't know?" "If he doesn't know, just how much can I tell without jeopardizing my job or my friendship?" "Since he may already know, should I set him straight on the pertinent facts of the matter and on my present condition?"

44. It is understandable that the state seeks to define radicals as mentally disturbed or as acting out of personal gain to detract from their attack on the system and the underlying problems at which these attacks are directed.

45. Warren and Johnson (1972) call for studies on the etiological theories used by deviants, and the possible contributions of social science theory and research to these etiological notions. To the extent this "transference" occurs, it is a second sense in which social scientists help to create and shape deviant careers. As noted in Chapter IV, the work of social scientists may also contribute to public stereotypes of deviant roles and help shape recognition and reaction to behaviors heretofore ignored.

46. One critic of labeling theory chastises it for a "lack of concern with the vulnerability of certain rule-breakers to self-labeling processes which may reduce the significance of *objective* labeling processes in determining deviant careers" (Mankoff, 1971:216). "Objective" here means public.

47. In Lemert's words, labeling theory represents "a large turn from older sociology which tended to rest heavily upon the idea that deviance leads to social control. [However] the reverse idea, i.e., social control leads to deviance, is equally tenable, and the potentially richer premise for studying deviance in modern society" (Lemert, 1967:v).

48. The terms "attachment" and "commitment" are used in the sense Hirschi uses them in his social-control theory of deviance (1969).

49. At times, access to deviant others may reduce labeling effects because the person can argue that he is not as bad as the rest. Imputations of a deviant essential self may be "defused," since there are clearly others who are "more deviant," which may increase the chances of reform.

50. "Overlap refers to the stress put upon two closely related themes: the marginal rather than gross differentiation *between deviant and conventional folks* and the considerable though variable *interpenetration of deviant and conventional culture*. Both themes sensitize us to the regular exchange, traffic, and flow—of persons as well as styles and precepts—that occur among deviant and conventional worlds. Thus, the conceptual distinction . . . recognizes the process of movement between the two realms" (Matza, 1969:68. Emphasis added.). In *Stigma*, Erving Goffman also notes the thin and variable line between stigmatized and normal; so variable, in fact, that any individual may be called upon to play either part in the "normal-deviant drama" (1963:133). "The normal and the stigmatized are not persons, but rather perspectives . . .; particular stigmatizing attributes do not determine the nature of the two roles, normal and stigmatized, merely the frequency of his playing a particular one of them" (*Ibid.*, p. 138).

51. This case is of interest to the social construction of reality question. The juveniles in the gang Reiss studied consistently engaged in what many would term antimasculine behavior (homosexual acts) while at the same time maintaining both individual and collective definitions of extreme masculinity. This was achieved by strict norms on appropriate partners, situations of contact and service, the monetary aspects, and the quick resort to violence when money or conditions of contact were violated. They were also very restrictive on the type of sexual role played such that anything but the inserter role was strongly sanctioned.

52. There appears to be less cultural tolerance of female delinquency. Given more stringent socialization of females, and lower tolerance levels for transgressions, the rule breaking of adolescent girls is seen as less transient, and consequently more serious (Goldman, 1969:285).

53. Self-perception appears to change more readily where there is low consensus among significant others as to the actor's essential self (Backman, *et al.*, 1963). If labeling reduces support for definition of the actor as conventional, we would predict recidivism; those who maintain support in spite of labeling are more likely to reform.

References

Backman, Carl W., Paul F. Secord, and Jerry R. Pierce
  1963   "Resistance to change in the self-concept as a function of
          consensus among significant others." *Sociometry* 26:102–111.

Ball, Donald W.
  1970   "The problematics of respectability." In J. D. Douglas (ed.),
          Deviance and Respectability. New York: Basic Books.

Becker, Howard S.
  1960   "Notes on the concept of commitment." *American Journal of
          Sociology* 66 (July):32–40.

  1963   *Outsiders: Studies in the Sociology of Deviance.* New York:
          Free Press.

  1967   "History, culture and subjective experience: an exploration of
          the social bases of drug-induced experience." *Journal of
          Health and Social Behavior* 8(September):163–76.

Bem, Daryl J.
  1972   "Self-perception theory." In Leonard Berkowitz (ed.), *Ad-
          vances in Experimental Social Psychology,* Vol. 6. New York:
          Academic Press.

Berger, Peter L.
  1963   *Invitation to Sociology.* New York: Doubleday-Anchor.

Bowers, Warner F.
  1960   *Interpersonal Relationships in the Hospital.* Springfield, Ill.:
          Charles C. Thomas.

Bryan, James H.
  1966   "Occupational ideologies and individual attitudes of call
          girls." *Social Problems* 13 (Spring):441–50.

Burgess, Robert L., and Ronald L. Akers
  1966   "A differential association-reinforcement theory of criminal
          behavior." *Social Problems* 14 (Fall):128–47.

Cameron, Mary Owen
  1964   *The Booster and the Snitch.* New York: Free Press.

Capote, Truman
  1965   *In Cold Blood.* New York: Random House, Inc.

273

Chambliss, William
    1969   *Crime and the Legal Process.* New York: McGraw-Hill.

Clinard, Marshall, and Richard Quinney
    1973   *Criminal Behavior Systems.* 2nd ed. New York: Holt, Rine-
            hart and Winston.

Cloward, Richard A., and Lloyd E. Ohlin
    1960   *Delinquency and Opportunity.* New York: Free Press.

Cohen, Albert
    1965   "The sociology of the deviant act: anomie theory and
            beyond." *American Sociological Review* 30 (February):5–14.
    1966   *Deviance and Control.* Englewood Cliffs, New Jersey: Pren-
            tice-Hall.

Cole, Stephen, and Robert Lejeune
    1972   "Illness and the legitimation of failure." *American Sociologi-
            cal Review* 37 (June):347–56.

Dank, Barry M.
    1971   "Coming out in the gay world." *Psychiatry* 34:180–97.

Davis, Nanette J.
    1971   "The prostitute: developing a deviant identity." In James M.
            Henslin (ed.), *Studies in the Sociology of Sex.* New York: Ap-
            pleton-Century-Crofts.

De Lamater, John
    1968   "On the nature of deviance." *Social Forces* 46 (June):445–55.

Duvall, Shelley, and Robert A. Wickland
    1972   *A Theory of Objective Self-Awareness.* New York: Academic
            Press.

Emerson, Robert M.
    1969   *Judging Delinquents: Context and Process in Juvenile Court.*
            Chicago: Aldine.

Empey, LaMar T., and Steven G. Lubeck
    1971   *Explaining Delinquency.* Lexington, Mass.: D. C. Heath.

Fisher, Sethard
    1972   "Stigma and deviant careers in schools." *Social Problems* 20
            (Summer):78–83.

Freidson, Eliot
    1966   "Disability as social deviance." In Marvin B. Sussman (ed.),
            Sociology and Rehabilitation. American Sociological Associa-
            tion.

Garfinkel, Harold
    1956   "Conditions of successful degradation ceremonies." *American
            Journal of Sociology* 61 (March):420–24.
    1967   *Studies in Ethnomethodology.* Englewood Cliffs, N.J.: Pren-
            tice-Hall.

Gecas, Viktor
  1971   "Parental behavior and dimensions of adolescent self-esteem." *Sociometry* 34 (December):466–82.
  1972   "Parental behaviors and contextual variations in adolescent self-esteem." *Sociometry* 35 (June):332–45.

Gergen, Kenneth J.
  1971   *The Concept of Self.* New York: Holt, Rinehart and Winston.

Giallombardo, Rose
  1966   *Society of Women.* New York: John Wiley and Sons.

Goffman, Erving
  1959   *Presentation of Self in Everyday Life.* New York: Doubleday-Anchor.
  1963   *Stigma: Notes on the Management of Spoiled Identity.* Englewood Cliffs, New Jersey: Prentice-Hall.
  1967   *Interaction Ritual.* New York: Doubleday-Anchor.

Goldman, Nathan
  1969   "The differential selection of juvenile offenders for court appearance." In William J. Chambliss (ed.), *Crime and the Legal Process.* New York: McGraw-Hill.

Gould, Leroy C.
  1969a   "Juvenile entrepreneurs." *American Journal of Sociology* 74 (May):710–19.
  1969b   "Who defines delinquency: a comparison of self-reported and officially-reported indices of delinquency for three racial groups." *Social Problems* 16 (Winter):325–36.

Haber, Lawrence D., and Richard T. Smith
  1971   "Disability and deviance: normative adaptations of role behavior." *American Sociological Review* 36 (February):87–97.

Hammersmith, Sue Kiefer, and Martin S. Weinberg
  1973   "Homosexual identity: commitment, adjustment, and significant others." *Sociometry* 36 (March):56–79.

Hartnagel, Timothy F.
  1970   "Father absence and self conception among lower class white and Negro boys." *Social Problems* 18 (Fall):152–63.

Heiss, Jerold, and Susan Owens
  1972   "Self-evaluations of blacks and whites." *American Journal of Sociology* 78 (September):360–70.

Hirschi, Travis
  1969   *Causes of Delinquency.* Berkeley: University of California Press.

Humphreys, Laud
  1970   *Tearoom Trade.* Chicago: Aldine.

Jensen, Gary F.
  1970   "Containment and delinquency: analysis of a theory." *University of Washington Journal of Sociology* 2 (November):1–14.

1972   "Delinquency and adolescent self-conceptions: a study of the personal relevance of infraction." *Social Problems* 20 (Summer):84–103.

Kitsuse, John
1962   "Societal reaction to deviant behavior: problems of theory and method." *Social Problems* 9 (Winter):247–56.

Lemert, Edwin M.
1951   *Social Pathology.* New York: McGraw-Hill.
1967   *"Human Deviance, Social Problems, and Social Control.* Englewood Cliffs, New Jersey: Prentice-Hall.
1972   *Human Deviance, Social Problems, and Social Control.* 2nd ed. Englewood Cliffs, New Jersey: Prentice-Hall.

Lofland, John
1969   *Deviance and Identity.* Englewood Cliffs, New Jersey: Prentice-Hall.

Lofland, John, and Rodney Stark
1965   "Becoming a world-saver: a theory of conversion to a deviant perspective." *American Sociological Review* 30 (December):862–75.

Lorber, Judith
1967   "Deviance as performance: the case of illness." *Social Problems* 14 (Winter):302–310.
1971   "Deviance as conformity." Paper presented at American Sociological Association Meetings in Denver.

McAuliffe, William E., and Robert A. Gordon
1974   "A test of Lindesmith's theory of addiction: the frequency of euphoria among long-term addicts." *American Journal of Sociology* 79 (January):795–840.

McCaghy, Charles H., and James K. Skipper, Jr.
1969   "Lesbian behavior as an adaptation to the occupation of stripping." *Social Problems* 17 (Fall):269–70.

McIntosh, Mary
1968   "The homosexual role." *Social Problems* 16 (Fall):182–92.

Mahoney, E. R.
1973   "The processual characteristics of self-conception." *Sociological Quarterly* 14 (Autumn):517–33.

Mankoff, Milton
1971   "Societal reaction and career deviance: a critical analysis." *Sociological Quarterly* 12 (Spring):204–218.

Maris, Ronald W.
1971   "Deviance as therapy: the paradox of the self-destructive female." *Journal of Health and Social Behavior* 12 (June):113–24.

Matza, David
1964   *Delinquency and Drift.* New York: John Wiley and Sons.

1969   *Becoming Deviant.* Englewood Cliffs, New Jersey: Prentice-Hall.

Matza, David, and Gresham Sykes
1961   "Juvenile delinquency and subterranean values." *American Sociological Review* 26 (October):712–19.

Messinger, Sheldon E., Harold Sampson, and Robert D. Towne
1970   "Life as theatre: some notes on the dramaturgic approach to social reality." In Gregory P. Stone and Harvey A. Faberman (eds.), *Social Psychology Through Symbolic Interaction.* Waltham, Mass.: Ginn.

Miller, Walter B.
1958   "Lower class culture as a generating milieu of gang delinquency." *Journal of Social Issues* 14:5–19.

Miyamoto, S. Frank, and Sanford M. Dornbusch
1956   "A test of interactionist hypotheses of self-conception." *American Journal of Sociology* 61 (March):399–403.

Osgood, Charles E., George J. Suci, and Percey H. Tannenbaum
1957   *The Measurement of Meaning.* Chicago: University Of Illinois Press.

Parsons, Talcott
1951   *The Social System.* New York: Free Press.

Petroni, Frank A.
1969   "The influence of age, sex, and chronicity in perceived legitimacy to the sick role." *Sociology and Social Research* 53 (January):180–93.

Phillips, Derek
1963   "Rejection: a possible consequence of seeking help for mental disorders." *American Sociological Review* 28 (December):963–72.

Reckless, Walter C., and Simon Dinitz
1967   "Pioneering with the self-concept as a vulnerability factor in delinquency." *Journal of Criminal Law, Criminology and Police Science* 58 (December):515–23.

Reiss, Albert J., Jr.
1961   "The social integration of queers and peers." *Social Problems* 9 (Fall):102–120.

Rosenberg, Morris
1965   *Society and the Adolescent Self-Image.* New Jersey: Princeton University Press.

Rosenthal, Robert, and Lenore Jacobson
1968   *Pygmalion in the Classroom.* New York: Holt, Rinehart and Winston.

Ross, Lawrence H.
1961   "Traffic law violation: a folk crime." *Social Problems* 8 (Winter):231–41.

Sampson, Harold, Sheldon L. Messinger, and Robert D. Towne
1961 "The mental hospital and marital family ties." *Social Problems* 9 (Fall):141–55.

Schafer, Stephen
1971 "The concept of the political criminal." *Journal of Criminal Law, Criminology and Police Science* 62:380–87.

Scheff, Thomas J.
1966 *Being Mentally Ill.* Chicago: Aldine.

1968 "Negotiating reality: notes on power in the assessment of responsibility." *Social Problems* 16 (Summer):3–17.

Schur, Edwin M.
1969 "Reactions to deviance: a critical assessment." *American Journal of Sociology* 75 (November):309–322.

Schwartz, Michael, and Sheldon Stryker
1970 *Deviance, Selves and Others.* Washington, D.C.: American Sociological Association.

Schwartz, Michael, and Sandra S. Tangri
1965 "A note on self-concept as an insulator against delinquency." *American Sociological Review* 30 (December):922–26.

Schwartz, Richard D., and Jerome H. Skolnick
1962 "Two studies of legal stigma." *Social Problems* 10 (Fall):133–42.

Sherwood, John J.
1965 "Self-identity and referent others." *Sociometry* 28 (March):66–81.

1967 "Increased self-evaluation as a function of ambiguous evaluations by referent others." *Sociometry* 30 (December):404–409.

Short, James F., Jr., Ramon Rivera, and Roy A. Tennyson
1965 "Perceived opportunities, gang membership and delinquency." *American Sociological Review* 30 (February):56–67.

Short, James F., Jr., and Fred L. Strodtbeck
1965 *Group Process and Gang Delinquency.* Chicago: University of Chicago Press.

Simmons, J. L.
1965 "Public stereotypes of deviants." *Social Problems* 13 (Fall):223–32.

1969 *Deviants.* Berkeley: Glendessary.

Skipper, James K., Jr., and Charles H. McCaghy
1970 "Stripteasers: the anatomy and career contingencies of a deviant occupation." *Social Problems* 17 (Winter):391–405.

Smith Paul E., and Richard Hawkins
1973 "Victimization, types of citizen-police contacts and attitudes toward the police." *Law and Society Review* 8 (Fall):135–52.

Strauss, Anselm L.
  1969   *Mirrors and Masks: The Search for Identity.* San Francisco: Sociology Press.
Szasz, Thomas S.
  1956   "Malingering: 'diagnosis' or social condemnation." *Archives of Neurology and Psychiatry* 76 (October):438–40.
Tangri, Sandra S., and Michael Schwartz
  1967   "Delinquency and the self-concept variable." *Journal of Criminal Law, Criminology and Police Science.* 58 (June): 182–90.
Taylor, Ian, Paul Walton, and Jock Young
  1973   *The New Criminology: For a Social Theory of Deviance.* London: Routledge and Kegan Paul.
Thorsell, Bernard A., and Lloyd W. Klemke
  1972   "The labeling process: reinforcement and deterrent?" *Law and Society Review* 6 (February):393–403.
Tucker, Charles W.
  1966   "Some methodological problems of Kuhn's self theory." *Sociological Quarterly* 7 (Summer):345–58.
Turner, Ralph H.
  1969   "The public perception of protest." *American Sociological Review* 34 (December):815–31.
  1972   "Deviance avowal as neutralization of commitment." *Social Problems* 19 (Winter):308–321.
Warren, Carol A. B., and John M. Johnson
  1972   "A critique of labeling theory from the phenomenological perspective." In Robert A. Scott and Jack D. Douglas (eds.), *Theoretical Perspectives on Deviance.* New York: Basic Books.
Weinberg, Martin S.
  1970   "The role homosexual: age-related variations in social and psychological characteristics." *Social Problems* 17 (Spring):527–37.
Williams, Colin J., and Martin S. Weinberg
  1971   *Homosexuals and the Military.* New York: Harper and Row.
Winich, Charles
  1964   "Physician narcotic addicts." In Howard S. Becker (ed.), *The Other Side.* New York: Free Press.
Wolfgang, Marvin E., Robert M. Figlio, and Thorsten Sellin
  1972   *Delinquency in a Birth Cohort.* Chicago: University of Chicago Press.
Yancey, William L., Leo Rigsby, and John D. McCarthy
  1972   "Social position and self-evaluation: the relative importance of race." *American Journal of Sociology* 78 (September):338–59.

The Total
Institution
and Its Impact

There is no human dialogue between the hospital psychiatrist and his committed patient; instead, the patient's talk is "clinical material." The mental patient is a living corpse, the words he utters the semantic exudates of his disease, to be examined, not heeded. Psychiatrists thus refer to the patient's speech as "productions," as if his words were sputum: they record it on magnetic tape, atomize it into linguistic bits and pieces, and replay his "tape" before students who listen to it as they would view tubercle bacilli under a microscope. These are the essential steps in the processing of man into mental patient. . . .

Thomas Szasz

The society, through its authorized social-control agents and agencies, *does something to* the individuals that come under its purview. At a minimum, a label is attached and no further action takes place: the outpatient goes home; the convicted criminal is granted a suspended sentence. At a maximum, the subject is hospitalized or incarcerated for the rest of his life. Between these two extremes, labeled institutional confinement ranging from a few days to several years may transpire, followed by a reentry into the society. Our principle concern at this point is with this midrange group—i.e., those who undergo significant amounts of agency-directed control ostensibly aimed at orderly adjustment to the day-to-day routines of the outside society. This rehabilitative premise rests upon the subject's cooperation and agreement, which in turn rests upon his granting the whole process a sense of legitimacy. The key issue of perceived legitimacy is the sense of justice produced by agency contact.

Sense of Injustice

To speak of a sense of injustice, one must come to terms with the concept of justice. David Matza, in a discussion of the sense of justice developed by the juvenile court, delineates five dimensions of fair-

Source: Thomas S. Szasz, *The Manufacture of Madness,* New York: Harper and Row, 1970, p. 283.

ness: cognizance, consistency, competence, commensurability, and comparison.[1] Each component may be used to indict juvenile justice agencies. Matza suggests that the very operations of the juvenile control system and its attendant ideology facilitate a neutralization of controls which may result in delinquency: "the ideology of child welfare supports the delinquent's viewpoint in two ways. It confirms his conception of irresponsibility and it feeds his sense of injustice" (1964:98). In a general sense, the same outcome is predicted for those social-control agencies which utilize processing stereotypes, engage in mystification and reification during case disposition, and impose corrective procedures upon the deviant.

Cognizance refers to perceptions of the legitimacy of surveillance of personal activity. A labelled deviant may feel it is unfair to be watched more closely than other individuals in society. Matza says the delinquent feels it is remarkably unfair to officially monitor his actions while the actions of other youth and many adults are not as systematically observed: "the delinquent may sense injustice because of the selective procedures inherent in any efficient system of enforcement" (Matza, 1964:108). Cognizance is influenced by the processing stereotypes of an agency in that these typified images determine, in part, what the agency will look for and where they will look. Thus, police "partition the city into areas of more or less anticipated crime [which] provides both police and probation officers with additional typifications about what to expect when patrolling. Thus the officer's preconstituted typifications and stock of knowledge at hand leads him to prejudge much of what he encounters" (Cicourel, 1968:67). These self-fulfilling aspects of surveillance and apprehension may result in vicious cycles of reaction to deviance (Lemert, 1951; Parsons, 1951; Pittman and Gillespie, 1967). In a similar sense, those with extensive contact with public agencies—e.g., welfare recipients—may have more of their behavior come under official observation. (See our discussion of visibility in Chapter IV).

Injustice may be the natural outgrowth of variation in societal expectations for certain groups. Delinquents, for example, are more subject to legal controls than adults because society has enacted status offenses—i.e., activities only illegal when carried out by persons under an arbitrary age limit. For example, the "delinquent tendencies" clause of delinquency statutes includes truancy, incorrigibility, running away, and other adolescent-specific offenses. Here, cognizance depends on a status characteristic (in this case age) and this exclusive focus comes to be seen as unfair. Another example would be the greater cognizance of probationers and parolees in both imposition of special, status-specific rules and closer observations of behaviors through supervision.

A third meaning of cognizance refers to what is selected and emphasized from a particular case. This form of selectivity is evident when the deviant feels that his biography has not been accurately rendered by control agents. This is likely to occur if the deviant realizes that "almost anyone's life course could yield up enough denigrating facts to provide grounds for the record's justification of commitment" (Goffman, 1961:159). In this case resentment is produced not by too much cognizance, but by selective attention to background characteristics such that negative aspects are over-represented.

Consistency of publicly espoused disposition criteria and procedure with actual practice facilitates a sense of justice. Yet, in settings such as the juvenile court and commitment hearings, this consistency may be largely absent: "the sense of inconsistency is likely to be heightened when legal agents possess great discretion or when the principles that guide decision are diffusely or mysteriously delineated" (Matza, 1964:111). It was suggested in Chapter VII that processing stereotypes are part of an informal system within processing bureaucracies which provide standardized guidelines to action when formal criteria for action are ambiguous or absent. The deviant may sense a high level of inconsistency when he is aware of the formal principles of the agency, yet observes decisions being made on seemingly unrelated criteria. This form of inconsistency is also evident in the adult legal system. The accused is supposedly judged in a system which assumes innocence until proven guilty, provides for trial by peers, and prescribes an adequate defense for the indigent. Instead, he finds a shuffling of legal categories based on a stereotyped picture of his case, a complex system of assuring guilty pleas, and a public defender more concerned with getting a reduction in the charge than with raising questions of innocence and how it might be proven in court.

One reason that the inconsistencies are so glaring, even to the first-time offender who is likely to suffer at the hands of bargain justice, is that society has perpetuated a due-process myth. The mass media cover large trials, in part, because of the difficulties involved in observing plea bargaining. Radio and television shows give the impression of automatic trials. Even the court itself helps to perpetuate the myth. Newman (1966) notes that the judge always asks the defendant who is entering a guilty plea if there has been any deal made. The accused is told beforehand to say "no" to this question. The judge and the accused, as well as other officials of the court, know a deal has been made but continue in the charade.

In addition, the bargain justice system tends to benefit the sophisticated criminal while going hard on the first-time offender who has not learned how or what to negotiate. Skolnick's (1966:167–81) study of the impact of bureaucratic pressures to improve the clearance rates by a police department (percentage of crimes known to the police which the police write off as solved) is an example of agency goal displacement. Since solving and thereby clearing crimes is a valued commodity within the police organization, those suspects who can provide information, or who are willing to admit to a large number of crimes, have the greatest bargaining power. The first-time offender who was unfortunate enough to be arrested after his initial burglary has nothing to bargain with. Thus, an ironic situation evolves where the more highly involved and sophisticated criminal comes off better in the control network than the first-time offender, who often has the book thrown at him. Here again, the inconsistent aspects of the criminal justice system do not go unrecognized by those deviants involved.

This form of inconsistency coincides with Matza's component of *commensurability*. Clearly, when the individual who admits one hundred burglaries comes out ahead of the individual who commits one, the resultant punishment has not fit the crime. The demand that the punishment fit the crime implies that the uniqueness of the case must be considered. This is especially true in juvenile court where the doctrine of individualized justice is professed, but it also applies to adult criminal court in terms of *mens rea*, mitigating circumstances and self-defense. However, processing stereotypes and the heavy reliance on records rather than on testimony tend to reduce and obscure the unique aspects of the case. In addition, processing stereotypes imply that typical cases get typical dispositions in terms of sanctions. Therefore, the deviant may conclude that his punishment was not commensurate with his actions, and a sense of injustice is generated.[2]

Feelings of consistency and commensurability are also violated when the court professes to make decisions on a certain criterion, but in fact uses unrelated factors to make decisions. Matza states that in juvenile court, the judge relies on parental sponsorship—i.e., typifications of the suitability of the family to control the delinquent—and residential availability—i.e., the amount of correctional space available so that incarceration can be ordered. The juvenile comes to see these as the principles upon which the court operates rather than the espoused principle of individualized justice. The perception of this inconsistency increases the sense of injustice. Matza states, however, that not all delinquents perceive these inconsistencies in the juvenile court operations. This is where the *comparison* element of justice plays a role. The experiences of one juvenile are compared to the experiences of others.[3] Even though only a small minority of youth actually see and understand the duplicity of the court, each shares his feelings with others. The delinquent subculture provides a means of comparison: "the subculture of delinquency is, among other things, a memory file that collects injustices" (Matza, 1964:102). This comparison function in the assessment of processing procedures has been found in other settings. Goffman (1961) mentions that mental patients use comparison to assess their positions in the hospital. Roth (1963) found that tuberculosis patients use comparisons of the treatment provided fellow patients as "bench marks" to structure their passage through the system. This comparison function is found in most total institutions (Brim and Wheeler, 1966).

The majority of delinquents are mystified by the operations of the court, by the legal rhetoric used by officials, and while they may not see the inconsistency in court decision criteria, the mystification itself may produce a sense of injustice. Blumberg (1967) has suggested that a major function of defense attorneys is to provide an interpretation of the proceedings such that mystification is reduced. These attorneys may be called upon to provide a "cooling out" function—i.e., to help their clients adjust to the estimated outcome.

The final component of injustice—the perception of *incompetence* of official control agents—is perhaps easiest to understand: police corruption, unenforceable laws, cries of police brutality and police hypocrisy, all operate to undermine the legitimacy of the law and the agents charged with its enforcement. Matza notes that the common complaints of control agents—e.g., low pay, high case loads, lack of autonomy, etc., may indirectly contribute to the sense of incompetence which may be imputed to the agents. The delinquent may conclude that if the job is so bad, the individual must be incompetent or he would have sought out a better occupation. Since many people in society feel that incompetence does exist in our control agencies, it is not difficult for the delinquent to generalize these feelings to justify his own law violations.

We have illustrated the five components of injustice in the area of crime and delinquency. We would predict that a sense of injustice is *less* likely to develop when the processing rubric is mental illness. Take, for example, our last point about perceptions of officials' competence. The mental health ethic and psychiatry in general receives widespread support from the public, hence the concept of corrupt or incompetent psychiatrists is barely entertained and never seriously considered. There are no equivalents to the Knapp Commission or the Walker Report (on Chicago police brutality) to discredit organized psychiatry. The main challenge to psychiatry has probably come from the voluminous writings of Thomas Szasz; yet he concentrates mainly on institutional psychiatry and involuntary commitment. His *Manufacture of Madness* (1970b) is a wide-ranging attack on the legitimacy and credibility of institutional psychiatry. As Szasz notes, the ties between psychiatry and religion help to legitimate the former in a highly Christian nation.[4] When this entrenched legitimacy is coupled with the intra-psychic biases of psychiatric ideology and treatment, there is little chance for a sense of injustice to develop. Also, psychiatry benefits from its inclusion in the medical area, a highly respected profession. For these reasons, we would predict that this strong societal support for psychiatry produces a differential in the sense of injustice for those processed in the criminal-legal and the medical realms. In the criminal justice system, the sense of injustice develops all along the processing route (see Casper, 1972; Irwin, 1970). In the case of medicalized deviance, this attitude may never form or would probably require extensive contact with control agencies under involuntary auspices—e.g., commitment hearing or total institution.

In general, we propose that feelings of injustice are more likely with greater exposure to social-control agencies. Such contacts should also have a great impact on self-conceptions. Only the social-control agency (in contrast to one's church, workplace, club, etc.) concerns itself directly, immediately, and fundamentally with the individual's very identity. Only there does the organization's primary function revolve around the construction of conscious, formal judgments concerning the nature and "goodness" of the individual. Given this unique, express function, the social-control agency can be expected to exert greater influence over personal identity than do social interaction settings in general. This influence is probably greatest in the setting of the total institution.

The Total Institution and Self-Mortification[5]

A total institution is a control agency where "inmates" (whether termed patients, prisoners, or clients) are restricted in their leave-taking and contacts with the outside world. The most "total" of these institutions would be prisons and mental hospitals, while boarding schools, colleges, ships, military bases, monasteries, and nursing homes may also be total in their effect (Goffman, 1961:4–5). Total institutions are characterized by control through a single authority structure, by the tight scheduling of inmates' daily activities performed in the company of large groups of others, and by forced activities which are "brought into a single rational plan purportedly designed to fulfill the official aims of the institution" (*Ibid.*, p. 6). The consequences of these practices for inmates are indeed awesome. The impact of control ideologies is perhaps most evident in the total institution, producing what Erving Goffman has termed "mortification of self":

> Upon entrance . . . [the individual] begins a series of abasements, degradations, humiliations, and profanations of self. His self is systematically, if often unintentionally, mortified. He begins some radical shifts in his moral career, a career composed of the progressive changes that occur in the beliefs that he has concerning himself and significant others. (1961:14)

The following factors inherent in the total institution contribute to the self-mortification process: depersonalization, behavior monitoring, the record, and "being on."[6]

Depersonalization

The daily round, and the actions of the control-oriented staff, produce a sense of depersonalization for the deviant. In prison, he is not a name, but a number; in a mental hospital he is likely to be referred to by psychiatric nomenclature—e.g., "the older psychotic in Ward B." Rosenhan (1973:256) describes the dehumanizing aspects of a psychiatric hospital:

> The patient is deprived of many of his legal rights by dint of his psychiatric commitment. He is shorn of credibility by virtue of his psychiatric label. His freedom of movement is restricted. He cannot initiate contact with the staff, but may only respond to such overtures as they make. Personal privacy is minimal. Patient quarters and possessions can be entered and examined by any staff member, for whatever reasons. His personal history and anguish is available to any staff member (often including the "grey lady" and "candy striper" volunteer) who chooses to read his folder, regardless of their therapeutic relationship to him. His personal hygiene and waste evacuation are often monitored. The water closets have no doors.

Generally, such deprivations have been legitimated by the need to control and protect inmates; administrators asked about the punitive

nature of such conditions are likely to respond "well, we're not running a country club here." An alarming trend in both prisons and
mental hospitals is that some of the deprivations described are now
being systematically used in the name of rehabilitation. Behavior
modification programs often make removal of deprivations contingent upon "good behavior"—i.e., conformity to institutional rules.
This, unfortunately, may inadvertently legitimate some of these conditions. Lawyers are now trying to curtail such treatment programs
in the sense of establishing certain minimum rights—e.g., an inmate
cannot be deprived of food, clothes, sleeping facilities and other
essentials. (See Wexler, 1973, for a review of such legal action.)

The dehumanizing conditions of the total institution produce depersonalization because inmates come to be treated as nonreactive
objects. Their cases are often discussed by staff *in their presence:* the
impression is given that they are not there,[7] or are incapable of
comprehending the discussion. This leads to a sense of "invisibility"
(Rosenhan, 1973). This compounds the feelings of transparency already present from self-labeling (see Chapter IX). In addition, contact between staff and inmates is highly superficial,[8] such that eye
contact is avoided, requests are ignored, and presentations of self are
not honored (Messinger, *et al.*, 1970). Personal and social space of
inmates are systematically violated, thereby destroying feelings of
personal autonomy and self-worth (Goffman, 1959:69).

Behavior monitoring

Surveillance of activity in the total institution is virtually complete;
staff observation, often facilitated by electronic means, is possible
because private places do not exist. The monitoring of behavior is
seen as part of the treatment mandate: progress, or more often the
lack of it, must be recorded so that case-related decisions can be
made (Stoll, 1968). Due to understaffing, however, the control agents
are "often too busy to record anything but acts of disobedience"
(Goffman, 1961:360). The corrective ideologies found in most total
institutions produce highly selective recording of behaviors consistent with the processing stereotypes of various cases.

Since total institutions are highly regimented and activities in such
places are carried out in blocks, the possibility of surveillance increases. These requirements, plus the extensive monitoring, put the
inmate in a *highly artificial situation.*[9] This heightens the visibility
of behaviors and exaggerates their significance. Inmates are super-
vised "by personnel whose chief activity is not guidance or periodic
inspection . . . but rather surveillance—a seeing to it that everyone
does what he has been clearly told is required of him, under condi-

tions where one person's infraction is likely to stand out in relief against the visible, constantly examined compliance of the others" (Goffman, 1961:67). In this situation, more is required, more is seen, and more is likely to come under organizationally imposed punishment for violations of "institutional rules." The result is likely to be classification as a "troublemaker" and the imposition of more restrictive controls: tranquilizing, punitive therapy—e.g., electroshock—or transfer to a more restricted ward.

The record

The data produced by the extensive monitoring end up on the behavioral record of the inmate. The case record comes to stand for, and eventually supplant, the inmate. All the selective aspects of biography building are present and in the extreme due to staff surveillance. The record increases self-mortification because it constitutes a "violation of one's informational preserve regarding self"— something generally accorded to people on the outside (Goffman, 1961:23). Through the case record, current behaviors are reinterpreted via the diagnostic category; the procedure "provides a means of systematically building up a picture of the patient's past that demonstrates that a disease process had been slowly infiltrating his conduct until his conduct, as a system, was entirely pathological. Seemingly normal conduct is seen to be merely a mark or shield for the essential sickness behind it" (Goffman, 1961:375).[10]

Rosenhan notes that the normal behaviors of his pseudopatients (confederates who posed as mentally ill to gain admittance to a hospital, but were instructed to then act normally) were reinterpreted by the staff as symptoms of pathology. The students were instructed to keep detailed notes on their observations and experiences, and many found their "compulsive" writing behavior appeared on the nursing records as an indication of their "disturbance." In short, the pseudopatients found that virtually *none* of their behaviors—perfectly acceptable on the outside—were seen as normal in the hospital setting. Furthermore, behavior was seen by the staff as the result of internal pathology, not as the normal responses to abnormal situations. In short, their behavior was not seen as contextually "determined" (Goffman, 1969; Melbin, 1969).

Because the staff brings a particular diagnostic set to both observations and records, inmates are often seen as shallow, one-dimensional persons—not as multi-faceted personalities who would have a chance of making the required adjustment back in society. These records become crucial in release decisions, as many states now require automatic case reviews at designated points in the hospital stay. To the extent records are both diagnostically slanted and more likely to detail rule violations than periods of conformity, they reduce the chances of release (Stoll, 1968). In a similar manner, records of prisoners' in-house behavior affect parole chances.

Official records are difficult, if not impossible, to refute. Records impart a legitimacy and authority to themselves, they have a quantifiable character and impose a permanence and finality to case decisions (Wheeler, 1969). The inmate is in no position to argue as to their contents or interpretations. The staff and record are always right in the total institution; the deviant is not likely to have his accounts and other remedial work honored, especially in regard to the record. If the inmate objects to the rendering of the record, it is to no avail. Protestations will only be used against him to document the underlying condition, in what Goffman terms a "looping" effect:

> An agency that creates a defensive response on the part of the inmate takes this very response as the target of its next attack . . . ; he cannot defend himself in the usual way by establishing distance between the mortifying situation and himself. (1961:35–36)

The record and other aspects of incarceration produce a sense of powerlessness in the inmates which increases the self-mortification.

Being "on"

We noted earlier that deviants, especially those officially labeled, develop an acute awareness of being "on" (on view). While in society they can gain time out from observation and evaluation, this is not generally possible in a total institution. The inmates come to see the importance of the behavioral reports which comprise the record and they recognize their vulnerability. "During hospitalization patients tend to construe all situations as, potentially, 'test' situations in which their 'sanity' is being assessed" (Messinger, et al., 1970:693).[11] The institutionally imposed demand to be "on" (with no time outs, no back regions to aid in staging, and very little team work) is very stressful.[12] As a consequence of constantly being on, "not only can the patient no longer trust others but, most devastating of all, he can no longer trust himself. He is, for a while, anxiously uncertain as to whether the 'normal character' he projects is his 'self' " (Messinger, et al., 1970:694). In this way, the total institution obfuscates the distinction between what is real and that which is staged.[13] The distinction is further complicated by the feelings of depersonalization, powerlessness, and invisibility already mentioned. "And the more he appears to himself as 'acting'—the more single-mindedly he strives for 'effect'—the more uncertain he seems to become" (*Ibid.*, p. 694). This may lead to a resignation and a passivity which comes to be seen as symptomatic of the "condition" (Erikson, 1957).

In these ways, self-image is threatened and self-esteem is likely to be reduced. The feeling of powerlessness will negatively affect self-worth; surveillance (with demands for performances) causes the inmate to severely question his self-image, his essential self. The mortification of self has been achieved, helping to assure engulfment in a deviant role. The result is a reduction in the chances that the deviant will be rehabilitated or prepared for confrontation with the outside world. We would also expect that elements producing self-mortification would reduce feelings of justice and, hence, the legitimacy imparted to the control agency. Now, some evidence on these assertions.

While there is some evidence that a sense of injustice is fostered during status degradation ceremonies (Matza, 1964), we propose that experiences in the total institution are the most powerful determinants of a sense of injustice. Baum and Wheeler (1968:171-72) found that within the first two weeks of incarceration, juveniles (while mystified by their juvenile court experience) did not see their institutional commitment as unfair (only 24 percent felt it was unfair). They were also more likely to blame themselves for their difficulties (83 percent) than to blame others or the system. This would preclude a sense of injustice (Cloward and Ohlin, 1960). Other studies of juveniles conclude that there is "a significant increase in spontaneous expressions of hostility toward the law and its agents as the length of imprisonment extends" (Maher and Stein, 1968:188). A study of adult inmates, interviewed within the first week of their prison stay, found 60 percent felt their sentence was fair. For those in the middle of their stay in prison, this percentage was 36 percent (Glaser and Stratton, 1961). This again suggests that time in the institution affects attitudes toward fairness. (However, the same study found the feelings of fairness increased prior to release. Among those to be released within the next 90 days, 70 percent described their sentence as fair.) Another investigation of a pretrial detention facility found that during the early stages of incarceration, inmate-inmate confrontations were the most prevalent offenses; later, offenses against the staff predominated (Olson, 1974:57).

We propose that a sense of injustice is related to "prisonization" —the development of antistaff attitudes and behaviors—and therefore studies of such processes qualify as indirect evidence on this phenomenon. Wheeler (1961) and Garabedian (1963) have discovered that prisonization fits a U-shaped curve, with antistaff attitudes and actions low at entrance to prison, high in mid-phase, and low again prior to release.[14] (Notice this parallels the sense of injustice in the Glaser and Stratton study). These findings suggest that feelings of injustice may be confined to the institution and may not be translated into antiestablishment attitudes and behavior on the outside.[15]

There are very few studies of the effect of the total institution on the inmates' personal identity: self-image and self-esteem. Karmel (1970) found that time in a mental institution reduced former social identities: "home world" identities were strong during the first month, but after one or two years in the institution, these identities dropped sharply—to the level of those spending fifteen to twenty years in the institution. A study of delinquents concludes that "arrest and a court appearance does not seem to change the offender's self-concept [he does not yet identify himself as a delinquent]: the change comes, apparently, with day-to-day living in the institution" (Maher and Stein, 1968:220). These findings are not inconsistent with Scheff's major proposition on labeling theory; he states that the residual rule breaker *may* accept the deviant role when first publicly labeled in a commitment hearing or court setting (1966:88). If the change in self-image does not occur here, he would predict it would occur in the total institution (*Ibid.*, pp. 84–86).

Self-esteem is also affected by exposure to total institutions (Kaplan, *et al.*, 1964). In a study of a minimum security narcotics hospital, Tittle found self-esteem of both male and female patients was affected by time in the institution under two important conditions. First, those patients having greater exposure to a purely custodial regime within the institution were more likely to experience reduction in self-esteem with greater time in the hospital[16] (Tittle, 1972:73). Second, the degree of affiliation with other inmates affected self-esteem scores. As time in the hospital increased, those who were isolated—lacking contacts with other inmates—developed lower self-esteem (1972:75). We can surmise that greater inmate contacts are characteristic of prisonization,[17] and that patients may have used this as a source of self-esteem—achieved through collective opposition to the total institution's deprivations. Here, as is true on the outside, deviant activity may become a source of self-esteem when other avenues are not available. The degree of influence on self-esteem will depend on the type of deviance involved. It appears that hospitalization of the mentally retarded may actually contribute to self-esteem (Edgerton, 1967).

Adaptations to
Self-Mortification

There are three major forms of inmate response to institutionally imposed self-mortification while the inmate remains incarcerated. First, inmates may completely abandon former self-conceptions and adopt the sick role (or prisoner role): performances are directed toward being a model patient (hospital) or a "square john" (prison) (Erikson, 1957; Schrag, 1961). The organization and staff pressures are directed toward this end:

> The therapist thus proceeds to set in motion a social act which has as its goal the effective cure of the patient's illness. In order for the therapist to enact his own role as medical practitioner, it is necessary for the patient to publicly accept his status in the hospital and *to develop a view of self which is in accordance with the therapist's*. In short, the patient must learn to view the hospital as a legitimate treatment source. In addition, *he must learn to view himself as mentally ill* and in need of treatment. (Denzin, 1968:349. Emphasis added.)

Evidence of the power of therapists and other staff to elicit such definitions comes from a study of a teaching hospital. Here, partly due to the demand for instructional materials, patients engaged in exaggerated behavioral displays of their illnesses when professional staff were present (Melbin, 1969; see also Erikson, 1957; Kaplan, *et al.*, 1964). At the extreme, this adaptive stance may entail the adoption of the corrective ideology of the institution; often inmates are rewarded directly by special privileges or jobs—e.g., trustee role in concentration camps (Bettelheim, 1965).[18]

Second, inmates may form an oppositional subculture (prisonization) which provides a source of recognition and prestige for the inmate. Self-esteem may be raised in part because feelings of powerlessness are reduced. The subculture may also reinforce and solidify feelings of injustice. In prisons, this produces the roles of "right guy" and "con politician." The former are completely dedicated to the oppositional subculture while the latter play both staff and inmate cultures for advantages (Scharg, 1961). Collective resistance to the staff may occur in the form of grievance campaigns, hunger strikes, or confrontations (Cohen and Taylor, 1974:140–46). There appears to be a major difference here between mental hospitals and prisons in terms of the collective response to self-mortification. The oppositional subcultures found in prisons are less likely to form in mental hospitals. First, patients are less likely to use collective methods of adaptation: "collective means of working the system seem not too common in mental hospitals" (Goffman, 1961:215). Collective responses, when they do occur, are likely to be *supportive* of therapeutic programs and staff.[19] One reason for this difference is that a sense of injustice is less likely to form in the medical setting of the mental hospital. As noted above, psychiatry is accorded more legitimacy in the general culture than is the case for the criminal justice system.

Finally, the adaptive response may simply be withdrawal. Selfisolates avoid contacts with both patients and staff. Here, feelings of self-esteem are low; self-esteem may have been low prior to entrance, and this produces isolation; but, regardless, we would predict self-mortification would further reduce feelings of self-worth. In these cases we would not expect a sense of injustice to develop.

We have suggested the ways total institutions affect the deviant's sense of justice and personal identity, and how the inmate may adjust to this mortification while in the institution. We now combine feelings of self-esteem[20] and the sense of justice in order to make some predictions about the deviant's behavioral response to institutional contact upon release. In short, we are interested in the types of adjustments made in future behavior as a result of a stay in a total institution. The possible combinations of self-esteem and perceptions of justice are shown in the typology in Figure I.

Perceptions of
System Legitimacy

		Justice	Injustice
Self-Esteem	High	A Cooperation Contentment	B Independence Defiance
	Low	C Compliance Accommodation	D Retreat Withdrawal

Figure I   *A typology of primary behavioral responses*

In the high esteem–justice situation (Cell A), the individual builds or maintains high self-esteem and perceives that he has been treated fairly, justly emerging from the labeling experience with feelings of satisfaction, or even of gratitude. This individual constitutes the true rehabilitative success. In extreme form, this labelee may become a proselytizer on behalf of the system. Such is the case of the ex-con, ex-alcoholic, ex-junkie, or ex-mental patient who openly discusses the sins of his past as part of an effort to steer others away from a similar fate. Kiwanis luncheons and school assembly programs are typical settings for such self-exposure at the most public level. Synanon and Alcoholics Anonymous organizations are examples of more limited public expression, and written testimonials permit a blend of wide audience contact and personal anonymity.

More commonly, the "contented" labelee simply holds a private gratitude for the perceived self-improvements or redirections resulting from the agency experience; there is no attempt to flaunt the evidence before others or to go out of the way to campaign for the system.[21] Midway between these two extremes we find the person who refrains from self-initiated disclosures but is selectively responsive to cues from others. For example, when a friend initiates inquiry into the labelee's experiences out of general concern or, especially, as overt solicitation of personal counsel and advice, the labelee responds with appropriate supportive commentary.

Moving to the perception of the justice–low self-esteem condition (Cell C), we find those who fatalistically accept the attribution of deviance as indicative of their proper and maximum station in life. The apathetic unemployed who slip into what Oscar Lewis calls the "culture of poverty" can be placed here, as can the "neurotic" housewife whose daily round of depression is broken only by weekly treks to the psychiatric couch. While the system continues to operate, the individual neither runs from it nor fights back at it but simply rolls with the punches. Goffman's notion of "defensive cowering" fits perfectly (1963:17).

This is perhaps the most pathetic behavioral response of all, in that quietude (accommodation, compliance) can be so easily mistaken for cure—i.e., many compliant types are lumped together with cooperators and regarded as rehabilitative successes. In the case of criminal behavior, this evaluative intermingling may be appropriate: if you're not committing crimes any more, you're no longer criminal. But disappearance from welfare lines is no guarantee of achieved affluence, and passive social behavior is an unreliable indicator of psychiatric vitality. To the extent that labeling experiences support and promulgate purely accommodative responses, they not only fail in their publicly expressed aims but (of greater concern) promote the illusory interpretation that they have achieved those aims.

Cell D (low self-image–perception of injustice) differs from Cell C as a behavioral response primarily in that the individual does *not* simply roll with the punches. While he too does not think highly of himself, he explicitly blames "the system" (rather than himself) for having produced the condition.[22] Consequently, out of fear, resentment, or some combination of the two, he takes extra precautions against the reoccurrence of agency contact by withdrawing, retreating, and isolating himself both psychically and socially. While we see this as the general trend, there are exceptions such as the Hell's Angels:

> The Angels have given up hope that the world is going to change for them. They assume, on good evidence, that the people who run the social machinery have little use of outlaw motorcyclists, and they are reconciled to being losers. But instead of losing quietly, one by one, they have banded together with a mindless kind of loyalty.... There is no talk among the Angels of building a better world ... [yet there is a] kind of suicidal loyalty [and the] feeling of constant warfare with an unjust world. (Thompson, 1966:265–66)

Whereas the "accommodator" may become asocial by default, the "retreatist" does so by design. This is a very risky enterprise, since very few of us are able to function for long as fully independent, asocial beings in a complex, technologized, high-density society. Thus, the retreatist exposes himself to a paradoxical Catch 22, particularly if he resides within a "therapeutic state": his very acts of intentional withdrawal subject him to imposed definitions of deviance which maximize the likelihood of his return to the settings he seeks to avoid! The Skid Row derelict provides one such example, as does the antiestablishment drug experimenter. The paradox in both cases is that the selected escape route may circle back to the heart and core of "the establishment" itself. This is well documented by the public drunk who is on the circuit (Spradley, 1970; Wiseman, 1970).

Only two devices realistically exist to preclude this course of events. First, the surrounding subculture may develop its own internal prevention and treatment techniques. Thus, the more experienced members of an urban drug scene may seek to (a) deemphasize enchantment with drugs and redirect participant motives and satisfactions (e.g., turn to religion) and/or (b) construct in-group programs of social support and counseling for those who demonstrate problem behaviors (e.g., Alcoholics Anonymous). Secondly, the larger society may overtly agree to "write off" a retreatist subpopulation as a lost cause, thereby declining to activate social-control measures that are otherwise available. This is the pattern in many urban settings where the afore-mentioned Skid Row becomes an institutionalized feature of the community landscape. High recidivism rates, unavailability of workable employment options, the cost of establishing and maintaining treatment and detoxification centers, and the difficulty of recruiting, training, and holding effective workers may interact to produce this phenomenon. It is at its peak when police are encouraged to curtail arrests for public drunkenness and when the deviant actors themselves have learned that they will be left alone as long as they stay within established territorial boundaries.[23]

Another case in point regarding the paradox of retreatism is that of the experienced psychiatric labelee who operationalizes his perception of injustice in the form of a belief that people are "out to get him." He may then generalize this sensitivity to noncontrol agents in his immediate environment, taking their objectively innocuous comments as cues indicative of involvement in a general conspiracy (e.g., question: "How are you today?" Answer: "Why do you want to know?"). As such interactions continue, the individual falls victim to his own self-fulfilling prophecy: others really *do* go out of their way to avoid him. As Lemert (1962) implies, many people who feel that others don't like them have simply sensed the fact that others indeed *don't* like them: they have seen to it by their own behaviors. At any rate, the psychiatric label "paranoid" exists for those who harbor such perceptions, and it may be freely applied irrespective of whether the expressed conspiracy is factually based or purely imaginary. The behavior clearly accelerates the likelihood that social interactants will perceive the actor as "abnormal" and "in need of help." Hence, pressures in the direction of renewed psychiatric care may be exerted in forms ranging from the subtle hint to formal commitment proceedings. When these pressures are successful, the ready label is applied and the individual's protests serve as verbal quicksand (e.g., "I don't belong here! The system is out to get me!" "Sure you don't. Sure it is. Now would you like to roll up your sleeve while I make a few notes on your chart?") The number of "career patients" that can be accounted for along these or similar lines is seemingly immune to accurate detection and count. One reason is that they may reject traditional methods of data gathering, questionnaires, and interviews, because these procedures have literally been used against them in the total institution.

Turning now to the final case, high injustice–high self-esteem (Cell B), we rely on a fictional account to highlight its implications. A recent episode of a television series depicted the unorthodox plight of a relatively orthodox unwed mother. Befriended by an innocent bystander as she waits her turn in an abortion clinic, our heroine (Barbara) is persuaded that she really should bear and love her child and is then deposited in a warm, supportive Home for Unwed Mothers. Subsequent to delivery, she is told that her child was stillborn, a story she will not accept since she herself saw the newborn alive and well. She meets with continuing rejection and rebuff as she seeks to rectify this perceived injustice. Assorted lack of sympathy and assistance prompts her to shoot two men with the pistol she has taken from the home's not-so-gentle-after-all matron, whom she has "done in" in what constitutes an act of involuntary manslaughter. As the pieces of the plot fall together, it turns out that Barbara has been victimized by a cleverly designed adoption racket and her baby has been sold for $3,000 to a nice couple residing on the San Francisco peninsula. The police arrive just in the nick of time and disarm Barbara in the midst of her attempt to recover her child at gunpoint.

Meanwhile, Barbara's callous mother (a University of San Francisco professor, no less) has informed us that Barbara underwent psychiatric care some years ago; hence, of course, she is likely to be a little unstable now. Dissolve to the epilogue, wherein Barbara emerges from the judge's chambers reconciled to the decision that she is to be sent to the state mental hospital while the nice couple continues to care for the baby—at least until Barbara "gets better," and then "we'll see what should be done at that point."[24]

Barbara qualifies as an example of the "independence" or "defiance" response (Cell B) in that she is both exceedingly self-confident and highly resentful of the "unjust" treatment she feels she has experienced at the hands of social-control agencies. Whether or not Barbara's initial psychiatric experience was justified, her current state of psychiatric health is good. Her experiences and her intelligence as applied to understanding the workings of the social-control system combine to tell her that a story about a mysteriously disappearing newborn infant will be received with a minimum of credibility. Thus, she senses that her only option is to take matters into her own hands. She initiates a series of behaviors so necessarily unorthodox that she ensures a return trip to the mental hospital when she is finally apprehended.[25] Injustice is thereby compounded: behaviors activated out of perceptions of injustice lead her directly to the outcome she seeks to avoid.

In order to double-check our typological model, let us speculate on Barbara's actions and fate had she characterized another cell type.[26] As a "cooperator," she would have been equally distraught about the abduction of her child, but perceptions of just treatment in the past would presumably have led her to the police rather than to her own devices, thus precluding criminal activity and incarceration or rehospitalization. As either a "complier" or an "isolate" (Cells C and D), the low self-image component leads us to expect a lowering of initiative of any sort on Barbara's part, but more in the former case than in the latter. In everyday language, if one does not feel "good" or "confident" about oneself and takes such feelings as indicative of personal inadequacy, inaction is more likely than if the same feelings are part of a resentful consciousness of having been "had" by the system.

We do, then, appear to have solid conceptual grounds for predicting a differential behavioral response to the same incident as a function of the two variables of our typology, with aggressive, autonomous behaviors at a peak in Cell B and most depressed in Cell C. This brings us a step closer to understanding some of the special irony and importance of Cell B (defiant response).

Sociologists in the areas of deviant behavior, criminology, and penology have long demonstrated a fondness for informing their students that our typical prison systems act as "colleges for crime." The point of this shocking pronouncement is that the best way to turn a novice criminal into a hardened master criminal is to place him in a setting where he is surrounded by already hardened criminals who can teach him the tricks of the trade. But prisons may operate as crime colleges in a far more subtle sense by imparting another kind of social learning: the rhetoric of societal injustice (e.g., Irwin, 1970). This education comes not only in the form of direct propaganda from angry peers but, perhaps more importantly, from first-hand involvement in a system that advertises fairness, equity, humanity, and rehabilitation but practices inequity, dehumanization, and retributional confinement. As he comes to see that wealth and social status strongly influence every aspect of surveillance and response from apprehension to sentencing, that prisons are poorly staffed, underequipped, and not actively concerned with meaningful personal retraining and redirection, and that the society goes out of its way to avoid reaccepting anyone with "a record," he needs little guidance from others to conclude that democracy and the golden rule find little reflection in his day-to-day reality. Under these conditions, recidivism should not be surprising.

While the criminal processing is likely to produce feelings of injustice in more cases than hospital treatment, perhaps the greater casualty of the mental hospital stay is the effect on self-image and self-esteem. Hospitalization means the patient learns how to falsify his presentation of self in all social settings where open display might be taken as symptomatic of pathology, perhaps managing to retain some private or small-group spheres for the display of his "authentic" self (Messinger, *et al.*, 1970). The behaviors learned in the institution do not prepare him for the outside world, so failures are likely to be encountered. It is not so much that fellow inmates teach the mental patient how to act "crazy" as it is that irrationality comes to be seen as the most rational response to an irrational set of surroundings.[27] When this confused sense of rationality is transplanted to interactions outside the institution, it will produce further negative sanctions and pressure to return to the hospital.

But what of the costs to society? While the criminal's undisclosed but continuing criminality imposes direct, objective costs upon the community (i.e., financial and property losses), the "psychotic's" undisclosed but continuing "psychosis" incurs no such clearcut loss. We might readily conclude, therefore, that everything is just fine: the individual can still "do his thing" selectively while the rest of the society is no longer burdened with having to put up with him. What this perspective fails to consider is that a much more subtle, indirect societal loss may be in operation. An appreciation of the nature of such a loss requires prior acceptance of the idea that societies benefit from diversity of personality types and life styles or, conversely, that the order-sustaining advantages of conformity have their limits. As we say in our earlier discussion of entrepreneurial work of control agencies, there exists a trend toward narrowing definitions and standards of normality such that fewer and fewer atypical behaviors are deemed broadly desirable or even acceptable. Going to extremes for purposes of argumentation, the ultimate extension of the therapeutic state would be a normatively restrictive society of robotized humanoids moving in lock-step, as commonly portrayed in futuristic science fiction scenarios. Few would disagree that such a society would be repressive, monotonous, and stagnant.[28] At the other end of the continuum, we are equally wary of a totally atomized anarchy of maximum personal freedom coupled with the absence of any social constraint whatsoever, where individuals are unguided and unprotected and where a quite different form of social stagnation sets in. What we are wrestling with here, of course, is the age-old problem of where society should draw the line between individual freedom and social responsibility. And what we are suggesting is that society deprives itself of the potential benefits of individual uniqueness, creativity, and spontaneity by organizing itself so that atypical behaviors are *assumed* (without adequate test) to be undesirable and destructive. By suppressing the innovator via social-control devices and later diverting him away from ongoing social interaction, real social losses are incurred amidst total lack of awareness that they are in process. To add self-insult to self-injury, in fact, the society goes further and congratulates itself that deviance has been quieted and brought under control.

An anonymous author recently explained the existence of U.S. urban slums by imagining what the devil might propose as a means of achieving a form of hell on earth (Economic Education Bulletin, 1974). The irony of the piece is that the devil suggests a complex of local, state, and federal programs, real estate codes, and tax systems identical to those that already exist. In other words, we could do no better job of slum creation if we had set out with the express goal of *creating* urban slums. By the same token, it appears that we could hardly do a better job of creating criminality and psychiatric deviance than what we currently accomplish with the interpersonal and organizational workings of our social-control systems. As society draws narrower normative boundaries and exposes more people to the injustices and inconsistencies of official processing, we expect more persons to develop a defiant response. It is not that "defiance" appears only as the result of social-control experiences. Rather, social-control experiences provide one of several routes to defiance. The possibilities of political deviance must now be examined.

Notes

1. "The major meanings of fairness are captured . . . in the following assertions: it is only fair that some steps be taken to ascertain whether I was really the wrongdoer (cognizance); it is only fair that I be treated according to the same principles as others of my status (consistency); it is only fair that you who pass judgment on me sustain the rights to do so (competence); it is only fair that some relationship obtain between the magnitude of what I have done and what you propose to do to me (commensurability); it is only fair that differences between the treatment of my status and others be reasonable and tenable (comparison)" (Matza, 1964:106).

2. "Commensurability refers to the relation between infraction and sanction. What you do to me should in some measure be related to what I have done. Moreover, the phrase 'what I have done' must be understood in context and full complexity" (Matza, 1964:159).

3. To the extent public and informal labeling force individuals into subcultures for support and defense, the sense of injustice is more likely to occur; these two factors operate to maintain the individual in the ascribed deviant role. For a description of the sources of injustice for adult felons, see Irwin (1970:50–60, 173).

4. "Modern psychiatric ideology is an adaptation—to a scientific age—of the traditional ideology of Christian theology. Instead of being born into sin, man is born into sickness. . . . [W]hereas in the Age of Faith the ideology was Christian, the technology clerical, and the expert priestly; in the Age of Madness, the ideology is medical, the technology clinical, and the expert psychiatric" (Szasz, 1970a:5).

5. This section relies heavily on Erving Goffman's classic, *Asylums* (1961). It is highly recommended for those interested in the complex implications of the total institution for identity and behavior. In addition, institutional effects in mental hospitals are graphically detailed in Kesey (1962), Green (1964), and Sechehaye (1970).

6. Not all agree that mortification *does* occur in total institutions. One investigator, using instruments only remotely relevant to Goffman's meaning of the term and applying them to subjects institutionalized for only one month, concludes that a slight *gain* in "self-esteem" takes place in the course of mental hospitalization (Karmel, 1969). Exclusive of methodological weaknesses, it is interesting to note the author's own comment that "what appears humiliating and role-dispossessing to an outsider may not appear as such to a mental patient" (p. 141). It would seem to follow that what does *not* appear humiliating and role-dispossessing to an outsider may appear as such to a mental patient. For methodological criticisms of this study, see Bohr (1970).

7. One observer in a mental hospital reported this incident: "a nurse unbuttoned her uniform to adjust her brassiere in the presence of an entire ward of viewing men. One did not have the sense that she was being seductive. Rather she didn't notice us" (Rosenhan, 1973:256).

8. Rosenhan states that the "heavy reliance upon psychotropic medication tacitly contributes to depersonalization by convincing staff that treatment is indeed being conducted and that further patient contact may not be necessary"

(1973:256–57). In prison settings, the presence of counselors and group therapy sessions may likewise mean that custodial staff depersonalize the prisoners.

9. "Artificial" in the sense there are few comparable situations of this type on the outside. However, the deviant's earlier "training" in covering and passing may be of some aid in these situations. The implications for self are discussed below.

10. As an illustration, one observer in a mental ward reported: "One psychiatrist pointed to a group of patients who were sitting outside the cafeteria entrance half an hour before lunchtime. To a group of young residents he indicated that such behavior was characteristic of the oral-acquisitive nature of the syndrome. It seemed not to occur to him that there were very few things to anticipate in a psychiatric hospital besides eating" (Rosenhan, 1973:352).

11. To have an analogous situation in a less total institution, college, students would be subject to surprise "pop quizzes" in all courses, and to be more accurate, at any time outside the classroom.

12. On the topic of presentation of self and the dramaturgical model, see Goffman, 1959, and a critique by Messinger, *et al.*, 1970. Wilkinson (1974), drawing on Thomas Scheff, has proposed that mental illness can be conceived as "dramaturgical incompetence." The mental hospital is hardly conducive to the development of competence in presentations.

13. Studies indicate that mental patients try to create back regions and time-outs by strictly defining "therapeutic" and "non-therapeutic" spheres. Sick role performances are demanded in the former, while relaxed in the latter (Erikson, 1957; Kaplan, *et al.*, 1964; Melbin, 1969).

14. For an exception to this pattern, see Atchley and McCabe (1968). Space limitations allow us merely to list the factors which may affect "prisonization": type of crime, prisoner's role (square john, right guy, outlaw, or con politician), prior prison experience, type of prison (state-federal), extent of inmate-inmate and staff-inmate contact, institutional type (punishment-treatment), institutional organization, and past association with criminal subcultures outside of prison. The last factor questions whether the oppositional subculture is imported to the prison or grows out of prisoner adjustment to the total institution. See Atchley and McCabe (1969), Schrag (1961), and Tittle (1969) for an introduction to these issues and the relevant literature.

15. John Irwin's research (1970) indicates that injustice does generalize to the outside and affect parole success. There is little systematic evidence on the sense of injustice and the probability of recidivism. We shall make some predictions of behavioral effects in the next section.

16. We see this as suggesting that the more custodial and restrictive the environment, the greater the feelings of helplessness and lack of power. As stated before, this should lower self-esteem. The setting of this study only minimally qualified as a total institution, since it included some voluntary patients (although 40 percent of these voluntary patients thought of themselves as prisoners). See Tittle, 1972:66–67.

17. As we shall see below, the contacts between inmates may not necessarily be to oppose the staff and the organization, but at times may actively aid it.

18. For documentation of adaptive responses to the extreme stress of concentration camps, see Bettelheim (1965), Bluhm (1964), Luchtenhand (1971), and Schein (1965).

19. For evidence, see Kaplan, *et al.*, (1964) and references cited there. For a case of an oppositional subculture in a mental institution, see Stoll, 1968. Goffman (1961) speaks of the underlife of the mental hospital, but it is not highly organized for collective implemementation.

20. We do not include self-image (deviant or conventional) because we feel the products of total institutions are likely to see themselves as deviant or "formerly deviant"—this becomes important to understanding of future actions.

21. This is not to say the agency will not try to use him to document their success. His story is likely to be repeated for the benefit of friends and supporters of deviants entering the total institution.

22. We have argued above that persons with low self-esteem are less likely to develop a sense of injustice, and so the number of persons fitting this cell may be small. When found, however, we would predict they would be *less* likely to seek a *collective solution* to the perceived injustice. It may also be the case that since low self-esteem is present, the actor may come to a very specific delineation of injustice—in other words, the actor may sense that he or she is getting a bum rap, but may not generalize this to others (generalized injustice). See our earlier comments on the comparison aspect of injustice.

23. At present, the public-at-large reflects the same set of tacit understandings in their agreement to stay out of certain parts of town. "The very anticipation of such contacts can . . . lead normals and the stigmatized to arrange life so as to avoid them" (Goffman, 1963:12). Parallel considerations apply to tacit boundaries surrounding other types of labeled deviants—e.g., "shantytown," "the other side of the tracks," the red light district, Harlem.

24. What is most disturbing about this fictional piece is not its ironic conclusion but the credibility apparently attached to the conclusion by the mass audience. Indeed, as this co-author bolted from his chair in anger, he simultaneously bolted into heated argument with a co-viewer who maintained that the outcome was as it should be: Barbara did, after all, have a psychiatric history, and the nice couple would surely make better parents than Barbara ever could.

25. Clearly, Barbara was a victim of extreme extenuating circumstances and should ideally be released outright with her infant in her arms. But if the society demands incarceration, she should be imprisoned, not hospitalized! She has engaged in no irrational behavior whatsoever. On the contrary, her acts were highly rational and carefully and intelligently planned. But she did kill one person and wound two others, and such behavior is against the law. At the same time, prison would not be a healthy, renewing experience for Barbara, as we see that psychiatric treatment has already taken a personal toll in her willingness to accept the judge's decision.

26. It is to be suggested that when response shifts occur, most of them will be from justice to injustice. This proposal is based upon our impression that generalizations of justice are inherently more precarious than are generalizations of injustice. That is, given a mixture of "good" and "bad" personal experiences, generalized anticipatory cynicism is more self-protective than generalized optimism—i.e., "expect the worst, and you'll never be disappointed whatever the outcome." Stated in another way, social beings may be more prone to conclude "On the basis of a single experience, I will assume that the entire society is evil" than "On the basis of a single experience, I will assume that the entire society is good." Among other assists, this formulation would help us account for those who show abrupt conversion to a radical political ideology when they themselves encounter a first-time personalized contradiction of the promises of the democratic creed.

27. See the work of R. D. Laing—e.g., *Sanity, Madness and the Family*, 1964; *The Divided Self: An Existential Study in Sanity and Madness*, 1965.

28. As deviance is suppressed, we are closer to what Robert Merton termed a "ritualistic society" (Merton, 1938).

References

Atchley, Robert C., and M. Patrick McCabe
    1968   "Socialization in correctional communities: a replication." *American Sociological Review* 33 (October):774–85.

Baum, Martha, and Stanton Wheeler
    1968   "Becoming an inmate." In S. Wheeler (ed.), *Controlling Delinquents.* New York: John Wiley and Sons.

Bettelheim, Bruno
    1965   "Individual and mass behavior in extreme situations." In H. Proshansky and B. Seidenberg (eds.), *Basic Studies in Social Psychology.* New York: Holt, Rinehart and Winston.

Bluhm, Hilde O.
    1964   "How did they survive? mechanisms of defense in Nazi concentration camps." In B. Rosenberg, *et al.* (eds.), *Mass Society in Crisis.* New York: Macmillan.

Blumberg, Abraham S.
    1967   *Criminal Justice.* Chicago: Quadrangle Books.

Bohr, Ronald H.
    1970   "On total institution and self-mortification." *Journal of Health and Social Behavior* 11 (June):152.

Brim, Orville G., Jr., and Stanton Wheeler
    1966   *Socialization after Childhood: Two Essays.* New York: John Wiley and Sons.

Casper, Jonathan D.
    1972   *American Criminal Justice: The Defendant's View.* Englewood Cliffs, New Jersey: Prentice-Hall.

Cicourel, Aaron V.
    1968   *The Social Organization of Juvenile Justice.* New York: John Wiley and Sons.

Cloward, Richard A., and Lloyd E. Ohlin
    1960   *Delinquency and Opportunity.* New York: Free Press.

Cohen, Stanley, and Laurie Taylor
    1974   *Psychological Survival: The Experience of Long Term Imprisonment.* New York: Vintage.

Denzin, Norman K.
1968 "The self-fulfilling prophecy and patient-therapist interaction." In S. Spitzer and N. Denzin (eds.), *The Mental Patient.* New York: McGraw-Hill.

Edgerton, Robert B.
1967 *The Cloak of Competence.* Berkeley: University of California Press.

Erikson, Kai T.
1957 "Patient role and social uncertainty." *Psychiatry* 20 (August):263–74.

Garabedian, Peter C.
1963 "Social roles and processes of socialization in the prison community." *Social Problems* 11 (Fall):139–52.

Glaser, Daniel, and John R. Stratton
1961 "Measuring inmate change." In D. Cressey (ed.), *The Prison.* New York: Holt, Rinehart and Winston.

Goffman, Erving
1959 *Presentation of Self in Everyday Life.* New York: Doubleday-Anchor.

1961 *Asylums.* New York: Doubleday.

1963 *Stigma: Notes on the Management of Spoiled Identity.* Englewood Cliffs, New Jersey: Prentice-Hall.

1969 "The insanity of place." *Psychiatry* 32 (November):357–88.

Green, Hannah
1964 *I Never Promised You a Rose Garden.* New York: Signet.

Irwin, John
1970 *The Felon.* Englewood Cliffs, New Jersey: Prentice-Hall.

Kaplan, Howard B., Ina Boyd, and Samuel E. Bloom
1964 "Patient culture and the evaluation of self." *Psychiatry* 27 (May):116–26.

Karmel, Madeline
1969 "Total institutions and self-mortification." *Journal of Health and Social Behavior* 10 (June):134–41.

1970 "The internalization of social roles in institutionalized chronic mental patients." *Journal of Health and Social Behavior.* 11 (September):231–35.

Kesey, Ken
1962 *One Flew Over the Cuckoo's Nest.* New York: Viking Press.

Laing, R. D.
1965 *The Divided Self.* Baltimore: Penguin Books.

Laing, R. D., and A. Esterson
1964 *Sanity, Madness and the Family.* London: Tavistock.

Lemert, Edwin M.
    1951   *Social Pathology.* New York: McGraw-Hill.
    1962   "Paranoia and the dynamics of exclusion." *Sociometry* 25 (March):2–25.

Luchtenhand, Elmer
    1971   "Prisoner behavior and social system in the Nazi concentration camps." In B. Rosenberg, *et al.* (eds.), *Mass Society in Crisis.* 2nd ed. New York: Macmillan.

Maher, Brendon, and Ellen Stein
    1968   "The delinquent's perception of the law and the community." In S. Wheeler (ed.), *Controlling Delinquents.* New York: John Wiley and Sons.

Matza, David
    1964   *Delinquency and Drift.* New York: John Wiley and Sons.

Melbin, Murray
    1969   "Behavior rhythms in mental hospitals." *American Journal of Sociology* 74 (May):650–65.

Merton, Robert K.
    1938   "Social structure and anomie." *American Sociological Review* 3 (October):672–82.

Messinger, Sheldon E., Harold Sampson, and Robert D. Towne
    1970   "Life as theatre: some notes on the dramaturgic approach to social reality." In Gregory P. Stone and Harvey A. Faberman (eds.), *Social Psychology Through Symbolic Interaction.* Waltham, Mass.: Ginn.

Newman, Donald J.
    1966   *Conviction: The Determination of Guilt or Innocence Without Trial.* Boston: Little, Brown.

Olson, Sheldon R.
    1974   "Minutes in court, weeks in jail: a study of pretrial detention." Working paper No. 8 in Russell Sage Program in Law and Social Science.

Parsons, Talcott
    1951   *The Social System.* New York: Free Press

Pittman, David J., and Duff G. Gillespie
    1967   "Social policy as deviancy reinforcement: the case of the public intoxication offender." In D. Pittman (ed.), *Alcoholism.* New York: Harper and Row.

Rosenhan, D. L.
    1973   "On being sane in insane places." *Science* 179 (January 19): 250–58.

Roth, Julius A.
    1963   *Timetables: Structuring the Passage of Time in Hospital Treatment and Other Careers.* Indianapolis: Bobbs-Merrill.

Scheff, Thomas J.
1966   *Being Mentally Ill.* Chicago: Aldine.
Schein, Edgar H.
1965   "Reaction patterns to severe, chronic stress in American
          Army prisoners of war of the Chinese." In H. Proshansky and
          B. Seidenberg (eds.), *Basic Studies in Social Psychology.* New
          York: Holt, Rinehart and Winston.
Schrag, Clarence
1961   "Some foundations for a theory of correction." In D. Cressey
          (ed.), *The Prison.* New York: Holt, Rinehart, and Winston.
Sechehaye, Marguerite
1970   *The Autobiography of a Schizophrenic Girl.* New York: Sig-
          net.
Skolnick, Jerome H.
1966   *Justice Without Trial.* New York: John Wiley and Sons.
Spradley, James P.
1970   *You Owe Yourself a Drunk.* Boston: Little, Brown.
Stoll, Clarice S.
1968   "Ward deviance and psychiatric decisions." *Journal of Health
          and Social Behavior* 9 (December):336–45.
Szasz, Thomas S.
1970a   *Ideology and Insanity.* New York: Doubleday-Anchor.

1970b   *The Manufacture of Madness.* New York: Harper and Row.
Thompson, Hunter S.
1966   *Hell's Angels.* New York: Random House.
Tittle, Charles R.
1969   "Inmate organization: sex differentiation and the influence of
          criminal subculture." *American Sociological Review* 34 (Au-
          gust):492–504.

1972   "Institutional living and self-esteem." *Social Problems* 20
          (Summer):65–77.
Wexler, David B.
1973   "Token and taboo: behavior modifications, token economies,
          and the law." *California Law Review* 61 (January):81–109.
Wheeler, Stanton
1961   "Socialization in correctional communities." *American Socio-
          logical Review* 26 (October):697–712.

1969   *On Record.* New York: Russell Sage Foundation.
Wilkinson, Gregg S.
1974   "Psychiatric disorder dramaturgically considered." *Sociologi-
          cal Quarterly* 15 (Winter):143–58.
Wiseman, Jacqueline P.
1970   *Stations of the Lost.* Englewood Cliffs, New Jersey: Prentice-
          Hall.

The Problem of Return: Options for the Deviant

Problems of Reintegration
Political Deviance
Politicized Deviants

Among the conditions that account for the relative stability of Western societies, one must perhaps count the neutralization provided by convincing so many otherwise politically available Actors that they have personal "problems" that have nothing to do with political process and social power. Hundreds of thousands, perhaps millions, of Actors who believe or at least fear that they are psychiatrically "sick" are not thereby strongly disposed to undertake political activity. There is a sense in which the social control establishment is "functional" to American civilization in reducing the pool of persons likely to be available for hypermoral politics. And normal-smith self-help groups are similarly functional in draining off moral heroism from politics into proselytization for groups that look inward rather than outward to the world of politics and power.

John Lofland

Problems of Reintegration

The deviant's problems are by no means over upon release from the total institution. For those attempting to return to conventional roles, a number of problems lie ahead, many being a continuation of labeling effects. Understanding these problems involves an explication of Thomas Scheff's assertion that deviants are punished in their attempts to return to conventional roles.

Our concern is with the problems of reintegration. Daniel Glaser (1971) distinguishes between rehabilitation and reintegration. For social-control institutions, "a change in the reference group and hence in the preferred self-label is the prime rehabilitative objective when dealing with deviants who have a stake in nonconformity because their reference group is deviant" (Glaser, 1971:75). When agencies speak of rehabilitation, what is actually being referred to is "attitudinal redirection"—i.e., a production of the desire to return to conventional roles (e.g., Cressey, 1955). However, good intentions

Source: John Lofland, *Deviance and Identity* (Englewood Cliffs, New Jersey: Prentice-Hall, 1969), p. 287.

311

are largely useless (and often counterproductive) unless coupled with the opportunity to enter these "new" roles, to be reintegrated into society. Measures of success in rehabilitation efforts generally involve recidivism rates—i.e., the proportion who return to deviant behavior. These measures are misleading in part because the rehabilitation may have been successful, but barriers to reintegration resulted in recidivism.[1] We shall not deal immediately with the question of whether social-control agencies rehabilitate, focusing instead on the problems of reintegration. (Indeed, without rehabilitation in the sense specified here, the question of reintegration is mute—the deviant is simply not interested).

Access to conventional roles

There is little or no concern with reintegration upon release from most total institutions. Erikson (1966) notes that in our society no formal ceremonies mark passage out of deviant roles. There are no activities parallel to the degradation ceremonies which publicly ascribed the deviant role. The records and corresponding stereotyped image of the deviant tend to follow the processee after release. Movements toward expungement of records have been largely ineffective (Kogan and Loughery, 1970). Furthermore, most prisons are not actively involved in job placement of paroled inmates, often leaving these tasks to a half-way house or to parole officers.[2] Mental hospitals may have outpatient clinics that supervise reintegration, but often patients are simply released to relatives.

Very real resistance to re-entry is encountered by the formerly institutionalized. Job opportunities are limited in a number of ways. The particular deviant label may automatically disqualify some from employment. Homosexuals are not employed in many federal jobs; the teaching vocation is likely to be closed to them. Convicted felons automatically lose certain rights—e.g., they cannot enter medicine or law, and in some states are excluded from barber colleges (by professional licensing requirements); they cannot drive a truck or cab (ineligible for chauffeur's license), cannot become messengers or delivery men (cannot be bonded), and may find themselves denied other occupations.[3] Those with a history of treatment for mental illness often cannot be covered by a company's health and insurance plans, making many jobs inaccessible. Legitimate occupations may also be closed off due to blatant discrimination against the formerly institutionalized (cf. Schwartz and Skolnick, 1962). Although some states now prohibit employers from asking about past arrests and convictions, long periods of unemployment (due to incarceration) may be very damaging to employment chances.

In addition to the very real problem of earning a living, others are encountered. Credit is difficult, if not impossible, to establish; requests to open checking accounts may be turned down.[4] Familiar social roles may be redefined or absent—e.g., the woman who returns to find her family no longer needs her, her roles having been taken over by others. Old associates may not be interested in reconstructing friendships, in part because they have found other friends, and in part because they do not know exactly how to relate to, or whether to trust, the releasee. The closure of old roles prompts the exploring of new ones. The deprivations of the total institution often make the search for new relationships a frantic one. Witness the comments of Harry King, a professional safecracker, who spent much of his life in the "joint":

> In prison everyone dreams about women. They dream so much about marriage and a home and all that, and when they come out they think all they have to do is go on into it. . . . They jump into something without any thought at all. And the results are —an unhappy marriage. (Chambliss, 1972:127)

Generally, experiences in the institution have not prepared the deviant to adjust to this wide range of failures. The new releasee is truly a marginal person; he is not tied to the inmate world, nor is he accepted by conventional society (e.g., Chambliss, 1972; Irwin, 1970). Total institutions, especially mental hospitals, produce role ambiguity for the patients; they are not sure who they are, nor whether their condition is amenable to change. Indeed, some institutions may inadvertently foster expectations of failure amongst their charges (Irwin, 1970:52–53). Observations in a Federal narcotics hospital bear this out.

> It was widely assumed among the inmates that readdiction was inevitable regardless of any rehabilitation activities in which they might participate. The patients were fond of citing a mythical failure rate of 95 per cent. (Tittle, 1972:272)

In this way the total institution may condition the releasee to failure (and thereby legitimize it and remove personal responsibility when it occurs).

Secondary rules

Another set of problems is precipitated for the releasee when he is subjected to secondary rules. These are special prescriptions and proscriptions assigned to his particular status—e.g., the technical rules of probation and parole.[5] The presence of secondary rules makes the deviant much more vulnerable to rule violations than are conventional persons. He simply has more rules—and more clearly articulated guidelines—which he is expected to follow. Behaviors freely available to conventional persons are defined as privileges for the former deviant. For instance, decisions to marry, to leave the city or cross state lines, or change residence, must now be cleared with a parole officer (see Irwin, 1970:208–211). The former prisoner may be returned to the total institution for a "technical violation," which oftentimes are violations of expected life styles. The parolee may find himself returned to prison for "going to the race track" or engaging in adultery. The latter is illegal, but seldom punished among respectable citizens; the former is simply indicative of the deviant's refusal to accommodate to a life style that is conducive to law-abiding behavior[6] (Duster, 1970:208)—a technical violation in the most literal sense of the word.

While these secondary rules are formalized for the ex-convict, they also exist for the ex-mental patient. Relatives are often informed by psychiatrists about what to look for in future behaviors of the patient, problems the patient will likely encounter, and things which the patient can be reasonably expected to do as well as things he may not be ready to handle. Such professional coaching may establish a self-fulfilling prophecy: the patient is not allowed to do certain activities and, over time, is seen as incapable or incompetent in these areas.[7]

Coterminous with secondary rules is increased observation of behaviors. The mental patient is more closely watched by friends and relatives after release, often with greater attention than existed prior to the agency referral. The family of the ex-convict may help the parole officer supervise his activities. One of the conditions of probation, especially for delinquents, is the requirement that adults monitor the deviant's behavior in some systematic way. The sense of being "on" which was present in the total institution thereby continues after release. This increased surveillance may affect the cognizance component of justice (see Chapter X) with resentment the result. Greater visibility of behavior occurs for those with criminal records for quite another reason. The police may periodically round up known criminals when a crime occurs. This comes to be seen as an efficient method of law enforcement, especially for difficult-to-solve property crimes. For this reason, as David Matza remarks, the labeled thief is put to work:

> Though he may resent the part he comes to play, the social use to which he will be put, though he may regard it as unjust, simultaneously he will concur in the common sense that, after all, there is a certain

> justice in employing an admitted thief whenever an
> account of theft is sought. Having been cast in a part,
> he should be put to work. The essential thief is em-
> ployed as a regular suspect; . . . . he now works for the
> state, literally, though without adequate recognition
> or compensation. (1969:180–81)

By being used as a regular suspect, and by subjection to secondary
rules, the deviant is constantly reminded of his or her essentially
deviant status—even though the deviant is officially "released" from
the machinery of the state.

Evaluation of self

Let us recapitulate to this point. We begin with a released deviant
who—for whatever reasons—is making an attempt to return to conventional roles. He experiences objective consequences such as job
denials and responsibilities withheld; he has a marginal status between the deviant and the straight world, with no strong ties in
either; he encounters the arbitrariness of secondary rules and attendant over-surveillance of his actions; he senses the stigma attached
to his labeled condition and his contact with control agencies. Assume for the moment he continues to strive to achieve an acceptable
role and identity. The question is now: how does the deviant come
to see himself in this return attempt?

We have specified the dynamics of self-labeling in an earlier chapter. Now we ask: To what extent are these processes operative in his
effort to acquire conventional roles, and how might they affect the
outcome? First, we examine what others are doing. Observers, many
of whom are supporters—i.e., sympathic—may selectively view his
behavior. They will be looking for signs and clues to his real intentions. They feel, due to official labeling and time in a rehabilitative
setting, that he was essentially deviant and may still be. We would
expect the audience to be critical, for they assume (perhaps rightly
so) that safety resides in vigilance. They must be *certain*. The neutralization process which originally protected his reputation may
now work against the deviant. Good behaviors may be explained
away: "if the person has a long history of inappropriate behavior, and
then starts to act in an appropriate fashion, others will . . . normalize
his behavior (still see him as inappropriate)" (Gove, 1970:882).

Moreover, the deviant is likely to become aware of the close observation and critical evaluation of his behaviors. Again, as in the situation of rule violation, he becomes extremely cognizant of the way he
appears to others. Observers will come to see him behaving in a
conventional manner because he is forced to do so; they will see him
as a "petty collaborator":

> They will gaze at him as he plays baseball or walks to
> school, or stands idly and they will literally observe
> someone in the act of refraining from doing bad
> things because he has been forcefully told to . . .
> [T]hey have noticed the subject "behaving himself"
> or as it is sometimes put, "keeping his nose clean."
> (Matza, 1969:174)

In attribution theory terms, his behavior is seen as externally motivated (cf. Chapter IV). His behavior is not genuine, but a forced performance. And perhaps because he has been forced to engage in such performances in the total institution, the deviant actor becomes quite unsure of self-evaluations. ("Perhaps they are right"—a conclusion he may come to upon reviewing his previous rule violations and his incarceration. After all, an integral part of his therapy may have been a definition of self as essentially deviant—sick, criminal, or whatever—but nevertheless redeemable through constant effort and hard work). Matza continues:

> The relevant matter is that *in his own mind,* the
> subject has glimpsed society as it caught him in the
> act of collaborating. He was playing baseball and
> they saw him doing something quite different,
> "behaving himself." (1969:174–75)

This realization that he is being seen as a collaborator by others may be the turning point in his own self-view; he may begin to give up on the possibility of return. Being constantly seen (by others) as good because he was told to be by the state may have self-fulfilling aspects. As the deviant comes more and more to see himself as collaborator, as forced to conform, he may (again) decide that he is basically, essentially, deviant and that his conformity is really *out of character.* In Daryl Bem's framework of self-attribution, the deviant comes to see his behavior as externally determined, and is less likely to ascribe the reasons for the conformity to choice, to a desire to be nondeviant (1972:39–40). He comes to conclude (as do many of the conventional persons witnessing his behavior) that his actions are indeed not genuine, that to strive for conventional roles and identity would be a further compounding of this forgery. The more he sees his behavior as due to collaboration, the more he feels he is the *type of person*[8] who must be forced to behave—thereby documenting his essentially deviant nature.

We have presented a very pessimistic view of the situation confronted by the "rehabilitated" deviant. The situation is one of almost constant jeopardy to deviant imputation and assault on conceptions of essential self. Our goal has not been to enumerate the size of groups of deviants who experience these problems compared to those who do not. Clearly, some never leave the total institutions of society. Others, because of radicalization during or before prison/hospital, may be unconcerned with reintegration; and still others experience societal intervention and clearly reform.[9] The point we wish to make is two-fold. First, control agencies would have us believe that most of the labeled deviants benefit from the total institution and reform, and that conditions in these agencies are conducive to success upon release. We have tried to show this is not the case. Second, and a point we now discuss in some detail, the sense of injustice fostered within control agencies (Chapter X) and reinforced by barriers to reintegration, may mean the deviant takes things into his own hands. He may continue in his deviant role, but now comes to use it as a means of attacking some of these barriers.

In the last two chapters, we have depicted the deviant as someone capable of making choices, directing label application, adjusting to societal intervention—in short, an active participant (rather than a passive recipient) in the labeling process. Here we again pick up that theme by examining conditions whereby collective responses to societal intervention may be adopted. To what extent do deviants use political means to adjust to societal reaction and reintegration problems? Can the oppressed organize to effect a change in the social-control machinery of society? What forms will this organization take? We want to caution the reader that our inclusion of this topic here (in a chapter on problems of return, and immediately following a discussion of the effects of the total institution) should not be taken to mean that political deviants must experience incarceration. While we feel that the sense of injustice created in all stages of processing is important, whether directly experienced or simply known about in the sense of a cognitive awareness of the potential threat of intervention, there are, of course, other sources of political response.

Political
Deviance

Previous labeling formulations imply a conflict model of deviance analysis.[10] This means that:

> the deviant behavior itself, and the actions of rule-makers to prevent such behavior [must be seen in political terms]. The political climate prescribes both

> what conflicts will occur between deviants and non-
> deviants, and the rules by which such conflicts will be
> resolved. The struggle of groups for legitimation thus
> constitutes an integral part of deviant behavior.
> (Horowitz and Liebowitz, 1968:282)

From this perspective, deviance is seen as a political act. Take, for
example, violations of the criminal law:

> In the broadest sense, it may be argued that all
> crimes are political crimes inasmuch as all prohibi-
> tions with penal sanctions represent the defense of a
> given value system or morality, in which the prevail-
> ing social power believes. . . . Taking this *ad absur-*
> *dum,* even a bank robbery, a shoplifting, or a rape is
> a political crime. After all, making them criminal
> offenses protects the interests and rights of the law-
> making power, which regards them as right and
> worthy of safeguarding with the threat of penal con-
> sequences. (Schafer, 1971:380)

We see little advantage in terming *all* crime political crime. We are
concerned mainly with the rule violator's orientation to the rule
prior to the act.[11] If a person engages in law violations for the purpose of attacking or changing the established order, we can speak of
political crime: the political criminal performs an illegal act out of a
sense of conviction; he is " 'convinced' about the truth and justification of his own altruistic beliefs" (Schafer, 1971:384) and violates
rules on behalf of others in his social group. His goal is not self-
interest, but social change for the communal good.[12] The strategy
may be to attack the entire system, as in the case of the Weathermen,
or only certain norms within the system, as with civil-rights demonstrators.

While political deviance is usually conceived of as civil-legal rule
violation, polite-interactional rules and background expectancies
may be systematically violated as a tactic of disruption and rebellion,
as evidenced by the activities of Jerry Rubin and Abbie Hoffman. See
Rubin's *Do It* and Hoffman's *Revolution for the Hell of It* for examples of these tactics. While these political dissidents were probably
not familiar with Garfinkel's work on violations of background expectancies, the disruptive nature of Garfinkel's experiment-demonstra-
tion has implications for politically engineered chaos. Alvin
Gouldner suggests that these tactical violations are better seen as
rebellion than as true revolution:

> Underneath the ethnomethodological demonstra-
> tion, then, there is a kind of anarchial impulse, a

> genteel anarchism ... [which will] appeal to youth and others alienated from the status quo, and that may also congenially resonate the sentiments of some on the New Left. It is a way in which the alienated young may, with relative safety, defy the established order and experience their own potency. The ethnomethodological "demonstration" is, in effect, a kind of micro-confrontation with and nonviolent resistance to the status quo. It is a substitute and symbolic rebellion against a larger structure which the youth cannot, and often does not wish to, change. It substitutes the available rebellion for the inaccessible revolution. (1970:394)

Since politically-directed rule violations may occur at any or all of these three levels of rules, we prefer the term "political deviance" to the narrower term "political crime."[13] To summarize, political deviants "often announce their intentions publicly, challenge the very legitimacy of laws and/or their application in specific situations, attempt to change the norms they are denying, lack personal gain as a goal and appeal to a higher morality, pointing out the void between professed beliefs and actual practices" (Reasons, 1973:474).

In order to place political deviance in context, let us return to the concept of label seeking described in Chapter IX. We propose that individuals may seek certain deviant labels as *a strategy of attacking the system.* When the question of intent (personal gain or attack on system's legitimacy)[14] is correlated with the degree of label-seeking, the typology shown in Figure I results.

Figure I   *Selective service rule: obligatory military service*

| | | Actor's intent in failing to serve | |
		Attack the system	Personal interest
	Sought	Draft resister	Doubly-labeled
Deviant labels			
	Unsought	Conscientious objector	Acceptable deferment

The typology is illustrated by reference to draft law violations. The typology should be seen as a heuristic device, and our cell entries should be seen merely as suggestive; we recognize that "failing to serve" may be motivated by both personal concerns and attitudes about the legitimacy of the draft system (and perhaps the government itself).

We would predict the draft resister would openly defy Selective Service directives. He may choose prison instead of military service and seek publicity for this decision. Or he may leave the country and show his resistance by forming groups to work against the system from without (e.g., helping others to leave the country). In either case, the true resister visibly refuses to serve, seeks and accepts the label "resister" (or more stigmatic ones such as "traitor") in order to inform the public of the injustices of the draft or the illegality of the war (in the case of Vietnam). The Conscientious Objector refuses to serve out of moral feelings against war, thereby indirectly attacking the system. He does not seek a deviant label, rather claims the legally protected right to refuse to participate.

In situations of self-interest, the doubly-labeled seeks a deviant label as a means of avoiding service. He may feign mental illness or mental retardation, or act out stereotypic images of homosexuality or transvestism, to be legally excluded.[15] Such a strategy makes him susceptible to informal societal reaction on two counts—e.g., being a homosexual and a draft-dodger—producing the double labeling. Finally, some may take a deferment strategy where relatively non-stigmatic avenues are used—e.g., physical illness or afflictions producing a IV–F or I–Y classification. There is evidence that entrance into the sick role increased during the escalation of fighting in Vietnam (Waitzkin, 1971). (This study also found blacks were less likely to be granted exemptions for medical reasons than were whites.) A reminder: we are speaking of those who intend to avoid the draft. Many deferments were quite legitimate in the sense they were not sought actively as a way out of service obligations. However, the sharp increase in application for, and granting of, sick role deferments during the Vietnam conflict suggests this was an active strategy of avoidance.

We note in passing that the state attempts to place all deviant actors in the rule-violation-for-personal-gain categories. Anti-establishment acts are officially interpreted as personal pathology or an outgrowth of selfish motivations. An excellent example is the role of campus psychiatry in getting students (and the general public) to see campus disturbances as due to the personality pathologies of a few marginal students: "the psychiatric framework of evaluation and explanation has increasingly led to those students [who pursue actions which threaten the university's structure] being discredited and channeled into 'safe' [from the university's perspective] medical treatment" (Maddison, 1973:130; also Horowitz, 1970).

The introduction of the label-seeking concept now permits the specification of two types of political deviants.[16] Traditionally, political deviants have been seen as individuals seeking to attack or destroy the system by remaining underground and avoiding apprehension. Bernadine Dorhn and other Weathermen(women), and more recently the S.L.A., carry out guerrilla warfare while seeking to keep activities and identities secret. In a sense, they operate *on only one front.* A second type of political deviant is the individual who violates rules and "seeks" official sanctioning to assure visibility of the act. These offenders wage their war *on two fronts:* against the system through rule violations and from within the official processing bureaucracies charged with their control.[17] Arrest, indictment, and trial are viewed as opportunities to inform the public of the cause and point up hypocrisy, injustice, and inconsistency in the reactive procedures. Often the state obliges them—e.g., the arrest of demonstrators at the 1968 Democratic National Convention, carried live on television, showed the brutality of the reactors, reinforcing the protestors' indictment of the system (see Walker, 1968). The zeal of the enforcers can be used to an advantage in gaining public sympathy. This two-pronged attack on the system means that societal intervention may become part of the arsenal of weapons used against the state. It is perhaps in this situation that the political dimensions of deviance are most visible.[18]

The political deviant attempts to make his agency contacts and processing as public as possible. The trial becomes a public forum where the deviant's cause is placed before the people (the political deviant does not plea bargain); the defense presents its case to two audiences: the jury and the public. The official labeling process is converted into an educational and propaganda tool to assert and seek support for the deviant's perspective. The goals of the assault on the system include: increased publicity and active proselytizing for the cause, a raising of consciousness for some segment of the population, and an attack on the credibility of the legal system and its agents[19] (e.g., Antonio, 1972). Perhaps the best example of confrontation tactics occurred in the Chicago Eight (later Seven) trial, but confrontation characterized other trials also: e.g., New York Panther 21 trial, the New Haven Panther 14 trial, "Catonsville Nine" or Berrigan trial (see Sternberg, 1972; also Epstein, 1971; Schervish, 1971; Silvergate, 1974). The tactics developed in Judge Hoffman's court served as a mechanism to convert the political trial into a "radical-criminal" trial.[20] The latter is characterized by courtroom disruptions, supportive "audience participation" from courtroom observers, attempts to reverse roles of judge, prosecutors, and defendants—in short, to put the state and its policies on trial. Use of the mass media by the defense to educate the general public is also an important aspect of these trials.

In these radical-criminal trials, the issues may take precedence over the defense of the accused. Strategies of defense are often selected with an eye to their proselytizing value rather than to the probability of winning acquittal. Schervich (1971) reports that in the trial of ten persons charged with removing and burning Selective Service records in Chicago in 1969, some defendants used a "cultural insanity" defense which allowed them to bring U.S. war policies into courtroom testimony. Others attempted to use jury nullification[21] as a defense strategy. Both these defenses were seen as having a lower probability of acquittal than, say, the traditional insanity defense. Generally, the personal risks of defendants are balanced against the potential payoff for the cause or movement. Conviction may even be "beneficial" in that "martyrdom may serve . . . to interest others in the given ideal and to recruit members for other convictional violations of the law" (Schafer, 1971:386).

To reiterate an earlier point, it is extremely difficult to delineate political deviance. First, it varies greatly in scope, from destruction of the status quo to illegal or disruptive action designed to gain more power or control within the established order (e.g., labor conflicts, some industrial sabotage, the blue flu among police, etc.). Second, participants will vary in their commitment to the goal from the "true believer" to the pseudo-convictional (who uses the movement for personal self-interest). It is quite easy to take the latter for the former. For example, delinquency experts predicted that delinquent gangs would become involved in more political-convictional crime during the 1960s and early 1970s. One observer comments:

> The predicted transformation of American youth gangs never occurred . . . ; the actual proportion of youth gangs involved [in political action] was small, with the greatest majority of gang youth remaining essentially unaffected by political/social activism. Even among those most affected, there is little evidence that activism replaced illegal and/or violent pursuits; rather, traditional activities such as theft, assault, extortion, and various "hustles" were carried on in conjunction with, and frequently as an intrinsic part of, political and social reform undertakings. (Miller, 1974:232–33)

For similar conclusions about the lack of true political action among urban gangs, see Short (1974) and Klein (1971).

Another problem is deciding the exact goals of political deviance. Following Schaefer, we have defined political deviance as "instrumental" crime directed at some communal end. There is evidence that much that passes for political deviance may not involve any concise, or even vague, set of goals. The deviance, in other words, becomes an end in itself. The student rebellions on college campuses have been so described: "it led not to organized political responses of a conventional variety, but rather to a celebration of deviance itself as the ultimate response to orthodox politics" (Horowitz and Liebowitz, 1968:289). Deviance may become a response to the absurdity of the established institutions—it is engaged in for fun (cf. Scott and Lyman, 1970).[22] This seems consistent with the Yippie Philosophy of "revolution" (Rubin, *Do It*). Even in the case of the more serious challenges to the established order, the political deviants may pull back from their espoused goals; for example, comments of a Weatherman regarding discussions on the bus to Chicago in 1968:

> The heaviest part of our struggle on the bus was the discussion on what "winning" meant in Chicago . . . we realized the reasons for our fear. *We were afraid winning in a particular tactical situation would entail the escalation of the struggle;* that is to say, the ruling class and their pigs would increase their attack on us. It would mean next time, we would have to fight much harder on a higher level. (Quoted in Walton, 1973:169. Emphasis in original.)

In addition to the problems of deciding what exactly qualifies as political deviance, we see that as defined above it may be a relatively rare species. We do not see a significant increase in the number of individuals who actively plan criminal and other deviant acts to achieve some communal end.[23] In the absence of any sweeping national issues, such as Vietnam, we see the numerical incidence of true political deviance as very small compared to another adaptation which entails the creation of "politicized deviants."

Politicized Deviants

The politicalization of deviants refers to groups of rule violators who organize and strive for collective goals, but do so largely *by utilizing legal means within the present political system.* Groups of deviants are now actively working for greater community tolerance of behaviors, legal rights equal to nondeviants, and more self-control in terms of directing their own rehabilitation—*when that is seen by them as desirable.* Groups of deviants were organized originally to provide subcultural support for the problems of labeling and re-entry. The focus was on self-help, whether simply informal friendship or self-controlled programs of treatment. Such organizations include ex-convicts (e.g., Seven Steps program), mental patients (Recovery Inc.), alcoholics (A.A.), and drug addicts (Synanon) (cf. Sagarin, 1969). These groups represent "an insistence that deviants themselves are best able to define their own problems and deal with those problems" (Horowitz and Liebowitz, 1968:282). Gaining control of their own rehabilitation may be a prerequisite to turning to other political aspects of the conflict with the larger culture.

We propose that the politicalization of deviant actors will affect the ways in which the deviant will manage his public identity, as well as attitudes about his deviant role. To illustrate these points, we turn to the case of homosexuality. Again we speak of label-seeking or the affirmation of a deviant public identity. A second dimension is the political orientation of the deviant: is he concerned with the collective plight and problems of those of his deviant category, or is he unconcerned about the problems and possible political solutions? These dimensions are depicted in Figure II.

Figure II   *Individuals who engage in homosexual acts*

		Politicalization on homosexuality[24]	
		Political	*Non-political*
Public identity	Homosexual (label sought)	Gay activist	Overt homosexual
	Not homosexual (label unsought)	Quiet reformer	Closet queen

The Gay Activist sees the promulgation of a public identity as homosexual as a means of raising the consciousness of other homosexuals,[25] of gaining public visibility for the cause, and of seeking a public definition as a potential voting block which would appeal to politicians. The activist also sees coming out of the closet as a prerequisite to any effective political organization which is required to bring about decriminalization, legal rights of marriage, inheritance and adoption, and an end to job discrimination. Gay liberation groups are concerned with gaining greater sexual freedom and tolerance within the American system. The homosexual who actively seeks a public identity as a means of producing social change through political means may, at some point, consider attacking the entire system (at which point he becomes a political deviant). Those in the gay liberation movement have apparently rejected this broader tack. Laud Humphreys reports that alliances with socialist, communist, and Third World political organizations were considered, but dismissed, in part because tolerance for homosexuals did not appear any greater under these regimes (Humphreys, 1972:158–62). This is not to say that Gay Activists may not violate laws (marching without a permit, trespassing, loitering, disturbing the peace, etc.), but such violations are at this point designed largely to produce changes within the present political system.

The Quiet Reformer is active in challenging the status quo through support of homophile groups, but maintains a public identity as heterosexual. We would expect the Reformer to be enjoined by activists within the homophile group to "go public," to openly declare sexual affiliation in order to support the cause. Shapiro (1972) argues that raising consciousness is a prerequisite to getting support for political organization of oppressed people. Gay activists, using slogans such as "better blatant than latent" and "out of the closets, into the streets," try to appeal to all homosexuals to become visible activists. We would expect greater pressure on the Reformer than on the Overt Homosexual, since the former is likely to be in closer contact with the Activist.

The Overt Homosexual may seek a public identity because his occupational group is more tolerant than others (e.g., Leznoff and Westley, 1956) or because he sees this as a viable adjustment to homosexuality. He may not develop a political concern over his status, since he is well-adjusted or may lack contacts with official control agencies (so a sense of injustice is less likely to form). The Closet Queen may avoid political involvement out of fear of discovery. We would expect the Closet Queen to be more isolated from the homosexual subculture, and thus less aware of the possible political responses to homosexuality and labeling. Also, he may be quite well adjusted in "passing," so that he does not experience any pressure to produce change as long as his deviance remains secret. Both types of nonpolitical homosexuals would probably be more likely to see their behavior as the result of a "condition" and would not see themselves as responsible for their sexual preferences. The politically active would be more likely to reject psychiatric views on homosexuality, stressing instead their role in choosing to engage in the activity. Based on our discussion in the last chapter, we would also expect that the politically active homosexual would probably have more contacts with official control agencies, and come to perceive the injustices in this processing. Finally, what may distinguish the Activist from the Reformer is the more positive self-esteem of the Activist. Activism reinforces that sense of high esteem and self-worth by providing a radical identity, collectively reinforced, and access to some feelings of political power.

We would predict that more groups of deviants will come to see their collective plight and the possibilities for collective action in the years ahead. The politicalization process involves a raising of consciousness, which may require public (visible) deviance for publicity and support. This produces (or permits) a political orientation among extant subcultures or facilitates the creation of a political organization from the ground up. A period of political confrontations likely follows attempts to gain power and social change, as well as financial support—e.g., Black Panthers enjoyed the monetary support of some wealthy white liberals; the NORML has received monetary support in a national campaign to raise funds to change marihuana laws. Politicalization may be fostered by what might be termed a chaining or modeling effect. Once a group organizes and produces some gains, others may follow their example. In this sense, the black power movement may have been a prelude to the gay movement and the women's movement (cf. Howard, 1974).

Second, we predict that, for the time being, the political activities of deviant groups will remain narrow, in the sense of the central concern being their own problems. Alliances between deviant groups are not likely in the immediate future as different groups may clash or, what is more likely, there may be ideological disagreements within the same movement. For example, there is some conflict between male and female homosexuals over the question of "sexism" within the gay movement (Howard, 1974:133). For similar reasons, we do not predict a movement away from politicized deviants to political deviance in the near future. For such an attack on the system, there would have to be some ideological development which would unite all deviant groups:

> Deviants are not organized to battle police, and they have no ideology which labels police as enemies to be attacked or destroyed. Police have legitimacy as long as deviants avoid rather than attack them. However, police traditionally mount an organized collective effort against deviants, who typically respond only as unorganized individuals. The existing conflict is a one-sided war. (Horowitz and Liebowitz, 1968:292)[26]

The only thing approaching an organized resistance has been some of the radical militant black organizations who have attempted to organize against the white "occupation forces" in their neighborhoods.

Probably the major determinant of what form the opposition of deviant groups will take in the future lies with the public reactions to the deviant activity and to the increasingly political tactics of deviant groups. Will community tolerance increase, and demands be met, or will society react with more repression? Recent setbacks in the battle for legal rights for homosexuals in such supposedly liberal places as New York City and Boulder, Colorado,[27] suggest that community tolerance limits have been reached (at least in these cities). Perhaps one reason for this intolerant response to gay activism is that the public *misperceives* its aims. They may see homosexuals as out to destroy the heterosexually-dominated culture and family structure. They may misinterpret consciousness-raising as blatant attempts to convert heterosexuals to this new sexual lifestyle (a view reinforced by the stereotyped images of homosexuals as the wanton seducers of little children). In short, activism may be seen by the public as an attack on the system, when in fact it is an attempt to establish equality as members in that system.[28] A second possible reason for intolerance is the negative stereotypes of the deviant activity and its participants. It is not surprising that marihuana penalties have been reduced in the wake of increased use by white middle- and upper-class youth. The supreme irony of the stereotypes of homosexuals (and of drug addicts) is that they have evolved from the very methods of control used by society. To the extent homosexuals are not allowed to marry, adopt children, and work in certain occupations, they are forced into more impersonal, impermanent sexual contacts—often in public places—producing the stereotype of the selfish, exploitative, completely sex-oriented homosexual out to seduce anyone of the same sex. Add to this the injustices and negative impact upon those officially processed, we predict greater numbers of individuals will choose one form of political action (either political deviance or politicalization) in response to societal designations and incarceration of deviant persons. Rule makers and rule enforcers will greatly influence which it will be.

Notes

1. For laymen, and most professionals, rehabilitation means returning the deviant to conforming roles, yet these dimensions are best treated separately; while few total institutions rehabilitate, we shall argue none are actively concerned with reintegration. For cogent discussions of the problems of defining rehabilitation and difficulties in using recidivism rates to measure success, see Empey and Erickson (1972), Glaser (1969), Levin (1971), and Tittle (1974).

2. Prisoners in the State of Texas Department of Corrections are given a prison-made suit, a small amount of money, and then taken to the local bus station where they are released. The Texas prison system does not have any work-release program, because as one spokesman said, "If they are ready for work-release, they are rehabilitated" (Personal communication).

3. For an extensive discussion of rights denied felons and other prisoners explicitly by law in various states, see Kerper and Kerper (1974).

4. In essence, the formerly institutionalized are denied opportunities to engage in the two most common activities of conventional persons: work and consumption (see Irwin, 1970).

5. Specific secondary rules also attach to status ascribed without a stint in the agency —e.g., welfare recipients are subject to regulations, greater observation (including midnight raids), and increased vulnerability to deviance imputation (Beck, 1967; Briar, 1966). Status offenses such as delinquent tendencies for youth are, in a sense, secondary rules (Green, 1970).

6. Other, less repressive, approaches have been tried in an attempt to launch the deviant into a respectable life style. One program involved paying ex-addicts a high salary on the assumption it would build stakes in conformity and foster middle-class values and life style. It did not work (see Bullington, et al., 1969).

7. Other factors which affect adjustment of mental patients include post-hospital performance levels, family tolerance of deviance, type of family (parental or conjugal), and extent to which others are present in the family to take over the patient's former roles (see Spitzer and Denzin, 1968:385–445). In general, social background characteristics and family variables have been found better predictors of rehospitalization than psychiatric diagnosis or prognosis. One finding is that rehospitalization is more likely in middle-class than in lower-class families. It may be that the middle-class family members, while being concerned with status and public image, are also more sympatic to psychiatric frameworks (Friends and Supporters). Consequently, they may cooperate more with the psychiatrist and more critically observe the patient's adjustment.

8. As noted elsewhere, we see the phenomenological availability of conceptions such as essential self or absolute character in a culture as a crucial part of the labeling process.

9. At this point, we are less concerned with the relative proportions of deviants in these various response possibilities, and more concerned with delineating the problems faced both within and outside the total institution and the processes

which are initiated which are likely to lead to recidivism rather than reform (cf. Chapter IX). Also, many of the studies required for such an enumeration have not yet been done.

10. The political nature of label making and label application is evident in Lemert (1951, 1967), Becker (1963), Erikson (1966), and Taylor, *et al.*, (1973). The conflict model in criminology was influenced by Vold (1958). More recently, the work of Horton (1966), Chambliss (1969), Turk (1966; 1969), Quinney (1970), and Chambliss and Seidman (1971) are extensions of conflict ideas. In psychiatry, the work of Szasz has conflict implications (especially 1970a, 1970b). See our discussion in Chapter VI.

11. Eldridge Cleaver (1968) has noted how interracial rape can be a political act; kidnapping and bank robbery may also be political in nature (e.g., S.L.A.). At this time, most political crime is *ex post facto* in the sense that a person sentenced to prison may be radicalized by various revolutionary groups within the prison, and as a result comes to define his armed robbery as "really" a political act. Anyone studying prison populations to ascertain the number of "convictional" criminals should be aware of this problem (Schafer, 1971).

12. It may be extremely difficult to distinguish the true political (convictional) criminal from an imposter: "many pseudo-convictional criminals simply use the convictional ideal as an excuse for their own selfish criminal acts" (Schafer, 1971:386). Schafer distinguishes three types of criminals: conventional offenders (violate law for personal reasons), pseudo-convictional (violate law out of self-interest but seek to have it defined as serving collective, ideological ends), and the true convictional offenders (see violation as a political act prior to the offense). For a discussion of the problems of making these distinctions in the case of industrial sabotage, see Taylor and Walton (1971).

13. We have defined political deviance based on the intent of the deviant actor. Another strategy would be to examine the state's action and intent: political crime exists when the state "invokes its laws to punish those who present a threat to the government" (Clinard and Quinney, 1973:154). Consistent with this view, any law may be enforced for political reasons. This definition would permit the study of those situations where the state attempts to control dissidents politically by invoking prosecution where, in fact, no law violation has occurred—e.g., some conspiracy indictments, frameups, etc. (cf. Reasons, 1973:475). Also, the state may move against certain individuals who have no direct political intentions—e.g., the police were found to write more traffic citations for drivers of cars carrying Black Panther bumper stickers than for cars in the same area without stickers (Heussenstamm, 1971).

14. This follows Merton's well-known distinction: behaviors designed for personal gain are termed "aberrant behaviors" and activities designed to change the system "nonconforming behaviors." (See Nisbet and Merton, 1971:829–32). Studies of deviance have generally ignored the latter types of acts. For one piece of evidence that most criminal behavior is directed at personal gain, see Casper (1972:169–70).

15. We are not making estimates about the number of individuals in each cell, but we would agree that "the number of people who adopt the traditional political path by refusing to serve and going to jail as political prisoners is small compared to the number who adopt the deviant path, using mental illness, homosexuality or drug addiction (whether these be real or feigned) to avoid serving" (Horowitz and Liebowitz, 1968:289–90). One indicator of the "radicalization" involved in any given rule violation would be a simple ratio of those who use the act to attack aspects of the system compared to those breaking the rule for self-centered purposes (assuming the pseudo-convictional violators could be discovered).

16. It also provides a way of relating labeling theory to the concept of political deviance at the micro level, something critics say has not been done. For example,

"the societal reaction perspective has failed to grasp the acceptance of, and seeking for, social reaction, which much political deviancy involves" (Walton, 1973:168; see also, Liazos, 1972:109).

17. There will, of course, be variation in the extent to which the political deviant seeks contacts with the authorities. The Chicago Eight probably did not plan to be arrested and indicted on conspiracy charges (indeed the defendants themselves said they could not agree on lunch). The type of political deviant under consideration here, however, will use the system once in it; political deviants usually realize that opposing the government carries with it the possibility of such prosecution.

18. For some, this confrontation is implicit in the definition of political deviant—i.e., "an individual or group who resist the label of the formal imputers and counterlabels these imputers by asserting the legitimacy of one value orientation and normative structure over another vis-à-vis some adjudicating third party" (Schervish, 1971:25). It must be noted that the political deviant who wages such a war over labels from within the processing machinery may be inadvertently legitimating its existence. (This may be one reason for the constant courtroom disruptions during the Chicago Seven trial: a purposeful rejection of the judicial process—a task aided by Judge Hoffman.) A parallel problem is posed to the activist lawyer who uses legal action to force change in treatment of the mentally handicapped —e.g., filing a class action suit on the right to treatment in effect legitimates the asylum through indirect recognition.

19. As an example of attacking credibility, dissidents can point to the failure of the government to get lasting convictions in most of the major conspiracy trials of the 1960s and early 1970s: these conspiracy cases served to demonstrate the government was willing to bring inadequate cases to trial. The ease with which the government brought cases, thereby tying up dissidents with conspiracy charges, impugned the credibility of the state and the criminal justice system. In this situation, the government experienced a form of the "boomerang" effect of labeling, where they are effectively denounced through counter-labeling (see Chapter IV).

20. The term is used by Sternberg (1972) to signal the many differences between the traditional criminal trial of political radicals and the more recent radical criminal trial where the attack on the state was made explicit and where many new weapons were introduced into the struggle. Silvergate (1974) delineates the tactics available to the state in this public confrontation.

21. William Kunstler, a vocal advocate of jury nullification, states concisely the basic argument: "because the jury is ideally a representative cross section of the community, it ought to be able to acquit a defendant who admits the commission of certain formally illegal acts, the commission of which the community, represented by the jury, approves. The major difficulty with this approach is that jurors, almost without exception, have no idea of the extent of their power in this respect, and under recent case law, they cannot be enlightened as to this power" (Kunstler, 1969:71). As Kunstler points out, its use is problematic because jurors do not know of the principle of ruling on the law as well as the facts, and most states prohibit attorneys from bringing up this point. Indeed, only two states, Maryland and Indiana, provide for judicial instructions to the jury which mention this principle (Scheflin, 1972).

22. This is perhaps the reason for delinquent gang involvement in the urban riots of 1967. Walter Miller observes: "in virtually no instance did the gangs 'start' the rioting—either in the sense that they agitated actively for the advent of riot conditions, or that incidents involving gangs served as major trigger events. Once the riots were under way, however, gang members were among the most ardent and energetic participants" (1974:231).

23. This is an admittedly tenuous statement, as data are simply not available. An indicator might be the number of police officers killed with no apparent motive (a figure which has increased in the past ten years, according to enforcement officials). We base our assertion on the demise of the anti-war movement (even before "peace" was declared), the calm on the campuses, and the relative lack of political action of a criminal nature (outside of the over-publicized S.L.A.). As of this writing, no one has taken to the street in violent protest over Watergate, I.T.T., Agnew, the Ellsberg break-in, or inflation.

24. Data on the extent to which homosexuals are politicized are difficult to acquire. Most studies draw their samples from the mailing lists of homophile organizations, which would present a very biased picture of the political sentiments of homosexuals. For an ingenious method of data collection using the patrons of gay bars, see Hammersmith and Weinberg (1973), although this procedure may bias the sample in the direction of the overt homosexual and against the covert, secret deviant. Samples of "closet queens" are, of course, largely inaccessible except through observations and contact in tearooms (Humphreys, 1970).

25. The methods of raising consciousness should be similar for all politically oppressed groups—e.g., blacks, Chicanos, native Americans, drug addicts, alcoholics, ex-convicts, mental patients, the blind, handicapped, and women, in addition to homosexuals (Shapiro, 1972).

26. It should not go unnoticed that the police themselves are becoming very political and are demanding greater control over their own profession (Skolnick, 1969).

27. Boulder residents voted two to one to reject an ordinance that would have forbidden job discrimination against homosexuals (*Newsweek*, May 20, 1974:76–77).

28. A similar interpretation has been made of the conflicts over the question of Prohibition. See Gusfield's discussion of the "enemy deviant" (1967:183–85).

References

Antonio, Robert J.
   1972   "The processual dimension of degradation ceremonies: the
             Chicago conspiracy trial: success or failure?" *British Journal
             of Sociology* 23 (September):287–97.

Beck, Bernard
   1967   "Welfare as a moral category." *Social Problems* 14 (Win-
             ter):258–77.

Becker, Howard S.
   1963   *Outsiders: Studies in the Sociology of Deviance.* New York:
             Free Press.

Bem, Daryl J.
   1972   "Self-perception theory." In Leonard Berkowitz (ed.), *Ad-
             vances in Experimental Social Psychology,* Vol. 6. New York:
             Academic Press.

Briar, Scott
   1966   "Welfare from below: recipients' views of the public welfare
             system." In J. tenBroek (ed.), *The Law of the Poor.* San Fran-
             cisco: Chandler Publishing Co.

Bullington, Bruce, John G. Munns, and Gilbert Geis
   1969   "Purchase of conformity: ex-narcotic addicts among the bour-
             geoisie." *Social Problems* 16 (Spring):456–63.

Casper, Jonathan D.
   1972   *American Criminal Justice: The Defendant's Perspective.* En-
             glewood Cliffs, N.J.: Prentice-Hall.

Chambliss, Bill
   1972   *Boxman: A Professional Thief's Journey.* New York: Harper
             Torch-Books.

Chambliss, William J.
   1969   *Crime and the Legal Process.* New York: McGraw-Hill.

Chambliss, William J., and Robert Seidman
   1971   *Law, Order, and Power.* Reading, Mass.: Addison-Wesley.

Cleaver, Eldridge
   1968   *Soul on Ice.* New York: Dell.

Clinard, Marshall, and Richard Quinney
  1973   *Criminal Behavior Systems.* 2nd ed. N.Y.: Holt, Rinehart, and Winston.

Cressey, Donald
  1955   "Changing criminals: the application of the theory of differential association." *American Journal of Sociology* 61 (September):116–20.

Duster, Troy
  1970   *The Legislation of Morality.* New York: Free Press.

Empey, LaMar T., and Maynard L. Erickson
  1972   *The Provo Experiment.* Lexington, Mass.: D. C. Heath.

Epstein, Jason
  1971   *The Great Conspiracy Trial.* N.Y.: Vintage Books.

Erikson, Kai T.
  1966   *Wayward Puritans.* New York: John Wiley and Sons.

Glaser, Daniel
  1969   *The Effectiveness of a Prison and Parole System.* Indianapolis: Bobbs-Merrill.

  1971   *Social Deviance.* Chicago: Markham.

Gouldner, Alvin W.
  1970   *The Coming Crisis of Western Sociology.* New York: Basic Books.

Gove, Walter R.
  1970   "Societal reaction as an explanation of mental illness: an evaluation." *American Sociological Review* 35 (October):873–84.

Green, Mark J.
  1970   "The law of the young." In B. Wasserstein and M. Green (eds.), *With Justice for Some.* Boston: Beacon Press.

Gusfield, Joseph R.
  1967   "Moral passage: the symbolic process in public designations of deviance." *Social Problems* 15 (Fall):175–88.

Hammersmith, Sue Kiefer, and Martin S. Weinberg
  1973   "Homosexual identity: commitment, adjustment, and significant others." *Sociometry* 36 (March):56–79.

Heussenstamm, F. K.
  1971   "Bumper stickers and the cops." *Transaction* 8 (February): 32–33.

Horowitz, Irving L.
  1970   "The brave new world of campus psychiatry." *Change* (January–February):47–52.

Horowitz, Irving L., and Martin Liebowitz
  1968   "Social deviance and political marginality: toward a redefinition of the relation between sociology and politics." *Social Problems* 15 (Winter):280–96.

Horton, John
1966 "Order and conflict theories of social problems as competing ideologies." *American Journal of Sociology* 71 (May):701–713.

Howard, John R.
1974 *The Cutting Edge.* New York: J. B. Lippincott.

Humphreys, Laud
1970 *Tearoom Trade.* Chicago: Aldine.
1972 *Out of the Closets: The Sociology of Homosexual Liberation.* Englewood Cliffs, N.J.: Prentice-Hall.

Irwin, John
1970 *The Felon.* Englewood Cliffs, New Jersey: Prentice-Hall.

Kerper, Hazel B., and Janeen Kerper
1974 *Legal Rights of the Convicted.* St. Paul: West Publishing.

Klein, Malcolm W.
1971 *Street Gangs and Street Workers.* Englewood Cliffs, N.J.: Prentice-Hall.

Kogan, B., and D. L. Loughery
1970 "Sealing and expungement of criminal records: the big lie." *Journal of Criminal Law, Criminology and Police Science* 61 (September):378–92.

Kunstler, William M.
1969 "Jury nullification in conscience cases." *Virginia Journal of International Law* 10 (December):71–84.

Lemert, Edwin M.
1951 *Social Pathology.* New York: McGraw-Hill.
1967 *Human Deviance, Social Problems and Social Control.* Englewood Cliffs, N.J.: Prentice-Hall.

Levin, Martin A.
1971 "Policy evaluation and recidivism." *Law and Society Review* 6 (August):17–46.

Leznoff, Maurice, and William A. Westley
1956 "The homosexual community." *Social Problems* 3 (April):257–63.

Liazos, Alexander
1972 "The poverty of the sociology of deviance: nuts, sluts and preverts." *Social Problems* 20 (Summer):103–120.

Lofland, John
1969 *Deviance and Identity.* Englewood Cliffs, New Jersey: Prentice-Hall.

Maddison, Simon
1973 "Mindless militants? psychiatry and the university." In I. Taylor and L. Taylor (eds.), *Politics and Deviance.* Baltimore: Penguin Books.

Matza, David
    1969   *Becoming Deviant.* Englewood Cliffs, New Jersey: Prentice-
             Hall.
Miller, Walter B.
    1974   "American youth gangs: past and present." In A. Blumberg
             (ed.), *Current Perspectives on Criminal Behavior.* New York:
             Random House.
Nisbet, Robert, and Robert K. Merton
    1971   *Contemporary Social Problems.* 3rd ed. N.Y.: Harcourt,
             Brace, Jovanovich.
Quinney, Richard
    1970   *The Social Reality of Crime.* Boston: Little, Brown.
Reasons, Charles E.
    1973   "The politicalizing of crime, the criminal and the criminolo-
             gist." *Journal of Criminal Law and Criminology* 64 (Decem-
             ber):471–77.
Saragin, Edward
    1969   *Odd Man In: Societies of Deviants in America.* Chicago:
             Quadrangle Books.
Schafer, Stephen
    1971   "The concept of the political criminal." *Journal of Criminal
             Law, Criminology and Police Science* 62 (September):
             380–87.
Scheflin, Alan W.
    1972   "Jury nullification: the right to say 'no.'" *Southern California
             Law Review* 45:168–26.
Schervish, Paul G.
    1971   "Deviance as a political strategy: the trial of the Chicago 15."
             Paper presented at the Annual Meeting on the Society for the
             Study of Social Problems.
Schwartz, Richard D., and Jerome H. Skolnick
    1962   "Two studies of legal stigma." *Social Problems* 10 (Fall):133–
             42.
Scott, Marvin B., and Stanford M. Lyman
    1970   *The Revolt of the Students.* Columbus: Charles E. Merrill.
Shapiro, David
    1972   "On psychological liberation." *Social Policy* 3 (July–
             August):9–15.
Short, James F., Jr.
    1974   "Youth, gangs and society: micro- and macrosociological pro-
             cesses." *Sociological Quarterly* 15 (Winter):3–19.
Silvergate, Harvey A.
    1974   "The 1970s: a decade of repression?" In R. Quinney (ed.),
             Criminal Justice in America. Boston: Little, Brown.

Skolnick, Jerome
  1969   *The Politics of Protest.* N.Y.: Ballantine Books.
Spitzer, Stephen P., and Norman K. Denzin
  1968   *The Mental Patient.* N.Y.: McGraw-Hill.
Sternberg, David
  1972   "The new radical-criminal trials: a step toward a class-for-
          itself in the American proletariat." *Science and Society* 36
          (Fall):274–301.
Szasz, Thomas S.
  1970a   *Ideology and Insanity.* New York: Doubleday.

  1970b   *The Manufacture of Madness.* New York: Harper and Row.
Taylor, Laurie, and Paul Walton
  1971   "Industrial sabotage: motives and meanings." In S. Cohen
          (ed.), *Images of Deviance.* Baltimore: Penguin.
Taylor, Ian, Paul Walton, and Jock Young
  1973   *The New Criminology: For a Social Theory of Deviance.* Lon-
          don: Routledge and Kegan Paul.
Tittle, Charles R.
  1972   "Institutional living and rehabilitation." *Journal of Health
          and Social Behavior* 13 (September):263–75.

  1974   "Prisons and rehabilitation: the inevitability of disfavor." *So-
          cial Problems* 21:385–95.
Turk, Austin T.
  1966   "Conflict and criminality." *American Sociological Review* 31
          (June):352–88.

  1969   *Criminality and Legal Order.* Chicago: Rand McNally.
Vold, George B.
  1958   *Theoretical Criminology.* New York: Oxford University Press.
Waitzkin, Howard
  1971   "Latent functions of the sick role in various institutional set-
          tings." *Sociology, Science and Medicine* 5:45–75.
Walker, Daniel
  1968   *Rights in Conflict.* New York: Bantam Books.
Walton, Paul
  1973   "The case of the Weathermen: social reaction and radical
          commitment." In I. Taylor and L. Taylor (eds.), *Politics and
          Deviance.* Baltimore: Penguin Books.

_____

  1974   "Homosexual Rights." *Newsweek* (May 20):76–77.

Chapter
XII

Trends in the Creation of Deviance

One who learns why society is urging him into the strait and narrow way will resist its pressure. One who sees clearly how he is controlled will thenceforth be emancipated. . . . The secret of order is not to be bawled from every housetop. The wise sociologist will show religion a consideration. . . . He will venerate a moral system too much to uncover its nakedness. He will speak to men, not youth. He will not tell the "recruity," the street Arab, or the Elmira inmate how he is managed. He will address himself to those who administer the moral capital of society. . . . In this way he will make himself an accomplice of all good men for the undoing of all bad men.

Edward Alsworth Ross, 1901

Every group in power—in a nation, a government, an economy, a political party or a revolutionary cadre—tells its story as it would like to have it believed, in the way it thinks will promote its interests and serve its constituencies. Every group in power profits from ambiguity and mystification, which hide the facts of power from those over whom power is exerted. . . . A sociology that is true to the world inevitably clarifies what has been confused, reveals the character of organizational secrets, upsets the interests of powerful people and groups. . . . Thus, work which is true to the world and explains the actual relations of power and privilege that envelop and determine what goes on in society will be politically useful to radicals, even though (importantly) those who do such work may not themselves be committed to radical goals.

Howard S. Becker and Irving L. Horowitz, 1972

Sources: E. A. Ross, *Social Control* (Cleveland: Press of Case Western Reserve University, 1969), p. 441. H. S. Becker and I. L. Horowitz, "Radical Politics and Sociological Research: Observations on Methodology and Ideology." *American Journal of Sociology* 78 (July 1972):48–66, p. 55.

The Creation of
Deviance

Our theme throughout this volume has been that society, in its attempts to control deviance, may increase the amount of deviant behavior and also force certain individuals into deviant careers. Let us now summarize these various methods of creation. First, and most evident, society creates deviance by the enactment of laws and the resultant setting of collective expectations. Emile Durkheim was one of the first to note that the establishment of a sense of community is facilitated by the creation of a class of actions and actors which are termed deviant. Unity is provided in a collectivity as they unite against what is felt a common threat to both morality and social order. Deviance thus provides a contrast function which demarcates normative boundaries thereby reinforcing the righteousness of the conformists[1] (cf. Erikson, 1966). In this view, a collective sense of morality is achieved, in part, by the creation of deviance.

The establishment of rules and laws not only creates deviance in a very direct sense, but legal policies may contain the seeds of other forms of deviance. This is seen most clearly in the phenomenon referred to as "secondary crime" (Schur, 1965). Secondary crime is the direct result of public policy on a particular behavior. The best example is the theft, burglary, armed robbery, and other crimes which drug addicts must carry out in order to acquire enough money to secure illegal drugs. Our legal policy of making narcotics unavailable by legally proscribing possession and sale of drugs and the possession of facilitating instruments creates a black market. This inflates the price of drugs, money for which must be obtained illicitly by users (Packer, 1968). This crime tariff not only produces secondary crimes by addicts, but allows organized crime to flourish. Another example of this phenomenon is the way in which bail and bonding practices may induce criminals to engage in theft or other illegal activities in order to pay the high bonds set by the court (Chambliss, 1969:375).

Legal policies may also force deviants into subcultures, as in the case of drugs, prostitution, and to some extent, homosexuality. The subculture may originally be a way of adjusting to the problems of legal harrassment and surveillance (i.e., the problems of secondary deviance). As we noted in Chapters IX and XI, subcultural membership may also serve to raise feelings of self-worth through acceptance of a deviant self-identity.[2]

Another source of deviance creation is found in the bureaucratic organization of the rule enforcers. Considerable entrepreneurial work occurs in the agencies charged with enforcement of various rules. Demands for agency perpetuation lead to larger populations of potential deviants being delineated and actively recruited; there is also pressure to subsume more forms of behavior under official control and correction. Organizational demands for efficiency and maximal processing of cases mean that pressures to enforce rules are constant; yet the commission of rule violations may not be constant. Erikson observes:

> The amount of men, money and material assigned by society to "do something" about deviant behavior does not vary appreciably over time, and the implicit logic . . . seems to be that there is a fairly stable quota of trouble which should be anticipated. (1966:24)

Our point is that agencies will find some law to enforce, some action to engage their attention.[3] Enforcement may turn to relatively petty or innocuous offenses, things which at other times would be ignored and probably normalized by the citizenry. For example, over 50 percent of the juvenile arrests in an affluent suburb of Phoenix, Arizona, are for curfew violations! (Personal Communication). Organizational demands to assess "efficiency" of control personnel often produce law enforcement where it otherwise might not occur. Traffic officers, for example, are expected to write a certain number of tickets for a given time period, producing what amounts to a quota system of arrests (Skolnick, 1966).

A fourth general way in which deviance is created demands an examination of the ways in which category systems used by formal agencies of social control are diffused, adopted, and applied by the general public. This diffusion means that laypersons see behaviors, formerly acceptable, as "symptoms" of a latent problem. That which was undifferentiated suddenly becomes a labeled condition. In addition to the propagation of category systems by control agencies, the formulations of social scientists, the stereotyped accounts of deviance in the mass media, and the general presence of stereotyped images of deviant roles in the folk culture also help to channel informal reactions to behavior. We have described how common citizens may become unwitting recruiters for control bureaucracies because of these influences; this also increases the chances that certain behaviors will come to official notice through various lay referral systems. Even when official action is not taken, the "informed" typifications of deviance held by the general population will probably mean that informal, largely private, remedial actions will be undertaken, and are likely to be more restrictive or punitive in effect. This leads directly to a fifth sense of deviance creation: the self-fulfilling prophecy.

Labels and categories set up expectations (conveyed in part by stereotypes of master status characteristics) which may be met due to a structuring of the situation—the removal of various opportunities for those suspected of deviance to do otherwise. Rosenthal's work on teacher expectations has demonstrated the subtle ways in which both positive and negative expectations may become manifest in student behaviors (Rosenthal and Jacobson, 1968). In similar ways those with devalued attributes, such as the blind or the mentally retarded, are often denied an opportunity to show they can function adequately in the world. These self-fulfilling conditions are set up at two levels. Friends and relatives of the rule breaker, having adopted all or part of the official typification, may alter reactions to the deviant (after an initial period of normalization and denial). At the level of official contact, the control agents themselves may set the stage for fulfillment of expectations. What is ironic is that control agents often realize this phenomenon occurs, but fail to see its wider implications. The psychiatrist who attempts to treat potentially suicidal patients realizes he must be careful not to suggest this diagnosis, or otherwise set up an expectation which the patient may feel obligated to fulfill (Light, 1972). Another example involves the case of child abuse. Bakan (1971:12) suggests that physicians who feel child abuse has occurred but are then not able to substantiate it, open up the possibility that the child will, upon release from the hospital, be attacked by the parent in response to the doctor's accusation. Doctors, sensing this possibility, may ignore certain cases where hard evidence is absent.

Sixth, the process of labeling itself (visibility, recognition, attribution of cause, motive, and essential self) creates deviance *differentially* in the sense that it makes certain segments of the population more liable to imputations of deviant character. For example, the lower-status individual is more likely to have his rule breaking attributed to internal causes, while conformity is likely to be seen as externally produced. The joint effect of such processes is the creation of deviance (in the sense of greater probability of assignment to deviant categories) for lower-status individuals and minority groups. It is not surprising that these segments make up the bulk of the natural resources of social-control agencies. These processes also mean that the discredited groups in society have difficulty achieving respectability (see Chapter IV).

We have proposed that proliferation of enforcement agencies and the greater contact which results increase the susceptibility to labeling and agency intervention—e.g., few learning disabilities or behavioral problems were discovered in the rural, one-room school compared to those found in the modern diagnostic and counseling offices of large suburban school systems. Those who rely on the public welfare system find that their behaviors are more visible since aspects of their condition may be referred on to other agencies (secondary visibility). Agency contact—whether voluntary or involuntary—also raises the possibility of imposition of secondary rules. The application of secondary rules is an example of pure deviance creation: imposing very restrictive conditions on an individual because of ascribed status—e.g., the parole regulations for released felons—simply compounds the expectations and demands placed on the deviant. Feelings of resentment, injustice, and perhaps rebellion may result. Agency contact may also have significant consequences for the actor's view of himself. The biography building which occurs may convince him of his essential deviant nature and force him to accept the deviant role. Many treatment programs demand that the individual completely accept the fact of his deviance, a flaw in character, as a starting point for rehabilitation. This may contribute to the failure of the treatment (Edgerton, 1967:212). To the extent that a rehabilitation program is not effective, an adoption of a deviant self-conception is facilitated, along with probability of continued rule violation.

One final (and probably the most ironic) sense in which society creates deviance involves the control agents themselves: they may engage in widespread rule breaking (illegal and extra-legal actions) while enforcing other rules. Our drug policies have produced an incentive for police corruption, well documented by the Knapp Commission. Other victimless crimes may lead to violation of rights to secure arrests, since willing complainants are not readily available. Organizational demands for a "good pinch" lead to police brutality and systematic violations of due process rights (Westley, 1953; Stark, 1972). The fear of crime may produce repressive legislation where personal freedoms are sacrificed for public safety, and such legislation is sometimes taken as a mandate for procedural law violations by control agents (Harris, 1969). For example, the misuse of the wiretap has continued even though greater powers have been granted for its legitimate use. The Watergate affair and related incidents showed that the rule breaking of the controllers could be virtually limitless. The White House tapes revealed that a fear of the anti-war movement and the New Left seemed to generalize to many

unlikely people (e.g., enemies list, wiretap list). Worry over dissent
within the country produced deviance within the government on an
unprecedented scale—a classic case of concern over one form of
deviance leading to a more extensive, and more threatening, pattern
of rule violations.

Some Disturbing
Trends

Given the many senses of the creation of deviance discussed above,
what are some possible future trends? Has society reached its potential in creativity? The following trends will affect the forms and rates
of deviance in society in the years ahead. These trends are largely in
the direction of greater deviance creation, and so our forecast is a
gloomy one. We shall, however, try to indicate some developments
which might reduce the generation of deviance. Two major trends
seem to assure that deviant behavior will remain a problem in the
years ahead: first, the proliferation of control agencies and their
influence, and second, the medicalization of many forms of deviant
behavior.

In terms of the three spheres of social control—legal, therapeutic,
and social welfare (see Chapter VI)—the size and scope of social-
control agencies in all three sectors seems to be increasing. Indeed,
it is difficult to think of any behavior which could not be brought
under the jurisdiction of some type of regulatory agency. In the legal
sphere, in addition to the large and pervasive public legal systems
(criminal and civil law), there are an increasing number of private
legal and quasi-legal systems such as workman compensation boards,
ethics committees for professions, tenure and promotion procedures
in universities, etc. Each new social problem produces a new set of
agencies (and a corresponding set of initials) which increases the pool
of controls and controllers. The recent concern with the environment has produced the Environmental Protection Agency (EPA), as
well as state and local agencies, to regulate air, water, and noise
pollution. Overnight a whole new range of human activity was
brought under bureaucratic control. Therapeutic and welfare realms
also expand to meet new social problems.

In addition to numerical expansion, control agency influence is
proliferated by a greater range of placement for its specialists in
deviance detection. John Lofland summarizes the situation
(1969:137):

In addition to their sheer numbers, the facilitative significance of sensitive specialists is increased by their institutional and territorial dispersion. The psychiatrist in the factory and the social worker (or even policeman) in the school, by their penetration of new institutional spheres, increase the visibility of the conduct of a larger number of Actors. They thereby collectively increase the number and range of Actors who are likely to be imputed. Such a dispersion of specialists, gives rise, in turn, to opportunities for collaboration and cooperation among them, even further increasing the possibilities for imputation.

Thus, even if there was a moratorium upon the creation of new control agencies, the influence of extant agencies would continue to expand, and deviance would continue to be discovered/created.

The expansion of control agencies, both numerically and in terms of territorial invasion, has been underwritten largely by the assumption that social problem areas can be remediated if they are subjected to a scientific and rationally based, bureaucratic program. Scientific rationality, embedded in a bureaucracy dedicated to efficiency, facilitated by an advanced technology (developed in war and space research), comes to be seen as the hope and salvation of man, a ready solution to societal problems. Because of its eager acceptance as a panacea by the general public, bureaucratic rationality may be compared to a pain-relieving, medically sound, but addictive drug. If the patient uses the prescribed amount for the specified ailment, his pain is eliminated and he functions more comfortably and more efficiently. If he takes the same medication for another ailment, however, the new pain is unaffected and, moreover, the problem is likely to increase in severity. Or, if the individual indulges in ever-increasing quantities of the drug because he finds it so pleasurable, he becomes addicted to it. Bureaucratic rationality, if utilized in non-production, non-business settings (such as social-control agencies) can constitute the organizational equivalent of "bad medicine." And if the society becomes addicted to bureaucratic rationality as a cure-all, the entire system can suffer. Nevertheless, the society at large clings to its love affair with bureaucratic rationality, oblivious to its dangers and misapplications. Population growth and concentration accelerates the taken-for-granted approach to all of a society's affairs by providing more people with more problems, which of course must be handled even more efficiently due to growing caseloads. We can expect, then, to see *more* standardized procedures rather than less, *more* labeling rather than less, and *more* career effects rather than less as we apply more bureaucratic rationality to more agency settings.

The recent stress on systems analysis, computer simulation, and mechanized data processing within control agencies indicates that advances in technology are seen as the road to greater rationality. No less a figure than Norbert Wiener, the acknowledged father of cybernation, warned years ago what is still being argued about today: that computers are merely highly efficient mechanical slaves which can be no smarter than the data they receive and the men who compile the data.[4] Nevertheless, there is probably not a reader who has not been told, at one time or another, "I'm sorry this happened to you, but it just couldn't be helped—the computer did it." The fact of the matter is that the computer *didn't* do it. Its program was designed by a human being and its output was relayed onward by other human beings. When input is designed for the convenience of the machine and when output is unquestioningly accepted as "objective finding," humane considerations and human complexities are largely ignored. Mechanized examination and computerized diagnosis, for example, have already begun to make an appearance on the physical illness front. There are undoubtedly those who anxiously await the transfer of such techniques to the precinct station (perhaps under the auspices of "preventive detention") and the psychiatric clinic ("preventive psychotherapy"?). At this writing, for example, the Columbia Region Information Sharing System (Portland, Oregon, metropolitan area) is preparing for the installation of a $1,499,332 computer system designed to *"automate processing of criminal information,* aid better dispatching of police forces, and *speed offender booking and disposition of court cases* through automated court scheduling" (*The Oregonian*, Oct. 1, 1973. Emphasis added.). The risks of such sophisticated equipment revolve around (a) the mechanical requirement that a diagnostic computer operate only in terms of a set of limited, fixed-input variables, thus bypassing "extraneous" information and automatically guaranteeing the "biography building" phenomenon, and (b) the likelihood that the computer decision *will be taken* as an objective, accurate, and sufficient basis for subsequent agency processing.

Another aspect of proliferation of control, which has ominous overtones, is what might be termed control by circumvention. This refers to the fairly widespread practice of using one set of rules to control other forms of behavior which may not be under regulation, or which have been exempted from regulation. Examples would be the use of loitering laws to control prostitution (at least streetwalkers) and street people and the use of zoning ordinances to keep out pornographic movies or bookstores and to control the placement of massage parlors. Another example is the control of topless dancing by threats of revocation of liquor licenses for violations (this usually occurs after local anti-topless ordinances are declared unconstitutional). The regulation of personal behaviors and lifestyle to "qualify" for welfare payments is a widespread form of circumvention. These forms of entrepreneurial work at the enforcement level expand agency jurisdiction and inflate the population of official deviants. Somewhat related is the possibility of a redirection or convolution of the entire enforcement machinery. The most vivid example of this occurred in the late 1960s when part of the intelligence division of the United States Army was shifted from background checks for security clearance of military personnel to a program of active spying and recording of activities by civilians during the anti-war movement. Observations of Earth Day activities, peace marches, and demonstrations, plus photographs and newspaper clippings, found their way into files and dossiers on civilians. In this case, the redirection was ordered from above; at other times, it may occur as a response by the organization to maintain survival.

There are, of course, other factors contributing to the proliferation of control agencies. One indirect factor is the increase in training programs for occupations related to people-processing agencies. One example is the large number of criminal justice programs, as well as police and correctional "science" degree programs, in universities and community colleges. This relates to the general movement toward a service society, with the attendant acceptance of and legitimacy accorded to various service agencies in the welfare state. This leads to a second major trend, the medicalization of deviant behavior.

There has been a shift in recent years in dealing with various types of deviant behavior from control by criminal sanction to a therapeutic approach to intervention and treatment. The underlying assumption of this divestment of criminal law and the substitution of what has been termed the "medicalization of deviance" (Pitts, 1968) is boldly stated by Karl Menninger: "according to the prevalent understanding of the words, crime is not a disease. Neither is it an illness, although I think it *should* be" (Menninger, 1969:254). We noted in Chapter VI that one of the reasons for the increasing acceptance of this sentiment is the failure of the criminal law (with its assumed punishment and deterrence aspects) to deal effectively with crime and other deviance. The shift is probably more the result of a desire to divert behaviors from the jurisdiction of the criminal law than to a careful consideration of what is implied in the alternative—the therapeutic state. We now review the characteristics of the medical model which underlie the therapeutic state and trace out its implications.

We have indicated throughout this book that considerable legitimacy and awe are accorded the medical profession and psychiatry. The medical model is embraced partly because of its favorable record in physical illness (compared to the relatively unsuccessful legal control of deviance). There is the appeal of a quick cure, and even preventive medicine (detection and prevention of anti-social behavior—e.g., the Hutschnecker plan described in Chapter VI). The medical approach also appeals to humanitarian concerns since punishment is ostensively replaced by treatment. The auspices of intervention are seen differently by the public, apparently because they draw an analogy to the private physician-patient relationship. In other words, the public assumes that medicalization of deviant behavior means voluntary treatment and a sincere concern on the part of the deviant individual to "get well." Even some social scientists have been taken in. Jesse Pitts (1968:391) claims the following advantages for the movement toward medicalization of deviance: (1) the medical professions will be more immune to political pressure and corruption than are agents of the criminal justice system; (2) the therapeutic ideology "creates an optimistic bias concerning the patient's fate;" (3) the deviant is denied the rationalization that he has been injustly treated, since intervention is not the result of a judgment of sickness, not moral evil (Supposedly medical decisions and diagnoses are free of moral judgments and, since no injustice and subsequent rationalization are possible, "[t]he medicalization of deviance results in the political castration of the deviant."); and (4) there is less stigma in medical intervention and labels than legal intervention and labels.

Hopefully the reader will realize, given the evidence in previous chapters, that each of these assumptions is patently false! The medical profession is open to influence and corruption when working as an agent of the state in a large control bureaucracy—e.g., the influence of the Army bureaucracy on psychiatrists (see research by Daniels). The medical model leads to systematic errors of diagnosis ("when in doubt, treat")—hardly a bias in favor of the patient. Medical judgments when dealing with deviant behavior are moral judgments (see Szasz), and a sense of injustice can be created in the processing of deviant behavior through medical channels. In addition, the use of psychiatry for political purposes, such as the control of campus radicals through referral to mental health clinics, may also serve to generate feelings of injustice. Finally, there is little evidence that medical labels are less stigmatic than legal ones (e.g., research by Phillips). In short, we reject the notion that salvation lies in the medical definition and treatment of rule violations (be they civil-legal, polite-interactional, or background expectancy violations).

A more realistic appraisal would note the following. First, the medical and legal models are similar in that the source of the problem is located in the individual and, hence, the individual is the target of the "treatment."[5] Our point, implicit throughout, has been that effective treatment must take into account the context of the rule violation and the role of reactors (official and unofficial) in the continuation of the behavior.

Second, the medicalization of deviance has occurred primarily in cases where offenders are seen as either "mentally abnormal (the mentally ill, the psychopaths, and to a degree alcoholics and drug addicts) or else chronologically immature (the juvenile delinquent)" (Kittrie, 1971:342). Anthony Platt describes this "medicalization" phenomenon in juvenile court:

> The child savers depicted delinquents as irresponsible and incapable of free choice, and as victims of uncontrollable forces. ... With this emphasis upon predetermined as opposed to volitional conduct, there was an accompanying tendency to regard delinquents as psychologically incapacitated and therefore not responsible. As a consequence ... , juvenile court judges were cast in the role of physicians whose task it was to diagnose social diseases and to recommend appropriate remedies. (Platt, quoted in Kittrie, 1971:343)

The outcome of such an assumption is that, as more behaviors come under medical rather than legal control, there will be a corresponding pressure to view more behaviors as the result of pathology[6] —a manifestation of abnormality or immaturity. This goes counter to the evidence cited here which stresses the importance of societal reaction in the creation of deviance. It also denies the actor's own role and possible choice in the rule violation. This fact not only prohibits an understanding of the act, but probably reduces the chances of changing the behavior pattern.

Third, the demands for benevolent treatment often mean that the rights of due process, recognized and secured in the legal model (albeit incompletely), are now largely absent in the medical model. Therefore, the most dangerous characteristic of the therapeutic approach is the failure to provide due process controls over both intervention and treatment activities (Murphy, 1969). The humanitarian underpinnings ("we are doing it for your own good") and the emphasis on public safety over individual rights have produced an ever-expanding social-control system with few procedural safeguards. Ironically, it was the injustices of the present punitive aspects of the criminal justice system which were cited by Menninger and other proponents of the therapeutic state as justification for the establishment of the medical approach. However, advocates of divestment have failed to realize that the prescribed remedy to the "crime of punishment" may involve many unjust and inhumane aspects (see Murphy, 1969). Nicholas Kittrie suggests some reasons why the therapeutic approach has developed without attendant safeguards:

> Bowing to the desires and ostensible good-faith opinions of the experts, the law forsook its role as the censor of the exercise of state power and left the therapists to devise their own means for bringing the therapeutic power to bear. Although legislators abetted this process by establishing special and informal administrative procedures for the therapists and appending no safeguards thereto, the absence of procedural safeguards in the therapeutic realm is equally the fault of the courts. They have withheld constitutional protections from putative patients on the basis that the proceedings were noncriminal, and have uncritically accepted the testimony and opinions of doctors, social workers, and others charged with the therapeutic mission. By abridging the individual's right to object and by neglecting to scrutinize the state's requests to exercise therapeutic power, the courts have placed the therapist outside societal controls. (Kittrie, 1971:371)

While the rights of due process are largely absent in most areas of therapeutic intervention, a recent exception is the juvenile court. Based on the principle of *parens patriae*, the court was originally envisoned as a "medical-welfare" rather than a legal approach to deviance (and thus the avoidance of the "trappings" of a criminal court). Recent Supreme Court decisions, however, have brought the child-saving movement full circle. The decisions of *Kent, Gault* and *Winship*[7] have restored most of the procedural safeguards of adult criminal proceedings, and therefore have moved the court closer to the legal model than the previously glorified medical model.

Finally, the medicalization of deviance is achieved in a number of ways. It may involve a complete divestment from the criminal law, as was attempted in the establishment of the juvenile court system. Or divestment may come about through court decisions which affect the power of the criminal law to impose punishment. For example, the Supreme Court stated that drug addiction was an illness as early as 1925 (*Linder v. United States*) and has more recently reaffirmed this view (*Robinson v. California*). Similarly court decisions have noted that chronic alcoholism is an involuntary condition (*Driver v. Hinnant* and *Easter v. District of Columbia*), although a later decision by the Supreme Court complicated the issue (see Kittrie, 1971: Chapters 5 and 6).[8] In the *Robinson* case, the state was not able to imprison Robinson under a statute making it a crime to be addicted to the use of narcotics (addicts may still be arrested for possession, sale, etc.). In sum, these cases imply there are advantages to treating alcoholics and drug addicts in a medical setting. More importantly, they set up the legal grounds for recognizing and legitimizing alternative treatment programs outside the legal area. This becomes another tie between the medical and legal models. The practice has been termed "diversion"—i.e., "the disposition of a criminal complaint without a conviction, the noncriminal disposition being conditioned on either the performance of specified obligations by the defendant, or his participation in counseling or treatment" (Nimmer, 1974:5). Another form of diversion includes post-conviction diversion, such as treatment programs entered into as conditions for probation (Vorenberg and Vorenberg, 1973).

Diversion can occur, therefore, at virtually any point in the criminal justice system with varying degrees of "force" involved (although programs are termed voluntary, entrance is seldom an open choice). The diversion is often to a medically-based treatment program. One reason for the popularity of this procedure is that it saves money.[9] It also reduces case loads within the criminal justice system. However, diversion does raise three serious issues: what are the guarantees of due process in the placement of a person in a treatment program, especially in cases where placement is made prior to finding guilt? What is the degree of voluntary choice? And what coercion may be present once in the program? The question of individual rights is indeed crucial here. For example, a homosexual may be given a choice of a "voluntary" aversive conditioning program or a prison sentence. In similar ways, drug addicts and those convicted of public drunkenness may be forced into voluntary programs where failure to complete the alternative treatment means return to the criminal justice system, which usually results in incarceration. Regardless of these civil rights questions, the trend is toward diversion, and we feel this will be a continuing impetus in the turn toward the medicalization of deviant behavior.

Some
Recommendations

Labeling theory is largely anti-establishment in implication and tone. It proposes that current policies of social control are instrumental in the production of deviant behavior in clear violation of their original mandate. Consequently, the theory is often seen as negative—i.e., highly critical of the present system, but offering no alternatives. While recognizing the importance of the "debunking" nature of the theory, we shall now try to draw out some implications for changing our public policies regarding deviant behavior. In doing so, we do not wish to be identified with the "positivistic correctional view"[10]—i.e., we are not interested in producing more effective and repressive social-control systems. We are somewhat disturbed that agencies of control might take our findings and use them in ways which would lead to more efficient and rigid controls: knowledge, of course, may be used for good or evil, liberation or repression. In this sense, all research can have political consequences (often unintended or un-recognized by the researchers). Our particular value stance might be summarized in the following way.

We believe that the labeling and processing of individuals as deviant is often unwarranted, and at other times, counter-productive. We are concerned with the negative effects of the labeling-reaction pro-cess—e.g., the creation of a sense of injustice, the forcing of many individuals into devalued deviant careers, and the subjection of per-sons to the deprivations of total institutions. Our concern is with the reduction of repression and injustice in society—hardly a new theme in philosophy or social science. We do not accept the myopic view that freedom is achieved through eradication of all control agencies. We feel that certain actions are problematic within society—e.g., threat to personal safety or property—and that protective agencies are a necessity at this point. However, we feel that the dynamics involved in the creation of deviance can be altered so that lives are not ruined, talents lost, nor violent repression legitimated. Such al-ternatives can be implemented at the organizational and social pol-icy level and, over the longer haul, at the societal level.

Organizational and
Policy Changes[11]

There are some things which can be done right now to reduce label-ing effects in social-control agencies. We shall now try to make explicit some points implicit in our earlier discussion of labeling and organizational processing stereotypes (which produce reified diagnoses and dispositions, and a correspondent sense of injustice). Simple things such as pay structure are important. Recall that Scheff found personnel at public commitment hearings were paid by the case, thereby establishing a situation where speed in processing was reinforced. Being paid a flat salary would at least permit more time to be spent on analysis of the details of a rule violation and the special characteristics of the offender. (This alone would be insufficient if case load pressure remains high.)

Another source of processing stereotypes is the organizational demand for efficiency, both in processing cases and in the evaluating performance by control personnel. Are there other ways of evaluting police performance besides volume of arrests (e.g., traffic quotas), removing crimes from the books (producing good clearance rates), or making a "big pinch" (regardless of the methods utilized)? One proposal is that police officers in the field be evaluated on the extent to which their patrol activities decrease or prevent crime in a neighborhood. However, arrest rates and other police data could *not* be used to make this evaluation: to do so would simply reinforce the ignoring or covering up of crimes. Independent indicators, such as victim surveys, would be required for an unbiased assessment of police behavior and crime prevention or reduction. In a similar way, evaluating public defenders and district attorney personnel by the number of convictions produces the plea-bargaining system, in turn maximizing case disposition in the shortest period of time. Other means of evaluation must be developed which will be free of these negative side effects.

Other changes which might be made include the decentralization of control agencies (e.g., Lemert, 1967). This would reduce reification of cases due to requirements of passing cases to other decision makers. Case loads must also be reduced; the usual recommendation here is to demand more money and personnel. We reject this solution because it simply produces a proliferation of control agencies. Rather, case loads can be reduced by decriminalization—i.e., removing many behaviors from control by the criminal law (Morris and Hawkins, 1970; Schur, 1965). Delinquent tendency and dependent child cases could be removed from the juvenile court. This would remove about two-thirds of the present cases. Public drunkenness, sexual behavior between consenting adults, drug use, gambling, and prostitution could be removed from criminal law control. Case loads may also be reduced by various diversion programs (Nimmer, 1974); but, as noted above, serious questions of procedural rights must be addressed if this policy is accepted.[12] Other behaviors might simply be ignored by officials, what Lemert terms "judicious non-intervention" (1967).

Another step involves the education of control agents as to labeling effects and the dynamics of processing stereotypes.[13] For example, anyone going to work in a mental institution should be required to read Rosenhan's "On Being Sane in Insane Places." Police officers would benefit from reading Skolnick's *Justice Without Trial.* Public defenders should be exposed to Sudnow (1965) and Skolnick (1967). Other methods of instruction might also be implemented. Rosenhan (1973:257) recommends that psychiatric personnel spend some time as pseudo-patients.[14] Similarly, law enforcement personnel might be incarcerated in various total institutions as a means of consciousness raising. (In this regard, some judges have volunteered to spend a *weekend* in jail—it would be instructive to study their sentencing and bail-setting behaviors before and after such an experience.)

Another strategy would be the removal of existing labels and diagnostic systems within the control agency. Abandonment of existing social-control labels would mean the disappearance of current psychiatric categories from "paranoid schizophrenic" to "sociopathic personality disturbance, anti-social reaction" and of certain criminal categories such as "incorrigible youth." In their place, agencies would relate the precise nature of the allegedly deviant behavior and leave it at that. Mary Jones' "paranoid schizophrenia" chart entry might become, for example, "thinks everyone is trying to destroy her, experiences visual and auditory hallucinations, and imagines herself to be the reincarnated Joan of Arc." Those readers who are already insistent upon the absurdity of this idea are probably focusing upon the cumbersome, wordy nature of our proposed substitute descriptions—they are simply not efficient! How can agency workers be expected to communicate effectively any longer? *That is precisely the point!* First of all, efficiency of communication need not be sacrificed one iota. Mary Jones is still Mary Jones and she can be talked about as Mary Jones rather than as "the paranoid schizophrenic." Furthermore, and of exceeding importance, when Mary Jones has no categorical label other than her name attached to her identity, others *cannot* engage in the restrictive perspectives prompted by a diagnostic label and *must* force their attention upon exactly what it is about Mary that constitutes problematic behavior. It would be instructive to note how control agencies would function if they were barred from a reliance upon categorization systems such that their actions had to be justified by means other than appeal to "standard procedure for patients of type A."[15]

If label removal is not facilitated, certain minimal safeguards should be set up. Patients should not be referred to by staff in terms of diagnostic labels (especially in their presence—a common practice in many hospitals; cf. Rosenhan). Biography building should be redesigned so that positive and negative information is included. Some type of adversary procedure may have to be instituted—e.g., one control agent, or an outsider, would be asked to search the biography for signs of "normality," to be counterbalanced with another person who looks for problems. Likewise, records of institutional behaviors should include both conforming and rule-violating incidents. Also, there should be stronger controls over information about patients or prisoners. Simple rights of privacy must be instituted: true expungement of records might reduce stigma. The return of full legal rights should also occur upon release.

Finally, there should be a move away from individual-centered treatment programs to a contextual, behavioral approach. The dynamics of the situation, the presence of others, and the role of the actor must be examined as to their separate and combined contributions in the etiology of the rule violation. (For a description of these forms of analysis and treatment, see Laing and Esterson, 1964, Lennard and Bernstein, 1969, Martin, *et al.*, 1968, and Tharp and Wetzel, 1969.) If those in charge of various treatment programs become aware of the importance of others' reactions in the maintenance of deviance, it may be possible to use these labeling effects to achieve the desired change in behavior. Levin (1971:36–37) suggests that positive labeling, positive self-fulfilling prophecies, and experimenter effects might be incorporated into probation programs to increase success rates. Rosenthal and Jacobson (1968) found that teacher effects had a positive outcome. Teachers in an elementary school were told at the beginning of the year that certain students would make great intellectual gains. This randomly chosen group designated as "spurters" did develop more intellectually than did the nonlabeled group as measured by standardized intelligence tests given at the end of the year (cf. Retish, 1973).

Broader
Implications

The creation of deviance is tied to community tolerance in two important ways. First, as indicated in our discussion of total institutions, one road to reducing labeling effects is to deinstitutionalize the handling of deviants. What is required is the development of community-based treatment and correctional programs, the use of outpatient clinics for mental illness, and the establishment of supportive communities for the criminal, the mentally ill, or the mentally retarded—e.g., Laing's use of apartments in London where those with behavioral problems learn to live together and adjust to society with the help of nondirective staff members. These programs often meet resistance from the larger community, out of fear for personal safety, concern with neighborhood reputation, or feelings that property values will decline (Empey and Erickson, 1972; Yablonsky, 1967).[16] When located amid a hostile citizenry, these programs are less likely to succeed because of the negative reactions of citizens to the persons in the program.[17] Yet, even with community resistance, these programs are more successful than total institutions (Empey and Erickson, 1972; Levin, 1971).

A second way in which community tolerance is important is implicit in our definition of deviance (Chapter III). Deviance can be reduced by expanding the tolerance limits of the group or society so that reactions do not occur. At issue here, then, is the initial deviance-creating power of society.

> The task is to create a society in which the facts of human diversity, whether personal, organic or social, are not subject to the power to criminalize. (Taylor, *et al.*, 1973:282)

In what ways, operating at the social level, might greater tolerance for behavior be created?

The logic of labeling theory implies that a reeducation of the public as to the myths and misguided stereotypes of persons designated as deviant would reduce labeling and increase tolerance. This is not likely to occur—given the vested interest of social-control agencies —and would probably not be that effective, especially if the powers of the control establishment continues to expand. Stated differently, the reduction of informal lay reactions may be offset by greater use of sanctions by professional control agents. Another possibility is that certain areas will develop tolerant attitudes toward deviance. For example, San Francisco has been characterized by the term "culture of civility" (Becker and Horowitz, 1971).[18] In the case of San Francisco, the reasons for the greater tolerance of deviance by the public and by officials are unclear: it may have been due to possible economic incentives—"deviance, like difference, is a civic resource, enjoyed by tourist and resident alike" (*Ibid.*, p. 210). Or, it may have resulted when the enforcers realized a policy of accommodation involved fewer "hassles." Apparently, both police and deviant groups negotiate problem areas rather than resort to conflict or law enforcement for resolution of an issue. However, even the culture of civility has limits to accommodation, and repressive responses still occur for most types of deviance. Indeed, a superficial air of tolerance may mask a deeper repression: "Is this no more than a clever trick, a way of buying off deviant populations with minor freedoms while still keeping them enslaved?" (*Ibid.*, p. 213).

Perhaps tolerance can only be achieved by changing the basic structure of American society (Quinney, 1974; Taylor, *et al.*, 1973). Some of the architects of such change may be those deviants forced toward a collective solution by the repressive response of society. The increasing militancy and political organization of deviant groups may produce changes more conducive to a tolerant attitude toward various life styles. It seems that the deviant will have to create his own tolerance in the face of public apathy and resistance from entrepreneurial control agencies. This leads to the final irony in the creation of deviance: impetus for the reduction of deviance may lie with the rule breakers and not the rule enforcers.

Notes

1. Durkheim, using a functionalist argument, suggested that any group or society must create deviance: "Imagine a society of saints, a perfect cloister of exemplary individuals. Crimes, properly so called, will there be unknown; but faults which appear venial to the laymen will create there the same scandal that the ordinary offense does in the ordinary consciousness" (Durkheim, 1964:68–69).

2. In response to societal reaction, a person may be forced into the company of like-minded others who have "adjusted" to persecution. Over time, deviance may continue because of factors growing out of the subcultural membership. For example, the prostitute gets to know other prostitutes, learns the techniques of fee collection and detection evasion, forms ties to other prostitutes while withdrawing from attachments in conventional society. She further learns a set of justifications which legitimate the activity. She may no longer care or think much about societal reaction, or at least this is not the main motivating force in continuation of the deviant career. The deviance has moved to a new phase (beyond secondary deviance, but nevertheless as a response to adjustment problems indicated by the term "secondary deviance"); a new set of determining variables has evolved. (This might be termed "tertiary deviance," although the term is less than appealing.) This does not deny the possibility of subcultural membership prior to extensive deviant acts, or even prior to official societal reactions (e.g., homosexual subculture). However, the distinction becomes important to understanding continuation in a career.

3. Kai Erikson, using records of crime waves in Puritan New England in the seventeenth century, found these rates were bounded by the capacity of the control agencies of the society. "When a community tries to assess the size of its deviant population, then, it is usually measuring the capacity of its own social control apparatus and not the inclinations toward deviance found among its members" (1966:25).

4. Social-control agencies, since they are staffed predominantly by "professionals" of one sort or another, have long been thought to be relatively immune to the notorious dehumanization features of technology, the thought being that "brain work" is far less susceptible than "brawn work" to displacement by machine. Thus, there has been no attempt to avoid record-keeping and information-storing functions of the new technology. Computer input necessitates the use of standardized forms, charts, and schedules for collecting information. In consequence, the perceptive set of agency personnel is unconsciously narrowed to the limits set by standardization; the way is paved for the abundance of biography building and process stereotyping that is blithely accepted as progressive, beneficial, and efficient.

5. There are situations in medicine where the environment is recognized and partially acted against—e.g., the policy of quarantine, and the medical concepts of "contamination" and "epidemic." A parallel within the legal model is the use of family courts to handle delinquency, where problem behaviors of the child are located in the dynamics of the family situation. Remedial action may be directed

to the family unit, rather than the child. These, unfortunately, are very limited exceptions to the general trend.

6. See Matza, 1969, for a critique of the pathology assumptions as applied to deviant behavior.

7. In 1966, the *Kent* decision on the transfer of jurisdiction from juvenile to adult court gave the following safeguards to the juvenile: (1) a full hearing on the issue of transfer to adult court; (2) the assistance of counsel at such a hearing; (3) full access to social records gathered and used by the court to determine whether transfer should be made; and (4) a statement of the reasons for jurisdiction waiver. In the *Gault* case of 1967, it was declared that the child and his parents must (1) be notified regarding the charges in advance of the hearing so that the defendant has a reasonable opportunity to prepare for it, (2) be informed of the right to be represented by counsel, or be provided with counsel if the defendant cannot afford one, and (3) be informed of the right to refuse to testify for fear of self-incrimination and (4) be granted the right to confront and cross-examine witnesses. Thus, *Gault* provided the delinquent with the due process rights which were applicable to adults. The *Winship* case in 1970 said the juvenile court was required, in cases of acts which would be crimes if committed by an adult, to prove guilt beyond a reasonable doubt, replacing the civil dictim of guilt by a preponderance of evidence criterion (Caldwell and Black, 1971:220–25).

8. In a complex case (*Powell*, 1968), the Supreme Court stopped short of overthrowing criminal punishment for actions of a chronic alcoholic. The earlier *Driver* and *Easter* cases applied only to selected Eastern states; hence, we have no definitive national policy divesting alcoholics from the criminal legal process. Each of these cases has served in limited ways as justification for doing away with arrests for public drunkenness in some cities and has prompted alternative treatment programs such as detoxification centers.

9. California recently provided monetary incentive to local areas to keep convicted criminals out of the state prison system: "In an effort to reduce the costs of supporting inmates in state prisons, the California Legislature authorized the payment of subsidies to the counties for each offender placed on probation instead of being sent to a state institution. Between July 1966, when the Probation Subsidy Program went into effect, and July 1968, the state saved approximately $10.5 million in the first 2 years of the program's operation" (Campbell, *et al.*, 1970:642).

10. For a critique of the corrective perspective in sociology of deviance, see Matza, 1969; Taylor, *et al.*, 1973; and Quinney, 1974.

11. We are immediately open to criticism from radical sociologists at this point because our discussion implicitly legitimates present methods of social control. This is not our intent, but we feel that to try to reduce injustices in the short run is preferable to idealistic discussions of a possible utopian world. Such a utopia, if achieved, is not likely to occur overnight. We see little prospect for an immediate and major revolution in American society. In a sense, the radical criminologist is "copping out" by ignoring the injustices in the short run. For an example of the role some British sociologists are playing in social action, see a description of the National Deviancy Conference in Mintz, 1974.

12. Perhaps the central dilemma of social control is to provide due process and procedural safeguards to the deviant, yet do so in a setting which is not so cumbersome as to produce stigma and other labeling effects. This difficulty is very evident in the history of the juvenile court.

13. Analyses of control organizations should focus on the following: how processing stereotypes evolve and are maintained by daily activities of control agents, how the processee develops a sense of injustice, how goal displacement occurs in large bureaucracies, and then how each of these factors sabotage the intended outcome of social control: reform and redirection of behavior patterns. Control agents must then be instructed on the results of such studies. If treatment programs have a

built-in evaluation research design, such questions could be incorporated within it.

14. Some students, after reading Rosenhan's study, suggested that new personnel be required to pose as pseudo-patients and that intake staff be informed of this possibility, which might lead to a reversal of the tendency to find illness among the populations they come in contact with. After this apprenticeship period, these new agents could be moved to intake roles as well as other positions in the mental hospital.

15. We do not hold out much hope for this "solution." The demands to categorize and label are central to the social construction of reality as we have noted throughout the book. Another tack might be taken—that is, the prevention of recording of certain types of information which are the basis of processing stereotypes. Intake forms could be modified so that superficial information is not gathered. Computer programs could be modified so that details of the setting of the rule violation were recorded rather than shorthand indicators such as traits or labels. Indeed, the storage capacity of computers should be exploited so that maximum information is available to inform decisions. (Granted, there would still be a summarization via the computer program which pulled out the data, but it need not be as narrow as present category systems.)

16. For a very complete description of problems encountered by one community-based treatment program, see Empey and Erickson (1972:155–75). These authors conclude: "(1) that it was difficult to sustain a high level of public support for this particular field study; (2) that the rules by which the scientific game were played were incongruent with the rules by which the political game was played; and (3) that, in the absence of effective and politically supported models for field experimentation, it was necessary for the investigator to play a host of conflicting roles: scientist, politician, public relations man, agent of social control, therapist, and others" (Empey and Erickson, 1972:172).

17. Movement to community-based treatment programs does not assure success, because labeling effects may still occur. It appears that one reason for the failure of the Cambridge-Sommerville Youth Study was the stigma attached to those boys in the program (Harris, 1968). Another community-based program had participants wear uniforms, a very visible form of stigmatization (Arnold, 1970:451).

18. Becker and Horowitz note that greater tolerance means that those with deviant life styles live more openly. Such openness should expel a number of the negative stereotypes about these groups, which, in turn, may lead to greater tolerance by the community.

References

Arnold, Robert
    1970   "Mobilization for Youth: patchwork or solution?" In H. Voss (ed.), *Society, Delinquency and Delinquent Behavior.* Boston: Little, Brown.

Bakan, David
    1971   *Slaughter of the Innocents.* Boston: Beacon Press.

Becker, Howard S., and Irving L. Horowitz
    1971   "The culture of civility." Pp. 209–215 in I. Horowitz and M. Strong (eds.), *Sociological Realities.* New York: Harper and Row.

Caldwell, Robert G., and James A. Black
    1971   *Juvenile Delinquency.* New York: Ronald Press.

Campbell, James S., Joseph R. Sahid, and David P. Stang
    1970   *Law and Order Reconsidered.* New York: Bantam Books.

Chambliss, William J.
    1969   *Crime and the Legal Process.* New York: McGraw-Hill.

Durkheim, Emile
    1964   *The Rules of Sociological Method.* New York: Free Press.

Edgerton, Robert B.
    1967   *The Cloak of Competence.* Berkeley: University of California Press.

Empey, LaMar T., and Maynard L. Erickson
    1972   *The Provo Experiment.* Lexington, Mass: D. C. Heath.

Erikson, Kai T.
    1966   *Wayward Puritans.* New York: John Wiley and Sons.

Harris, David B.
    1968   "On differential stigmatization for predelinquents." *Social Problems* 15 (Spring):507–508.

Harris, Richard
    1969   *The Fear of Crime.* New York: Praeger Publishers.

Kittrie, Nicholas
    1971   *The Right to be Different: Deviance and Enforced Therapy.* Baltimore: Johns Hopkins Press.

Laing, R. D., and A. Esterson
    1964   *Sanity, Madness and the Family.* London: Tavistock.
Lemert, Edwin M.
    1967   "The juvenile court—quest and realities." In *Task Force Re-port: Juvenile Delinquency and Youth Crime.* Washington, D.C.: U.S. Government Printing Office.
Lennard, Harry L., and Arnold Bernstein
    1969   *Patterns of Human Interaction.* San Francisco: Jossey-Bass.
Levin, Martin A.
    1971   "Policy evaluation and recidivism." *Law and Society Review* 6 (August):17–46.
Light, Donald W., Jr.
    1972   "Psychiatry and suicide: the management of mistakes." *American Journal of Sociology* 77 (March):821–38.
Lofland, John
    1969   *Deviance and Identity.* Englewood Cliffs, New Jersey: Pren-tice-Hall.
Martin, John M., Joseph P. Fitzpatrick, and Robert E. Gould
    1968   *The Analysis of Delinquent Behavior: A Structural Approach.* New York: Random House.
Matza, David
    1969   *Becoming Deviant.* Englewood Cliffs, New Jersey: Prentice-Hall.
Menninger, Karl
    1969   *The Crime of Punishment.* New York: Viking Press.
Mintz, Robert
    1974   "Interview with Ian Taylor, Paul Walton, and Jock Young." *Issues in Criminology* 9 (Spring):33–53.
Morris, Norval, and Gordon Hawkins
    1970   *The Honest Politician's Guide to Crime Control.* Chicago: University of Chicago Press.
Murphy, Jeffrie G.
    1969   "Criminal punishment and psychiatric fallacies." *Law and Society Review* 4 (August):111–22.
Nimmer, Raymond T.
    1974   *Diversion: The Search for Alternative Forms of Prosecution.* Chicago: American Bar Foundation.
Packer, Herbert
    1968   *The Limits of the Criminal Sanction.* Stanford: Stanford University Press.
Pitts, Jesse R.
    1968   "Social control: the concept." *International Encyclopedia of the Social Sciences.* New York: Macmillan. (Volume 14, pp. 381–96).

Quinney, Richard
    1974   *Critique of Legal Order.* Boston: Little, Brown.
Retish, Paul M.
    1973   "Changing the status of poorly esteemed students through teacher reinforcement." *Journal of Applied Behavioral Science* 9 (January-February):44–50.
Rosenhan, D. L.
    1973   "On being sane in insane places." *Science* 179 (January 19): 250–58.
Rosenthal, Robert, and Lenore Jacobson
    1968   *Pygmalion in the Classroom.* New York: Holt, Rinehart and Winston.
Schur, Edwin M.
    1965   *Crimes Without Victims.* Englewood Cliffs, New Jersey: Prentice-Hall.
Skolnick, Jerome
    1966   *Justice Without Trial.* New York: John Wiley and Sons.
    1967   "Social control in the adversary system." *Journal of Conflict Resolution* 11 (March):52–70.
Stark, Rodney
    1972   *Police Riots.* Belmont, Calif.: Focus Books.
Sudnow, David
    1965   "Normal crimes: sociological features of the penal code in a public defender office." *Social Problems* 12 (Winter):255–76.
Taylor, Ian, Paul Walton, and Jock Young
    1973   *The New Criminology: For a Social Theory of Deviance.* London: Routledge and Kegan Paul.
Tharp, Roland G., and Ralph J. Wetzel
    1969   *Behavior Modification in the Natural Environment.* New York: Academic Press.
Vorenberg, Elizebeth W., and James Vorenberg
    1973   "Early diversion from the criminal justice system: practice in search of a theory." In L. Ohlin (ed.), *Prisoners in America.* Englewood Cliffs, New Jersey: Prentice-Hall.
Westley, William A.
    1953   "Violence and the police." *American Journal of Sociology* 59 (July):34–41.
Yablonsky, Lewis
    1967   *Synanon: The Tunnel Back.* Baltimore: Penguin Books.